The Democratic Imperative

THE

DEMOCRATIC

IMPERATIVE

Exporting the

American Revolution

GREGORY A. FOSSEDAL

A NEW REPUBLIC BOOK

Basic Books, Inc., Publishers   New York

Library of Congress Cataloging-in-Publication Data

Fossedal, Gregory A.
  The democratic imperative.

  "A New republic book."
  Bibliographical notes: p. 247
  Includes index.
  1. United States—Foreign relations.   2. Democracy.
3. World politics—20th century.   I. Title.
E183.7.F743   1989   327.73   88–47905
ISBN   0–465–09801–0

CONTENTS

I

THE ENDS

II

THE MEANS

III

THE HEARTS AND MINDS

I

THE ENDS

A great democratic revolution is taking place in our midst; everybody sees it, but by no means everybody judges it the same way.

Some think it a new theory and, supposing it to be an accident, hope they can check it; others think it irresistible because it seems to them the most continuous, ancient, and permanent tendency known to history.

—ALEXIS DE TOCQUEVILLE

1

OPPORTUNITY

ON CHRISTMAS DAY 1936 a ship set sail from New York City, carrying several hundred Americans bound for Paris. From France, the Americans smuggled themselves across the border to a training camp in Villanueva de la Jara, Spain. They went there to aid the Loyalists in their civil war against the Fascists. Eventually, several thousand Americans crossed the ocean to work as nurses, mechanics, combat soldiers, even financiers, in the service of a common cause: a democratic republic in Spain.

They called themselves the Abraham Lincoln Brigade, and while about one in three was a blue-collar worker, leading intellectuals were also among them, including Ernest Hemingway, whose reporting helped popularize the struggle, and James Benét, who left a comfortable job at *The New Republic* to fight for an all-American unit of the First Transport Regiment.[1] At a time when such association carried little stigma, roughly half were members of either the Communist Party or the Young Communist League, including such commissars as Steve Nelson and Dave Doran.[2] Many, though, were registered Democrats or Republicans, and others were U.S. citizens denied the right to vote in their own country, a category that apparently included Commander Oliver Law, who may also have been the first black man to lead white Americans into battle. The one striking characteristic shared by nearly all the members of the Lincoln Brigade was a lack of military experience. The first commander to be appointed was a former teaching assistant at the University of California at Berkeley, Robert Merriman, chosen because he had gone through four years of part-time college courses for the Reserve Officers Training Corps.

Like other American crusades for democracy—some would place Woodrow Wilson's League of Nations atop the list; others, perhaps, our assistance to South Vietnam in the 1960s—the Lincoln Brigade was at best somewhat impractical, and at worst misguided, even according to many of its members. Within months of their arrival, the Americans found themselves increasingly intimidated and eventually dominated by the Soviet dictator who was supplying many of their arms, Joseph Stalin. On April 25, 1937, Roldan Cortada, a leading communist, was shot in Barcelona. In May, full-scale civil war erupted within the Spanish left, pitting true democrats (those not already forced to flee) against Soviet-directed agents whose vision of postwar Spain little resembled that of the Lincoln Brigade. By the summer, the Stalinists had won. Prime Minister Francisco Largo Caballero, who resisted the Soviet bid for domination,[3] was removed as de facto head of the Republicans and replaced by a man handpicked by one of Stalin's agents, Juan Negrin.[4] On June 14, Negrin ordered the secret roundup of members of the Marxist Partido Obrero de Unificación Marxista, or POUM, deemed to be insufficiently subservient to Moscow, and in the next eighteen months thousands of POUM members were executed or tortured in communist prisons.[5] History recorded ample and timely notice that the Republican cause was being subverted. George Orwell, for example, published a major exposé of the unfolding tragedy in the *New English Weekly.* Alas, his warning seemed to fall on deaf ears in the West. In a 1986 article for the *Washington Post,* Ronald Radosh concluded that well before the end of the war, the Spanish Republic had become "what its enemies called it, a puppet of Moscow." Even Bernard Knox, in an essay for the *New York Review of Books,* concluded that "by late 1937, the Communist party and its Comintern and Russian 'advisers' were in firm control of the Republican armies and were exercising civilian political control through a Russian-style secret police."[6]

The Americans of the Lincoln Brigade were slow, as many were, to see the dangers of communism. Unlike most Western peoples and governments, though, they were quick to see the even more imminent dangers of fascism. Like Winston Churchill across the Atlantic, they fought a lonely battle to alert their countrymen to the meaning of Franco, Mussolini, and Hitler. Like Abraham Lincoln, they saw that there could be no real freedom or security for one group of people while others were in chains. They were willing to risk their lives because they believed in the dictum of the Declaration of Independence that "all men are created equal," with rights given by God that no state can justly deny. "Few, if any, went to Spain as a way of furthering socialism," writes Robert A. Rosenstone. "Knowing little of Spanish politics or Francisco Franco, they were internationally minded enough to believe that anyone supported by Hitler and Mussolini was an enemy of civilization."[7]

By the end of the decade, they were proven right—as the fascists turned their guns on most of the free nations of the world.

The Lincoln Brigade, then, was one of the first enterprises of its kind: an active American attempt to extend democracy beyond its own shores. There was no thought of territorial expansion or national gain, but only a genuine, unselfish concern for extending the rights of man. And while it once seemed that this hope for democracy might be forgotten or quixotic, events years later have made the example of the brigades seem still relevant and alive.

The Winds of Freedom

In 1986, almost five decades after the founding of the Lincoln Brigade, the people of the Philippines—a former U.S. colony with Spanish roots—joined what seemed to be an equally hopeless drive for democracy in their own country. The election held on February 7, 1986, appeared to be just another sham, a show of democracy without the reality of a fair choice. The contest pitted the country's aging, authoritarian president, Ferdinand Marcos, against the wife of a former opposition politician assassinated by top Marcos aides in 1983, Corazon Aquino. Though observers from the United States and other countries, and from an independent group of Filipinos, all pointed to widespread fraud in the proceedings, the country's National Assembly proceeded with ballot counting as usual and declared Marcos the comfortable winner on February 15.

This time, however, forces intervened. The Catholic Church, always powerful in the country but also traditionally nervous about political involvement, weighed in heavily for Mrs. Aquino. So did the U.S. government. In the weeks following the election, a stream of messages and U.S. envoys arrived in Manila telling Marcos that he could no longer rely on American support. Secretary of State George Shultz and President Ronald Reagan both asked Marcos to resign. The U.S. Senate condemned his reelection and also called for resignation. As the day scheduled for the Marcos inauguration neared, thousands of Filipinos gathered around the presidential palace in Manila to protest. Some chanted "Co-ry, Co-ry, Co-ry"; others walked through the streets praying with rosaries.

Partly as a result of U.S. pressures, partly as a result of the defection of two key military advisers, and partly, perhaps, because of the chants and prayers, Marcos stepped down on February 25. And a democracy—embattled, fragile, and impoverished, but miraculously free—was born.*

As the 1980s aged, other U.S. allies in Asia, spurred by the Philippine example, seemed to be moving toward free elections as well. On February 24, 1986, South Korea announced it was loosening restrictions on opposition parties and reiterated its promises of constitutional reform leading up to a 1988 election. The timing suggested, as an editorial in the *Wall Street Journal*

---

*Within months, the U.S. Senate twice rejected a badly needed package of relief aid. Readers may wish to compare this blasé response to democracy with the predictions of continued Marcos rule that dominated the U.S. beforehand.

argued explicitly, an alertness to the example of Marcos.[8] A year later, the regime agreed to a revision of the election system, which had been heavily weighted to favor the ruling party. True, President Chun Doo Hwan continued to harass the opposition, repeatedly arresting such dissident leaders as Kim Young Sam and Kim Dae Jung. Even so, debate over political reform took place in a remarkably public way. Opposition leaders, allowed to sit in the existing parliament, united on various constitutional demands and frequently boycotted talks, led rallies, organized petitions, and debated their positions in a press that was supervised by the government but by no means dominated to the degree seen in Nicaragua or Chile.[9] Indeed, when opposition leaders found themselves stifled at home, they met frequently with U.S. diplomats and were able to publicize their case throughout the West, producing a steady pressure on the government to keep the reforms moving. On March 6, 1987, President Chun repeated his pledge to hold free elections and step down by 1988 to Secretary of State Shultz.[10] Meanwhile, as the *New York Times* noted, economic growth in Korea "liberated powerful new social forces. A growing urban population no longer passively accepts a self-perpetuating regime based in the military."[11] Korea appeared to be well on its way to full-fledged democracy.

Another authoritarian but prospering regime, the ruling Kuomintang Party in Taiwan, was ultimately forced to respond to the pressure of an increasingly vocal opposition, which met regularly with supportive U.S. politicians such as Congressman Stephen Solarz. In April 1986, the government created a twelve-member commission to consider removing the ban on new political parties and other political reforms.[12] Before the panel could report, however, opposition politicians announced the formation of the Democratic Progressive Party to challenge the Kuomintang in the December 6 legislative elections. Although the new party was not formally recognized, the government allowed its candidates to run, taking care to boost its own popularity with the announcement, in October 1986, that it was lifting martial law. The new DPP took 21 percent of the votes and twenty-three seats in the National Assembly and the Legislative Yuan.[13]

Accompanying these formal changes in the rules of electioneering were economic and social developments that fostered the evolution of democracy. In the 1970s and 1980s, the size of the middle class grew from 15 percent to nearly half the population, consisting of "bureaucrats, intellectuals, workers, and businessmen," according to sociologist Hsin-Huang Michael Hsiao of National Taiwan University.[14] The new class, chafing under the undemocratic restrictions of the past, began to organize and speak out for free-speech rights, and formed labor associations, control and environmental groups, and a consumer protection foundation—all unheard of in a country once obsessed with survival, cultural unity, and reclaiming the Chinese mainland. "The society," wrote journalist Georgie Anne Geyer, "now has reached a new stage of political participation," a likely precursor of further democratization.[15]

Similar developments, if less visible, could be seen in such countries as Pakistan, Chile, and South Africa. In late 1985, Pakistan lifted martial law and allowed the safe return of Benazir Bhutto. Bhutto, daughter of former Prime Minister Zulfikar Ali Bhutto, removed in a 1977 coup and later executed, quickly demonstrated charisma and skill in pressing for reform.[16] Though disgruntled at U.S. support for ruling President Mohammed Zia ul-Haq, she refrained from open criticism and in fact criticized the burning of American flags by some Pakistani leftists, alienating many natural supporters. "Pro-Americanism is difficult politics for her," observed Mahnaz Ispahani in *The New Republic,* "but she is clinging to it."[17] With a 1988 election widely praised as fair and open under its belt, Pakistan seemed ready to join the democratic league of nations. Pakistan is a particularly relevant example because of its tenuous geopolitical position. Large, militarized, and traditionally hostile neighbors—China, Iran, the Soviet Union, and India—all lurked nearby, as does Soviet-occupied Afghanistan. If democracy may be hoped for in Pakistan, it may be hoped for in even the most pressing circumstances.

In Chile, the struggle to establish free institutions continued despite regular crackdowns on dissent by ruling President Augusto Pinochet, who promised that Chileans would live "under a full democracy" after his term of office expired in 1989. In January 1986, pointing to recent evidence of a deterioration of human rights, the United States announced a program of increased support for the beleaguered opposition groups.[18] In March, the United States supported a United Nations resolution condemning Chile. That August, General John R. Galvin, chief of the U.S. Southern Command, met with Pinochet to stress the U.S. government's belief that there was an "urgent need" for Chile to at least begin democratization. He specified legalization of political parties, the initiation of voter registration, an end to torture by security forces and of press restrictions, and the opening of talks between government leaders and the opposition.[19] That fall, the United States threatened to cut off credits through international lending agencies and the U.S. Overseas Private Investment Corporation,[20] and while the United States ultimately acquiesced in a controversial World Bank loan of $250 million, the message of American seriousness was getting through. In the coming months, Pinochet released several thousand political prisoners and approved a long-promised law permitting the legal formation of political parties.[21] The best evidence that the growth of such institutions mattered came from Pinochet and his allies in the United States, who issued bitter accusations of "U.S. interference" with each new statement or action of support for the Chilean democrats.[22]

The same could be said for South Africa, where even incremental relaxation of that country's policy of racial segregation produced howls of protest from die-hard supporters of apartheid.[23] Black trade unions were legalized in 1979, and job-reservation laws (saving jobs for whites) were eliminated in most industries. In 1983, the white electorate of South Africa approved a referendum establishing a weak, but symbolically significant, branch of parliament to include Indians and persons of mixed race. In May 1985, a law banning multiracial parties was repealed; in June, interracial sex and marriage were legalized; in September, discussions were initiated on restoring citizenship to 8 million blacks in the so-called homelands, regions where they had been forcibly moved or retained as part of a strategy to maintain apartheid's racial division while changing its legal form. In February 1986, downtown commercial districts were opened to members of all races; in April, the government announced it would abolish "pass laws" restricting the movement of blacks. "I have a respect for Botha," South African Bishop Desmond Tutu told an interviewer in 1986. "The most revolutionary step he has taken is to declare once and for all that the future of South Africa will not be determined by whites alone."[24]

It's important to stress that none of these developments eliminated the possibility that governments challenged by the democratic tide would simply seek to roll it back. The making of promises and the growth of independent organizations—churches, unions, civic groups, political parties, the press, and others—by no means guarantee democracy. Nor does the enactment of a democratic constitution mean we can stop worrying about the Philippines, where opponents of Mrs. Aquino have staged several coup attempts, and Marxist guerillas continue to control vast areas of the countryside. Yet the growth of free institutions is an essential component of the gradual process of liberalization. The presence in the Philippines, for example, of strong trade unions, a powerful Catholic Church, and a feisty independent press gave the United States greater leverage in pushing for reform, and helped it to sidestep the old and awful choice between a pro-U.S. tyrant of the right and a pro-Soviet tyrant of the left.

The Third World is widely supposed to offer only flinty soil for the growth of freedom. Yet from 1976 to 1986, according to an annual survey by Freedom House, more than a dozen countries made the leap from "unfree" or "partly free" states to "free" states, none of them prosperous.[25] In 1977, more than a tenth of the world's people became part of a democracy when Prime Minister Indira Gandhi allowed free elections, was voted out of office, and conducted a peaceful transfer of power.

Many of the new democracies took root in Latin America, where freely elected presidents replaced military governments in the Dominican Republic (1978), Ecuador (1979), Peru (1980), Honduras (1982), Bolivia (1982), Argentina (1983), El Salvador (1984), Panama (1984), Uruguay (1985), and Guatemala (1985). The people of Haiti deposed the Duvalier dynasty in 1986, and voted in a new constitution in 1987. What surprises is not that further coups and setbacks may follow but that the strength of the democratic impulse can remain so strong even among the poor and long-tyrannized Haitians. With Brazil's elections in 1985, and the inauguration of its first civilian leader in twenty-one years, observed Fred C. Iklé, "90 percent of the people in the region south of us [live] under democratic rule, compared with about 40 percent [in 1974]."[26] In the decade that followed the inauguration of President Jimmy Carter, the world, in the words of Ronald Reagan, "witnessed one of the greatest expansions of democracy on record. Latin America, once the bastion of the *Caudillo*—the Latin strongman—is now, for the most part, democratic territory."[27] What is more, as Adam Meyerson observed in *Policy Review*, "with the exception of Grenada and Guatemala, most of the recent transitions to democracy have been achieved without force of arms. The democratic revolution has taken place because military regimes have relinquished power voluntarily."[28]

Even Mexico, where economic agonies and one-party politics produce chronic instability, offered reason for hope. In the 1980s, the country's National Action Party, or PAN, emerged as a strong opposition to the ruling Institutional Revolutionary Party, or PRI. In July 1986, PAN candidate Francisco Barrio Terrazas lost a hotly disputed election for state governor of Chihuahua. Widespread reports of election fraud became a major embarrassment for the PRI, threatening badly needed international credits and prompting broad concern among U.S. journalists.[29] The party's heavy-handed tactics also produced defections within the PRI ranks. In 1987, Cuauhtemoc Cardenas, leader of a reform wing of the party, broke with the PRI over what he described as its "authoritarian" and "treacherous" dealings.[30] The depressed state of world commodity prices worked great hardship on Mexico in the 1980s, but the rise of PAN and other opposition groups offered a glimmer of hope.

Perhaps the worst news for freedom came from Africa, where in January 1984, a military dictator seized power in one of the world's most populous democracies—Nigeria. The episode was a shameful one in many ways. Having brought on a world surge in commodity prices in the 1960s, and having urged Third World commodity exporters to incur heavy debts in the inflationary 1970s, America decided to clamp down in the 1980s, thus helping to topple Nigeria's civilian government. Equally culpable were the negotiators of the International Monetary Fund and other lending agencies, who had made it clear that their concern for short-term interest payments greatly outweighed any long-run interest in a just political order. Worst of all, these events drew not a loud cry of protest from Western governments but a whimper or two from the editorial pages of the *New York Times* and the the *Wall Street Journal,* both of which, after writing obligatory editorials in January 1984, scarcely mentioned the subject again. "Against all the to-do over Grenada," writes Jonathan Kwitny, "the coup in Nigeria—far more important in the world scheme of things—got scant attention."[31]

Even Africa, though, offered some hopeful examples. Senegal held scrupulously fair presidential and legislative elections every five years, prompting Charles Bray, U.S. ambassador from 1981 to 1985, to proclaim her "the Costa Rica of Africa."[32] In 1981, Senegal came to the armed assistance of neighboring Gambia, turning back a Marxist junta that had overthrown President Dawda Jawara and was calling for Soviet aid. Democracy also thrived in Botswana, despite harsh weather that damaged the farm economy and occasional military strikes from neighboring South Africa. From 1983 to 1985, farmers in this agrarian country lost more than 80 percent of their annual crops. Those that survived fetched little exchange given the slump in world commodity prices. Yet in 1984 Botswana held its fifth consecutive open election since 1966, returning President Quett Masire's ruling Botswana Democratic Party to power.[33] Kenya, the Ivory Coast, the Sudan, Liberia, Zambia, and Zimbabwe all held elections in the 1980s, and though these were generally limited to a single party, all these countries have adopted sufficient democratic practices to qualify as "partly free states" in the annual Freedom House index.[34] Considering the unfortunate economic policies adopted by many African countries, too often promoted by our own banks and lending agencies, it was remarkable that so many democracies were able to hold their own on the troubled continent.

North of Africa, in Europe, democracy made two great leaps forward. In 1975, Spain and Portugal both surged toward freedom when military dictatorships of long standing relinquished power to civilian governments. By the 1980s both countries had held several elections between contending parties and could be counted as solidly free. For the first time in history, all of Western Europe was democratic. It did not take long before this development seemed commonplace, a homely datum in a world of evil dictators and daring freedom fighters. The democratization of Europe, however, was anything but assured in the aftermath of World War II. The efforts to save Western Europe from Soviet domination were viewed at the time as bold and risky ventures offering no guarantee of success. Almost six months after Harry Truman announced a program of major aid to Turkey and Greece, for example, the issue remained doubtful to correspondent Robert Low of *Time* magazine:

> The $300 million American aid-to-Greece program is failing. . . . Once you get outside Athens, you realize that the situation is the worst it has been since October 1944 when the Germans left. . . . Two reports, issued the same day last week, show how fast guerilla destruction is outracing U.S. reconstruction. . . . Perhaps the worst problem is the 300,000 refugees from guerilla country. . . . In Salonika, a

top police officer told me: "If ever there has been a fertile breeding ground for Communism, it's among these refugees."[35]

A decade after Franco, many observers regarded his death and the death of one-man Spanish rule as necessarily identical. Yet it certainly did not seem so to one great American journalist. In 1975 George Will wrote:

> It has been well said (by British Prime Minister Stanley Baldwin) that a durable despotism is like a great tree, majestic in its way like any extravagance of nature, but like everything in nature, mortal. And when it blows down you see that nothing has grown beneath it to replace it; the saplings have died or been stunted for want of air.
>
> Where the public landscape has been kept flat, producing only untested leaders and conspiratorial organizations, gusts of passion encounter nothing to deflect and temper their sweep. And there is no reason to believe that Franco's deep freeze of political life did anything to alter the fact that excess is the distinguishing mark of the Spanish spirit. So there is reason to believe that Franco's caretaker regime will prove to have been only a long parenthesis between turmoils.[36]

Europe's second great leap took place behind the Iron Curtain. There, elites confronted with a decaying system enacted a series of reforms that moved their countries a marginal distance in a revolutionary direction: toward democracy. Hungary, where a bid for freedom was crushed in 1956, embarked on a sustained program of economic reform, becoming, in the words of Xan Smiley, "the most liberal economy in Eastern Europe."[37] The government, starting in the late 1950s, allowed small agricultural plots to flourish. Jobs in the country's "second economy," based on individual enterprise, were legalized or, where not legalized, winked at: By 1982, an estimated three families out of four worked in the second economy at least part time, where wages were often three to four times as high as in state-run entities.[38] Hungarian leader János Kádár gradually squeezed party bureaucrats out of sinecures and into the private economy, leaving only 800,000 party members in a country of 11 million people. Another Kádár reform allowed workers to lease equipment or whole plants for private use in their "off" hours,[39] when they often worked their hardest. Beginning in the 1970s, the state broke up large enterprises, decentralized them, and even sold some to private investors in an embryo bond market started in 1983.[40] From 1980 to 1983, Hungary broke eleven trusts and twenty-five large companies into more than two hundred competitive units.[41]

Thus, from 1971 to 1980, Hungary's gross national product grew at twice the rate of that of the Soviet Union.[42] And these official figures tended to understate the growing gap between the Soviet Union and its satellite, since Hungary's growth was taking place precisely in the unofficial, hard-to-measure, private economy. For the official statistics to be correct, it would have to be the case, as a muddled correspondent for the *Financial Times* of London put it, that "state and collective enterprises still account for about 95 percent of national income," a figure few experts would take seriously.[43] A more accurate measure of Hungary's prosperity might have been found on its shelves, which, in contrast to those of most of Eastern Europe, were well-stocked.[44]

Hungary wasn't the only Soviet satellite to outgrow the imperial center. Poland, the only Soviet-bloc country with a powerful Roman Catholic church, also outpaced the Soviet economy, as did Romania and East Germany.[45] In Poland and Hungary, moreover, where economic freedom grew fastest, calls for political freedom followed close on the heels of privatized production capital or free labor unions. In Poland, the beloved Solidarity Union established important possibilities for an independent organization in a communist country, winning official concession of its right to exist, propagate its views, and compete in elections. The union's activities were greatly curtailed after the government's martial-law crackdown, yet Solidarity chief Lech Walesa continued to criticize particular policies, and underground radio broadcasts and samizdat bulletins were unabated.[46]

In Hungary, political reform was less striking than in Poland, but no less real. Many of the economic reforms initiated by the government met repeated resistance from party cadres, who managed to roll back liberalization measures in 1976, and again in 1981. Some mechanism was needed to root out foot-draggers and advance reformers, and in 1983 the Communist Party of Hungary drafted an experimental law calling for competition between two or more individual candidates for each office.[47] By 1985, the law had its first test, and it also turned out, according to the *Wall Street Journal,* that the party was conducting public-opinion polls to gauge the reaction of Hungarians on everything from which kind of diapers they preferred to what they thought of the 1986 Reykjavík summit between Ronald Reagan and Mikhail Gorbachev.[48] Polls, of course, are hardly a perfect tool for effecting democracy, but their presence suggests an elite that is unusually interested in learning more about popular opinion. In 1985, Hungary, which traditionally allowed Western broadcasts through the Voice of America and Radio Free Europe to enter the country freely, even permitted direct phone contact between its major cities and West Germany. By 1986, Radio Free Europe had set up a telephone comment line and was receiving hundreds of calls a day.[49]

These incremental changes in socialism provoked heated debate in the West, with some observers warning that communists had pulled the same tricks before—for example, Lenin's New Economic Policy, Khrushchev's speech on Stalin to the Party Congress, and so on—only to revert to centralized planning. Great attention was focused on whether the Soviet leader in power—Andropov, Chernenko, or Gorbachev—was a liberal or not, and whether he intended to bring about democratic capitalism or only patch up the Soviet system to make communism work better.

OPPORTUNITY

To a large extent, all these speculations were irrelevant. The fact that previous, equally tentative reforms were reversed did not mean that the tentative reforms of the 1980s would be. Nor was the intent or sincerity of Soviet leaders at issue. It could hardly have been clear on the day the British king and several noblemen signed the Magna Carta, to take a magnified example, that many centuries later there would be a representative parliament serving all the essential functions of the crown. Yet the Magna Carta played an important role in that development.* "It doesn't matter if Gorbachev is a liberal," observed the Russian scholar and journalist Strobe Talbott. "The question is, is he liberalizing? It doesn't matter either if his reforms are 'just economic.' Economic reforms, in about 5 minutes, run into the bureaucracy, and necessitate political reforms."[50] What is more encouraging? A Soviet leader who ponders complete and rapid democratization of the system, a program unlikely to be sustained, or a Soviet leader who ponders gradual but real steps that amount to a shift toward democracy—not out of a sudden conversion to the thought of Jefferson and Lincoln, but simply because such measures seem to him pragmatic, sensible ways to advance "socialism"?

It seemed evident that the young ruler who took control of the Kremlin in 1984, Mikhail Gorbachev, was not the first kind of reformer. But might he be the second? In 1986, Gorbachev announced a policy of *glasnost,* or openness, presented as a means of producing a "broad democratization" that the Soviet leader said was "irreversible." The first front was economic, and similar to the

---

*It is vital to remember that this document, the very foundation of common law and the realization of natural rights for Englishmen—and later, for their cousins on the American continent—was born of what its authors deemed a pragmatic compromise. Those who initiated the reforms of the Magna Carta had no more intention of promoting a democracy in Great Britain than some communist may in Russia or China of the 1990s; but the principles the document propounded proved more powerful than the intent of the signers.

The process began with the rising complaints of thirteenth-century British nobles that they were being overtaxed. King John thought he could deflect their demands for limits to his royal authority when he pledged allegiance to the crusades of Pope Innocent—and invoked excommunication upon his opponents. But the barons, backed by Bishop Stephen Langton, continued to press. The key point in the struggle came when Langton, an expert in church teaching on natural law, convinced the barons that the king and the pope would have a more difficult time resisting their reforms if they represented not just the narrow economic demands of a few elites but a statement about the God-given rights that ought to limit all kings. On June 15, 1215, King John and several clergymen reluctantly sealed the original "Articles of the Barons" on which the Magna Carta was based, guaranteeing rights to a fair trial, freedom from the arbitrary seizure of property, and the autonomy of local churches and towns.

Thus the thing to watch when concessions are made by monarchs, whether they assert the divine right of God or of Marx, is what they do and what they say—not necessarily what they think the impact will be. For, as Winston Churchill noted of the Magna Carta:

The leaders of the barons in 1215 groped in the dim light towards a fundamental principle. Government must henceforward mean something more than the arbitrary rule of any man, and custom and the law must stand even above the king. It was this idea, perhaps only half understood, that gave unity and force to the opposition and made the Charter [the barons] now demanded imperishable. In the future ages it was to be used as a foundation of principles and systems of government of which neither King John nor his nobles dreamed.

(See Winston S. Churchill, *A History of the English-Speaking Peoples,* vol. 1, *The Birth of Britain* [New York: Dodd, Mead, 1956], pp. 252–56.)

reforms in Hungary. Not long after taking office in 1985, Gorbachev visited Hospital Number 53 in Moscow, where he learned that the chief surgeon, performing complicated, life-or-death surgery, earned less than five rubles for each operation. Shortly thereafter, the Politburo raised salaries and heightened incentives for doctors, a concept later broadened to other fields.[51] Writing in the monthly journal *Kommunist,* Tatiana I. Zaslavskaia, an economic reformer and adviser to Gorbachev, noted with alarm polls showing that most Soviets didn't want a "promotion"—that is, more work and responsibility without a commensurate increase in pay. Mrs. Zaslavskaia suggested wider wage differentials as the correct remedy.[52] Legislation passed by the Supreme Soviet in November 1986 legalized twenty-nine different types of private enterprise, including house and car repair, tailoring, and driving a taxi. The new law also permitted people to hold more than one job, an important feature.[53]

Quickly, though, Gorbachev found that even these incremental changes ruffled the feathers of party bureaucrats; he responded with a flurry of political *glasnost.* The government released leading dissidents such as Andrei Sakharov, who promptly called for more *glasnost* at a Moscow forum on arms control.[54] Candor crept into Soviet journals and TV and radio broadcasts. On December 18, 1986, the Soviet news agency Tass carried an unprecedented report on major riots that had taken place the previous day in Alma-Ata, the capital of the Kazakh Republic, after a top Moslem official was replaced with an ethnic Russian.[55] In February 1987, Soviet TV aired a speech by Gorbachev that conceded division within the Politburo over his own reform program. "Arguments are part of democracy," he told the weekly *Moscow News.*[56] At about the same time, *Pravda, Izvestia, Trud,* and other publications all ran exposés on the wide gap between Soviet workers and the ruling *nomenklatura.* By 1988, Russians selecting local party leaders for more than 30,000 posts could choose between competing candidates—with about one-third opting to toss out their incumbents in that fall's election. (In an appeal that resembled one of Ronald Reagan's addresses to the nation, Gorbachev went on national television that summer to urge citizens to vote for officials who would support further reforms.) Arnold Beichman, a scholar at the Hoover Institution not known for optimism about Soviet reform drives, wrote: "For the moment, at least, Mr. Gorbachev's new line may herald some amazing changes in Soviet life."[57]

Everything that has been said about the pace of reform in the Soviet Union is doubly applicable to the growth of democratic capitalism in the China of Deng Xiaoping. Unfortunately, all the same qualifiers would apply. By 1986, the dynamic of capitalist growth was manifesting what Marxists like to call its "inherent contradictions" in China. Party elites suspicious of the new ways launched a counterattack, removing key architects of the Deng reforms. It was not clear whether economic reforms would produce a shift to political democracy. It was clear, as students and other reformers took to the streets to demonstrate peacefully but firmly for free elections, that without such political measures, the economic reforms themselves rested on sandy ground.[58] "We have not yet established a rigorous system and procedure for policy decision-making, nor have we had an adequate consultancy system, appraisal system, supervision system, and feedback system for the purpose," Vice Premier Wan Li told the New China News Agency. "There is no scientific way of testing the soundness of a policy decision made in that manner."[59]*

While the Chinese groped forward toward a "feedback system," another democratic force struggled at the periphery of the Soviet empire to find food, shelter, and guns. Freedom fighters took up arms against the Red Army and its surrogates—Cubans, Syrians, East Germans, Czechs—in Angola, Afghanistan, Nicaragua, Mozambique, Ethiopia, and Cambodia. It was possible that none of these movements would succeed. It was also quite arguable that not all of the freedom fighters sincerely sought a democratic outcome for their country. Their mere existence, however, put a new twist on the old misunderstanding of liberation movements: Here were men and women, in substantial numbers, willing to fight and die to combat communism and promote democracy against rather tall odds.

Two hundred years ago, a small nation of several million people was virtually the sole analogue to the freedom fighters of the modern era and that nation, the United States, would not abolish slavery for another century. In 1987, however, fifty-six nations outside the United States were free; another fifty-seven were partly free; another fifty-three were not free, but in many cases

*Some of the more amusing affirmations of the potential for totalitarianism's evolution consisted in the reaction of Western Marxists to even the highly qualified actions and statements made by Chinese and Soviet leaders on behalf of bourgeois democracy. Petra Kelly, founder of West Germany's Green Party, responded with horror when a group of Soviet dissidents she met in Moscow pulled out packs of Western cigarettes and pleaded with her to "thank President Reagan" for hard-line policies they felt helped prompt their release. For Kelly, Gorbachev's perestroika erred in going far too far, raising the specter of visitors to Lenin's tomb waiting in line to view socialism's George Washington while munching on a Big Mac.

Similarly, Alexander Cockburn fretted in *The Nation* that Gorbachev might be giving away the ideological store by calling into question such "legitimate revolutions" as the communist coups in Afghanistan and Nicaragua. Cliff Du Rand, a Marxian philosophy professor at Morgan State, noted with some trepidation the emergence of Lockean concepts of the legitimacy of private and exclusive use of property. And where exclusive use treads, he observed, old-fashioned ownership may soon take up residence. "While often still under *de jure* social ownership," he wrote, "the right to use is being privatized. . . . These long-term leases already have some of the features of private property. . . . Only the future will tell whether the process of privatization [China's leaders] have set in motion can later be reversed and property resocialized, or whether it will lead not only to a reconstitution of private property but also to a capitalist society." There goes the neighborhood.

(An excerpt of Kelly's remarks was printed in *Harper's* magazine, May 1988, p. 27; Cockburn's piece ran in *The Nation* on 18 June 1988 ("Glasnost at Home and Abroad"); Du Rand's paper to the Southeast Marxist Scholars Conference at the University of South Florida, delivered on 19 October 1985, was adapted and published as "The Reconstitution of Private Property in the People's Republic of China: John Locke Revisited," *Social Theory and Practice* 12, no. 3 (Fall 1986): 337–50.

were becoming significantly more free over time. According to the annual Freedom House survey, the share of the world's population living in "not free" regimes was at its lowest recorded point: 39 percent.[60] Even that figure, one might argue, understates the rise of democracy. China's population of more than 1 billion is by no means "free," but it is certainly not as "unfree" as it was twenty years ago. A similar observation might be made about the Soviet Union or South Africa, countries that, however slow to mend their ways, were evidently much more hospitable places to live in the 1980s than in, say, 1948. Men born unfree are throwing off their chains.

Whatever democracy's prospects for the future, the winds of freedom should be a source of joy, pride, and inspiration to the United States. America is now the oldest democracy in the world. We were, as Ezra Pound put it, the first to "make it new." The mere example of America matters. What is more, America has played an active role in promoting democracy elsewhere around the world. American troops twice saved allies in Europe and the Pacific from tyranny. American aid rebuilt Allied and enemy countries alike after World War II. An agreement negotiated at a lodge in New Hampshire, by Britain's Lord Keynes and America's Harry Dexter White—the Bretton Woods accord—established a quarter century of free trade and economic growth around the world. Persistent pressure on our friends in Latin America and Africa in the 1970s and 1980s helped deliver more than a dozen nations to freedom, as the grateful testimony of such leaders as Raul Alfonsin of Argentina attests.[61] In the early 1980s, the United States blocked coups planned against democratic governments in El Salvador, Honduras, and Bolivia,[62] and directly aided the fragile but real progress toward democracy in Haiti, the Philippines, and Grenada.

In short, America has powerful tools with which to influence how our neighbors will be governed. This is not to say we have always, or even usually, used those tools wisely. Often, from Vietnam to Eastern Europe, American power has been used ineptly; but this being conceded, doesn't it make sense to focus our studies on the occasions when it was used well? The proper study of economists, as Michael Novak has argued, is not poverty, since even if we discover its most hidden and subtle "root causes," it will do us little good. As Novak asks, "What will we do then—make more poverty?"[63] Rather, the proper study of economists is wealth. It follows that the proper study of American foreign policy is democracy, and as we have seen, there has been ample evidence in recent years to help us learn how democracies flourish.

But before examining the deeper causes of this tide of freedom, and considering how we can aid its advance, let us consider a strange yet persistent theme in the debate over American foreign policy—a theme whose very existence would seem to cast into doubt everything that has been observed to this point.

2

SKEPTICISM

"**D**EMOCRACY**," writes the respected French author Jean-François Revel, "may, after all, turn out to have been a historical accident, a brief parenthesis that is closing before our eyes." In the first chapter of his book on *How Democracies Perish,* Revel chisels democracy's epitaph:

> In its modern sense of a form of society reconciling governmental efficiency with legitimacy, authority with individual freedoms, it will have lasted a little over two centuries, to judge by the speed of growth of the forces bent on its destruction. And, really, only a tiny minority of the human race will have experienced it. ... The combination of forces—at once psychological and material, political and moral, economic and ideological—intent on the extinction of democracy is more powerful than those forces bent on keeping it alive.[1]

Revel's vision of democracy is shared by many leading intellectuals in the West. Throughout the twentieth century, writes the British historian Paul Johnson in *Modern Times,* "the power of the State to do evil expanded with awesome speed. Its power to do good grew slowly and ambiguously." Western might and resolve withered in tandem to the point that "the American Century seemed to have ended only twenty-five years after it began."[2]

George F. Will, perhaps the premier journalist of his age, has described democracy as a "servile state" dedicated to "the stimulation of consumption."[3] In his newspaper columns and the widely read *Statecraft as Soulcraft,* Will fills a catalogue with democracy's flaws. "Liberal democratic societies," he writes, are "ill-founded." Politics in a democracy quickly lowers itself "to the strongest and commonest impulses in the mass of men," instead of concerning itself with "the best persons and the best in persons."[4] These appetites organize into special pressure groups that dominate democracy: "Today's servile state . . . sees itself as an undignified broker between clamorous interests." Manners decline: "The United States has . . . many people who lack the economic abilities and character traits necessary for life in a free society." Perhaps worst of all, Will argues, a government that can never ask for sacrifices, or even prudent risks, becomes unable to repel deadly enemies. "Internationalist foreign policy has been possible," he writes, "only when Americans have subordinated their natural isolationism to their tradition of deference to the foreign policy elite. Vietnam destroyed that tradition." Thus, the United States of the 1980s saw the end of "unnatural internationalism, and the rebirth of the nation's natural isolationism."[5]

Indeed, while admiring many of democracy's features, most political philosophers have harbored grave doubts about it as a system of government. Neither Plato, Aristotle, Hobbes, or Locke considered what they called "democracy" the ideal form of government. And while Rousseau found democracy suited to some climates and countries—such as small northern republics of limited wealth—even he found little use for it in many others. "If there were a people of Gods," Rousseau wrote in *Du Contrat Social,* "it would govern itself democratically. . . . Government so perfect is not suited to men."[6] Indeed, as historian Harry Jaffa has pointed out, from the growth of Greek democracies in the fifth century B.C. to the publication of *The Federalist Papers* in 1787, scarcely any writer of note advocated the idea of democracy as the correct system for a government under natural law.[7] (Spinoza would be a debatable exception, though his vision of democracy, based on the Hobbesian idea of an "equal fear of death," makes him less a champion of the right to self-government than of raw pragmatism.) "Until the emergence of the United States as the first mass democracy," writes Jeffrey Bell, "virtually no one believed the system could exist in an entity larger than a city state."[8]

It is interesting to note, however, that many of the historical arguments against democracy—on which our modern political philosophers draw heavily—either were not meant to apply to what we now call "democracy," or are growing rapidly obsolete. When Plato and Aristotle fretted about rule by the mob, they literally meant a mob. The democratic assemblies of many city-states involved actual town meetings, or direct democracy, and orderly discussion was sometimes impossible. Moreover, large classes of people were excluded, either because they lacked property or proper birth, or even because they lived in outlying areas that made it difficult to attend meetings of the assembly. Thus, as H. G. Wells observed, the complaints against "democracy" by many of the ancients apply with much less force in an age when ideas are communicated to millions in their own homes, ballots cast in a private booth with virtually universal enfranchisement, and laws passed in special assemblies of those chosen to lead. "Aristotle," according to Wells, "would have enjoyed the electoral methods of our modern democracies keenly."[9] Modern representative democracy would have been called an "aristocracy" by Aristotle, an "elective aristocracy" by Rousseau, and a medium between "democracy" and "oligarchy" by Plato.[10] The founders of the United States clearly had this distinction in mind. Defending their new design in the debate over the Constitution, James Madison wrote, "In a democracy the people meet and exercise the government in person; in a republic they assemble and administer it by their representatives. . . . A democracy, consequently, must be confined to a small spot. A republic may be extended over a large region."[11]

Plato worried that democracy would rapidly become vulnerable to demagogues, who would spur their country to "love of wealth" and incite those "eager for revolution."[12] But such blatant electioneering becomes difficult as wealth, information, and political power diffuse throughout a society, as they did in modern America and Europe.[13] Plato was concerned, as were Europeans seeing the rise of democracy in America, that if common men were given rights, they would abuse them. Indeed, he saw democracy as likely to evolve as a result of a revolution by the poor. By the nineteenth century, however, Alexis de Tocqueville could answer that fear by turning it on its head. De Tocqueville noted that once men had rights—he used the Lockean term "property," with the broad meaning Locke intended for it—they had reason to behave responsibly, and did. "Among civilized nations, only those who have nothing to lose ever revolt," he wrote. With wealth and power distributed broadly, by contrast, "every citizen of the United States transfers, so to speak, his attachment to his little republic into the common store. . . . In defending the Union he defends the increasing prosperity of his own state or country, the right of conducting its affairs, and the hope of causing measures of improvement to be adopted."[14] Rousseau voiced a more modern version of Plato's fear when he warned that in a large democracy, "corporate interests," by which he meant any collection of voters with some common bond distinct from the "general will"—what we now call "special interests"—would undermine democracy, twisting it to their own ends.[15] This process would be abetted as communications increased and these special interests—companies, labor unions, single-issue groups, and others—learned to cooperate and form dominant coalitions. Readers will recognize many of the criticisms leveled at today's political action committees and television advertising. Yet however imperfect campaigns in America are, the fact is that the voters enjoy far more information about candidates than those of any other democracy in history. They are thus far more immune to base appeals, with the modern press, and even the much-maligned TV-spot commercials, providing a bridge over narrow interests and allowing candidates to communicate a broad message based on Rousseau's general will.

An American president, for example, has what Harvard historian Doris Kearns describes as a great "tool" for promoting the general welfare: He can "focus attention" on his own "agenda," rallying the country around a broad appeal to the good of all.[16] In the twentieth century, American presidents used that tool to force Congress to deal with proposals, from the New Deal to the Marshall Plan to civil rights legislation, that would otherwise have been ignored. Even when leaders would not listen, voters managed to place issues and proposals of concern to them on the national agenda. The tax revolt consummated under Ronald Reagan, for example, began in the mid-1970s, when California passed a radical referendum on property-tax reduction. The nuclear-freeze movement of the 1980s was initially sparked in the town meetings of Vermont and New Hampshire. Mr. Will's complaints about the "Balkanization" of America into special-interest groups, unable to act in the general interest, seem hollow in light of the sweeping tax reform passed by Congress in 1986.[17] Since the critics were wrong about democracy in the context of domestic tax debates, they might also be wrong about a related aspect of democracy, namely its potential for reproduction.

That, of course, is our main concern: the notion that democracy, however efficient at producing justice and prosperity—and partly because it is so efficient at these tasks—is ill equipped to defend itself, let alone recreate itself abroad. Yet despite their reservations, neither Will, Revel, nor Johnson, has suggested abolishing elections, nor do those who complain of the weakness of our existing system propose radical changes in the constitutional order of the United States and its allies.* Why not, if the present construction of "democracy" may self-destruct?

Even its critics seem to agree that democracy as we know it is, in fact, the best possible system, or at least, as Churchill put it, the worst except for all the others that have ever been tried. These observers are genuinely distressed by what they see as a pair of inherent and reinforcing flaws: (1) where democracy exists, they say, it seems unable to defend itself; and (2) where democracy does not exist, it seems unable to take root, since these countries often lack the stable middle class, the free press, and the other traditions they deem necessary to make democracy work. Often there is no viable option of a democratic government, or "third force," only a U.S.-backed dictator and a Soviet-backed guerilla movement. This tone of defeatism is espe-

---

*Well, not generally. On the other hand, historian Brian Crozier writes in *National Review* (28 August 1987): "The Constitution that was relevant to the citizens of a country who had chosen to reject the 'rather modest tyranny' of George III is now outdated because it is incapable of meeting the needs of a superpower under global threat."

cially pronounced when it comes to America's foreign policy; it is manifested not only in what is said, but in what is not. Essays and speeches are filled with passages stressing the limitations of U.S. influence—without an equally needed emphasis on its possibilities. American successes, if they are remembered, are not so much studied as cited and sloganized: We need an Apollo approach to this, a Marshall Plan for that. Failures, by contrast, are quickly grafted with either a suffix (-gate, -amok, -scam, -aquiddick) or a prefix (the lessons of, the reality that) and given a full autopsy. Let us examine how this tendency has developed, first from a broad, strategic perspective, then from the standpoint of actual operations.

The Architects

From World War II into the 1980s, the debate on U.S. foreign policy was frequently governed by the phrase "containment." In the words of George F. Kennan, author of the original doctrine, "The main element of any United States policy toward the Soviet Union must be that of a long term, patient but firm and vigilant containment of Russian expansive tendencies." The early advocates of this strategy saw containment of communism as eventually, over many years, prompting the growth of democracy. Lacking legitimacy at home because of its inability to supply justice and prosperity, the Soviet government, proponents argued, must rely on constant foreign advance to sustain its rule. Halt advance, and the system would perforce "turn inward," as Kennan argued in an article for *Foreign Affairs:*

> [The] United States has it in its power to increase enormously the strains under which the Soviet policy must operate, to force upon the Kremlin a far greater degree of moderation and circumspection than it has had to observe in recent years, and in this way to promote tendencies which must eventually find their outlet in either the break-up or the gradual mellowing of Soviet Power.[18]

Over time, however, the strategic idea of advancing democracy became subsumed more and more by the tactical emphasis on the defensive and the reactive. Even when containment was challenged, its assumptions remained intact and guided actual policy. When Dwight Eisenhower's secretary of state proposed that unfree nations be liberated, the policy was explained as an effort to "roll back" communism. Unfreedom, in other words, was to be torn down— a noble goal, but one still fixated on what we oppose rather than what we are for. In any case, this approach, with its suggestion of military confrontation, proved too dull an instrument for use. In the 1960 election, John F. Kennedy proposed a new policy of "flexible response"—again, a worthy initiative, yet still no "flexible creation," if you will, of democracy.

This type of rhetoric matters a great deal (witness the furor that ensued when Ronald Reagan described the Soviet Union as an "evil empire"). Far from being misleading, however, the argot of American strategy has been a fair reflection of the general thrust of policy. Even as democracy itself battled ahead, the boldest thinkers on foreign policy mentioned the possibility of its triumph only with great hesitation, and more often, they explicitly renounced it. In his book *Game Plan,* Zbigniew Brzezinski, the national security adviser to President Carter and a leader of his party's hawkish wing, wrote:

> The U.S.-Soviet rivalry has been transformed into an endless game. . . . This unusual game, with no victory of the traditional type in sight . . . remains predominantly a mobile contest of maneuver, pressure, and even occasionally of force. Not to lose is the first objective.[19]

Lest anyone find this vision unduly sanguine, or sanguinary, Brzezinski later added, in an interview with reporter David K. Shipler: "[Our] task is to design a longer-range geostrategy which enables us to compete with the Soviets on an enduring basis . . . and perhaps eventually prevail. However, I have to add immediately that prevailing has to be viewed as something quite different from traditional victory."[20]

To be sure, Brzezinski's idea is not in formal contradiction to that of one who might say, "My strategy is to use peaceful tactics to produce slow and marginal changes in unfree states, including the Soviet Union—until one day, they are democratic." Yet Brzezinski takes great care to explain that his approach rules out the possibility of "traditional victory." That he does not have in mind a victory by democracy is stated clearly. What he does have in mind comes out only in puffs of smoke. What would "prevailing" mean, if it does not mean a "traditional victory"? A Soviet Union that remains communist, but no longer attacks other nations? An expansionist Soviet Union, but without Marxism? A Soviet Union that allows some mild reforms, but is still very much a totalitarian state? Brzezinski comes closest to a clear definition when he states, "Prevailing means creating international conditions congenial to our values and encouraging change within the Soviet Union which makes the Soviet Union more accommodating in regard to such international arrangements."[21] If this means that America can use tactics short of war to encourage democracy, however, one would expect an articulate man such as Mr. Brzezinski to say so.

SKEPTICISM

Brzezinski's dance has been dealt with at some length because compared with other policymakers, his analysis is one of the most clear, positive, and ambitious. Henry Kissinger, who has equally solid credentials as a thoughtful hawk, described his strategic vision during his tenure as national security adviser from 1969 to 1977 in similar terms:

> The United States as the leader of the democracies had a responsibility to defend global security even against ambiguous and seemingly marginal assaults. We would have to do this while simultaneously exploring the limits of coexistence with a morally repugnant ideology. We would have to learn that there would be no final answers. I was convinced then—and remain so—that we cannot find our goals either in an apocalyptic showdown or in a final reconciliation. Rather, we must nurture the fortitude to meet the Soviet challenge over an historical epoch at times by resistance, at times by negotiation.[22]

If there were tools other than "resistance" to Soviet initiative, on the one hand, and "negotiation" on the other, Kissinger was not at pains to point them out. All that remained, it would seem, was a period of several centuries of near-constant U.S. vigilance, during which, if our defensive efforts were wholly successful, some crack of hope for democratic change might emerge.

Contain, react, defend, respond, negotiate firmly—these constitute the most robust strategies for promoting freedom contemporary U.S. strategists have been able to come up with, and more pessimistic outlooks on America's potential for influence abound. To many observers, the problem is not just that the U.S. has limited influence, but that where it exists, it has generally been used for ill. Jonathan Kwitny, a respected investigative reporter, sees America not only failing to aid democracy, but rather, creating *Endless Enemies.*[23] Richard Barnet did observe a kind of *Global Reach*—but the reach belonged to corrupt multinational corporations that transcend and eventually dominate U.S. policy.[24] Jimmy Carter described U.S. foreign policy from the 1950s to his own presidency as often lacking any commitment to freedom and democracy. "Much of the time we failed to exhibit as an American characteristic the idealism of Jefferson or Wilson," he wrote in his memoirs. "Instead of promoting freedom and democratic principles, our government seemed to believe that in any struggle with evil, we could not compete effectively unless we played by the same rules or lack of rules as the evildoers."[25] Yet when Carter tried, or at least professed to try, to promote human rights, his efforts became, according to the scholar Joshua Muravchik, an *Uncertain Crusade,* a case, in the less favorable assessment of Jeane Kirkpatrick, of *Dictatorships and Double Standards.*[26] No wonder Yale professor Paul Kennedy found America one of history's "declining empires." The same general gloom emerged if one turned one's glance from foreign policy generally to the regions in which it operated. There was, for instance, Latin America, where James Chace, an editor of the *New York Times Book Review,* observed the United States involved, over "more than a hundred and fifty years," in an *Endless War.*[27]

The more common theme of foreign-policy discourse, however, has not been that U.S. influence is large and evil, but good and small; we have benign ends, but few means. Hodding Carter, a spokesman in Jimmy Carter's State Department, described it well: "You do get a sense from listening to these debates that nothing works. Nobody actually says, 'nothing works,' but if you add up what they do say it just about comes to that." To be sure, different schools of thought tend to stress America's impotence in different spheres. Opponents of Carter's human rights policy, as former Carter aide Leslie Gelb notes, tended to stress America's inability to influence allies; Carter and his supporters, meanwhile, tended to downplay our leverage over the policies of enemies such as the Soviet Union. Thus, when a 1986 editorial in the *Wall Street Journal* sighed that the country is "subject to very little, if any, U.S. influence," it meant Pakistan; when the *New York Times* said that "we're stuck with . . . their system," it meant the Soviet Union. The sum of these parts is a psychology of profound impotence. Ronald Reagan, surely one of the most optimistic and activist leaders of his time, put it this way: "Perhaps the most important reality facing us today is the shrinking global influence of the West. The signs of it are all about us."[28]

This sense of paralysis can also be seen from the perspective of the actual tools of foreign policy, from economic aid to arming freedom fighters. Name the lever, and the conventional wisdom among Western leaders is likely to be: It won't work.

The Tools

"Sanctions rarely work," wrote the historian Paul Johnson. In the case of alleviating apartheid in South Africa, at least, Suzanne Garment of the *Wall Street Journal* considered them "just a sideshow . . . trivial." They don't do much good against communists, either, concluded *The New Republic:* "The fact is that anti-Soviet sanctions don't work." Richard Nixon, evaluating the denial of most-favored-nation status in the Jackson-Vanik Amendment in 1973, argued, "I knew that it was utterly unrealistic to think that a fundamental change in the Soviet system could be brought about because we refused to extend MFN status." Jack Kemp agreed: "Sanctions don't work. You can't keep things like grain out of the free market."[29]

Now, the authors of those sentences did not actually say that there are no circumstances in which sanctions might work. Their words, perforce, are plucked from context, often from a long comment or an essay or book containing numerous qualifiers and nuances. No doubt they did not intend to inculcate the idea that sanctions never, under any circumstances, work. The problem stems from the likely effect their words will have on all but the most careful reader or listener, and thus, on the public debate.

To give but one example: The first quotation from Paul Johnson is not part of a general essay on economic sanctions in which the author, after an exhaustive view of their use, concludes that they "seldom work." It is, rather, an aside—part of Johnson's discussion of the events leading up to World War II. What Johnson has in mind is a discussion of a single episode: The imposition of sanctions on Italy following her attack on Abyssinia of October 3, 1935. (Italian exports, we should note, fell by nearly 50 percent in the months after the penalties took effect.) To Johnson's credit, he notes that sanctions can "damage, infuriate, and embitter," and there are certainly instances when this might be our main goal. What Johnson does show is that sanctions, in this case, did not prevent or reverse Italian aggression, yet as he himself notes, it is not clear that sanctions were in fact used against Italy in any meaningful sense. "France," he writes, "would not agree to oil sanctions (the only type likely to have any impact on events) and America, the world's greatest oil producer, would not impose sanctions at all." Johnson is one of the more careful writers cited, which is why his claims are amenable to a closer examination. This very qualified analysis of a single episode, however, is not what will stick in the minds of most readers. Rather, many of us will remember that according to a justly esteemed historian with a sharp pen, "sanctions rarely work."[30]

If not the stick, what about the carrot? Alas, while economic aid has enjoyed a slightly better reputation than sanctions, its actual effects are viewed with little enthusiasm. Our leaders seemed to view foreign aid as a nice idea in symbolic terms, but one almost bereft of positive impact. "The American government's efforts to bring relief, prosperity, and security to impoverished peoples in other countries have gone seriously wrong," concluded Nick Eberstadt of the Harvard Center for Population Studies. "Far from contributing to the goal of self-sustained economic progress in the low-income regions, our funds are instead being directed to a tragic extent into the construction of barriers against such progress, and in some cases may actually be paying for the creation of poverty."[31] Douglas Bandow, a senior fellow at the Cato Institute and special assistant to the president during the Reagan administration, studied foreign aid for the Heritage Foundation. "Does foreign aid work?" he asked. His answer: No. "The proposition that free or cheap money from abroad does not necessarily encourage economic progress seems counterintuitive. Yet logic shows why foreign assistance fails."[32] When not being misdirected at the recipient end, some argued, foreign aid was tailored to respond to narrow constituent interests by the donor.

Melvyn Krauss, a leading analyst of foreign-aid programs, catalogued various deleterious effects of aid in his book *Development Without Aid.* U.S. assistance, he argued, causes the recipient's currency to appreciate, making it more difficult to sell exports. It also permits governments "to pursue policies that damage economic growth." Rather than helping the needy, our money "winds up being used by the governments of poor countries to subsidize the politically powerful middle class and keep themselves in power." His conclusion: "Foreign aid hurts, not helps!" tempting one to ask Krauss if the United States should therefore ship massive amounts of aid to the Soviet Union in order to undermine communism.[33] Of course, the United States already did provide some assistance to Soviet-bloc countries through such institutions as the International Monetary Fund,* where its chief effect, according to Senator Phil Gramm of Texas, is to "support communist dictatorships."[34]

To be fair, one should note that many of these writers, all justly respected in their fields, propose alternative policies that they say would work. Yet their attitude remains fundamentally negative. Krauss recommends virtually cutting off U.S. foreign aid except in the case of dire, short-term emergency assistance. Bandow, besides supporting Krauss's recommendation that most aid be terminated, suggests that the United States encourage free trade. As evidence of the potential impact, he cites a World Bank study which estimated that increased protectionism might stunt Third World growth by as much as 0.4 percent per year. Yet Bandow also writes that "global economic events, particularly recessions and recoveries," have an impact of up to several percentage points per year—several times the estimated impact of trade barriers. So in Bandow's own terms, anything the United States can do to positively influence events is trivial. What we must really jettison, he argues, are not just certain failed programs, but "the even more basic assumption that foreign assistance necessarily helps anyone."[35]

---

*The IMF is a multinational, not a U.S., institution, but its voting shares are weighted to reflect the contributions of member states. In practice, the United States can largely determine IMF policy, though our domination falls short of total, direct control: Major IMF questions require an 85 percent majority, and the U.S. voting share exceeds 15 percent.

SKEPTICISM

Facts and Words

If not sticks or carrots, one might hope that words—facts, rhetoric, threats, and promises—would have some utility. One finds little faith in their effectiveness, though. Certainly one of the most important ways our voice reaches other countries is through such public-diplomacy efforts as Radio Free Europe, the Voice of America, Radio Liberty, and other activities of the U.S. Information Agency. These services broadcast news about world events and U.S. policy to virtually every country on the globe, and they constitute, according to the great Soviet writer and dissident Aleksandr Solzhenitsyn, what may be America's most "important" and "valuable" tools.[36] Supporters of such efforts, however, viewed their effectiveness as limited. Others are even less optimistic: in 1986, Caspar Weinberger doggedly resisted efforts to transfer a small portion of the Defense Department budget to the Radios, which had been hit by an unexpectedly deep drop in the dollar, telling National Security Adviser John Poindexter, "Those are nice, but it's the Soviet guns I'm worried about."[37] It is hard to find many such frankly negative statements about these efforts; there is little explicit opposition to the broadcasts as such. Yet even supporters offer only a bland, highly qualified assessment of their potential. Max Kampelman, a Democrat who served ably in the Reagan administration as a human rights and arms-control negotiator, said in an interview that "I'm a big supporter of the Voice of America and Radio Free Europe, but it would be wrong to overstate what they can do. They're a good, but very limited, tool."[38]

Of course, broadcasts and other information programs to undemocratic nations constitute only one type of public diplomacy. Another involves the issuance of private and public criticisms, threats, and other actions, which under the Carter administration became known as a "human rights policy." Did the Carter idea work? Again, some of the most damning testimony on the impotence of this lever came from the faint praise rendered by its defenders. Two years after Jeane Kirkpatrick's celebrated criticism of Carter's policy as involving a damaging "double standard," *Commentary* magazine held a symposium on human rights. The task of defending Carter was not small. Scholars contributing essays critical of Carter labeled the policy "unrealistic . . . naive . . . hypocritical."[39] Against this backdrop of harsh and specific criticism, Brzezinski wrote:

> The Carter policy was far from perfect. We did not succeed in overcoming the
> inherent contradictions that such a policy has to confront, and no doubt we made
> some mistakes. Nonetheless, we did make significant progress in enhancing the

scope of individual freedom in a variety of places in the world. Thanks to our efforts, thousands of political prisoners were released in several countries in Latin America and Asia. We enhanced the scope of personal freedom in South Korea. We obtained the release of five key dissidents from the Soviet Union (but, alas, the Soviets did crack down on the exit of Jews and on human-rights dissidents within the Soviet Union itself). We quietly obtained the release of some Jewish women from Syria, and so on.[40]

Now, all of these events are to be cheered. Yet at the time Brzezinski wrote, the Carter human rights policy was charged with crimes far greater in scope, including the loss of Nicaragua, Iran, and indirectly, several other countries to communist regimes with even worse human rights practices than their predecessors. Considering the severity of these accusations, Brzezinski's list of triumphs appeared rather mundane. He was, however, more positive than Princeton political scientist Richard Falk, another writer with broad sympathies for the Carter administration and its policies. Falk stated: "The Carter approach to human rights could not finally be reconciled with a world view of states or with the practical pursuit of U.S. interests in the world."[41] Jimmy Carter himself, answering the charge that human rights pressure simply alienated friends and complicated negotiations with enemies, offered little more than Brzezinski in the way of specific gains attributable to his human rights policy. In his memoirs, Carter wrote:

> What would have been the fate of these . . . persecuted people if we had stayed mute on the subject? How many others would have been abused? There is really no way to know. . . .
> It will always be impossible to measure how much was accomplished by our nation's policy when the units of measurement are not inches or pounds or dollars. The lifting of the human spirit, the end of torture, the reunion of a family, the newfound sense of human dignity—these are difficult to quantify.[42]

The critics of human rights were hardly criticizing the policy in terms of "inches" or "dollars." Their claim was that human rights policy of the Carter variety was making human rights worse, causing a decline of "the human spirit" in places like Iran and Nicaragua. As with economic aid, there was a detailed critique asserting that such policies have either little influence or an essentially negative one, and that they failed to produce any concrete, tangible results. There was no corresponding positive assertion that human rights policies can, in the real world, promote human rights.

SKEPTICISM

The Impotence of Arms

If not words, or economic butter, then guns, one might hope, might serve as a tool to aid the spread of democracy. Yet the conventional wisdom is that arms shipments won't work. Not in El Salvador: "American military aid ends up more or less equally in the hands of the insurgents and the Government," Senator Daniel Patrick Moynihan argued. "More of such aid will simply increase the level of violence and reduce the possibility of a settlement."[43] Perhaps, then, America should arm not rickety governments but Third World freedom fighters, such as the antigovernment rebels in Nicaragua. Alas, many leaders insisted that arms won't work there, either. Military aid simply meant "a continuation of a conflict that cannot be won by the contras," according to a proposed "Democratic Foreign Policy" drafted by Congressmen Les Aspin and Stephen J. Solarz.[44] Colleague Victor Fazio agreed: "These bands are not going to be turned into an effective fighting force with mass appeal by giving them more U.S. aid that is wildly unrealistic. Rather than being an effective military threat to the Sandinista regime, the Contras have largely waged war against civilian targets."[45]

Other self-described freedom fighters provoked less controversy in Congress, but little more hope for a democratic victory, as in the proposal for aid to Jonas Savimbi, leader of the National Union for the Total Independence of Angola, or Unita. "After a decade the fighting drags on," wrote a correspondent for *Time* magazine, "with no prospect of victory by either side."[46] Congressman Solarz argued that aid to Savimbi was actually counterproductive: "Instead of producing a reduction in the number of Cuban forces in Angola, it will undoubtedly result in an increase in the number of Cuban troops."[47] The assumption that Savimbi could not win was shared even by many who supported the aid. A 1986 analysis by the State Department and the Central Intelligence Agency reportedly concluded that Savimbi "can't win and can't force a coalition government." This judgment accompanied an "optimistic" reading attributed to the Defense Intelligence Agency which said there was a "fairly strong" prospect that Unita could achieve a "stalemate."[48]

A similar calculus seemed to apply to the freedom movement in Cambodia, which received an estimated $3 million to $5 million in U.S. aid in 1986 and 1987, to fight an occupation force from Vietnam, a country receiving in excess of $300 million per year in direct Soviet aid.[49] Solarz, a leading proponent of aid to the Cambodian rebels, conceded the seeming implausibility of a rebel victory: "Critics of the Cambodian aid proposal have suggested that the noncommunist resistance is no match for the Vietnamese. . . . It is too early, however, to write off these groups." Why too early, many asked, if the freedom fighters cannot triumph? In a major article for *Foreign Policy,* Solarz tried to answer, but retreated into the same vague rationales he himself ridiculed when advanced on behalf of aiding other can't-win resistance movements: "make Vietnam pay as high a price as possible . . . increase the pressure on Hanoi and give it an incentive to work toward a political settlement," and so on.[50]

Now, most of those cited never said outright that U.S. aid to freedom fighters cannot, on principle, produce a victory for democracy. It is the assumptions behind their arguments that are so troubling. The critics of aid to the contras, for example, may have felt there is a freedom-fighter movement elsewhere that can win, but if so, they did not identify it. Similarly, those who opposed giving aid to Savimbi used the inadequacy of a certain amount of aid not to argue for more, but for none, while stating clearly that if aid were raised, it would not be supported by the American people, or simply would be matched by the Soviets. It was hard to find anyone who, on principle, opposed aid to freedom fighters. It was hard to find anyone who was willing to argue that aid could have any concrete, positive results.

Laws Without Police

With so many tools rusty or discredited, international law—the use of treaties, courts, conferences, and the United Nations—seemed to be the sole arrow in democracy's quiver. International law is not supported by recognized international adjudication or law enforcement. Serious advocates, therefore, should presumably be searching for or propose ways to create enforcement. Instead, proponents have urged that international law be given a try, without making contingency plans for when—inevitably—it fails.

Often, international law is used not as an active tool to produce real gains for democracy, but as a means to curtail the use of other tools. International law was used, for example, as an argument against the U.S. mining of the Nicaraguan harbors. The proponents of international law showed no such vigilance, however, in attempting to apply its strictures to the shipment of arms by the Soviet Union, Cuba, and even the Palestinian Liberation Organization into Nicaragua. This is not to say the proponents of international law would have opposed, say, action by the World Court or the United Nations. But they were not loud in demanding it. Nor, interestingly, could any of a number of critics of the harbor mining be seen advocating any reforms to give the World Court's rulings, which are purely advisory, any enforcement teeth. Columnists Anthony Lewis of the *New York Times,* James Schlesinger of the *Wall Street Journal,* Alexander Cockburn of *The Nation,* and Michael Kinsley of *The New Republic* all blasted the United States as an outlaw nation following the World

Court consideration of our mining of the Nicaraguan harbors, or in the wake of the U.S. invasion of Grenada, or both. Yet not one of these writers proposed adding any force to the court's decision.[51] They seemed to like international law just as it was: absent and weak around the world, but present and sometimes powerful as an argument against U.S. action.

If this was all the enthusiasm for real international law that could be mustered by proponents, the public should be forgiven for thinking it a dull instrument. And then there were the opponents. Caspar Weinberger described the efforts of a U.S.-Soviet body that discusses alleged arms-treaty violations, the Standing Consultative Commission, as a farce. "The SCC," Weinberger wrote in a November 1985 memorandum to the president, "has become a diplomatic carpet under which Soviet violations have been continuously swept, an Orwellian memory hole into which our concerns have been dumped like yesterday's trash."[52] Weinberger proposed no actions to strengthen that body, however, and it was not surprising that when his top aide on arms treaties, Richard Perle, was asked to cite his major accomplishments from 1981 to 1987, he responded: "First, we have passed through six difficult years without concluding an arms control agreement that damaged our national security."[53] Ronald Reagan's ambassador to the United Nations, Jeane Kirkpatrick, reacted similarly when asked to list some of her achievements at the U.N., citing a pair of resolutions noxious to U.S. policy whose passage our lobbying was able to prevent.[54]

In the midst of what might be called the Democratic Century, then, conventional wisdom found the cupboard of U.S. influence nearly bare. Even the Reagan presidency, which at the least demonstrated the potential for a rebound, failed to change establishment thinking decisively. By the end of the 1980s, talk of deficits, arms-deal fiascoes, and an allegedly lagging U.S. economy prompted many to argue, as John McLaughlin put it, that America is "going to the dogs . . . demoralized . . . [its] role as the world's economic and military superpower shrinking."[55] When something went right in the world, Western elites rushed in to assure us that suddenly global events had no connection to U.S. diplomacy. (Thus the rise of Gorbachev and his reformist supporters was attributed to a kind of spontaneous combustion—rather than as a response, at least in part, to a partial revival of U.S. will and might and vigor in the 1980s.) What prevailed, as Robert W. Tucker of Johns Hopkins has noted, was the view that "reality" has already "largely foreclosed" any ambitious goals for American foreign policy:

> This view is shared by otherwise very divergent groups in the foreign policy spectrum. It is emphasized both by those who believe we must adjust our interests and behavior to the more modest position we now occupy in the world and by

those who believe we can and must recapture the position and leadership we once enjoyed. . . . What is no longer open to question is the decline in the nation's power and position that has occurred.[56]

A Common Thread

So far, we have been examining this strain of thinking in quite separate instances. Yet there may be a common strand of thinking woven into all of these arguments. If we tug at the strand, we will be able to see this argument more clearly.

When the *Christian Science Monitor* says of proposals for U.S. assistance to Jonas Savimbi, for example, that "military aid likely would lead not to victory but to stepped-up assistance to the Angolan government from Cuba or its Soviet sponsor," it cannot seriously mean that no matter what the United States does, the Soviet Union will match it.[57] Once we assume there is an upper level of Soviet response, even if it is 100 percent of total Soviet output, then the questions become (1) "At what point will the Soviets stop responding?" and (2) "Are we willing to provide assistance up to that point?" A more persuasive essay might have considered the Soviet commitment to communism in Angola, and balanced this against the American interest in democracy, comparing the likely costs of different outcomes from a total Soviet or U.S. victory to a negotiated settlement enforced by U.S. involvement.

It is quite possible, of course, that the author of the editorial in question at least considered these issues, and that the *Monitor* may be interpreted as saying, in shorthand, something like, "Savimbi would need so-and-so many dollars to defeat his adversary, but the United States is not willing to provide that amount of assistance; therefore, it is fair to say we cannot aid Savimbi enough to make a difference." If we look at this reformulated version of the argument, though, several assumptions reveal themselves. One has to do with the power of democracy in Angola itself, the assumption being that however much some Angolans desire freedom, either their desire lacks sufficient strength among the people, or the people themselves lack sufficient courage or bravery to overcome material disadvantages and see that desire realized. A similar assumption is made with regard to the United States, whose citizens are understood to support the idea of democracy, but are not willing to sacrifice material comforts, or risk far worse suffering, to the degree needed to help democracy triumph in Angola. There is even an assumption made about democracy in the Soviet Union, where the people are widely perceived as not having enough influence to prevent their government from meeting whatever challenge democracy poses in Angola. Indeed, in the view of many Western leaders, American actions against the Soviets or their clients, as George Ball wrote in 1983—be they sanctions or covert operations or aid to freedom fighters—tend only to call up an equal and opposite response from the Soviets. "It has substantial freedom to do so," Ball concludes, "for, unlike the leaders of democracies, the masters of the Kremlin can largely ignore public opinion in allocating resources."[58]

These assumptions are common; their net result is to see democracy as a potential liability in the United States, the Soviet Union, and the rest of the world. Consider this excerpt from an endorsement by *National Review* of Philippine ruler Ferdinand Marcos:

> With a growing Communist insurrection on his hands, Marcos . . . is now asking the voters to choose between an experienced (if much tarnished) longtime ruler and a political naive. From a U.S. strategic view, a Marcos victory is preferable. He has promised to preserve the status quo on the Clark Air Force Station and Subic Bay Naval Base; Mrs. Aquino favors a plebiscite on the question.[59]

The case for Marcos, depending on one's reading, either stated or assumed that the value of democracy in the Philippines was questionable. Voters there might not see that Corazon Aquino was "naive," as the editors of *National Review* did. The people of the Philippines might, if allowed to vote directly on the question, actually eject U.S. military bases. Nowhere did this editorial state that the people of the Philippines have no right to decide if their country will have U.S. bases, although even were they acknowledged to have such a right, it was assumed they might exercise it stupidly—not seeing the need for U.S. protection as clearly as William F. Buckley and his colleagues could.

The same kind of thinking was at work in 1984, when Meg Greenfield and the editorial writers of the *Washington Post* recommended that the United States take action to prevent the election of Roberto D'Aubuisson in El Salvador and to encourage the selection of his opponent, Jose Napoleon Duarte.[60] Why was the *Post,* and many other respected journalists, backing what amounted to U.S. intervention in a foreign election? Because D'Aubuisson had been "linked to the death squads" in that country—not by any court of law, and not by Duarte, who praised D'Aubuisson as a legitimate democrat, but by U.S. journalists themselves. (An article in *The New Republic,* a magazine that also backed a lean toward Duarte, conceded that "none of the many allegations about his involvement with the death squads . . . [has] ever been proved.")[61] The core assumption, as an editorial of mine in the *Wall Street Journal* pointed out at the time, was that the people of El Salvador were unequipped to judge whether D'Aubuisson was a fascist murderer. The editorial concluded:

> It occurs to us that Americans . . . might let Salvadorans decide about the death squads. Given the case that appears so far, we suspect that the best judge of Mr. D'Aubuisson is not the State Department or U.S. press, but the Salvadoran people. If in fact Mr. D'Aubuisson is a pathological killer, it's hard for us to imagine his winning on a democratic ballot. And if he wins, it's equally hard for us to imagine he's a pathological killer. Maybe we're wrong, but democracy gambles that the people are the best jurors, and we're willing to gamble on democracy.[62]*

*It strikes me that this thing the author is urging American foreign policy to promote, "democracy," has not yet been defined. In this book, the term refers to a political system run by leaders chosen in periodic elections open to general participation and free debate. Those leaders serve a government of limited powers, with certain rights such as free speech, a fair trial to those accused of serious crimes, and so on, the denial of which is beyond even the state's reach. It is assumed that with those rights intact, voters will be able to choose the optimal arrangements for, say, economic freedom. Yet it is important to note that historically all these freedoms and rights—political, civil and economic—seem to go hand in hand; a state that seizes property or earnings, or quashes dissent, is likely to be in some degree of trouble. But at least a regime with voting rights intact can throw out the leaders who impinge on other liberties. Hence by this definition, democracy would be less threatened by arrangements in Sweden, where economic rights were curtailed substantially in the 1960s and 1970s, or in European and Asian countries that restrict severely the criticism of government war operations in the press, than by the regime in Chile, where citizens may enjoy more economic freedom than in Sweden but where their whole person may be deprived of all rights by an unelected government, or by South Africa, where there are honest elections but the majority of the population, which also is deprived of most economic and civil rights, may not vote.

For the purposes of this book, where an advance of economic or civil freedom occurs, even without the formation of a representative body, it will be equated with an advance of "democracy." This shorthand might be questioned by some, but there is some justification for it. For one thing, it is easier than saying "freedoms that tend to go hand in hand with democracy." For another, an expansion of economic opportunities is an expansion of democracy itself. Insofar as a citizen's earnings, or savings, or property, is made relatively more free from the dictates of the state, and more responsive to his will, he enjoys greater control over his own life. Insofar as he becomes more free to criticize his government, even if that government is a king or a dictator, he gains greater influence over its operations.

Others might use a different term than "democracy" to describe this cluster of freedoms and label the key principle "republicanism," since democracy per se might simply mean government by town meeting with no other freedoms. Yet there have been many republics that were not democracies, and few if any democracies that were not republics. Since our concern is with the freedoms and rights granted by democracy, rather than the constitutional form per se—however important that form may be to the maintenance of such rights—it seems more reasonable to abbreviate "democratic republicanism" to "democracy" than "republicanism." Others might object that what is really meant here is "repesentative democracy" rather than the "direct democracy" of the ancient Greek city-states and modern towns in Vermont and New Hampshire. And so it is, the conduct of an actual direct democracy being impractical for all but the smallest nations today. Hence the author will not be offended if readers mentally scribble in the word "representative" before the word "democracy" wherever it appears throughout most of the book. This is hardly necessary, though. Twentieth-century Britain, France, and the United States are commonly referred to simply as "democracies." For a more extensive discussion of the relationship between rights and democracy, see chapters 4 and 9.

3

IDEOPOLITIK

MIGHT, like wealth, is not chiefly material, but metaphysical. Nations poor in resources—Britain, Germany, Japan—have grown to great power. Amply endowed nations—Brazil, Russia, Iran—have floundered under unjust and inefficient polities. The most monstrously efficient police state can collapse once the delicate web of human relationships on which the system depends breaks down. Democracy, despite miscues by individual leaders, churns out wealth and power unconsciously, because it does not have to rely on fiat or compulsion to issue instructions to the inherently complicated machine—or rather, organism—that is a modern state. In a sense, the best proofs of democracy's power are precisely its drawbacks and errors. If democracy can survive blunders from Versailles to Yalta, and maniacal geniuses from Hitler to Stalin, then it is a virile form of government indeed.

Perhaps this notion is best understood in comparison to those theories of raw power grouped together under what the Germans labeled *Geopolitik.* "The destiny of a state," Napoleon reportedly said, "lies in its geography." Not every student of geopolitics would go quite so far. It is fair to say, however, that geopolitics seeks to find the factor or factors that are at the crux of the world balance of power, or, as Sir Halford J. Mackinder put it, "the geographical pivot of history." Mackinder, in fact, thought he had discovered it in 1904, when he lectured the Royal Geographical Society that "certain aspects, at any rate, of geographical causation [are] universal in history." "Who controls the Heartland"—a strip of productive and strategic land from Berlin to Moscow—Mackinder wrote, "controls the World Island" of Eurasia; and "who controls the World Island controls the world." A grave prediction, since the region of Eastern Europe he considered the Heartland came under near-complete Soviet rule in 1945.[1]

Others, of course, proposed pivots of their own. Not long before Mackinder's paper appeared, Alfred Thayer Mahan, a captain in the U.S. Navy, outlined the "profound determining influence" of sea power upon history.[2] Not long after Mackinder, a host of theorists asserted the primacy of air power: American pilot William "Billy" Mitchell, Italian strategist Giulio Douhet, and military analysts Louis A. Sigaud and Alexander P. De Seversky, among others. In any war in the foreseeable future, Douhet wrote in 1921, "the Air Force will be decisive."[3]

By the 1940s, the dominant school of thought involved abstraction from the events of the battlefield, arguing that control was contigent on general economic strength—a theme sounded by such diverse leaders as Franklin Roosevelt, Harry Truman, Winston Churchill, Dwight Eisenhower, John Kennedy, and Richard Nixon. Within this economic school of geopolitics, it should be noted, there were variations. Churchill, who steered Britain toward weapons breakthroughs with the tank in World War I and air defense in World War II, and Eisenhower, who successfully pushed for deployment of the first intercontinental missiles and nuclear submarines, both placed heavy emphasis on the technological cutting edge of the military-industrial complex. So, in the 1970s and 1980s, would such advocates of a Star Wars defense as Daniel O. Graham and Ronald Reagan. Graham also articulated, as a corollary, an extraterrestrial geopolitics, calling space "the high seas" of the coming era. Another variation on the economic thesis focused on supplies of critical commodities, such as energy and key industrial minerals, and these strategists set forth to defend key "choke points"—such as the Persian Gulf and South Africa—through which movement of those materials depended.

By the great upheavals of the 1970s, the economic model in one form or another reigned supreme in the world of *geopolitik*. The key fight was not for the world island, German Prime Minister Helmut Schmidt argued, but for "the world product." It is "the economy," echoed columnist William Safire, "on which all potential domination rests."[4]

Yet however vital the issue of where power resides and how it is exercised, there is a prior, more fundamental question suggested by these theories of *geopolitik*. Given that there is some "pivot of history," some key determinant of the balance of power, which sort of polity will tend to find and dominate it? The answer to this question is contained in what may be labeled a theory of *ideopolitik*.

For many modern strategists, study of the various types of power has become an end in itself. They hold vast conferences with huge maps containing great red and blue arrows, or black symbols for strategic minerals (all minerals in these games seem to be "strategic"). Interestingly, though, many of the great geopoliticians arrived at the conclusion that a nation's system of political economy is the critical determinant of its power, and nearly all of these found democracy the superior order. Mackinder's most popular work on the subject is entitled *Democratic Ideals and Reality*. The book concludes with essays on "The Freedom of Nations" and "The Freedom of Man," setting out the political model by which democracies can triumph. For the West, Mackinder said, preventing Russian or German domination of the heartland depends on ensuring that "men and women of the democracies" become "more free," promoting "balanced economic development," while voiding "undue centralization." Democratic polity, for Mackinder, was the key to the key, the social crux behind the geopolitical crux of the World Island:

> Human riches and comparative security are based today on the division and coordination of labor, and on the constant repair of the complicated plant which has replaced the simple tools of primitive society. In other words, the output of modern wealth is conditional on the maintenance of our social organization and capital. [Without this] the machinery becomes so much scrap metal.[5]

Mahan, too, emphasized the polity which underlies military strength. "The empire of the sea," he wrote, "is doubtless the empire of the earth."[6] The question then became, "Who shall rule the seas?"

For Mahan, the answer lay not in the sheer size of one's military armada, but in a vast infrastructure of shipbuilders, sailors, and merchants. A mere program to "increase sea power" would not do. Spain, France, and Germany all launched vast, centralized efforts with this aim, yet they failed to match the English, the Dutch, and later, the Americans. Mahan underlined the fact that both Britain and Holland were widely discredited as "nations of shopkeepers." "But the jeer, in so far as it is just, is to the credit of their wisdom," he continued. "They sought riches not by the sword but by labor. The instinct of the born trader, shopkeeper if you will, sought continually new articles to exchange; and this search combined with the industrious character evolved through generations of labor. . . . The tendency to trade, involving of necessity the production of something to trade with, is the national characteristic most important to the development of sea power."[7]

And what, in turn, makes for a nation of shopkeepers? Less democratic governments, such as that of Spain, tended to oppress commerce and the spirit of freedom that accompanies it. In Britain and Holland, by contrast, "the State was republican in name" and allowed large scope to "personal freedom and enterprise." National policies were developed more rapidly, and accurately reflected the popular will. In short, Mahan found the crux of naval power to lie in the national character:

> In the matter of sea power, the most brilliant successes have followed where there has been intelligent direction by a government fully imbued with the spirit of the people and conscious of its true general bent. Such a government is most certainly secured when the will of the people has some large share in making it.[8]

De Seversky echoed this theme in his *cri de coeur* of 1942, *Victory Through Air Power,* in which he argued that the essential ingredient was not sheer production—at which Germany and Japan had demonstrated considerable determination and skill—but the ability to outthink and outplan the enemy, discarding old strategies and shifting to new technologies at top speed. Free, democratic institutions, providing constant feedback and forcing rapid revision of errors, held a major advantage in a contest of air power. "Americans are the natural masters of the aerial weapon and therefore the destined victors in a technological contest," he wrote.[9]

Even the study of might apart from right, then, when well conducted, becomes the study of might as a consequence of right: *ideopolitik.*

A New Age?

With the advent of nuclear weapons in 1945, of course, democracy faced a new challenge. Mankind is now in the "nuclear age," living "on a precipice" under the threat of "doomsday." To many, this "inescapable reality" has altered the very nature and foundation of foreign policy.

Such millenarian rhetoric, however, overstates the change. Contrary to a widespread cliché, for example, it cannot fairly be said that nuclear weapons have "kept the peace," freezing the democracies and their opponents into a kind of cement pond—a Lake of Cocytus—where neither side is able to move. During the 1970s, several dozen conventional wars raged, on every continent but Australia. The number of terrorist incidents and assassinations grew by a factor of more than ten.[10] In the killing fields of Cambodia's civil war, millions died; millions more probably perished, in combination, in bloody conflicts between Iran and Iraq, between the Soviet Union and Afghanistan, and in civil wars and induced famines across Africa. By 1983, 45 of the world's 164 countries were at war against either an external foe or a sizeable internal guerilla army. From 1945 to 1987, more than 81,000 American servicemen died as a result of hostilities that were wars in all but name: Korea, Vietnam, Lebanon, Grenada.[11]

Nuclear weapons, and the fear of them, did help prevent an all-out war among the major powers. What Metternich was to the nineteenth century, Einstein was to the twentieth. Yet in the 1980s, virtually every nation thought to possess nuclear weapons used military force against another country, including France (against Libya in Chad), the United States (against Grenada and Iran and Libya), the Soviet Union (Afghanistan and China), Britain (Argentina), South Africa (against several neighbors), Israel (Syria and Lebanon), India (Pakistan and Sri Lanka), and China (Vietnam, Cambodia, Soviet

Union). This list includes only direct and well-publicized uses of force by a government's own agents; if we were to include proxy forces, arms shipments, armed alliances, paramilitary training efforts, smaller border skirmishes, and intelligence arrangements, one could easily paint the picture of a third world war, albeit at a low level of intensity. Hence, nuclear weapons have tended not to prevent war, but to push the conduct of war, and of foreign policy more generally, into what Richard Nixon called a new twilight struggle. "There is today a vast gray area between peace and war," Nixon wrote, a struggle between democracy and communism in which proxy armies and arms shipments, propagandists and spies, terrorists and police fight for supremacy but not in open conflict. "The struggle will largely be decided in that area."[12]

In this gray area—under the shadow of nuclear weapons, one might say to complete the Nixonian metaphor—democracy faces substantial disadvantages. Total war became "unthinkable." Threats are likely to be ambiguous, as Henry Kissinger observed, and therefore difficult for a democracy to combat until the hour is too late. The United States seems unable, as in Vietnam, to maintain commitments to far-flung regions. That the enemy is no longer bent on immediate domination through rapid, frontal assault makes the problem in some ways more difficult. "The Soviet practice," Henry Kissinger wrote, "is to promote the attrition of adversaries by gradual increments, not to stake everything on a single throw of the dice."[13] This poses a special problem for democracies, which do better against clear, brazen enemies. Besides pushing conflict into the difficult "gray area," moreover, nuclear weapons often made the West afraid to act even within that gray area. The West, as journalist and Reagan administration aide Phil Nicolaides argued, often resembled a frightened animal—petrified in the dark as a bright light, the threat of annihilation, is pointed into our eyes. Meanwhile, according to Nicolaides, the Soviet leaders move about freely—provided they keep the light trained.[14]

History seems to confirm the fear that Marx and the atom were a deadly combination. At the beginning of the First World War, Marxism was in place approximately nowhere. By 1985 it ruled more than half the surface and population of the globe. In between lies a long list of casualties to communism, from the tiny republics of Latvia, Estonia, and Lithuania to Poland, Hungary, East Germany, Cuba, and Vietnam. Worse still, these advances strike many as being immutable. "A success" for American foreign policy, argues Irving Kristol, "would be for a country governed by a Marxist-Leninist regime to undergo a political transformation. We have had no such success in the postwar period." Kristol would not go so far as to say there had been no Soviet setbacks, but others did. Indeed, the idea has been advanced most strenuously by those who view the Soviet gains as most pernicious. Once they have established a clear grip on a piece of real estate, Jean-François Revel writes, what the Soviets gain is never challenged: "The primarily territorial nature of Soviet

Concessions and Retreats:
Soviet Thrusts and Setbacks of the Postwar Era

Iran, 1946—The Soviets withdraw several thousand troops from occupied area, allowing this strategically important country to pass to British and U.S. control.

Berlin, 1946—The Soviets attempt to shut off Western land traffic to West Berlin. Truman responds with an airlift to keep the city supplied. The Soviets allow traffic to resume.

Yugoslavia, 1948—Marshal Tito breaks with the Soviet-dominated Comintern and establishes his country as a communist state, but one often hostile to Soviet objectives.

Greece and Turkey, 1945–50—Under the Truman Doctrine, the United States ships billions in aid, and commits U.S. ground advisers, to governments fighting a civil war against Soviet-backed rebels. The Soviet forces are eventually defeated, and by the 1980s, both countries hold elections relatively free of corruption.

Korea, 1950–52—Troops backed by the Soviets and the Chinese brazenly assault South Korea, pushing the country's army into a small foothold in the south. United Nations troops, deployed largely thanks to the United States, push the invaders far back into North Korea. Eventually, the war is settled with the partition of Korea into two countries—a setback for the Soviet aim of a united, pro-Soviet state.

Austria, 1955—Thousands of Austrians, wanting to establish a neutral democracy, take to the streets to protest, march, and pray the rosary. To widespread astonishment and joy, the Soviets withdraw.

Eastern Europe, 1945–70—Facing general insurrection, and with the United States promising to intervene on behalf of local dissidents, the Soviets must initiate what they greatly preferred to avoid: a crushing, all-out assault on Hungary in 1956, construction of the Berlin Wall in 1961, the invasion of Czechoslovakia in 1968. Stalin won't even bring the East German Communist Party into the Comintern in 1947, convinced that the West would insist on legitimate elections. The West fails to capitalize on the opportunities presented by these brutal repressions. Even so, in each case, the Soviets must leave behind a vast occupying force and incur lasting enmities. In addition, the Kremlin, its resources stretched to the limit, is forced to allow a series of experiments with democracy and capitalism, particularly in Hungary, East Germany, and Poland.

Cuba, 1962—Having established a client state in 1959, a clear victory, the Soviets try to achieve a rapid shift in the balance of nuclear power by placing nuclear weapons in Cuba. A U.S. naval blockade forces the Soviets to reconsider and the weapons are withdrawn. President Kennedy, in also legitimizing the continuation of an aggressive Marxist regime by extending U.S. security guarantees, may well have squandered the fruits of a great and achievable victory. Strategist Harold Rood argues this case forcefully. But again, we seek here to test the thesis that Soviet policy never retreats or contemplates retreat—no more.

China, 1959—The approximate climax of a long-simmering Sino-Soviet split, in which the most populous nation on earth abandons its alliance with the Kremlin. By the 1970s, China is a quasi-ally of the United States. In the 1980s, she conducts a great experiment, one that may test whether any nation conceived in Marxism can make a peaceful shift to democracy.

Western Europe, 1950–72—Two major offensives by the Soviet Union are crushed. The first involves efforts to seize power through the election of Eurocommunists, especially strong in Italy, France, and Greece. After posting impressive gains through the 1960s, these parties eventually become isolated and discredited. The second offensive involved an attempt to intimidate Western Europe by waging a campaign of terrorism on the West's own soil. This, too, backfired: West Germany and Italy in particular quashed the domestic threat.

The Congo, 1960–65—Communist guerillas aided by Che Guevara and supported by the Soviet Union face off against the remnants of Belgium's former colony, which has recently gained independence. Instead, nationalist Joseph Mobutu takes power—

hardly a Western, democratic leader, but a defeat for Soviet designs on what is now called Zaire.

Latin America, 1965–75—Saying that Latin America is "ripe" for subversion, Castro acquires Soviet arms designed to foment revolution in Peru, Colombia, and Venezuela. All turned back the violent threat and are essentially democratic states by the late 1980s.[a]

Seven Days in 1967—Israel decisively pounces on a planned invasion by Soviet-backed Arab states and occupies important new territories on the West Bank.

Egypt, 1972—More than 50,000 Soviet advisers and military personnel are expelled from the Kremlin's major ally in the Middle East. They leave behind an expensive arsenal.

Chile, 1973—Salvador Allende, a Soviet-backed Marxist who threatened to subvert Chile's democracy, is removed by a military *junta,* probably with extensive U.S. support. The resulting dictatorship of Augusto Pinochet was no democracy, but it was fiercely anti-Soviet.

Spain and Portugal, 1974–77—Two states threatened by Soviet subversion give birth to democracy.[b]

Angola, 1976 to . . .—Cuban forces and Soviet advisers occupy this African state for more than a decade but cannot subdue the rebel forces of Jonas Savimbi, a former Marxist.

Afghanistan, 1979 to . . .—An all-out Soviet invasion cannot crush the brave resistance of the mujahedin and other freedom fighters.

El Salvador, 1979 to . . .—Soviet-backed rebels establish a foothold but the country holds free elections in 1982, 1984, and 1986, and the movement, though alive, is on the defensive.

North Yemen, 1972—The Soviets back guerillas, tribes, and South Yemen with arms in an attempt to unify Yemen under a Kremlin-dominated government without success.

Uganda, 1978—Idi Amin, famous for his cruelties and backed by Soviet arms, is deposed.

Somalia, 1977–78—A country once aligned with the Soviet Union and backed by Soviet advisers launches a guerilla war on another Soviet satellite, Ethiopia. Ethiopia triumphs in the short run with massive Soviet-Cuban assistance, but her continuing instability convinces many Africans that the notion of Soviet invincibility is a myth.

Poland, 1979 to . . .—A free trade union including more than one-third of the nation's population, and commanding the sympathy of probably 90 percent of its population, is established, wins important changes in Polish society, and holds a union congress demanding freedom of speech, civil rights, and an elected parliament. In the fall of 1981, alas, the Reagan administration fails to assist Solidarity with the critical information that authorities plan to establish martial law. Yet Solidarity, and a web of samizdat journals and church leaders, survive, a constant force for freedom.[c]

Zimbabwe, 1980—A Soviet-backed guerilla faction led by Joshua Nkomo loses out in a power struggle to Chinese-backed Robert Mugabe.

Nicaragua, 1981 to . . .—A Soviet client state comes under assault from a band of freedom fighters, the contras, who enjoy U.S. backing. By 1987, Nicaragua requires an estimated $1 billion in annual military aid, and the contras remain, bravely hoping to revive resistance in the future.

Lebanon, 1982—The Soviet-backed Palestine Liberation Organization is swept to the sea, though the West unwisely rescues much of the PLO in a kind of save-the-terrorists Dunkirk from the port of Beirut.

Grenada, 1983—The United States leads a multinational invasion to liberate an outright Soviet-Cuban satellite.

[a]Truly a Soviet defeat? See Jean-François Revel, *How Democracies Perish,* trans. William Byron (New York: Doubleday, 1984), pp. 114–15.

[b]Ibid., pp. 94–95.

[c]This chilling account of a U.S. sellout of Solidarity, alleged by defected Polish Colonel Ryszard Kuklinski, was first reported in the *Washington Post* on 4 June 1986. Eric Chenoweth and Jerzy B. Warman of the Committee in Support of Solidarity repeated the charge in an article for *The New Republic* on 14 July 1986. Kuklinski outlined the tragic, needless decline of Solidarity in a long interview for a Paris-based Polish magazine, *Kultura,* Spring 1987.

imperialism is one of the secrets of its irreversibility." George Bush in 1980 bemoaned the fact that "terrible as it is, the Brezhnev Doctrine," which asserts that no communist-bloc state will ever become democratic, "has been carried out. It would be hard to name an exception."[15] The irony is that by asserting the irreversibility of Soviet conquest, these leaders helped induce a paralysis nearly as great as that produced by those who claim there have been no Soviet gains at all, or that such gains are negligible. One way to freeze a nation into inaction is to insist that its opponents are not worthy of concern. But where apathy is absent, despair will do, and in painting the Soviet Union as a sort of infallible, monolithic giant, anticommunists in the West promote the same result.

Fortunately, Soviet postwar foreign policy has hardly been characterized by unbroken successes. The chart on "Concessions and Retreats" considers just some of the setbacks suffered by Soviet Marxism in the nuclear age. Bear in mind that we are not for the present examining Western victories. Nor need we concern ourselves with the complicated debate over which side has enjoyed greater relative gains. We are interested in whether the Soviet Union, the chief rival to the democracies, is so relentless a foe as to never retreat, even sometimes in humiliation.

Soviet leaders have proclaimed, and will continue to proclaim, that they intend to convert the world to communism, using whatever methods are available. There is good reason to deal cautiously with a power that even advances such claims, yet as strategic expert Kenneth Waltz has written, "Her sporadic successes should not obscure the fact that what the Soviet Union has done mostly since 1948 is lose . . . and her recent slight successes bear no more promise of longevity than earlier ones did."[16]

Freedom Fighters Without Guns

Wee Willy Keeler once summarized his batting strategy as: "Hit 'em where they ain't." By the 1980s, the Soviets had been reduced to something resembling this strategy for undermining democracy: Subvert it where it ain't. This strategy wasn't hard to carry out—authoritarians are easier to subvert than democratic governments—yet it also limited Soviet advances to a narrowing sphere. Indeed, it would be hard to name an established democracy—a nation in which there have been meaningful transfers of power under free elections— that has fallen under Soviet domination.

By the same token, no states that endured more than a decade of Soviet domination have become democracies, either. The problem for both systems, then, and for the world generally, is that by the 1980s there were few easy pickings left. With the gradual consolidation of most states into solid democracies or Soviet satellites, the region of the world where both communism and democracy ain't is shrinking. Monarchy and fascism are dying out. "At the beginning of this century," notes political activist and analyst Jeffrey Bell, "ruling monarchy was the dominant system of mankind, except in the Western hemisphere and a small minority of the population of Europe. By 1950 it had little importance outside the Islamic world. By 1980 kings ruled in only three Arab countries—Morocco, Jordan, and Saudi Arabia." Fascism, in the form of military dictatorships, lived in only a few nations, and unlike the fascism of Hitler, was defended only in terms of some emergency, real or invented. Autocratic rulers such as Chile's Pinochet or Marcos of the Philippines proclaimed themselves bridges to an eventual return to free elections. "No one is writing books advocating permanent army rule as the answer to the world's or even a single region's problems," Bell noted, "and most of the ruling generals see themselves as caretakers."[17] Democracy and communism, meanwhile, gradually expanded and consolidated. (Readers may want to consult the world maps of democracy from 1875 to the present, on pages 242–244.)

Even this observation overlooks an important development: For in countries neither wholly democratic nor wholly aligned with Soviet communism, vast changes were and are taking place. This plays to democracy's greatest strength—its advantage in the ideopolitical struggle for freedom, in which popular and efficient political systems grow and thrive. One example of this phenomenon is communication. In 1950, few families even in America owned television sets. Today they are common in the developed world, with more than one set per family in such new industrial powers as Korea and Taiwan. By one estimate, 70 percent of all East Germans receive Western television broadcasts. Even in Russia, Cuba, China, and Soviet-occupied Europe, the overwhelming majority of families own radios, on which they can listen to Western radio broadcasts. By 1980, the circulation of samizdat journals topped 100,000 in the Soviet Union; in Poland, thanks to the continuing network of factory workers and farmers of Solidarity, small underground fliers and broadcasts reached "the majority of the population," according to one activist. And an increase in accuracy and honesty under various Soviet "openness" initiatives made even the state-run media more informative. Less-developed countries feel the impact of improved information delivery, too. Many African villages, previously cut off from the world almost entirely, are now easily reached by telephone or radio. Literacy rates are above 90 percent in most countries of the world, with many poor nations outperforming the United States. Small villages that cannot afford a huge library suddenly have access to up-to-the-minute, exhaustive information on medicine, farming, and other practical questions through the personal computer, an electronic version of the Peace Corps.[18]

These trends help democracy in a number of ways. In the democracies themselves, better information has meant better policies, and a more rapid transmission of effective policy around the world. By the time the United States completed its revolutionary tax reform of 1986, France, Britain, West Germany, and Japan had already announced their intention to adopt similar changes. The civil rights gains of the 1960s, the environmental protection movement of the 1970s, and the desire for stronger American defenses in the 1980s owed much to the improved information provided to American voters. They saw blacks ill-treated in their own homes, heard frightening reports about the impact of pollution on their own lives, and read jarring statistics about the growth of Soviet military power. Political action followed.

Improved communication also makes the peoples of less democratic nations more aware of, and thus more eager to share in, the benefits of freedom. Leaders in Korea and Taiwan, which announced major democratizing moves of their own in 1987 and 1988, admit they were powerfully influenced by the popular cries for democracy in their country that followed the fall of Ferdinand Marcos in 1986. Marcos himself illustrated another important effect of information: Americans more aware of his undemocratic rule were less willing to support aid to his regime, and helped pressure the Reagan administration to pressure Marcos to leave the country. Even the Soviets, while obviously not subject to the full force of these pressures, found increasing incentives to relax controls on dissidents. When they released longtime critics of the regime from jail, they were rewarded with front-page headlines in the West. When Soviet police brutally suppressed Jewish dissidents protesting for the right to emigrate, the same front-page headlines denounced them vigorously. On the margin, then, communication has aided democracy in significant ways.

Of course, communications technology has more sinister uses; it can make the police state more efficient. One of the happy realities of information, however, is that a more efficient transfer mechanism only makes the system as a whole work better if the facts you put into it are generally true. Moreover, the greatest benefits of information come when it is not only true, but readily available, when facts can be plugged in and taken out freely. It does your local K-Mart no good to have a 50 percent markdown sale on records if no one is aware of it. And it does a centralized economy little good to have individuals cranking out brilliant new methods of production that aren't speedily made available to production plants. Yet the rapid transfer of accessible and accurate information is precisely what a totalitarian regime must seek to prevent. When it does not, the result can be a popular movement such as Solidarity in Poland, which was heavily dependent on the country's telephone system. Tyrants naturally try to reap the fruits of information technology without granting increased freedom, just as Lenin envisioned vast wonders for the Soviet economy from the determined production of electricity, or as Peter the Great sought to infuse his country with Western innovation without Western liberty. But new technologies such as the computer do not ease the dilemmas faced by central authorities; they heighten them. James V. Ogle, a former CIA agent and expert in computers and East-bloc development, explains:

> In today's world, computerization is an economic necessity. However, as industrialization does continue, the Soviet bloc faces even larger contradictions. . . . Computerization brings with it a transformation which is just the opposite of that projected by George Orwell in *1984*. Big Brother—the party leadership in Moscow—can no longer watch the whole society. Tens of thousands of computers in the hands of analysts and technicians dispersed all over the continent are watching Big Brother, creating new opportunities for decentralization and debate. . . . The de-Stalinization of data increasingly deprives the political leadership of that arbitrariness which is part of the definition of tyranny.[19]

A second, related factor that is strengthening democracy is its own popularity. Related, yet not identical, because communication could aid democracy even without convincing people around the world explicitly that democracy is a better system, and, conversely, because the belief that democracy provides a superior model is not simply due to better communication. Information about communism and democracy was widely available in the 1950s and 1960s, but many countries nevertheless found the Marxist model attractive. Today, almost no one does, as Irving Kristol emphasized when he wrote an "obituary" in 1976 proclaiming that "socialism is dead."[20]

By the 1980s, despite massive diplomatic and financial investments, Moscow was losing influence on most continents. Latin America was united in its opposition to Soviet regimes in Cuba and Nicaragua, the latter two forming an increasingly costly burden; whatever their differences with the United States, Latins sought close ties with us, and distance from Moscow. So did most of Africa. "These days," reported Michael Kaufman of the *New York Times*, "it is commonplace to hear that, among activist powers in Africa, the Soviet Union is generally ranked below South Africa, France, and Libya," not to mention the United States. Libya, a quasi-client of the Soviets, was repeatedly repulsed in its efforts to dominate Chad, which had aid from the United States and France. And despite much anti-American rhetoric, African governments were eager to expand their economic ties with the West, and reduce them with the USSR.[21] Leslie Gelb, a journalist and former State Department aide, noted the same trend in Southeast Asia: Though a few countries fell like dominoes in the 1970s, many more rallied to resist a similar fate, relying on

U.S. or Chinese assistance to remain free of Soviet domination. "Ten years after the defeat of South Vietnam," Gelb wrote, "there is widespread agreement that the position of the United States in Asia is stronger now than at any time since the end of World War II. . . . Vietnam, the Soviet Union, and most communist movements in Asia tumbled from victory or ascendancy into decline, while the United States moved from defeat to a position of strength." By the 1980s, the nonaligned movement was actually becoming nonaligned, calling for the withdrawal of Soviet forces from Afghanistan, for example, at a 1983 meeting.[22]

A third force for democracy is religion, the death of which, as Paul Johnson has written, is the "outstanding nonevent" of the twentieth century.[23] In countries such as Russia and Poland, any institution free of the domination of the state will attract people. But religion, with its claim to a higher morality than a capricious bureaucracy or an arbitrary "dialectical materialism," is a particular thorn. In Poland, the strength of the Catholic Church helped create Solidarity and, despite the government crackdown, set important limits on how far the government could go. In the Soviet Union, refusenik Jews, because they have education and skills the regime badly needs, were able to win concessions from the government concerning emigration abroad and dissent at home. In a number of Third World countries—Argentina, South Africa, Chile, and Nicaragua, for example—church groups helped pressure for human rights. In the Philippines, the church was critical in the country's transition to democracy. And whereas a number of religious leaders once opposed democracy, more and more support it, including Pope John Paul II and a number of protestant and Jewish clergymen. Even Islam, while sometimes taunting the West as a Great Satan, is not theologically antithetical to representative democracy and it is certainly inhospitable to atheist Marxism. For all the scorn heaped on the notion of moderates existing in Iran, the Ayatollah Khomeini rules over an elected parliament where debates are bitter and disagreements real. He also faces an armed resistance movement claiming several thousand members—a group whose recognition was urged by more than fifty U.S. congressmen.[24] By the late 1980s, such countries as Turkey and Egypt, with large Moslem populations, showed promise of becoming solidly democratic.

A fourth ideopolitical advantage the democracies enjoy is demographic. Misery makes a poor aphrodisiac, and Marxism has produced a demoralized people uninterested in reproduction, plagued by chronic health problems and below-replacement fertility rates. From 1970 to 1980, the Soviet Union added 23 million people to the working-age population. From 1980 to 1990, according to an estimate by the Central Intelligence Agency, the country would add 5.3 million. It isn't just that the country has a falling birth rate—down to 19.4 births per 1,000 residents, or well below the world average. In a trend unique in the developed world, the Soviet Union has actually endured rising infant mortality and declining life expectancy since the 1960s. Infant mortality rose from a rate of less than 23 deaths per 1,000 births in the 1970s to 26 deaths per 1,000 births in 1985. (The U.S. rate was 10.6.) Life expectancy for males dropped to 62 years in 1980, from 67 years in 1964. From what we know of Soviet culture in the 1980s, that decline has almost certainly continued. Between 1965 and 1985, cigarette use per adult rose by nearly a third in Poland and more than 50 percent in Soviet-occupied Germany. In 1980, per capita consumption of alcohol was more than 70 percent higher in Eastern Europe than in Western Europe. By some estimates, half the Soviet population has a drinking problem, and the average woman has more than one abortion in her lifetime: 181 abortions per 1,000 fertile women per year. Of every 100 known pregnancies in the Soviet Union in 1982, 68 ended in abortion. All this, mind you, despite furious efforts to raise fertility rates and health-care standards in most of the Soviet-bloc countries. Such statistics attest to a profound cultural and demographic malaise.[25]

As America and Europe learned in the 1970s, highly successful and developed societies also face a demographic problem, since rising prosperity generally prompts declining birth rates. In recent years, much attention has focused on this phenomenon, in large part thanks to the publication of Ben Wattenberg's popular book, *The Birth Dearth.*[26] There are, however, several important ways in which Wattenberg has overstated the problem, particularly as it relates to the struggle between communism and democracy. Demographics is a highly speculative business, yet by far the most frightening of Wattenberg's projections, as he was careful to make clear, have to do with population declines that would occur in the West *if* present fertility and death rates remain roughly the same through the year 2100. Keeping things "roughly constant" always sounds reasonable, but in reality, most of these demographic variables are highly volatile: There would not be what Wattenberg called a "birth dearth" to begin with if Western fertility rates had remained "roughly constant" since the 1950s. Wattenberg's projections extended complex variables as far into the future as the Civil War is in the past—highly speculative stuff. More academic treatments of the subject voice much less alarm about the West's population level,[27] and even as Wattenberg's book was being published there were signs that the birth dearth was turning around. For all the talk of selfish American yuppies remaining unmarried, statistics pointed to another pendulum swing. The median age at first marriage in 1985 was 22.5 years for women and 25.2 for men; the comparable figures for 1890 were 22 and 26 years. In 1985, birth rates reached their highest level since 1965, with 3.75 million babies born. "Millions of women," chirped *Cosmopolitan,* "feel an *urgent* need to reproduce." Pollster Lou Harris reevaluated Census Bureau statistics and concluded that one marriage in eight, not one in two, was ending in divorce.[28] Even using Wattenberg's assume-rates-don't-change-much model, here is his projection for the year 2010: Population of the industrial communist world, 450 million. Population of the Western democracies, 791 million.[29]

The real growth in world population, as Wattenberg noted with some alarm, is taking place in the Third World. Yet much of the Third World, as we have noted, is becoming democratic, and a sizeable portion of it is moving to the democratic West: an estimated 400,000 to 800,000 legal immigrants coming to the United States alone each year.[30]* If we assume a flow of 1 million immigrants a year—well below the historical highs as a share of the U.S. population—then the U.S. population, rather than leveling off at 260 million, would reach a robust 400 million in the year 2080.[34] The question posed in Wattenberg's subtitle, "What happens when people in free countries don't have enough babies?" thus becomes something like, "What happens when countries having lots of babies are becoming more democratic—and sending lots of people to the free countries?" And the answer is, the free countries benefit greatly.

For the Soviets, even solving the demographic problem is a problem: New babies and immigrants are coming from Moslem ethnics not friendly to Soviet values or desired by Russian elites. By the 1980s, Soviet officials already spoke warily about the year 2000, by which, it was estimated, the Russian ethnic share of the total Soviet population would fall below 50 percent.[35] For America, immigration is at worst a mild social canker due to atavistic prejudices against foreigners. Even so, immigrants are readily assimilated and, once here, are a tremendous boon to the economy.[36] Demography, then, offers communism an awful set of trade-offs, and the West, some happy choices.

This is particularly so because of a fifth ideopolitical asset. Like religion, nationalism has been the object of many obituaries. Yet it breathes. Now, nationalism in its narrowest sense can be an enemy of democracy. The twisted nationalism of trade protectionism, for example, is a threat to economic prosperity, as is the impulse to lock out immigrants. Yet nationalism at its best is simply a broadened pride in community values and culture, embracing the local and the particular. When warped into a desire for the domination of others, nationalism can of course lead to war, but then it tends

---

*Wattenberg cites polls—a crude tool at best for making political policy projections—to argue that immigration to the West is unlikely to increase.[31] But there is little evidence that this public sentiment influences voting patterns. (Quick: How did your congressman vote on the Simpson-Rodino bill?) Of the people who consider immigration an important issue, the majority may favor more open borders. And such unfocused public xenophobia, while unfortunate, has not in the past blocked wave after wave of immigration. Even an ill-advised anti-immigration law passed in 1986 has not radically reduced the flow of human capital to the United States.[32] Indeed, by 1982, the Asians that America unwisely tried to exclude in the 1920s were the fastest-growing ethnic group in the United States. They also had the highest median family income of any ethnic group in the country: $22,075 compared with $19,908 for the nation as a whole.[33]

to put tyrants at the throat not of democracies but of other tyrants. Stalin and Hitler came to blows within two years of their nonaggression pact. In the 1970s, Iran hoped to spread a glorious Islamic revolution throughout the Middle East. Instead, she became bogged down in a war with Soviet client Iraq that wiped out half a generation of her youth. Libya, Syria, and Jordan, for all the threat they pose to Israel, spend much of their energy fighting among themselves, as do tyrants across Africa.

By contrast, consider how the force of nationalism is manifested in the Western alliance. U.S. troops in Europe and Korea, and nuclear weapons sometimes stationed in the Pacific, often seem to prompt what is called anti-American resentment, yet this reflects a positive nationalism. The people of those countries want to be free to pursue a more independent policy, and they are willing to purchase this freedom by bearing a greater share of their own defense burdens. This hardly harms the interests of America or democracy: Strong countries make good allies. In the 1980s, even as many U.S. hawks fretted about a lack of resolve in Europe, Britain went to war to defend the Falkland-Malvinas islands; France intervened in Chad and elsewhere in Africa; Germany, Spain, and Italy, as noted earlier, dealt forcefully with Soviet-backed efforts to spread terrorism; and even Japan, the smallness of whose defense budget was in large part thrust upon her after the war, voiced interest in exercising more military responsibility.

There is a simple reason why America can welcome Western debate over particular policies, and cheer the growing might and assertiveness of its friends: Our allies share our values and view our system as legitimate. In 1985, Europeans were asked whether their values resembled those of America or the Soviet Union. The response is shown in table 3.1.

The Soviets, by contrast, are saddled with a system that is not viewed as legitimate even by their own subjects. In the early 1980s, several different research institutes polled people of the Soviet bloc traveling through Western Europe. When people from Czechoslovakia, Hungary, and Poland were asked how they would vote in a free election, more than 80 percent chose one of several democratic labels, from "Conservative" to "Christian Democrat" to

TABLE 3.1

Western Europeans on American and Soviet Values

	Britain	France	Germany	Italy
What Americans value is similar or somewhat similar to own country's values	60%	25%	46%	54%
What Russians value is similar or somewhat similar to own country's values	14%	4%	8%	9%

SOURCE: *Public Opinion,* March–April 1987. Reprinted with permission of American Enterprise Institute for Public Policy Research.

"Democrat Socialist," while fewer than 5 percent said they would vote "Communist." Another question posed to people from the same three countries was: "Should a serious conflict develop between the United States and the Soviet Union, would your sympathies be with the United States, the Soviet Union, or with neither side?" Fourteen percent had no opinion, 33 percent would side with neither, and 48 percent would side with the United States.The number who would side with the Soviet Union: 5 percent.[37] People in these countries cannot change government policy as peacefully and directly as citizens in democracy, but their hostility to the Soviet model was a source of constant tension between the Kremlin and its Warsaw Pact satellites.[38]

The forces we have considered so far consist of more or less predictable phenomena: the resentment nations feel under an occupation regime, the inefficiencies of central planning, and so on. Yet history tends to move in unpredictable ways. It creates Churchills who will never give in, and Gandhis who will challenge even a seemingly invincible empire. It throws sand into the machinery of dialecticians—and beyond a certain mechanical opportunism, tyrannical regimes are uniquely unsuited to adapt. Discarding one way of thinking and adopting a new approach is a wrenching experience for any institution. People with a stake in the status quo, be it economic, bureaucratic, or intellectual, resist. Public sentiment, with a natural Burkean caution, demands reasons and justifications for the *novus ordo.* In democracy, the need for change is met by noisy debates. The popular will is exercised often, and thus becomes agile and muscular. In communist societies, the process lags. Richard Pipes, a leading expert on the Soviet Union at Harvard and a top adviser to Ronald Reagan, put it this way:

> The superiority of the democratic system of government and of the market economy consists [chiefly] in their greater realism, namely their ability to legitimize change, the inevitable concomitant of life. In this manner they prevent small, everyday crises from developing into cataclysms. An American thinker had this in mind when nearly two centuries ago he compared monarchies to majestic sailing ships that command the waves but once they hit rocks go down without trace, and republics to rafts in which your feet are always wet but you never sink.[39]

By the 1980s, even Soviet leaders broadly conceded the need for the Soviet system to evolve. Mikhail Gorbachev himself launched policies of economic "restructuring" and of "openness" to criticism, defining them as the "necessary condition" for the "democratization of our society."[40] Skeptics of the latest wave of Soviet reforms point out that such words have been used before,[41] but this should not be interpreted to mean that they should be ignored. "Even from a practical point of view," political analyst and activist Jeffrey Bell points out, "it is arguable that embracing a concept is hardly the most effective way of crushing it."[42] The likelihood is that in the modern world even undemocratic leaders feel they have no choice: the idea of self-government, they sense, is unassailable.

The Practical Populist Imperative

Despite their weaknesses, it is conceivable that undemocratic leaders could compete with the democracies in terms of negotiating treaties, carrying out covert operations, conducting unpopular wars, spreading false information, and so on. In fact, it is their only hope. Politicians in undemocratic governments, after all, engage in backroom power plays all the time; it is their principal source of strength. Democratic statesmen, by contrast, while they must certainly be capable of bargaining and negotiating, tend to rise to power by virtue of their skill in communicating ideas and enacting effective policies. It follows that a global strategy that makes use of these advantages must focus on popular forces, becoming, as Jeffrey Bell wrote in an important 1981 article for the *Wall Street Journal,* a "populist foreign policy."[43] For some, the term "populist" carries negative connotations, conjuring images of xenophobic demagogues and fast-talking snake-oil salesmen. It is used here in a literal sense—and in direct comparison to an "elitist" strategy—to characterize a foreign policy that places somewhat greater emphasis on public diplomacy, on explaining and strengthening the democratic idea throughout the world.*

No foreign policy is likely to be completely elitist or completely populist. We are not choosing between two distinct and inseparable options, but rather between degrees of emphasis. A populist foreign policy would place relatively strong emphasis on such levers of influence as the Voice of America, Radio Free Europe, Radio Liberty, and other means of reaching the people of other countries; an elitist foreign policy would place relatively less emphasis on these levers. An elitist diplomacy would be conducted more by professional diplomats and negotiators. A populist negotiating strategy would seek to change popular forces that all leaders, even undemocratic ones, must take into account

*Once upon a time, Republicans such as Bell did not have a monopoly on this sort of ambitious design for foreign policy. Consider this excerpt from a 1964 report by the Democratic-controlled Foreign Affairs Committee.

> For many years military and economic power, used separately or in conjunction, have served as the pillars of diplomacy. . . . But the recent increase in influence of the masses of the people over governments, together with greater awareness on the part of leaders, has created a new dimension for foreign policy operation. Certain foreign policy objectives can be pursued by dealing directly with the people of foreign countries, rather than with their governments. . . . It is possible today to reach large or influential segments of national populations—to inform them, to influence their attitudes, and at times even to motivate them to a particular course of action.

(Committee on Foreign Affairs, Report no. 2 on "Winning the Cold War . . . The U.S. Ideological Offensive," 88th Cong., House Report no. 1352, 27 April 1964, pp. 6–7.)

as they negotiate. An elitist approach tends to assume that an unpopular policy has simply been "misunderstood," or perhaps "misrepresented" by competing politicians, the press, and other elites. The populist would consider these possibilities. Yet if he had made reasonable efforts to describe and defend his position, and it still proved unpopular, he would rapidly reevaluate the position itself.

In a sense, populist thinking only underlines the importance of leaders in the political process. Imagine a small town where the favorite dish of the majority of the people is roast beef. The local diner, however, has for years served only chicken, pork chops, and a diet plate. Now, most people are not likely to walk out of a restaurant unless they find something horribly wrong, so customers continue to show up—everyone likes a night out now and then— and divide their preferences roughly equally between chicken, pork chops, and the diet plate. If everyone is at least comfortable with one of the three dishes, this situation might persist for a long time before there is any obvious sign of the advantage of a change. A few customers who are fervent red-meat eaters might mention that they wish roast beef were on the menu, but an unsophisticated manager might even find in this support for the present menu: After all, one-third of the people order chicken, one-third pork chops, and one-third the diet plate; only a tiny, radical "pressure group" is demanding roast beef. But a waitress with a sensitive ear might notice that people chronically hesitate when choosing among the dishes listed. She might begin to probe actively to find the real sentiment of the restaurant's electorate: If there were roast beef on the menu, would you order it? This hypothetical might be a little too abstract for some customers—they might like roast beef only if it is prepared a certain way, or might simply have forgotten about the possibility of restaurant roast beef over the years. So an even better restaurant leadership might try putting roast beef on the menu once a week, or travel to a nearby town to see how the restaurant leaders there handled their menu.

This analogy, if anything, understates the importance of leadership in foreign policy. When we order food, we place heavy weight on our own knowledge and prejudices. When voters "order" foreign policy, though, they naturally tend to defer to their leadership, which the voters select precisely because they know they do not have the time or knowledge to study the intricacies of tribal warfare in North Yemen, or the efficacy of the Stinger antiaircraft missile in use against Soviet air patrols, or the relative merits of fixed international rates of currency exchange. Moreover, whereas everyone is familiar with roast beef, there may be foreign-policy options that voters would like if someone suggested them but which they have never seen.

In many ways, foreign policy is becoming more populist whether leaders choose to make it so or not. An expanding share of the contacts between nations is between individuals from those nations, and not their governments.

IDEOPOLITIK

Every American businessman who travels to Korea or Taiwan is an ambassador for his country, just as every American (or Soviet) university is an ambassador to the Chinese or Nicaraguan student who studies there.

A concrete example makes this reality vivid. In 1985 and 1986, the U.S. Congress debated hotly the subject of providing aid to the Nicaraguan contras, assistance totaling roughly $120 million over two years. At the same time, however, private citizens from various countries, chiefly America, were providing up to an estimated $50 million a year in aid of their own, while groups opposed to the contras estimated they had raised a like amount—$50 million in the first half of 1987, though this was probably an overstatement—raised to help the Sandinistas.[44] Elitists on both sides of the debate, of course, took objection to such activities. Sandinista backers complained of a "privatized foreign policy" well before the Iran-contra scandal became public, objecting to the very idea of American citizens donating food, guns, helicopters, and bandages to a group of rebels abroad. Contra backers, meanwhile, railed against the cities and towns that adopted a "sister city" in Nicaragua to provide assistance, or denounced the "radical chic" parties at which Hollywood movie stars wined and dined Nicaraguan strongman Daniel Ortega.

A populist sensibility, however—a contra-supporting populist in my case—tends to look with equanimity on such activism, from whatever quarter. True, the rough-and-tumble of contra aficionados and Sandinista sympathizers produces a great deal of noise and confusion, making it more difficult for the United States government to pursue a clear set of objectives. Yet, as observers from de Tocqueville to Revel have told us, democracies are no good at carrying out elaborate, all-embracing schemes anyway. A hundred White House speechwriters and Capitol Hill lobbyists working for ten years probably couldn't have produced a movie as useful to Ronald Reagan's foreign-policy ideas as *Rambo* or *Red Dawn*. Central planning makes lousy cars, guns, refrigerators, and military toilet-seat covers; why should we assume it will perform better the far more subtle and elaborate task of promoting democracy? Dispersed power and the seeming chaos of the marketplace make for an efficient and happy society; isn't it possible that they can, steadily but unconsciously, advance freedom through the thousands of decentralized contacts and transactions abroad that democracy itself encourages? Eduardo Ulibarri, editor of *La Nación* magazine in Costa Rica, argues that a dependence on diplomatism, as traditionally understood, is a distinct weakness in U.S. foreign policy: "The U.S. has relied too much on governmental, official relations, and they should rely a little more on other kinds of relations and other ways to promote democracy, by building links between U.S. institutions and Latin American society and institutions."[45]

By tradition, foreign policy has a strong elitist bias. One reason is that diplomats constitute an elite. Poets think in terms of words and rhymes and meter; businessmen focus on profits; democratic politicians keep an eye on voters. Diplomats, quite naturally, concentrate on their daily meetings and annual summits, on treaties and protocols and agreements—the things that, as diplomats, they can most directly and obviously influence. There is nothing sinister about this. It is a grave error, though, as Irving Kristol has warned, to confuse these tools of foreign policy with foreign policy itself. The very fact that terms such as "diplomacy" and "foreign policy" are so often used interchangeably is evidence of such confusion. Jonathan Kwitny captured this truth in his book *Endless Enemies:*

> We constantly overlook the distinction between what a country's government says, and what the people of the country do. Newspapers report that "Brazil believes . . . ," and what the newspapers mean is that a relative handful of Brazilian generals and rich businessmen believe. *Brazil*—a consensus of its 125 million people—may well believe that those generals and businessmen should be lined up against a wall and shot. But only the government's views get reported, until suddenly, to everyone's surprise but the Brazilians', a rebellion starts.[46]

An overly elitist tilt especially afflicts our thinking on the important subject of the Soviet Union, with unfortunate consequences. Elitist thinking views Soviet reforms, for example, chiefly through the eyes of the Soviet leaders. Nothing can "force" the Kremlin to reform, the dovish *New York Times* argues. "Those in a position of power," says the more hawkish scholar Seymour Martin Lipset, "do not want to give them up."[47] Both statements are true; both statements are irrelevant. Many democracies evolved precisely because emperors not compelled to reform chose to do so. And many of their most important acts were undertaken out of a desire for more power, not less. Since many of the ideopolitical forces that shape Soviet reforms are popular in nature, elitist thinking, while an important component in dealing with the Soviets, misses many critical events. Hence, as Yale sociologist Jan T. Gross put it, "We must shift the [very] focus of foreign policy from governments to societies, for it is within those societies, rather than their governments, that there are forces of emancipation and democratization. . . . The defense of human rights is our only sensible *Realpolitik.*"[48]

Ambassador Jeane Kirkpatrick's famous distinction between totalitarian (Cuba, Vietnam) and authoritarian (Chile, Taiwan) regimes neatly illuminates the problem. Mrs. Kirkpatrick has often been attacked as if she had invented some monstrously contrived dividing line between polities essentially the same. In fact, the problem with her taxonomy, if we apply it to, say, the Soviet Union, Poland, and China, is that it does not allow for distinctions that are fine enough. Would that there were not two, but hundreds of different terms, to capture fully the myriad possible degrees of freedom possible. Populists think in terms of a finely graded continuum, and thus are alert to slight moves toward democracy that the elitists dismiss. Different populist camps may draw different lessons from these shifts, the populist doves arguing that marginal reforms make the Soviet Union less threatening, while populist hawks note that if the Soviet leaders are so reasonable, then surely the West can vigorously promote its values without threatening World War III. All populists, though, share an optimism about the ability of the Soviet and American people to change things.

Today *glasnost,* tomorrow democracy. The Soviet road to democratic capitalism will be paved with socialist slogans.

The elitist assumptions about the Soviet Union, in turn, have produced an elitist strategy. Broad and bitter feuds often occur over particulars, but elitists from across the spectrum all advocate a policy variation of containment. Some containment advocates would seek to combat Soviet expansion everywhere it occurs, on the spot. Still others, notably John Kennedy, have advocated a doctrine of "flexible response." All these variations of containment, however, are essentially responsive. They seek to convince Soviet leaders that any aggressive actions on their part will be met with steel-like resolve on the part of the West. Even if this strategy could be upheld consistently, it offers little hope. The resulting dilemma was captured well by political scientist Aaron Wildavsky: "If the rules of the game are that I can take your marbles but you cannot touch mine, it is only a matter of time before I win. . . . And since retaliatory measures are ruled out, the Soviet Union can afford to fail. So long as its side wins now and again, it is able to cumulate all its winnings. Containment, pure and simple, is a losing game."[49]

Nevertheless, it is possible for leaders to do the right thing for the wrong reason, and American foreign policy has enjoyed many successes. The happy, dirty secret of postwar diplomacy is this: America has not pursued a containment policy. Containment assumptions, strategy, and rhetoric have dominated the articulation of policy, it is true. But the Marshall Plan, Bretton Woods, Radio Free Europe, Kennedy's Alliance for Progress, Nixon's China opening, Ford's Helsinki accords, Carter's Middle East initiative, and Reagan's freedom-fighter doctrine—none of these could properly be called exercises in mere containment. Democracy's leaders have often proven better than their ideas; they have been more successful than even they themselves, perhaps, understand.

These noble efforts, and the heroism of people throughout the world, have laid a solid foundation for democracy, to the point where one can actually envision an entire world in which all men enjoy the right to determine their own destinies. America can help build such a democratic world. Let us examine the tools at our disposal.

II

THE MEANS

The best service peace research could offer to
the world today probably consists, not so
much in understanding conflicts better, as in
providing politicians with an enormous
repertoire of actions short of violence that can
be applied in conflict situations.
— JOHN GALTUNG
"On the Meaning of Nonviolence,"
Journal of Peace Research

4

WORDS INTO DEEDS: THE EVOLUTION OF HUMAN RIGHTS

FOREIGN-POLICY tools do not operate in isolation. A boycott against one country making war on its neighbors alerts other countries that launching a similar war may carry penalties. Nor are economic penalties our only recourse. American diplomats can criticize another government's treatment of its citizens. We can meet with opposition leaders, and assist unions, political parties, civic groups, churches, the press, and other democratic institutions. Our president can urge another leader to reform undemocratic practices, through emissaries or in person, or in published reports. As Patricia Derian, Jimmy Carter's assistant secretary of state for human rights, has noted aptly: "The whole of society . . . is based on ideas, and you do something about ideas with words."[1]

Such advice and assistance constitute an approach to international affairs that under President Jimmy Carter became known as human rights policy. Although the Reagan administration applied the policy with considerable differences in tone and emphasis, large elements of the Carter idea survived. From the late 1970s into the 1980s, U.S. diplomats have actively encouraged human rights on a broad scale. Countries that violated human rights faced a cutoff of U.S. assistance, and U.S. representatives to such institutions as the World Bank often voted to deny them other credits as well. The State Department has issued annual human rights reports criticizing countries where respect for freedom deteriorated and praising those where it improved. Those reports have often swayed the outcome of congressional debates on U.S. assistance. Hence it can be said that a decisive shift in U.S. foreign policy took place in January 1977, remaining largely intact for more than a decade. This provides an opportunity to step back from individual cases and consider whether human rights policy, in a broad context, can achieve its desired end.

A Matter of Measurements

Scholars who studied Carter's policy initially did not give it high marks. Jo Marie Griesgraber, former deputy director of the Washington Office on Latin America, found in 1979 that at the end of the first flurry of human rights interest, "there was little to show for congressional human rights efforts."[2] Scholar Joshua Muravchik, author of a leading book on human rights policy, *The Uncertain Crusade,* studied twenty-eight countries against which the Carter administration applied punitive measures of one sort or another. In the beginning of 1977, those countries had an average rating of 11.7 in the annual Freedom House survey, with 2 being the best possible score for a country's freedom, 14 being the worst. At the beginning of 1981, Muravchik found, the same countries had an average rating of 11.9.[3] Stanley Heginbotham of the Congressional Research Service performed a similar analysis on fifteen countries and found: "The record on direct and explicit use of foreign assistance as leverage to bring about specific improvements in human rights conditions . . . is hardly encouraging. In only five or six instances did we find evidence that actual or explicitly threatened reductions in aid played a significant role in bringing about changes."[4]

There are, however, several problems with these surveys. Heginbotham's finding, for example, that direct pressure led to specific human rights improvements in 33 percent to 40 percent of the cases, strikes me as a good batting average. Leaders do not often capitulate to outside pressure in so recognizable a fashion. There is, furthermore, a conceptual problem in looking only at countries that were the object of sanctions, since some nations may have noticed sanctions being applied to others and changed their practices in order to avoid them. Thus, the Muravchik model ignores Ecuador, the Dominican Republic, and Peru, where military governments held free elections during Carter's term. Did Carter's policy play a role? General Edgardo Mercardo Jarrin, who was critical to the shift to democracy in Peru, argued in 1986 that "the U.S. human rights policy was absolutely critical. We had our eye on the other countries, like Chile, where democracy was overthrown and the friendship of the United States suffered."[5]

In other countries, human rights may deteriorate markedly in a given year, leading the United States to step up its efforts. El Salvador and Argentina would be examples of how a deterioration of human rights led to sanctions, not the other way around. Then, too, even where human rights policy begins to work, we must remember that governments do not often change their very form in a matter of weeks or months. Yet the Heginbotham model condemns a policy just begun in 1977, and extended in 1978, for producing visible results in "only" one of three countries by 1979. If we take the same twenty-eight countries viewed by Muravchik, and look at their Freedom House ranking for 1987, we see that their average declines from an initial 11.7 to 10.4, a marked improvement.[6]

Even this recalculation of Muravchik retains the other flaws mentioned earlier. It leaves in a number of communist countries, which can give misleading results. Yet Muravchik, despite obvious care and thought in constructing his model, factors in more than a dozen countries—including Vietnam, Afghanistan, and South Yemen—that were essentially Marxist dictatorships when they became the object of human rights penalties. This tends to water down an average rate of improvement which was quite dramatic for a number of other states. El Salvador, Guatemala, and Uruguay all declined from Freedom House ratings of 12 or higher to ratings of 6 or less by 1987. Much of this improvement is attributable to the interest in human rights that survived Carter's egress, interest on the part of the Reagan White House and State Department, the Congress, and the American public. Adam Meyerson, editor of the Heritage Foundation's *Policy Review,* notes the impact of human rights policy on Latin American countries where the tentative shift to democracy was well under way by the end of Carter's term:

> Brazil's soldiers . . . have long been planning to leave the government, and have been slowly and deliberately opening up the political system since 1974. . . . In El Salvador and Honduras, the military faced a double realization: democracy would be a valuable weapon in mobilizing popular opinion against communism, and it was also probably necessary for securing American aid. . . . The Carter Administration's emphasis on human rights led to humanitarian improvements in Argentina, and provided an important boost of morale for democratic forces there.[7]

Critics of human rights policy, of course, take issue not with the existence of a broad trend toward democracy, but with the notion that Carter should get credit. His detractors, such as former United Nations Ambassador Jeane Kirkpatrick, have often had their views misstated, so before even evaluating their model, it is important to review what they actually said and what they did not. These critics did not claim, though the words were often stuffed in their mouth, that the United States should never pressure for change, especially in countries that generally support American foreign policy. Kirkpatrick's celebrated attack on Carter in *Commentary* magazine, "Dictatorships and Double Standards," for example, was not so much prescriptive as descriptive. She argued that Carter had produced defeats for human rights in countries such as Iran and Nicaragua, not that human rights ought not to be pursued. "No problem of American foreign policy is more urgent," Mrs. Kirkpatrick wrote, "than that of formulating a morally and strategically acceptable, and politically realistic, program for dealing with non-democratic governments who are threatened by Soviet-sponsored subversion." She went on to observe that "authoritarian" regimes can more readily evolve into democracies than "totalitarian," communist ones. This is reasonable: There are many examples of the former, few of the latter. She then faulted Carter, not for applying pressure to authoritarian regimes per se, but for pressuring countries which in her view contained no reasonable hope of a democratic outcome. One might disagree with Mrs. Kirkpatrick's judgment about whether a given country has such a democratic force. Even when dictators in the Philippines and Haiti were ousted by leaders apparently committed to democracy, Mrs. Kirkpatrick found these cases "an exception" and noted, "We do not yet know what will come after Marcos and Duvalier." That is not a very satisfying model for foreign policy, since Ronald Reagan had to decide in 1986 what to do about those dictators; he could not wait for three years to offer his assessment of the results in the pages of *Commentary*. The Kirkpatrick doctrine, however, hardly amounts to "stand by your strongman," as reporter Sidney Blumenthal characterized it in the *Washington Post*. In a symposium on human rights, in fact, she proposed "aggressive statements in information programs, and official pronouncements of the case for constitutional democracy." Her argument was simply that in the case of a friendly, authoritarian regime, with only a weak or nonexistent third force for democracy, friendly and private persuasion would prove a better and safer remedy than explicit, public pressures. It is this model, and not some caricature of it, that should be scrutinized.[8]

When the democratic revolution swept across more than a dozen nations in the 1980s, Kirkpatrick and her followers were quick to claim vindication for their own analysis. "The effort to give Carter policies credit," Kirkpatrick wrote, "is as bold as a bank robbery in broad daylight."[9] Disciples of the Kirkpatrick doctrine tended to find in the growth of democracy an affirmation of their faith. As *Wall Street Journal* columnist Paul Gigot argued:

> When [Asia's leaders] believe America stands by them firmly as an ally . . . they
> are more likely to be politically tolerant at home. The transfer of power in the

Philippines from Ferdinand Marcos to Corazon Aquino is a dramatic confirmation of Jeane Kirkpatrick's observation that pro-Western authoritarian regimes can and often do evolve into freer societies. If we compare the political situation in the late 1970s with the situation today, it is clear that the phenomenon Mrs. Kirkpatrick described is occurring throughout the region.[10]

Indeed it was. Yet the same examination reveals a number of regimes that were the object of human rights penalties under the Carter administration, and of continuing pressures to improve from the Reagan administration, Congress, and the U.S. public. In Korea, for example, Gigot saw signs of a "marked liberalization," including relatively open elections in 1984. That liberalization was carried out, however, by President Chun Doo Hwan, who came to power in a 1979 coup that replaced Park Chung Hee. Park was one of the earliest and most prominent targets of Carter's human rights policy. Carter sought the removal of U.S. troops from South Korea in 1977 and 1978, and when he encountered resistance from Congress, he put a cap on U.S. bilateral assistance. At the time, of course, Carter's notion that there could be a third force for democracy was ridiculed. "The Koreans have never had a democratic or constitutional system," wrote Masataka Kosaka, a professor at Kyoto University. "Viewed in this context, the dictatorship of Park Chung Hee in the South was very natural. . . . Korea's tradition of authoritarianism poses a formidable obstacle to the establishment of a democratic system." Fuji Kamiya, a professor at Keio University, agreed: "Both Koreas have felt that need for a dictatorial system. . . . [I]t is inappropriate for Carter to expect the Koreans to practice democracy."[11] If authoritarian Korea evolves into a stable democracy in the decades to come, part of the reason will be that both the diagnosis and the prescription offered by these Kirkpatrick doctrine enthusiasts were ignored. This is not to say that human rights policy was the only reason that democratic forces exerted themselves in Korea, or even that encouraging those forces was necessarily the central goal in Jimmy Carter's mind. It is hardly fair, though, for those who criticized the general drift of U.S. policy for many years to spin about and cheer the results of that policy as an affirmation of their own model. During the Reagan administration, U.S. spokesmen from the Secretary of State on down met frequently with leading opposition figures, criticized the government for slow progress toward democracy, and cheered reforms as they accelerated in 1986 and 1987. They did so loudly and publicly, and for this they should be praised; but so should the Carter doctrine that the Reaganites, to some extent, were applying.

Similarly, Kirkpatrick singled out Taiwan as a place where the Carter administration's "ideological" approach made it "blind" to the "reality" that pushing for change might well lead to a communist takeover. The United States certainly pushed: From the late 1950s through the Carter presidency,

Taiwan was gradually cut off from U.S. economic assistance, multilateral lending agencies, and the United Nations. Even during the Reagan administration, there was a constant threat that arms sales regarded as critical by the Kuomintang would be cut off or diminished. Consequently, there was great pressure on the government of Taiwan to conform more closely to U.S. human rights standards. Again, U.S. foreign policy diverged substantially from what Kirkpatrick recommended, or at least seemed to recommend. It was partly thanks to this that Gigot could write in 1987 of "local elections last year, that were, by all accounts, remarkably free."[12]

Of course, the outstanding shift to democracy during the Reagan administration—tentative but remarkable—took place in the Philippines. The fall of Ferdinand Marcos, to be sure, demonstrated the veracity of Mrs. Kirkpatrick's observation about the mutability of authoritarian regimes. The change, however, took place in large part due to U.S. pressures, which Kirkpatrick remained strongly opposed to until the end.[13]

Rereading Kirkpatrick's critique of Carter human rights policy, one is struck by how nondoctrinaire her doctrines really were. In 1980, shortly after Jimmy Carter was swept from the White House, Kirkpatrick sat down to clarify her own alternative conception of an effective human rights policy for Latin America, which was published in *Commentary*. The "first step" in building an effective human rights policy, Kirkpatrick argued, was "intellectual. It requires thinking more realistically about the politics of Latin America." Fair enough. "The second step is to assess realistically the impact of various alternatives on the security of the United States." Okay—we are all thinking and assessing more realistically. What next? "The third step is to abandon the globalist approach which denies the realities of culture, character, geography, economics, and history." Hmmm. And what will we replace it with? "A foreign policy that builds (again [quoting Edmund] Burke) on the 'concrete circumstances' which give 'to every political principle its distinguishing color and discriminating effect.' "[14]

In sum, the Kirkpatrick doctrine: Think realistically, so that you can assess realistically, which will enable you to reject a globalist approach that is unrealistic and embrace a foreign policy based on concrete circumstances—that is, reality. Nebulous this model is; rigid it is not.

Nor Carter nor Kirkpatrick

The rise of Asian and Latin democracies, then, cannot be attributed to the Kirkpatrick doctrine, either as vaguely expressed by Kirkpatrick or as concretely distorted by her critics. Neither, however, was it an outgrowth of the

Carter human rights policy, at least as articulated at the time. Carter's human rights policy, in fact, tended to focus not on political structures but on particular abuses. Carter opposed dictators, but argued that efforts to spread a "particular form" of government would involve "an imposition" of American values on others. His human rights policy, then, was designed to reduce torture, support due process, and promote economic equality, but there was little emphasis on expanding democracy. Carter himself later wrote:

> We were inclined to define human rights too narrowly. [Encouraging] human rights was not merely a matter of reducing the incidence of summary executions or torture of political prisoners. It also included the promotion of democratic principles . . . expressed in our Bill of Rights, the right to emigrate and reunite families, and protection against discrimination based on sex, religion, or ethnic origin. These were the issues on which public attention was concentrated, but the right of people to a job, food, shelter, medical care, and education could not be ignored.[15]

Even this reformulated version sounds as much like a plea for specific social programs and penal reforms as it is an endorsement of democracy. Carter never mentions the right to choose one's own leaders as an important, let alone central, part of America's democratic principles. Indeed, most of his chief foreign-policy spokesmen explicitly renounced such a goal. "For Americans to inject into American external relations the ideological claim that the contemporary world struggle is between liberal democracy and various forms of despotic statism," National Security Adviser Zbigniew Brzezinski wrote, "would create a doctrinal coalition against the United States." His view fit right in with the rest of the Carter team. Secretary of State Cyrus Vance warned in a memorandum: "There can be no exclusively American solutions. There can only be international answers or there will be no answers at all." Stanley Hoffman, an academician whose writings greatly influenced the administration's foreign policy, denounced efforts to launch a "democratic crusade" as a "vindictive defense" of our system of freedom.[16]

Simple pragmatism, one might think, would have argued for a focus on democracy as the key to human rights progress. History records few undemocratic regimes that do not eventually violate humanitarian standards, and no examples of enduring democratic regimes where human rights violations persist for long. Yet the Carter human rights policy eschewed such an emphasis.

Many strains of thinking came together to frustrate what would have been a broader, and more effective, approach. In part, Carter sought to avoid the charge that he was engaging in ideological imperialism. A policy based on consensus, at home or abroad, is likely to enjoy greater support. Yet not all countries agree that democracy is the best system, and even many Americans harbor doubts about their own institutions. So the Carter administration, in an understandable effort to avoid divisiveness, tried to promote at least particular practices that enjoy near-unanimous support. "Human rights violations," Derian argued, "do not really have much to do with the form of government or the political ideology or philosophy."[17] Carter's policy therefore emphasized particular human rights abuses, rather than focusing on the systems of government that generate such abuses habitually. "We believe that human rights transcend ideology," Vice President Mondale said in 1977. "We believe all nations, regardless of political systems, must respect those rights." The administration thus sought, as Carter put it, to promote rights recognized by international conventions and treaties.[18] It's hard to deny that it would be nice if all governments respected human rights, or that there are some rights that even totalitarians pay lip service to, as in the United Nations Charter. Yet different ideologies view human rights differently, and undemocratic governments are entirely capable of ignoring them altogether.

Besides an aversion to being or even seeming unduly ideological, Carter also seemed driven by a desire not to be, or appear, tactically aggressive. To assert the primacy of democracy, in a sense, is to interfere in the affairs of others. Of course, such meddling is, as Carter State Department aide Leslie Gelb observed, almost a definition of diplomacy, "All foreign policy," he argued, "is the extension of one's internal policies into the internal politics of another nation."[19] Yet a consistent emphasis on democracy would have created tensions between the United States and the Soviet Union—tensions that, in Carter's view, could have undermined other important objectives such as arms reduction with the Soviets, halting the spread of nuclear weapons to other countries, and avoiding conventional conflicts in trouble zones such as the Middle East and Latin America.

In the fall of 1977 the State Department proclaimed in an outline of U.S.-Soviet relations: "We do not seek to change the Soviet political system, nor do we wish to single out the USSR for special criticism."[20] Translated by Carter and his advisers, that statement, itself a questionable policy, came to mean: We do not even seek substantial improvement in human rights within that system, and will in fact give it special immunity from criticism. Cyrus Vance says in his memoirs that he was "in accord" with Carter's "strong" feelings about human rights. "I pointed out, however, that we had to be flexible and pragmatic."[21] And pragmatism, it turned out, consisted in accepting the notion that we can't have much impact on the Soviets anyway. Carter argued: "Our influence could be much more effective [with allies] than in communist countries, where repression was so complete that it could not easily be observed or rooted out."[22]

Jimmy Carter had good firsthand evidence to reject the canard that we can have little influence on the Soviets. Their furious reaction to his early criticism should have told him that the conventional wisdom about U.S. lack of influence was wrong. For a mix of reasons, he never reached that conclusion, and gradually his human rights policy retreated from a broad, evenly applied concern for human rights to a stick for demanding this or that change from only some regimes.

Finally, Carter's human rights policy not only denied the important connection between political systems and human rights; it denied the U.S. had the power or the right to shape these. As Carter put it, his foreign policy was based on a notion "that was to prove painfully unpopular: limits. . . . Americans were not accustomed to limits—on natural resources or on the power of our country to influence others or to control international events."[23] All of which makes it difficult to give him central credit for the broad improvement in human rights that took place in the 1980s.

The Abrams Doctrine

Ronald Reagan took office in 1981 approaching America generally, and its human rights policies specifically, from an almost diametrically opposite viewpoint. Where Carter stressed limits, Reagan was optimistic about America's ability to shape destiny, even the democratic destiny of other nations. Where Carter wanted to speak out against human rights violations, but was inclined to avoid friction with the Soviet Union, Reagan was eager to criticize the Soviets, and had contempt for a human rights policy he felt had subordinated the top goal of fighting communism to a petty search for the misdeeds of friendly allies. Early in his administration he selected Mrs. Kirkpatrick as U.S. ambassador to the United Nations, a sign that he shared her rejection of Carter and his "predilection for policies that violated the strategic and economic interests of the United States."[24] A paper by his top advisers for Latin America policy, the Committee of Santa Fe, emphasized that Carter's stress on human rights "must be abandoned." Secretary of State Alexander Haig, in a speech to the Trilateral Commission, turned the Carter rhetoric of U.S. impotence against human rights, noting, "There are limits to what we can do or should do to transform other cultures." He promised at his first news conference that "international terrorism will take the place of human rights in our concern."[25] It was soon apparent that this rhetoric would in fact be administration policy, at least initially. Kirkpatrick visited Chile and Argentina, where she praised ruling juntas but declined to visit with some human rights groups. Then–Vice President George Bush traveled to Manila, where he toasted Ferdinand Marcos for his "adherence to democracy." The White House requested resumed military aid for a number of Latin and Asian countries, no strings attached.

Shortly after embarking on this course, however, Ronald Reagan's thinking began to shift. No doubt one factor was simple pressure. Congress refused to approve aid for El Salvador, an embattled regime fighting a Soviet-backed insurgency, unless Reagan could certify the government was making human rights progress. Serendipity also played a role, in the person of Elliott Abrams, then a State Department aide focusing on international organizations. Abrams, an intellectual with a keen mind and a slightly more inclusive approach than Kirkpatrick's, saw a chance to fuse the administration's anticommunism with human rights: the very opportunity Carter sometimes had missed. In October 1981, Abrams drafted a memorandum arguing that "human rights is at the core of our foreign policy."[26] After all, there was no contradiction between fighting communism and advancing freedom. The two work hand in hand. And historically, the system that best protects freedoms is democracy. "Other human rights goals such as an end to physical brutality by the police, or an end to torture, or the right to form free trade unions, can sometimes be gained for a moment without a system of free elections. But without free elections these gains are ephemeral: They can disappear as quickly as they had appeared, for they come only as the gift of the ruled."[27]

It was no accident that at almost exactly the same time, Kirkpatrick articulated a similar redefinition of human rights around a more Reaganesque core of democracy. "Only democracies do a reliable job of protecting the rights of all their citizens," she wrote. "That is why their survival must be the first priority of those committed to the protection of human rights."[28] Democracy as the key to human rights gave the Reaganites a way to out-Carter Carter, but without giving an inch in the ideological struggle with the undemocratic Soviet Union. Within months, Abrams had been nominated as assistant secretary for human rights. And in 1982, Ronald Reagan stood before the British Parliament, calling for a new effort by the West to promote the "democratic revolution."

The administration quickly found that its rhetoric was being compared to its actions. The annual human rights reports were read with particular scrutiny in 1983 and 1984 to see if the Philippines, South Korea, South Africa, and Chile would be criticized. They were, though not to a degree that pleased all of Reagan's critics. "In the eyes of the Administration's critics," Tamar Jacoby noted, in an important article for *Foreign Affairs,* "open contempt and disregard for human rights issues had been replaced by a hypocritical show of interest. . . . [C]ivil libertarians who dominate the leading human rights monitoring groups also felt that the focus on democracy was a way of evading many of the human rights concerns that had prevailed in international forums and in the Carter years."[29]

Political motives, of course, are always multifaceted, particularly in relation to a whole government or administration. The persistent lobbying of the human rights groups was an important factor in getting Reagan to at least pay attention to the issue. Once attention to the human rights issue was forced upon him, however, the president's decision to add a democratic twist was vintage Reagan. Ronald Reagan has always been understood best as a radical, in the best sense of the word: going to the root of a dispute and taking a clear stand. You can disagree with Reagan's convictions; you can find his thinking lazy, muddled, and contradictory at times, as some of my own newspaper columns have insisted; but this is a man who believes what he says, with a steady confidence. To think that he embraced Abrams's sweeping notion of putting human rights at the core of foreign policy, and democracy at the core of human rights, as a cynical ploy—using "human rights as a mere tool of geopolitics," as Jacoby put it—is to profoundly misunderstand both Reagan and the idea itself.[30]

Whatever the motives and intentions of the administration, the new doctrine offered a standard for judgment. Reagan would have to show skeptics that building democracy was not simply a clever diversion. The 1983 State Department report on human rights offered early evidence that the standard would be applied to friend and foe alike, even though this would sometimes mean "trouble," as the Abrams memorandum had put it.[31] The report criticized El Salvador for "serious human rights problems," though noting, accurately, that the incidence of torture and political killings had declined markedly in 1982. It blasted South Africa, where only 16 percent of the people were allowed to vote, and life was marked by "continued erosion of the rule of law and its replacement by administrative fiat." On the Philippines, another agonizingly hard case for Reaganites, the report said: "Political opposition is tolerated, but within a limited scope. . . . Abuses by some military personnel, including torture and summary executions, continue to be reported."[32]

Moreover, while the new policy differed considerably in tone and strategic goals from the Carter era, the old tactical pressures were by no means discarded. In 1983, the military leader of Guatemala, General Efrain Rios Montt, reportedly had a U.S. ambassador thrown out of his office because of America's continuing calls for democracy. The incident, widely discussed in Guatemala, offered great encouragement to civilian and military leaders pressing the government for free elections for it showed an American State Department willing to insist on democracy over narrow diplomatic or "strategic" concerns. Indeed, Guatemala, facing a Marxist insurgency, had to ground its helicopters at one point because the country couldn't obtain spare parts from the United States. Lucy Martinez-Mont, a businesswoman and human rights advocate in Guatemala, noted that U.S. pressures "were basically in effect from 1978 through 1985. . . . It was due to the Carter policy. In the State Department, it wasn't such a great change when Reagan took office, with regard to [Latin] countries."[33]*

Guatemala was only one example of America keeping its mouth and money in line with human rights. In 1984, Everett G. Martin of the *Wall Street Journal* surveyed U.S. policy in Latin America and found many of the Carter tactics intact:

> Last fall . . . a State Department Counselor was dispatched to Santiago to voice U.S. support for elections and urge that President Augusto Pinochet reach an agreement with his opponents. . . . State Department officials say Uruguay's rulers have received a similar exhortation. In Paraguay, U.S. Ambassador Arthur Davis has been outspoken in contending that President Alfredo Stroessner, who has ruled the country for 30 years, should consider a return to democracy.
>
> As a reward for returning to democratic forms of government, the administra-

---

*Mrs. Martinez-Mont was one of a number of civic and government leaders who agreed to participate in a survey on the 1980s surge of Latin democracy, conducted by the Alexis de Tocqueville Institution from 1986 to 1987. Both its process and its findings merit mention here.

The idea was first suggested to me by Robert Pastor, the scholar and Carter-era official in the National Security Council. Pastor shared my frustration with much of the analysis of increasing respect for human rights in the Americas. Both the *New York Times* and the *Wall Street Journal,* for example, had done interesting pieces on the spread of democracy in the region, quoting various scholars from Harvard and Princeton and the like on the implications of this trend, its connection to the policies of Carter and Reagan, or lack thereof, and so on. What was notably absent from those articles and the literature generally, however, was any comment from Latin Americans themselves—especially on the important question of which U.S. initiatives, if any, helped catalyze the change. "Why don't you ask some people in Brazil or Argentina or Costa Rica what they think?" Pastor suggested, and that is what we did.

First, Pastor and several Hoover colleagues advised me on a simple list of standardized questions. Pastor and David Asman, the editor of the *Wall Street Journal*'s "Americas" column, both suggested possible interviewees and also generously opened their respective Rolodexes to help us get in touch. Finally, Joe Anderson, a Hoover Institution research assistant fluent in Spanish, helped me conduct more than three dozen interviews with business, political, labor, and academic leaders from more than ten key countries.

The interviews generally confirmed my sense of Latin opinion formed after attending a 1986 conference on human rights that Pastor had helped organize at the Carter Center in Atlanta. Seven of the thirty-eight people to whom we spoke strongly emphasized the role of Carter's policies in the rise of democracy. Most of these were from Argentina, Brazil, or Peru; many related personal experiences with military regimes they might not have outlived save for Carter's intervention. These respondents tended to attribute any further application of human rights policy under Reagan to mere continuation (often seen as grudging) of Carter policies. Eight respondents, by contrast—mostly from Central America—voiced an equally strong belief that Reagan's policies were a vast improvement on Carterism, and deserved the bulk of the credit for democratization. These persons, as one might expect, tended to find communism a greater and more present threat, and hence found Carter's fear of communism inordinately small. They also laid greater stress on economic freedom as both important in its own right and as a promoter of civil and political rights.

A solid majority of those we spoke to—twenty-five of thirty-eight—argued that the rise of democracy, insofar as it was attributable to U.S. policy, was a reflection of elements of both administrations: the Abrams doctrine. This feeling was particularly strong in such countries as Chile, where there has been experience with tyrannies of both the left and the right, and where Carter and Reagan policies were sincerely vigorous in exporting democracy.

One strain of thinking that did not emerge also stands out. None of those interviewed questioned the presence of a strong democratic tide; all debate focused on its causes, not its existence. And only a handful, two persons, doubted that U.S. policy was one of its prime movers; sharp disagreements about which U.S. acts hurt or helped democracy took place against a background of near-unanimous agreement that what America does matters.

tion, without prodding from Congress, metes out generous assistance programs. U.S. aid to Peru is now one of the highest per capita in the world. . . . By contrast, aid to Chile and Uruguay, still under military dictatorships, has been pared back sharply.[34]

The more the Reagan human rights policy evolved, the more there was for human rights enthusiasts to like. In December of 1985, Secretary of State George Shultz refused to certify human rights progress in Haiti—and dictator Jean-Claude Duvalier began packing his bags. The following March, the Reagan administration blasted Chile's human rights record, prompting Pinochet to call an emergency cabinet meeting.[35] By the spring of 1986, the Reagan administration proclaimed and was carrying out the Abrams doctrine with elegant simplicity: "The American people believe in human rights and oppose tyranny in whatever form, whether of the left or the right."[36] Even critics hailed what Jacoby called the Reagan turnaround on human rights. "Major Shift in Emphasis" cheered a front-page headline in the *New York Times.*[37] Michael Posner of the Lawyers Committee for Human Rights agreed: "The Reagan Administration must now be viewed as a significant force for international human rights."[38]

Endowing Democracy

Besides the new strategic emphasis on democracy, Reagan added an important tactical twist to human rights policy. Even members of the Reagan administration often described this in elitist terms. "We find that quiet diplomacy is more effective with friends," as Abrams put it.[39] Maybe so. The vital shift effected by Reagan, however, was to switch the focus of human rights tactics away from simply influencing the dictators directly, and toward the people living under them. While the United States continued to criticize the bad, in public and private, Reagan launched substantial new efforts to create the good—to feed and nurture the institutions and ideals that help create democracy. Thus, in the fall of 1982, following his speech to the British Parliament, Reagan convened a conference on free elections attended by diplomats from Europe, Asia, and Latin America. The State Department sponsored a similar meeting; its refreshingly radical purpose was to "identify and develop means to promote democratic development under communist regimes."[40] The next spring, Congress approved the creation of the bipartisan National Endowment for Democracy, or NED, a series of private institutes that receives government funding to carry out its mission. One branch, directed by U.S. labor leaders, seeks to promote the development of free labor unions abroad. The Republican and

Democratic parties each operate their own divisions of NED, offering support and advice to foreign political parties. The NED has also sponsored smaller private groups, and one-shot projects, such as an effort by American attorneys to help blacks in South Africa set up their own law practices.[41]

A few examples give the best picture of how the endowment works. In Asia, the NED helped maintain anti-Soviet resistance by establishing schools, printing textbooks, and even training freedom fighters to use minicameras to provide the world with a visual record of the war in Afghanistan. The endowment offered training in democratic theory, and building political party strength, in India, Turkey, and South Korea, where the political opposition has been traditionally weak. NED was the chief source of voter education in the fledgling democracies of Haiti, Guatemala, and Grenada. In Nicaragua, NED helped fund *La Prensa,* one of the few voices of opposition to the Sandinista regime. The endowment helped black unions in South Africa train and attract new members, and provided legal assistance to jailed members of the Polish union Solidarity while helping their families make economic ends meet. It assisted in the publication of prodemocracy magazines in Poland, Hungary, and Czechoslovakia, and prepared videotapes on democracy for distribution in the Soviet Union.[42]

On one level, such efforts have a kind of goody-goody ring to them. Yes, it's nice for us to help build labor unions, publish a few samizdat magazines, support political parties, and help count ballots. But what good are high-school civics lessons to countries where there are no elections anyway? How much does it help South African blacks to know more about unionizing when they can be tossed in jail at the moment the apartheid state decides they are becoming too effective?

The answer to those questions, it seems to me, is to turn the questions around. How can we expect democratic forces to grow strong, to provide a choice other than Marxist dictators and fascist dictators, unless such institutions are strengthened? How can democracy emerge and thrive in the absence of actual practice in the arts of democracy?

One illustration of the importance of the NED's work was in Chile, where peaceful opposition parties tried to maintain themselves over more than a decade of rule under the military junta of Augusto Pinochet. On August 26, 1985, representatives of eleven major Chilean political parties—all but the most extreme ends of the spectrum—met in Santiago with representatives of the NED present. With the urging and the assistance of members of the endowment, the opposition leaders hammered out a joint plan and plea for "a transition to full democracy." The document recorded their unanimous support for a reform of Pinochet's 1980 constitution to allow for a popular vote for president.[43] This event was barely covered in the United States, but it should have been front-page news. By agreeing on a peaceful program for political reform, whatever their differences on other policies, the opposition groups demonstrated their own vitality as a third-force movement that could now approach Chileans, Pinochet, and countries such as the United States, as a united front. For Pinochet, the important effect was to undercut severely his argument that to pressure his regime was to turn Chile over to the communists. "It is part of Pinochet's strategy, and that of most dictators, to crush the center—to force opponents to one violent extreme or the other," notes J. Brian Atwood, head of the Democratic Party's branch of the NED. "When social democrats are able to agree on continued pressure for democracy, they weaken the following of the radical Marxist groups. When even some of the people on the right who support Pinochet's economic policies say that he must reform the political system, they weaken his own camp. The democratic center expands."[44]

In country after country, NED and NED-style programs run by other branches of government, the two parties, and the AFL-CIO have been busy at the critical business of building democratic forces. El Salvador, for example, was troubled by death squads of both Marxist guerillas and angry landowners and military officials. One possible response to such activity would be to cut off U.S. aid until the situation improved, as the U.S. Congress threatened to do. Instead, the United States intervened directly, providing intelligence information and lists of persons suspected of death-squad involvement while agents of the Federal Bureau of Investigation were sent to San Salvador to help show local security forces how to battle the problem. Similarly, in the late 1970s and early 1980s, labor unions in Honduras, frustrated by years of undemocratic rule, were growing increasingly attracted to the Marxist model of confrontational politics. A human rights policy that ignores democratic forces might have simply squeezed Honduras, and in fact the Carter administration did apply the usual range of pressures. While Carter was pressuring, however, the AFL-CIO was busy showing union leaders how to achieve results without bloody revolution, and educating workers about what tends to happen to unions the minute Marxists take over. By 1983, the unions were solidly in the social democratic camp. "If the AFL-CIO hadn't come here," said Andres Victor Artiles, a labor leader in Honduras, "our labor movement would be communist."[45] And the choices for American policymakers would have been much more agonizing.

The NED was also busy in Korea, another friendly authoritarian regime where repeated crackdowns threatened to drive democrats into violent opposition. In 1985, the government called a snap election for the Korean parliament. Opposition groups such as the social-democratic–style party led by Kim Dae Jung were convinced that the indirect format of the election would undermine their chances of victory, and threatened to simply boycott. Besides, the government was allowing only a few weeks for campaigning before the vote. Kim sympathizers at the NED understood the complaint, but argued that the party could still poll enough votes to demonstrate its own popularity and thus increase its strength in negotiating further changes toward direct elections and a full Korean democracy. The endowment offered some last-minute help and Kim's party participated in the election.[46] (The nature of such help, it should be noted, is generally directed at increasing participation, not promoting victory by one side or the other. While the Democrats of NED were helping parties in line with their philosophy, the Republicans were doing the same. Both parties know that blatant electioneering would undercut support for the NED in Congress.)[47] Though getting only 33 percent of the seats because of a system that was weighted against opposition parties, Kim's New Korea Democratic Party won 50 percent of the national vote. The party's higher profile in the parliament, and its obvious popularity, played a critical role in convincing the government to keep negotiating, ultimately promising to switch to a direct presidential election system in the spring of 1987. The floor leader of the NKDP credits "major U.S. support" for helping keep Korean democratic hopes alive "at a time when our young people are growing increasingly skeptical about the United States's role."

The continued vitality of the democratic opposition in turn helped convince the Reagan administration to keep up the Carter-style pressures on South Korea. In the spring of 1986, NED's Democratic branch proposed a conference for Korean opposition leaders. The State Department initially balked, insisting that the Korean government be informed of the conference. So it was; the conference went ahead. Gradually, the State Department revised its assessment of the Korean opposition and grew much bolder, in 1986 and 1987, in pressing for election reforms.[48]

Korea thus illustrates an important unintended consequence of human rights policy as it evolved in the Carter-to-Reagan era. Promoting democratic institutions has an important feedback effect on our willingness to apply pressures to dictators. The Reagan administration, seeing the strength of opposition groups in places like South Korea, abandoned some of its fears of pressuring authoritarian regimes. The Carter policy, we should note, had a similar, reverse effect. One of the things that helps a third force to grow is if its leaders remain alive. Yet in 1979 and 1980, Korean leaders hinted that they would have to execute Kim and other opposition leaders in order to prevent a communist takeover. Carter, focusing on his own brand of human rights promotion, vigorously lobbied the Koreans not to carry out the threat. He was joined by President-elect Reagan, who sent a message of his own to the Korean leaders in the fall of 1980.[49] Evidently, the pressures worked; Kim survived to lead his party and promote the evolution of Korean democracy. Hence the important lesson that pressuring dictators can help the growth of democratic third forces, even if this was not a conscious strategic goal on the part of the Carter administration.

The emergence of democracy in Brazil and Argentina in the 1980s likewise was thanks to the Carter pressures to reduce torture and political executions in the 1970s. "Jimmy Carter literally saved my life," one grateful Brazilian told former Carter aide Robert Pastor.[50] Jose Zalaquette, an attorney in Chile active in human rights issues throughout Latin America, credits State Department aide Pat Derian with blocking the execution of a number of South American dissidents. "If it weren't for Pat Derian, you would probably not be able to be writing about democracy in Argentina, because too many of the democrats would be dead. That woman was pushing very strongly for human rights in Argentina at a time when Argentina was not so clearly on the map of human rights violators, and when the U.S. didn't have any [obvious] geopolitical stake." Even Muravchik credits Carter human rights policy with producing an "improvement" in Argentina—a critical improvement, in retrospect. "It is plausible," Muravchik writes, "that the administration's successful efforts to bring about a reduction in violations of the integrity of the person was one stepping stone on the path to the restoration of Argentine democracy."[51] Ms. Derian might find it obnoxious to be given partial credit for Argentine democracy along with the Reagan administration, just as some members of the Reagan administration would object to the notion that some of their successes were made possible by Jimmy Carter. Whether they like one another's company or not, however, the Reagan and Carter human rights activists—Derian and Abrams, Pastor and Kirkpatrick—often acted in unconscious concert, and they made good music.

Third Force, First Priority

In fact, if we look at the successes of the first decade of human rights policy, from 1977 to 1987, an interesting pattern emerges.

The key early victories took place in countries where Carter went beyond passively criticizing dictators and actively engaged himself and the full might of the United States in supporting democracy. The later victories occurred when the Reagan administration, having convinced itself that there was an alternative other than status quo authoritarianism versus Marxist dictatorship, applied some of the old Carter pressures.

Carter's most clear-cut success came in the Dominican Republic in 1978. President Joaquin Balaguer foresaw a defeat to opposition forces and his army began confiscating ballots in order to rig the results. Now, there would have been nothing inconsistent with the Carter policy had the United States simply watched this happen, and then, in the weeks and months to come, threaten to cut off assistance to the new military regime. Indeed, to do much more than this would in a sense have violated the spirit of Carter's approach, which repeatedly assured foreign dictators we had no intention of interfering in their system. Yet violate his own approach is exactly what Carter did. He picked up the telephone, phoned Balaguer, and persuaded him that there would be serious consequences if the ballot counting by civilians did not resume unmolested. Weeks later, Antonio Guzman was sworn in as the new president of the Dominican Republic. As Jo Marie Griesgraber wrote: "No Marines were sent in, no assistance programs were added, suspended, or deleted. Only words were exchanged. But, given the context, they exerted a strong influence on the results."[52] Carter does not mention the Dominican incident in his memoirs, nor does he take credit for the rise of Latin democracies as such. Yet as the shift became more pronounced, Carter's own thinking seemed to change. In 1986, the former president held a conference of Latin leaders to discuss human rights in the hemisphere. The title: "Reinforcing Democracy in the Americas."[53]

Reagan's human rights successes involved a similar willingness to combine pressure against dictators. Their distinguishing characteristic, however, was an attentive eye on a country's democratic forces.

Again, many commentators and analysts missed this important development. They saw events in the Philippines, for example, as a shift, because in the final days of the Marcos regime, Reagan pressed for change. What brought Reagan to that point, however, was a policy that extended back over several years, aimed at creating a viable democratic alternative.

The effort began shortly after the assassination of Benigno Aquino, Mrs. Aquino's husband, in 1983. By 1985, the United States government was actively seeking to locate and strengthen the democratic center. Central Intelligence Agency analysts held a weekly meeting devoted solely to the Philippines. Both the Pentagon and the State Department established special task forces. "The intelligence officials and policymakers are discussing ways to influence the next elections, and some even advocate getting rid of President Ferdinand Marcos," reported Raymond Bonner in a 1985 article for *The New Republic*.[54] The NED channeled money to Philippine unions and political parties, many of whom signed a Declaration of Unity calling for political and economic reforms. U.S. officials leaked documents that were widely interpreted as disproving Marcos's claims to have been a World War II hero, and planted "confidential" reports indicating that the Reagan administration hoped to ease Marcos from power as the best hope of undercutting support for a growing communist insurgency.[55]

Eventually, it took a push from the administration and Reagan himself for Marcos to see the handwriting on the wall and leave the country. That push, however, came as the result of several years of working for democracy in Manila. Reagan's "turnaround," if there was one, took place not in February of 1987, but years before. And with a new democratic alternative, Reagan was more willing to pressure an old dictator.

Lessons Reconsidered

Sometimes the United States pushes a dictator out of power only to find that there is no democratic force ready to take his place. The syllogism runs something like this: (1) the United States pulled the rug out from under our ally in Country X; (2) in that country, an even less humane dictator, or a Soviet puppet, took over; therefore (3) we were wrong to push for change in the first place.

This is the standard analysis of both Nicaragua and Iran, generally cited as clear-cut examples of the danger of human rights policy. One cannot deny that something failed in both cases. Both countries were, to at least some degree, subjected to pressure for reform by the Carter administration. Both wound up with governments that can hardly be called superior to what they replaced: the Ayatollah Khomeini and his violent revolution in Iran; Daniel Ortega and his Sandinista Marxists in Nicaragua. It does not necessarily follow, however, that their triumphs were the inevitable result of U.S. pressure. The possibility should at least be considered that there were bona fide forces for democracy in both countries. If so, the United States may have erred not in pushing out the authoritarians but in failing to support the democrats.

In Nicaragua, a truly broad-based group of revolutionaries were fighting against the aging dictator Somoza. By as early as 1977, and surely by 1978, a Sandinista victory was a clear possibility. Was a Sandinista victory in the U.S. interest? That depended largely on the character of the Sandinista government to come. One possibility was a state dominated by the Marxist elements of the movement. Another was that the true democrats, men like Arturo Cruz and Adolfo Calero who opposed Somoza and later led the contra effort against them, would at least be strong enough to maintain a pluralist society and press for free elections, which the Marxists had promised and would likely lose. The focus of the Carter human rights policy, however, was not what would follow Somoza, but Somoza himself. When he refused to yield to U.S. pressures to hold a fair vote on his own rule, the United States turned, in 1978 and 1979, to sanctions, cutting off military aid that Somoza needed to survive.

Here was the time, if not sooner, for the U.S. to begin actively exerting its influence on the Sandinistas, to ensure a democratic outcome. In for a dime, in for a dollar. Yet as Shirley Christian records in her history *Nicaragua:*

Revolution in the Family, Carter hesitated at precisely this point. Playing an active role in the transition would have involved the United States in choosing which system the Nicaraguans would live under. For Carter, the only moral choice was not to meddle in the succession battle, or even to push out Somoza, but to let him fall. Anything more would be interventionist. Christian reports a key meeting at which the options were discussed by Robert Pastor and Viron Pete Vaky, two of Carter's top advisers on Latin America policy. "Pete felt we could and should force out Somoza in the fall of '78, and I felt that we couldn't and shouldn't," Pastor recalls. "I felt that Carter should not overthrow a government. I felt we were in the business too long and it was time to get out."[56] Not everyone would agree with Christian about the timing. William Sullivan, the U.S. ambassador to Iran when the shah fell, argues that the United States pushed too hard too fast in Nicaragua. "When it recognized Somoza's weakness, the United States moved so quickly to be rid of his regime that the moderates remaining had no time to organize, and the Sandinistas and the Cubans moved in by default."[57] We are not primarily interested in timing, of course, but focus. A true third-force doctrine, in fact, would have been interested in promoting a democratic opposition in Nicaragua well before 1978. Where Sullivan and Christian agree is that the United States had a chance to promote a democratic outcome but failed to seize it.

Still another opportunity came with the fall of Somoza himself in 1979. By now the effect of U.S. pressure against Somoza was clear; he was leaving. Having helped to produce his exit, Carter had a right if not a duty to intervene on behalf of the democrats seeking to enter. Again, though, the United States hesitated. Daniel Oduber, the president of Costa Rica from 1974 to 1978, recalls this critical opening: "After Somoza was overthrown, in July 1979, the moment came to move in and try to create a democratic alternative. Venezuela, Panama, and to a certain extent Costa Rica. . . . We tried, as Arturo Cruz knows. Social Democrats, liberals, Christian Democrats—everybody moved in. But it was not enough."[58] Timely intervention by the region's major power, in other words, was needed. Why wasn't it taken? In 1986, Carter said that such action was considered but rejected. Asked why the United States didn't move to block the rise of the Marxist government in Nicaragua, Carter answered: "I never tried to act unilaterally in the case of Nicaragua. . . . We applied pressure against Somoza, but jointly. . . . We did propose to Somoza that he hold an election or plebiscite, and that this be monitored." But what about the period when it was clear Somoza would fall, and the critical weeks and months after he did? "I consulted very closely with the leaders of the other democrats in this hemisphere, with the OAS, Colombia, Venezuela, Costa Rica, Mexico, Panama . . . and we put together about a dozen people to work on the problem. This is the group that we dealt with. We never sought to impose by American might a particular form of government on the Nicaraguan people."[59] It is interesting that Carter instinctively equated allowing Nicaraguans to select their own government peacefully with an imposition of American might. Carter, it seems clear, was not even thinking in terms of what he might have done differently, seven years after what he knew was regarded as one of the great failures of his human rights policy.

If human rights policy failed in Nicaragua, however, it is important for us to understand why it failed. Strangely, Carter and such critics as Kirkpatrick seem agreed that from 1978 to 1980, the only likely outcomes were dictatorship by Somoza or dictatorship by Ortega. This is precisely where they are all wrong. It was not that Jimmy Carter hated tyranny too much, but that he loved democracy too little. Ambassador Sullivan captures the lesson of Nicaragua well:

> Few Americans would endorse a political platform at home that time after time argued that the only policy approach to a dangerous domestic challenge was either fatalism or repression; nor should they abroad. There is ample basis for assuming that American diplomacy, skillfully, decisively, and wisely deployed, can assist in the constructive, peaceful restoration of democracy in countries with which the United States has friendly relations.[60]

Iran is at once more distant and more complicated than Nicaragua. Well, not to everyone. The standard 1980s view of Iran resembled the stereotypic 1950s view of the Soviet Union. "There are no moderates in Iran," Defense Secretary Caspar Weinberger flatly told the congressional Iran-contra investigating committee. "In Iran," writes Charles Krauthammer of *The New Republic*, "there simply was no democratic center."[61] Notably, those who were present at the creation of the first Iran disaster—Vance, Brzezinski, Carter, and Sullivan—tend to think that it need not have been a disaster, that a different use of U.S. influence might have produced something other than the Islamic despotism of Ayatollah Khomeini.[62] Scholars who have studied the fall of the shah, such as William Forbis, Grace Goodell, Michael Ledeen, and William Lewis, agree.[63] If there were in fact democrats in Iran from 1978 to 1979, establishing a stable government, then the standard view that Carter erred chiefly in pushing for change, or at least in not giving the shah sufficient backing, may itself be in error.

One complicating factor is that the Carter administration did not apply with full force the usual human rights pressures. Military sales to Iran continued at a level of several billion dollars per year. Although Carter pressed privately with the shah for human rights improvements, the public rhetoric of the White House and even the State Department stressed our support for the shah, "an island of stability" in a troubled region, as Carter put it at a 1978 New Year's Day toast.

Still, there were some punitive measures. At a potentially critical point in the Iran crisis, the United States denied tear gas to the shah's troops. Instead, the military used real bullets, precipitating the bloody Friday in which hundreds died in Jaleh Square. There is, moreover, little doubt that the administration's general human rights rhetoric convinced the shah and many observers that despite such encomia from the president, America's support for the shah was less than complete and less than enthusiastic. Perhaps the best summary is to say that both U.S. support for the shah and U.S. pressure on him were applied halfheartedly.[64]

Besides, the shah was improving human rights, especially in the two areas stressed by the Carter administration: rights involving the sanctity of the person, such as freedom from torture, and what were called economic rights, particularly as realized in the enactment of social programs. Iranian spending on social services and development ran about $2 billion a year in the early 1970s, but grew to $25 billion for fiscal 1979—compared to $10 billion on military expenditures.[65] The shah also launched a vast land-reform program greatly admired by State Department officials. Unfortunately, the land reform seized vast tracts from the church, enraging the rural clergy. And like many land-reform plans, the shah's was a collectivization scheme. The small farming units formed by individual producers, it was held, weren't advanced enough to make use of advanced farming techniques, and Iran's small villages and peasant societies weren't of an efficient size for setting up health clinics, schools, and other services under direction of the central government. So the shah, with help from Western development experts, drove the peasants into vast cooperatives, "agribusiness units," and state-run corporations. Bulldozers plowed through some 67,000 small villages to remold them into 30,000 big ones, uprooting families, mosques, and other vestiges of communities. Some of those rounded up from the farms went to work at Iran's new automobile factories; gold, salt, and copper mines; or one of several nuclear power plants—all part of a forced industrialization process reminiscent of 1930s Russia. Others festered in the cities, a stagnant pond of unrest for exploitation by Khomeini and other radicals. "There's never been so much change in 3,000 years," the shah chirped, calling his White Revolution a mix of "capitalism . . . socialism . . . even communism."[66] In the economic sphere, the ruler of the Peacock Throne was carrying out his own concept, and to a large extent Carter's, only too well.

Moreover, despite the abuses of the shah's dreaded secret police, the rights of person Carter liked to stress were respected more often in Iran than in many Middle Eastern countries. The shah granted amnesty to hundreds of dissidents, such as Khomeini, a move that probably would have led to front-page headlines if made by a Soviet premier. He ordered the termination of torture in Iran's prisons shortly after Carter took office, and introduced reforms in the legal system.[67]

All this has led to a lively historical debate over the timing of the shah's reforms. The problem with the reforms, though, was not that they were too fast or too slow, but too stupid. There was no political change to give the burgeoning middle class a voice in the government. In fact, insofar as the shah's social programs tended to disrupt the community and centralize the economy, the average Iranian lost more control over his own life than he gained. Hence as the shah relaxed the grip of the military and the secret police ever so slightly, he simply weakened his own ability to crack down on dissent—without giving it the peaceful, positive outlet of elections, parties, and meaningful debates among leaders with a real voice in national policy. Intermittently, the Carter administration would hint at the need for systemic political changes. Such moves toward democracy as did occur, however, were quickly reversed, with little protest from the United States. In 1975 and 1976, for example, the shah allowed a throne-sanctioned opposition party, the Rastakhiz party, to form, and relaxed limits on other organizations. The following summer the shah reversed himself, restricting even the Rastakhiz, but the Carter State Department made no protest over these important political moves. State Department reports criticized Iran, but mainly for the abuses of SAVAK, the secret police.[68] Carter seemed pleased, in fact, with the other changes under way in Iran. "During 1978, the Shah attempted to respond to demands from his people for a greater voice in public affairs," Carter notes approvingly in his memoirs, but he cites as evidence the release of several hundred opposition leaders and the greater tolerance for marches in the street—not any concrete moves toward or even promises of democracy as such.[69] Brzezinski is regarded as the hardliner in the Iran fiasco for his recommendation that the United States support a crackdown by the military, followed by reforms. But he shared the ethos concerning which reforms mattered. The key, Brzezinski argues, was to advance "socioeconomic modernization" with a move toward "greater political pluralism." Thus, he also praised the shah for "positive changes in the role of women" and "more widespread education."[70]

Carter's own human rights focus was reinforced by the U.S. intelligence and foreign service community, which adopted an elitist focus that ignored and discounted the potential of popular, third-force movements. It's worth noting that those who followed the forces of dissent in Iran, from radical mullahs to true social democrats in the middle class, spotted signs of trouble at a time when conventional wisdom saw the shah as firmly in control. Gary Sick, a top adviser on Iran for the National Security Council, reports a conversation in early 1978 with an Iran expert who predicted the shah would last less than two years. Most of these people, though, were human rights hard cores in the State Department or academia, and their analysis was dismissed. The conventional view of the CIA and the diplomatic community didn't even include input from the key players in Iran, as Sick reports:

> For at least a decade the United States had viewed its relations with Iran almost exclusively as relations with the person of the shah. There probably was never a formal order to avoid contacts with Iranian opposition groups, but there was a clear awareness that the shah was annoyed and suspicious about such contacts and they gradually dried up. . . . That decision was made easier by the fact that the disparate array of opposition groups had been operating to no apparent effect.
>
> In late 1978 the question of "domestic instability" in Iran was assigned a priority of three (on a scale of six) and on another, a priority of three on a descending scale of one to three. . . . Washington received little reliable information about the activities or intentions of opposition groups during the early stages of the revolution.[71]

Hence there was little knowledge about the democratic forces in Iran, much less active encouragement of them. An August 1978 State Department survey concluded that "Iran is not in a revolutionary or even a 'prerevolutionary' situation."[72] Had there been an interest in actively engaging the opposition groups, of course, we might have learned a number of useful things. We might have been able to render confident judgments about Khomeini. Was it possible to deal with him? If so, we could have been doing so early in the process, as Sullivan recommended.[73] Was it impossible? If so, we might have blocked his return to Iran.

We would, in any case, have known better who the fanatics and the moderates were in Iran, and how much strength the democrats had. Moderates and democrats in Iran? Yes. From the afternoon of September 7, 1978, when the shah declared martial law in the face of strikes, marches, and mounting unrest, through the seizure of the embassy and into 1980, a number of moderates rose to power; they might have remained, and been joined by others, with U.S. help. There was Ali Amini, the prime minister during a 1960s fling with reform who at one point agreed to help the shah form a consultative council with opposition groups. Karim Sanjabi, head of the National Front, may or may not have been a moderate. The shah eventually thought he wasn't, but he released him from prison and met to discuss forming a democratic coalition. Gholam Hossein Sadiqi and Shapour Bakhtiar, other National Front members, seemed clearly in the camp of the democrats. The shah met Sadiqi in December and found him agreeable to a government with the shah as a titular constitutional monarch. And he eventually handed power over to Bakhtiar. Ardeshir Zahedi, Iran's ambassador to the U.S., was a close friend of Brzezinski's and the shah's. Whether the shah considered him a potential successor depends on whether you believe Zahedi (who says he was) or the reports of the shah's opinions that came back through Sullivan and a dozen-odd special envoys sent over to assess the situation (they said he wasn't). There was little doubt that Zahedi believed in Western democracy and could have played a role in creating one with substantial help from the United States. Mehdi Bazargan, another moderate in Iran, engaged in a long war of nerves with Bakhtiar, taking power from him in February of 1979, then with Khomeini, a delicate battle that Khomeini won, and the U.S. and the moderates lost. Even after the seizure of the American embassy officials as hostages in November of 1979, Iranians elected as president Abolhassan Bani-Sadr, who took office in January of 1980 and immediately began to negotiate with the Great Satan for the release of the hostages.

For each of these moderates in Iran, there was a plan in the U.S. government to help them. Ambassador Sullivan proposed negotiating with Khomeini, the military, the shah, and other relevant actors for a coalition government headed by Bakhtiar.[74] Brzezinski first wanted a strong show of force by the shah, followed by democratization; then he favored a military coup, followed by liberalization. The notable common assumption of both plans was that the Iranian military, if it had firm backing from the United States, could combine with moderates in the religious community, the bureaucracy, and the private sector to avoid tyranny.[75] George Ball, more dovish, didn't think draconian force was necessary. He proposed that a council of notables be composed among several dozen moderate leaders from different walks of life in Iran to draft a proposal for a new constitution.[76] State Department aide Henry Precht, apparently unaware of the Ball proposal, proposed a similar but smaller committee of six notables.[77] Precht's colleagues agreed that the shah should be urged to relinquish power to the "secular political opposition." Vance agreed with Brzezinski that the United States needed to back the shah first, then prompt reform. Yet Vance, too, saw hope for a third force. "The shah's best chance," he wrote, was "to share enough power with a coalition government to split the moderate nationalists off from the Khomeini followers."[78] Still others, such as Sick, felt that by the fall of 1978, "the moderates were too weak." Yet Sick offered one of the most dramatic plans of all. The United States, he said, should call for a return to the constitution of 1906. Such a sweeping gesture, he argued, just might work, since it was "widely regarded as an acceptable political goal by much of the opposition."[79]

Any of these plans might have worked. All were rejected; or rather, none was enacted. Sullivan was told to hold off as the administration waited to hear back from Ball and other special emissaries. Besides, there was little stomach in the fall of 1978 for giving the shah a decisive push.[80] Even in December, there was still hope that the shah could work out an acceptable transition. So we waited. When the shah left, the administration held off to see if Bakhtiar could either win Khomeini's backing or outmaneuver him. He couldn't. When he stepped down on February 11, 1979, we looked to see if Bazargan would establish civilian control. He didn't, and we didn't help him. "I had hopes that the Ayatollah would stay in the holy city of Qum," Carter said. "It became obvious, however, that no government officials were to be in control of the country." As the bloodbath heightened in the fall of 1979, anti-Khomeini demonstrations broke out across Iran. We watched. Months later, Bani-Sadr was elected president, taking office in January of 1980. Here was yet another opportunity for action, but by this time paralysis had set in. Bani-Sadr tried to negotiate the release of the hostages, but ultimately was driven from Iran.[81]

There were two problems common to virtually all of the plans to shore up the democratic center in Iran. All of them resisted rethinking the assumption that the shah was still the center of power, and all of them avoided contemplating even a minimal use of force. "Since any substantial change in policy involved actions that were certain to be distasteful or worse," Sick writes, "people were inclined to keep their thoughts to themselves. The combined effect was to encourage procrastination in the hope that the situation would resolve itself somehow. . . . Neither Carter nor most of his key advisers were philosophically prepared to entertain the idea of massive U.S. intervention."[82] This throw-up-your-hands-and-hope-for-the-best attitude was best captured by Carter himself, in repeated assertions of U.S. powerlessness. Jimmy Carter on November 13, 1978: "We support the Shah . . . recognizing that we don't have any control over the decisions ultimately made by the Iranian people."[83] Jimmy Carter on December 7: "This is something that is in the hands of the people of Iran. We have never had any intention and don't have any intention of trying to intercede."[84] As late as January 7, 1979, Carter said: "We have no intention, neither ability nor desire, to intervene in the internal affairs of Iran."[85] In fact, of course, we were intervening every day, through emissaries, intelligence agents, and generals trying to sort out events and encourage a stable transition. What Carter had no intention of doing was intervening decisively or effectively.

In retrospect, of course, deterministic pronouncements often seem correct. Violence always seems to have been inevitable, from the French Revolution to Kerensky. But the evidence is that Kerensky could have survived, with only a light application of force at the right place and time. It is quite possible that what was needed in Iran was not the hundreds of dead on bloody Friday, or the thousands in the revolutionary courts of 1979, but rather one firm action against the radicals in 1978. What might have been in Iran? Heavy weight must be given to the opinion of James Bill, the Iran expert who warned Sick in early 1978 that the shah would soon fall. His conclusion: With U.S. backing, members of the National Front, the military, and the clergy could have been induced to agree to a transition to democracy, based on a restoration of the constitution of 1906.

WORDS INTO DEEDS

Reagan's Irans

Though less noted, two comparable failures of human rights policy took place during the Reagan administration. In one, a country with nearly as much oil as Iran, and many more people, fell to a military coup in the early hours of 1984. That country was Nigeria, the most populous country in Africa, and until the collapse of the Second Republic, one of the largest democracies in the world. The United States was responsible for the coup—though we by no means directly encouraged or sponsored it—in at least two ways. First, our Federal Reserve Board engineered a global collapse of commodity prices, including the price of oil. The proximate result was economic chaos in Nigeria and other countries dependent on commodity export for their economic liveli-hood—as a later chapter will describe in more detail. Second, we paid little attention to brewing dissent in the country. Corruption in the Nigerian govern-ment had reached epic proportions by 1982. Many Nigerians mistrusted the very mechanics of free elections. The United States could easily have offered assistance in conducting a fair vote. A few election observers, as in the Philip-pines, might have been, in the words of political scientists Larry Diamond and Seymour Martin Lipset, "of real and even potentially decisive significance."[86] But Nigeria, unlike Iran, didn't show up on any of the big maps with choke points and stickpins and flashing lights, and the Reagan administration was busy with other crises. Days after democracy perished in Nigeria, the West sent in not the marines, nor its diplomatic corps, but its bankers, to make sure that the country's debt would be rescheduled in an orderly fashion. When George Shultz showed up for consultations with the government in 1987, he complained not about the country's lack of democracy, but its insufficient efforts to cut down on heroin exports.[87]

The even greater tragedy took place in Poland, where the thriving labor and political movement of Solidarity was stalled (though not killed) by the imposi-tion of martial law in December of 1981. For all his anticommunist rhetoric, Ronald Reagan lost Poland. A Polish military officer, Colonel Ryszard Kuk-linski, who later defected to the United States, told the story. According to Kuklinski, who sat in on many of the sensitive deliberations of the Polish government in the fall of 1981, the plans for martial law were drawn up, and even Xeroxed, in the Kremlin. For several months, Kuklinski warned his CIA contacts of the impending crackdown. At one point, he was even smuggled out of the country when it appeared his life was in jeopardy. Kuklinski passed on the detailed scheme—almost everything but the precise date—to his U.S. contacts.[88] Precisely what happened to this critical information is difficult to determine. Reliable sources at the National Security Council and the State

Department later told me that the information went to Secretary of State Alexander Haig, who neglected to pass it along to the president on the ground there was nothing "realistic" we could do anyway. And CIA analysts evaluating the plans failed to take them seriously. What did not happen is clear. The United States did not act, either through private communication with the Soviets or by publicly announcing the plans, or both. "We waited for some kind of announcement from Washington," Polish government spokesman Jerzy Urban recalls. "But time passed and the United States was silent, so the plans were put into effect."[89]

None of this contradicts, and indeed much of it supports what Haig writes in his memoirs. "There were clear danger signals. On November 13, I wrote to the president," Haig recalls. "Once again, I reminded the president that our ability to influence events was limited." Like Eisenhower and Hungary in 1956, Haig saw few U.S. options in between a U.S. invasion and mere polite protest. Indeed, when Haig was later asked if Kuklinski's account was accurate, he drafted a carefully crafted letter to me that seemed to confirm Kuklinski's story—by denying numerous petty details from press accounts, but not taking issue of Kuklinski's claim that the United States sat and watched as martial law was imposed. "I do not know Colonel Kuklinski," Haig wrote. "Nor have I read a direct account of his remarks," he continued. Yet this evades the question of whether, as secretary of state, he had seen reports of Kuklinski's findings. He did not deny that the administration knew of, and did nothing to block, martial law. Richard V. Allen, Reagan's national security adviser at the time, also was kind enough to write to me about the Kuklinski account. He said simply, "I believe that the *New Republic* article," which cites Kuklinski and blames the Reagan administration for allowing the crushing of Solidarity, "fairly states the case."[90]

From both the failures, and the far more numerous successes, of human rights policy, a simple rule suggests itself. The rule is to locate and then build forces for democracy—a free press, political parties, unions, business groups, churches, and other private institutions—with words at first, and with other levers if necessary. Building democratic institutions over time succeeds in creating a third force of sufficient strength to obviate the unpalatable tripartite choice between dictatorship, communism, or a bloody U.S. intervention. Even where it does not, such a strategy can provide information that may be critical in a crisis. It can tell us whether the insurgents fighting a dictator are true democrats; generally anti-Western, but open to pluralism and democracy; or unremittingly hostile to freedom. Probing for the third force, moreover, will not only tell us about its character, but its might. This is critical to an assessment of whether it can triumph all by itself, with a little help, or only as the result of a major American exertion. Seldom is it a question of whether any democrats and moderates exist. There are always multiple actors of ambiguous commitments and debatable influence competing for power against a dictator whose own inclinations and influence may be unclear. The question, then, is not whether there is any third force at all, but how strong it is, and what sort of commitment is needed from the United States to help it find its voice. If they keep these central questions in mind, U.S. leaders will seldom go wrong.

5

TUNING IN TO GLASNOST: AMERICA'S RADIO VOICES

ON NOVEMBER 4, 1956, Soviet tanks rolled into Hungary to suppress a twelve-day-old revolt for liberty. Westerners tuning in to Hungarian radio frequencies heard repeated pleas for help from freedom fighters who had seized transmitters across the country. "Peoples of Europe!" one broadcast began. "Listen to the tolling of Hungarian bells warning of disaster!"[1]

But one by one, Russian troops located the stations and snuffed them out. At 9:35 A.M. on November 7, Radio Free Rákóczi issued one of the last recorded cries. If you go over it slowly, it almost reads like a poem.

Must we appeal once again?
Do you love liberty? So do we. Do you have wives and children? So have we.
In the name of all that is dear to you, we ask you to help. Do you not realize that those who have died for liberty are accusing you—who are able to help and who have not helped? . . .
Or shall we lose faith in the world's conscience and decency when we are fighting for world freedom?
S.O.S.! S.O.S.! Save our Souls! . . .
Pray for us.
And pray for yourselves.[2]

TUNING IN TO GLASNOST

We may never be sure what would have happened had the United States and Western Europe responded to those poignant appeals. There was ample reason for caution. At the time of Hungary's revolt, the United States was involved in a major dispute with its allies: the Suez crisis in the Middle East. Armed intervention, Dwight Eisenhower argued, would have been a difficult geographic prospect, involving Western troop movements either through communist Czechoslovakia, Titoist Yugoslavia, or neutral Austria. Moreover, as Eisenhower notes in his memoirs, the Soviets had by now tested atomic weapons. A policy of support for Hungarian democracy, Ike concludes, "would inevitably" have produced a "major conflict."[3]

In retrospect, then, the Kremlin's successful use of force to crush Hungary seems almost inevitable, but as journalist Michael Kinsley has observed, invasions always seem that way in retrospect.[4] At the time, the Kremlin faced immense difficulties in Hungary, and its action was in no way predetermined. After all, the Soviets had just allowed the evolution of a democratic government in Austria in 1955, and of a nonaligned socialist state in Yugoslavia. They seemed to be facing a second Yugoslavia in Poland, where Soviet troops were trying to maintain control. Berlin was persistently unstable, with riots in 1953 and again in 1955. Thus, for days after the beginning of the Hungarian uprising, on the evening of October 22, Khrushchev probed for the reaction of the United States, Western Europe, Yugoslavia, and China. The Soviet Presidium's decision to intervene, evidence suggests, was not taken until October 29—a week after the first mass meetings.[5] Inside Hungary, events were clearly slipping out of control. Eighty percent of the Hungarian army had defected.[6] Later polls of Hungarian refugees found that about one-third of the population had taken the risky step of actively supporting the revolution; an estimated 60 percent neither actively supported nor opposed it; and a mere 2 percent, mostly communist party officials, actively worked against it.[7] International opprobrium against the Soviets was universal outside their own rickety empire. The United Nations voted 50 (most of the world) to 8 (the Warsaw Pact) for a resolution calling for the withdrawal of Soviet troops. Though the Russians had tested nuclear explosions, the ability to deliver actual nuclear weapons could still be described fairly as a virtual U.S. monopoly.

Equally questionable is the notion that the United States had no choices in between an immediate overland invasion and polite protests. Bennett Kovrig, a professor of political economy at the University of Toronto, lists just some of the options:

> A firm, early, and secret warning from Eisenhower to refrain from force could have had a salutary effect. The United States could also have capitalized on the favorable status quo in Hungary by formally recognizing the Nagy government

by October 27 or 28 and by promptly acknowledging Hungary's withdrawal from the Warsaw Pact. . . . A U.N. delegation could have been dispatched to Hungary while the Nagy government was still in office . . . to enhance the inviolability of Hungarian sovereignty. Finally, a review of European security, which was a standing Soviet proposal, could have been linked by the United States to the strategic and political implications of Hungarian neutrality.[8]

Such actions might not have produced a different outcome. On the other hand, they might have. "According to the conventional wisdom," argues Jiri Valenta, a scholar at the Rockefeller Foundation who studied Soviet decision making during the crisis, "the invasion of Hungary was inevitable. . . . But [it] was not. If some of the key factors had been different, the sum of Soviet measures could have been different as well."[9]

Once revolt was under way, the response of the United States can best be described as one of ambiguous ambivalence. On the one hand, U.S. officials cheered on the Hungarians and at least seemed willing to assist. On October 27, John Foster Dulles delivered a speech in Dallas promising that East European nations could "draw on our abundance" during their "adjustment." Although only economic aid was intended, Dulles also asserted the right of the Warsaw Pact nations to "independence." He said the United States would take the matter to the United Nations—a formulation that to many suggested a parallel to Truman's dispatch of troops to Korea. Eisenhower himself reiterated his 1952 pledge to seek liberation for enslaved peoples "by all means in our power." On the other hand, Eisenhower and Dulles both warned that the United States contemplated no military intervention. Dulles stressed that the United States did not see these countries as "allies," but as part of a more "stable" European system. Eisenhower approved a cable to the Soviets emphasizing this part of the speech was official policy.[10] The net impact was probably the worst of both worlds, at once sparking unjustified hope among the Hungarians while assuring the Kremlin that our warm words were mere hot air. "The failure of the United States to have a plan or plans of action concerning Hungarian events," concluded the House Foreign Affairs Committee, "indicates either a serious weakness in our intelligence service or a serious misapplication . . . of facts reported."[11] Once again, ignorance of the strength of democratic forces allowed the lazy assumption there were no U.S. options, which encouraged ignorance of the democratic forces, which reinforced the lazy assumption there was "nothing we could do"—the old vicious cycle of reactive containment.

Reasonable people can disagree about whether the United States could have done more to aid the Hungarians without running a genuine risk of war. Yet one thing is clear: the situation in Hungary evolved largely as the result of a well-conceived U.S. effort to promote democracy. At the heart of these efforts were the Western radio services, among them Radio Free Europe, the Voice of America, and the British Broadcasting Corporation, which provided Hungarians throughout 1956 with what has proved to be perhaps freedom's most potent usable lever in the nuclear age:

Facts.

Broadcasts and Balloons

In the case of Hungary, simple facts helped bring a nation to the edge of liberation in two ways. First, our broadcasts armed Hungarians with the knowledge that even Soviet-dominated states can evolve toward independence and democracy, a fact that was being demonstrated regularly in Communist Europe from 1953 through 1956. The emergence of independent socialism in Yugoslavia, and democracy in Austria, has already been mentioned. Protests and labor stoppages also persisted in Berlin and Bulgaria. Nikita Khrushchev opened the door to reforms in his famous speech to the 20th Party Congress of February 1956, where he officially accepted the doctrine that there are "different roads to socialism," and thus implied that Soviet satellites might carve out different, more democratic approaches. Finally, days before the uprising in Hungary, Poland's communist leaders began taking that doctrine to its logical conclusion. On October 19, 1956, Poland's Central Committee voted to name popular dissenter Wladyslaw Gomulka to a post in the party secretariat, and was about to oust Marshal Konstantin Rokossovsky, a Russian national who both symbolized and embodied Moscow's dominance. Khrushchev rushed to Warsaw to block any such move, declaring that if the Poles went ahead, "we will crush you." The Poles went ahead. "The Polish people will defend themselves with all means," Gomulka told a cheering crowd on October 20. "They will not be pushed off the road of democratization."[12] That afternoon, Soviet troops crossed the border from East Germany. The Poles fired back.

These and similar events were the major theme of Western radio broadcasts to Hungary from 1955 up to the outbreak of revolution on the evening of October 22, 1956.[13] The strategy, as recalled by Allan A. Michie, a journalist with *Life* and *Reader's Digest* and later a Radio Free Europe official, was to provide people in the Soviet empire with ideas and information that would help them to make concrete advances toward democracy.

Its first fruits came in Czechoslovakia, where Operation Veto helped spur democratic changes on the margin. Under Operation Veto, U.S. broadcasts were supplemented by a creative program to collect and publicize demands for change made by local dissidents. The United States collected secret literature and scattered Western reports of the various suggestions for communist evolution raised by Czech dissidents. The most common were condensed into a list, and drummed in through frequent broadcasts about the Ten Demands. The United States even floated balloons—containing information pamphlets on the Ten Demands—that released hundreds of parachute boxes, which would open up as they neared the target, releasing smaller boxes with their own parachutes. The pamphlets, along with little palm-sized stickers with the number "10" on them, became peaceful fact-bombs, drifting all over the cities and countryside of Czechoslovakia. By mid-1954 they were ubiquitous and were regularly denounced in government propaganda media. A lively debate ensued between the candidates for office as to the merits or demerits of the Ten Demands. Even though every single official running in the election was a Communist Party member, discussion as to just what the nature of "communism" should be enabled voters to support more reform-minded candidates. Naturally, the Ten Demands were not explicitly granted. In the months that followed, however, the new National Assembly made grudging concessions to the opposition, allowing, for example, more autonomy for labor unions.[14]

Poland and Hungary were the next major tests. "It was the first sustained effort," Michie writes, "to get across to peoples of . . . the captive nations that their road to freedom lay not in waiting for the day when a 'war of liberation' would rescue them but in achieving by themselves a series of day-to-day advances; that they should work for specific, short-term reforms in their regimes . . . that would gradually lead to the whittling away of Communist authority."[15] If that was the goal, the program worked. The Hungarians who took to the streets demanding independence on October 22 and 23 clearly took their inspiration from other reformers in the Soviet empire. "Hurrah for the Poles!" read one banner. Another echoed Khrushchev, urging: "Do Not Stop Half Way: Away With Stalinism."[16] Gyula Háy, the Nobel Prize–winning author, told Hungarians at an open meeting on October 22 in Győr: "Yugoslavia has succeeded in protecting her complete independence and Poland and China are on the way to developing socialism based on national characteristics."[17]

Of course, Hungarians might have learned something about these events from their own government-run media—but not much. What little information about dissent within the Soviet bloc did creep into the censored news reports was in large part an effort to refute facts that were being broadcast by the West. Khrushchev's "different roads to socialism" speech, for example, was unknown in most of Hungary. Then Radio Free Europe obtained a copy of the speech and broadcast it repeatedly over all services; the East bloc was abuzz. Khrushchev himself was forced to respond to the unexpected publicity, warning communists not to air their "dirty linen" abroad.[18] Surveys conducted among those who fled Hungary after the invasion suggest that Western broadcasts were the major source of reliable information. More than 97 percent of the respondents said they had listened to Western broadcasts, with 72 percent listening "every day."

By contrast, when the refugees were asked to assess how many members of certain population groups were influenced by domestic propaganda, more than 75 percent of the refugees estimated that "few" or "hardly any" farmers, workers, educated people, or middle-class people were influenced.[19]

Once the revolution started, facts provided by Western broadcasts played a second critical role, keeping Hungarians informed about first hopeful, then confusing, then ultimately tragic events. With communications lines often cut, and the internal situation confused, Hungarians often found that Radio Free Hungary or the Voice of America was the only comprehensive source of information. One of the first actions of the rebels, after seizing stations of their own, was to shut down jamming facilities used by the government in an effort to block Western broadcasts.[20] Western radio stations were on the air twenty-four hours a day during the crisis. Correspondents from across Europe rushed to Budapest, and from their reports, together with the scattered broadcasts of the freedom stations, Radio Free Europe and the Voice of America were able to compile detailed accounts of the fighting and the events in the capital. RFE officials carefully pieced together the demands—chiefly, the withdrawal of Soviet troops, a nonaligned foreign policy, immediate scheduling of free elections, and rights to organize unions, own property, and criticize the government—and rebroadcast them, so that all Hungary could understand the program being advocated by various rebel groups. As in Operation Veto, there was as much emphasis on good listening as there was on talking. "These were not airy-fairy slogans cooked up by American advisers in Munich," Michie recalls. "They were formulated to represent the chief complaints and grudges of the people."[21] Émigré freedom fighters later said that often their only contact with one another during the critical days of resistance was the Western broadcasts themselves. RFE consequently became "a critically important communications channel for the revolutionaries," writes Sig Mickelson in his history of the service. Information about the revolution that would have required listening to dozens of scattered voices at once thus reached most Hungarians rapidly through one source.[22]

Even critics of what the Radios said, and of the overall Eisenhower policy in Hungary, recognize the impact of Western broadcasts, though of course their tone is more plaintive. "Radio Liberty," writes Katrina Vanden Heuvel in *The Nation,* "and to a greater extent Radio Free Europe, played an inflammatory role during the uprising, the latter broadcasting promises of Western aid."[23] Richard Holbrooke, a high State Department official during the Carter administration, writes: "1956 was a tragedy for many people in Hungary who were misled by the words which the United States government had no intention of backing up."[24] Interestingly, though, a number of reviews of Radio Free Europe and the Voice of America during the crisis found that they made little effort to foment disobedience. Radio Free Europe, which bore the brunt of the attacks, reviewed some 308 scripts broadcast from October 23 to November 23 of 1956. Of these, only four were found to contain material that violated RFE's policy of not encouraging listeners to rebel or promoting specific tactics for doing so. Three scripts, while not promising U.S. aid, contained thinly veiled advice for Hungarians on techniques being used for the do-it-yourself sabotaging of rail and phone lines and destruction of Soviet tanks. In the fourth, a Hungarian RFE editor speaking on November 4 concluded his world press review by quoting from an analysis published in the British newspaper *The Observer* which argued that once the American election was out of the way, Eisenhower and Congress might provide support. The RFE broadcaster then went on to summarize Western opinion in his own words: "In the Western capitals a practical manifestation of Western sympathy is expected at any hour."[25] This statement clearly went too far, summing up complicated expectations so matter-of-factly—though it is true that many observers, including *The Observer*, did believe such a "practical manifestation" was imminent. Still, the total of four excessive items, out of 640 hours of high-pressure broadcasting, hardly seems high. Independent committees appointed by the United Nations, the government of West Germany, and the Council of Europe all studied Western broadcasts during the revolt, finding little direct efforts to foment dissent. American scholar Robert William Pirsein reached the same conclusion when he studied the broadcasts of the Voice of America for the same period.[26] What these observers did find was that Hungarians expected the West to intervene because they believed the statements of Eisenhower and Dulles, accurately reported in our broadcasts, pointed in that direction. Both RFE officials and a private research institute later surveyed Hungarians to see if outside broadcasts had incited revolution. Only one refugee in sixteen felt that Western broadcasts themselves led to expectations of aid.[27]

Simply by passing along facts, Western radio broadcasts helped the Hungarian people to come within a whisker of freedom. An official of the Hungarian Ministry of Defense aptly summarized their effectiveness, well before the revolution, when he commented in 1953: "The most dangerous effect of Radio Free Europe is not that it results in organized resistance (which is easily detected and suppressed), but in personal resistance, which it is difficult to control."[28]

Establishing a Voice

If this is how Western broadcasts can be most effective, it is not necessarily the vision that inspired their creation. The Voice of America, whose job it is to tell "America's story" abroad—describing conditions in America as well as explaining and advocating our government's viewpoint on various events and issues—began broadcasting as part of the Office of War Information in 1942.* The idea was to counter Nazi and Japanese propaganda, partly by getting the truth to our own troops, but also by demoralizing to some extent the soldiers of the Axis Pact nations. Decades later, the VOA still used some of the same broadcast facilities employed by Hitler and seized by America after the war, a transmitting anachronism that seemed to symbolize its unusual character and mission. This is not to say that the VOA, even in its infancy, sought to use the same nefarious tactics used by Nazi propagandists. The strategic conception of VOA, however, did rely heavily on what communications specialists call the "bullet theory,"[29] which sees propagating information as having immediate, predictable effects on whole populations, in much the same way one can point a gun at a specific target, pull the trigger, and predict a specific result. In its most extreme form, the theory becomes ridiculous almost on its face: "If only the Russians knew what life in Russia is like, they would change Russia overnight." Even the most enthusiastic proponents of radio broadcasting and other public-information campaigns would not go this far, but their view of how broadcasts can work is often based on the same assumptions of mass persuasion that underlie the bullet theory.

Radio Free Europe and Radio Liberty, writes Sig Mickelson, former president of CBS News and of RFE-RL, had similar elements of "illicit" parentage. These stations were created in large part through the efforts of former officers of the Office of Strategic Services, America's master spies during the war, and of the newly formed Central Intelligence Agency. One reason was the feeling that the Voice was not tough enough. "The Voice of America, because it is an arm of government," complained Frank Altschul, perhaps the chief progenitor of RFE, in May of 1950, "is not in a position to engage in hard-hitting psychological warfare."[30] New services, he argued, could fill the broadcast gap. One such enterprise was already under way. In 1948, George F. Kennan, then in the State Department, held a series of discussions with leading citizens about the emerging division of Europe and the proper American response. Among those present at the creation were Henry Luce of *Time* magazine; Hamilton Fish Armstrong, editor of *Foreign Affairs;* and DeWitt Wallace of the *Reader's Digest.* They formed the National Committee for a Free Europe, out of which

---

*For the purposes of this book, which examines the potential for facts generally to act as a wedge for freedom in unfree societies, there will not be elaborate distinctions made between the different functions of U.S. broadcast services, though care will be taken to label which is which. But the reader should be aware of their different roles. The Voice of America is designed to function as both a voice of America and about America. Its guidelines call for the service to explain America to foreign peoples, including U.S. policy. The various services of RFE and Radio Liberty focus on providing news and features of interest to particular audiences. They are supposed to act as a kind of surrogate domestic radio—providing, as best they can given limited access and resources, what a Polish or Russian or Bulgarian radio station might provide if they were free to do so in these relatively unfree countries. Indeed, the staffs of RFE and RL consist in large part of foreign émigrés, who speak to their former countrymen over the U.S.-sponsored services.

grew Radio Free Europe. Most of the service's early monies consisted of private donations.[31] The emerging radio was given a boost and a powerful raison d'être by a National Security Council directive of April 14, 1950, that called for a nonmilitary counteroffensive against the Soviet Union in Europe.[32] "The intention," recalls one former RFE official, "was to hit hard and not be worried about the niceties of broadcast ethics . . . an image of bare fists and brass knuckles." From then on, both Radios were funded, covertly, by the CIA until 1971. So confident were some officials of the immediate, bulletlike potential of the Radios, that early facilities were housed in convertible modules and trailers. "It was still the established wisdom," recalls Mickelson, "that East European Communist regimes would soon fall . . . and there would be no further need for an RFE."[33]

The Voice of America, too, has tangled roots. More than a year before America declared war on Japan and Germany, the United States was becoming concerned about the progress of German fascist propaganda in Latin America. Franklin Roosevelt ordered the establishment of a new agency to deal with the problem: the Office for Coordination of Commercial and Cultural Relations Between the American Republics. Nelson A. Rockefeller was named the "coordinator" of the office, making him, it would seem, the coordinator of the Office for Coordination of Commercial and Cultural Relations Between the American Republics.[34] Despite this unwieldy title, Rockefeller quickly worked out a program to relay American broadcasts to Latin America, working with the networks—ABC, CBS, and NBC—and a private institute called the Worldwide Broadcasting Foundation. Well before there was an official "Voice of America" station, he had set up a vast public-private operation that delivered U.S. and private transcripts and broadcasts to Latin and U.S. stations for retransmission. "The whole venture was probably illegal," opined VOA official Wallace Carroll, because Rockefeller had to circumvent Civil Service rules by hiring foreign nationals to work on the broadcasts.[35]

The story of the Radios since then is rich with similar ambiguities, contradictions, and unintended consequences. During World War II, for example, the Voice naturally leaned somewhat toward good news over being purely objective. Yet when American forces suffered a major setback in Burma, the VOA aired the news immediately. By establishing the Voice's credibility, this broadcast probably did more to enhance the war effort than a dozen sugarcoated assessments would have. In his celebrated hearings of the early 1950s, Senator Joe McCarthy attacked the management of both the VOA and RFE-RL as riddled with subversives, saying they took too soft a line. McCarthy's intention was to strengthen the content, facilities, and personnel of the VOA, RFE, and RL, yet funding levels for the three services combined actually declined, in inflation-adjusted terms, by more than 15 percent from 1953 to 1961. Morale plummeted. Some scholars blame the McCarthy attacks, and the

Eisenhower administration's reluctance to carry through on its ambitious "rollback" rhetoric, for undermining the radios during the 1950s.[36] When the Radios had their greatest impact, as in Hungary, it was thanks in large part to the fact that RFE and the Voice had begun shifting to precisely the opposite approach, emphasizing information over direct persuasion.[37] By the early 1960s, the shift to an emphasis on facts rather than exhortations, and liberalization rather than liberation, was solidified under the leadership of Edward R. Murrow, JFK's first head of the new U.S. Information Agency. Murrow believed, along with Robert Sherwood, that "the truth, coming from American sincerity, is by far the most effective means of propaganda." The result of this seemingly more modest ambition was that the radios grew more effective, achieving what scholar James L. Tyson calls "new heights."[38] Despite the appeal of democracy made manifest in Czechoslovakia in 1968, however, U.S. broadcasts received little attention during the détente period of 1969 to 1980. Richard Nixon and Henry Kissinger, while in office, took no interest in such populist endeavors, operating a foreign policy that emphasized elite negotiations. Enter Ronald Reagan, who praised the Voice and RFE-RL as tools by which to aggressively press the democratic revolution, thereby seeming to portend a shift toward more blatant, tendentious broadcasting. Yet the men who executed the shift were by and large careful professional journalists of the emphasize-the-facts school, such as *Reader's Digest* editor Ken Tomlinson, one of the heads of the Voice under Reagan, and former NBC newsman Eugene Pell, the president of Radio Free Europe. Both stressed that the Radios, while certainly not bashing democracy, are there to broadcast facts.

By the late 1980s, the U.S. broadcasting services already mentioned were part of a large complex of Western efforts to spread facts and ideas. The U.S. Information Agency maintained libraries in dozens of countries, and conducted speaker tours by defenders and critics of U.S. policy to explain America abroad. In addition to the Voice and RFE-RL, listeners even behind the Iron Curtain could pick up international broadcasts by Deutsche Welle of West Germany, Kol Israel, Radio Peking, the Catholic Church's Radio Vatican, and numerous protestant services and private television and radio broadcasts. Radio Martí, a new broadcasting service set up by Reagan, pointed its beam at Castro's Cuba, and the U.S. State Department was busy helping antigovernment guerillas in Nicaragua initiate their own radio station.[39] For Americans, who live in a society saturated with information of all sorts, it's hard to conceive of the importance of a few short-wave radio broadcasts. Most Americans don't even own a radio capable of picking up the Voice of America. Yet *The Economist* of London, generally known for its dry-martini editorial tone, has called Radio Free Europe the greatest act of statesmanship since World War II, declaring that: "Radio Free Europe is more than an organization for the diffusion of news and political propaganda. . . . A determined and surprisingly successful attempt has been made to create complete, free broadcasting stations for several of the East European nations."[40]

Unlike many foreign-policy initiatives, the idea of broadcasting vital facts to unfree peoples has enjoyed near-universal support in the United States since we set up our own program in the 1940s. The CIA funding scandal of the 1970s is one of the exceptions that proves the rule, for it did not lead to the demise of the stations. If there is little question about the desirability of having broadcasts, however, it is partly because they are not taken seriously by much of the foreign-policy establishment. Yes, it's a nice thing to create a free press for communist countries, the feeling goes, but now let's get back to issues concerned with the real levers of power, such as where to hold the next summit and how to interpret the meaning of the last treaty. That is not my view. To me, if the Radios are mere words and symbols, we ought to consider canceling them, for in that case, they greatly complicate the execution of more formal diplomacy while doing little good. But they are much more than that. As Anatoly Shcharansky (later Natan Sharansky) has said, our broadcasts are perhaps America's "most powerful" tool, often more important than alliances, treaties, or military arsenals.

The Iron Strainer

There are several kinds of evidence of the importance of Western broadcasts. Each single piece can be questioned, but the web of proof that results from combining all the individual pieces is quite strong.

One indication that our broadcasts work is the massive effort the Soviets make to counter them. All told, the combined budget for various aspects of U.S. public diplomacy—including Radio Free Europe, Radio Liberty, the Voice of America, other USIA operations, and the National Endowment for Democracy—was less than $500 million in 1985. The Soviets spent more than $3 billion on comparable operations.[41] They spent an additional $300 million to $1.2 billion just to jam Western broadcasts.[42] (For technological reasons, it actually costs more to jam a signal than to broadcast one.) It's worth noting that despite these efforts RFE-RL in the 1980s still enjoyed a "channel effectiveness" of 30 percent for the Western half of the Soviet Union and 50 percent to 80 percent for the rest of Communist Europe.[43] Even where broadcasts are jammed, many listeners tune in during the early evening when broadcasts may enjoy a "twilight immunity" from most interference. Others listen to the fuzzy broadcasts two or three times, taking careful notes of the different scraps and eventually piecing together the entire newscast for the day. In other words, the

Soviets spend a great deal of money not to block out the broadcasts entirely but to reduce somewhat their effectiveness.[44]

The Soviets manifest great concern with Western broadcasts in their own propaganda organs, which regularly spew out bitter denunciations of the Voice and RFE-RL.[45] Ironically, the attacks sometimes backfire, since denunciation of a certain story on the Voice of America informs many Russians who didn't even hear the VOA broadcast of its content. Much of the Soviet effort to counter our broadcasts in Russia and around the world, however, is not directed at Soviet citizens. In fact, scholars who have studied the content of Radio Moscow and other Soviet propaganda say that a major purpose is not to sway listeners to the communist view—very few people listen to the stations outside the Eastern bloc, despite their vast expenditures—but to cast doubt on whether the West's own, much more effective, services are worthwhile. "For the communists," communications expert and author Julian Hale writes, "propaganda directed at the west is very much a rubber sword. . . . But the Russians want to build up a lobby, particularly in America, Britain, and West Germany, to persuade those who provide the money and the facilities for all the major western services that it is money not just wasted but misapplied."[46]

The Soviets also place great stress on Western broadcasting in formal negotiations. During the 1970s, the Soviets made repeated approaches to the U.S. government promising better relations if the West would muzzle its voice.[47] Andrei Gromyko pressed Alexander Haig to turn down the Radios at a 1982 meeting reported by columnists Rowland Evans and Robert Novak. When the United States and Israel announced plans to construct a powerful joint transmitter for RFE-RL and the Voice, the Soviets leaked word that they were considering construction of a powerful jamming transmitter in Syria.[48] In 1986, the Soviets and Israel held rare talks concerning the establishment of formal diplomatic relations at Helsinki. The Soviets raised two "main obstacles" to better relations. One was Israel's participation in Ronald Reagan's strategic defense plans. The other was the new radio transmitter.[49]

A second kind of evidence comes from extensive listener surveys conducted since the 1950s. How do you conduct a survey of listening habits in a communist country? Some are sponsored by the U.S. government among emigrants and tourists from the Eastern bloc. A few come out of private think tanks. The communist governments themselves have even held a few. Listenership varies widely from year to year, depending on world and national events, station content, and whether a given service is being jammed in a given country. Table 5.1 is designed to show the general impact of the stations over a prolonged period, illustrating both the lowest and highest recorded percentage of people who were regular listeners to a given service, from 1956 to 1986.

One last piece of evidence that the broadcasts have a sizable audience

TABLE 5.1

Eastern Audience, Western Broadcasts
Percentage of Adults Listening Regularly

	VOA	RFE-RL	BBC
Soviet Union	12–14	9–12	6–10
Poland	45–53	40–68	33–37
Romania	20–21	44–61	15–20
Czechoslovakia	13–37	23–65	16–30
Hungary	18–22	44–52	13–25
Bulgaria	19–21	22–33	20–23

SOURCE: Composite of surveys compiled by the author.[50]
NOTES: Since some people may listen to more than one foreign station, the numbers may add up to more than 100 percent.

During an important event such as the Cuban missile crisis, listenership can jump up to a level higher than 90 percent. The figures above omit such short-term blips and refer to average listenership over several months or more.

One should not use these numbers alone to form conclusions about the quality of different stations or language services. The Soviet Union jams heavily, and Western broadcasts aim chiefly at the Western one-third of the country; it's only natural listening levels are lower there. Hungary usually doesn't jam; listenership is higher. The VOA and the BBC broadcast fewer hours to most East European countries, and don't tailor their broadcasts as carefully to particular audiences; that's part of the reason their ratings are lower for Poland and Czechoslovakia. But those two services often aren't jammed in the Soviet Union, while Radio Liberty almost always is—hence they often do better in Russia than RFE-RL. Listenership can also vary, probably inversely, with the speed, quality, and accuracy of domestic media. In the 1980s, RFE listenership in Hungary had fallen off. But one reason may have been that Hungary's own media had become much more open and responsive to the past effectiveness of Radio Free Europe.

These figures should not be taken as precise measurements in the way we might view a Gallup poll taken in the United States. They are, rather, a solid but merely general indicator that the Radios reach many people. Then, too, studies of actual listenership omit what many experts regard as the most important medium of communication in a closed society: word of mouth. "Even those who do not listen to RFE hear about its broadcasts from others," a Polish architect told interviewers in 1964. "If for some reason I am unable to listen to RFE on a certain day, I learn about the latest news and commentaries when I get to the office. Wherever people meet you can hear them discussing what RFE said yesterday." Indeed, an estimated 55 percent of Polish listeners, and 67 percent of those in Czechoslovakia, said they discussed RFE broadcasts outside their family.[51]

consists of the phone calls and letters that flood the offices of the BBC, the Voice of America, and Radio Free Europe every day. The BBC alone received more than 250,000 such letters in 1972.[52] In the early 1980s, Bulgaria, Czechoslovakia, and Hungary introduced an automated telephone system that enables listeners to phone RFE directly and from the summer of 1985 to December 1986, listeners from those three countries alone left more than 50,000 messages.[53] Some correspondents impart information: "The party is going to publish a stricter law on dissent. It will be in the newspapers later this week." Some have very specific questions they would like answered on the air: "I would like to know in detail what the most favored nation status means." Many have thanks and praise.

By contrast, the sluggish television and radio newscasts force-fed by Soviet-bloc governments appear to produce little bang for the buck. There are few published surveys, but those that exist reinforce what Western scholars suspect from their own study of communist society. In 1968, the State Committee for

TABLE 5.2

The Nielsonovich Ratings
Preference of Soviet Citizens for Selected Domestic Broadcasts

Program Type	Like	Neutral	Dislike	Rarely Watch
Sports	84	5	1	10
Game shows	81	9	2	8
Variety	71	19	2	8
TV plays	61	17	2	20
News and current events	38	20	27	18
On-the-spot news coverage	36	24	7	33
Political themes	16	21	9	54
Serious music and opera	15	14	25	47

SOURCE: Survey by Soviet scholar Boris Firsov, in "There Is No 'Average' Viewer: A Soviet TV Survey," *Zhurnalist,* December 1967.

Radio and Television asked Soviets where they get their information. Except for Communist Party members, 70 percent or more were less than satisfied with the reporting, interpretation, and comment on international affairs. The author of the survey concluded, "Among all audience groups there are serious complaints with radio and television concerning the volume and information on foreign affairs and the credibility of the commentary."[54] When people do listen to domestic communist media, they tend to focus on the "soft" news— the exact opposite of Western broadcasts, where hard news is the most valued item—as evidenced in a survey in which Soviet citizens were asked how they react to state television programs on various subjects, outlined in table 5.2.

Obviously this is not the kind of preference that party leaders would hope for as they seek to inculcate Marxist values. Soviet print media such as *Pravda* and *Izvestia,* which are carefully censored and may thus be regarded as a close reflection of official opinion, point to deep concern that despite massive efforts the Russian people greet their own media with a collective yawn. In 1970, *Pravda* chastised radio broadcasters for failing to "reflect the urgent problems of concern" to listeners. The piece expressed particular concern that information is not "timely." The complaint is old, but totalitarian societies have not found a way yet to deal with it. As the Hungarian Central Committee noted back in 1965: "It is especially important to report on events and explain our policies without delay. There is no vacuum—whenever we fail to inform the population quickly . . . the enemy's explanation and interpretation reaches them promptly and easily."[55]

A third kind of evidence that radio broadcasts are a vital tool comes from third-force leaders, who issue persistent and ringing testimonials to their impact. The great Soviet author Aleksandr Solzhenitsyn: "If we hear anything about events in this country, it is through . . . the Radio Liberty broadcasts."[56] A board member of the Polish trade union Solidarity: "It [Western broadcasting] takes away from the government its monopoly on information . . . the best thing you could do." Ludmilla Alexeyeva, a Soviet human rights activist who emigrated to the United States in 1977: "Foreign radio was the basic source from which we gleaned knowledge of democracy and human rights, the values for which our movement came to stand. . . . They also enabled the movement to spread, by transmitting information about persecution of human rights activists and data collected by the activists about human rights violations in the USSR and the campaign against such violations."[57] These endorsements—echoed by Anatoly Shcharansky, Lech Walesa, and other well-known dissidents—are not decisive proof. And yet, given their passionate support of democracy, they have no reason to promote measures that won't materially help produce it. One thing that strikes me about those who have risked their lives to fight tyranny is that they are not frivolous—and that such leaders endorse the broadcasts so unequivocally may be the most persuasive evidence of all.

What a Difference a Datum Makes

If the West manages to smuggle facts to the people of unfree countries, do they do any good? In Hungary, it would seem, facts did all they could, yet proved a poor match for tanks. Or did they? The Hungarian revolt, although brutally repressed, was not without benefits. From the start, the Soviets felt compelled to pump in aid to the victims of the war; they did not attempt a return to the status quo of the early 1950s. In the years that followed, moreover, Hungary reformed its economy to allow measures of private enterprise, and in the early 1960s offered a sweeping amnesty to some five hundred to a thousand persons jailed since the revolution. In 1962, the government began to appoint noncommunists to leadership posts. "Who is not against us," proclaimed Party boss Stanislaw Kádár, "is for us." In 1963, the government allowed more noncommunists than communists to stand for election to the new parliament—something no other communist country has ever done. Still broader economic reforms followed in the 1960s, along with a decision to allow Radio Free Europe broadcasts to enter the country unjammed. By the late 1970s, less than a generation after the revolution, one could make the case that Hungarians enjoyed a greater degree of electoral democracy, more civil rights, a freer press, and a higher standard of living than the citizens of any other country in the Eastern bloc. The Hungarian freedom fighters, then, did not die for nothing.

If we take a broad view of events since World War II, we can observe a number of reforms and revolts in totalitarian societies that seem to be similarly connected to the radio broadcasts of the West. Just as there is strong evidence that our broadcasts reach people, so, too, there is evidence that the broadcasts actually enable them to influence events.

In the 1960s, both the Voice and RFE-RL continually stressed news about liberalization within the bloc that had been a factor in the Hungarian reforms,[58] an initiative fostered in large part by Edward R. Murrow. According to Allan Michie, the broadcasts sought to "exploit the possibilities for 'cross fertilization,' telling the Poles what the Czechoslovaks have been able to obtain in the way of 'liberalization,' and telling the Hungarians what the Poles and the Czechoslovaks have done. This sets up a chain reaction pressure. . . . For instance, when the Czechoslovak regime a few years ago intensified its campaign to drive all its farmers into collective farms, RFE countered with accounts of the success which Poland had achieved by turning away from the collective idea."[59]

This focus on facts about liberalization was of particular interest in Czechoslovakia, where Radio Free Europe's audience shot up from 33 percent of the population in 1962 to 51 percent in late 1967. This was the backdrop to the liberalization of 1968, when Alexander Dubček announced plans for a new constitution to include secret ballots, freedom of speech, and decentralization of the party's control of key industries. Interestingly, listenership fell somewhat in 1968, probably because the Dubček reforms also included a relaxation of censorship of the domestic media, making foreign broadcasts, happily, less essential. When the Soviets found this new manifestation of the democratic impulse intolerable, and invaded in late 1968, the audience tuned back in to the West in even larger numbers, with listener figures of 65 percent for Radio Free Europe, 42 percent for Radio Vienna, and 35 percent for the Voice.[60]

The same pattern repeated itself in Poland in 1970. In December, the government announced it was raising prices on basic consumer goods, including food. Riots broke out across the country, with the first protests taking place along the Baltic seacoast. Local police moved in quickly and the government shut down most news coming from the area, but Radio Free Europe carefully monitored local bulletins and relayed the facts about the riots, the demands of the workers, and the brutal response of the authorities. As Julian Hale notes: "This news was not put out in full detail on the Polish national channels. . . . Fifty-seven percent of Poles questioned . . . said they first heard of the Gdansk riots through RFE, which picked up the news by tuning into the local radio station."[61] Within days, Party Secretary Wladyslaw Gomulka had been ousted, replaced by Edward Gierek, who had learned the lesson of Hungarian food-price riots and relaxed central control of the economy and of political discussion. In the decade that followed, Poland was hardly a democracy, but like Hungary it was a much better place to live than most other Soviet-bloc countries. It is no coincidence, as the Marxists like to say, that Poles have been among the most enthusiastic listeners to the Voice of America, Radio Free

Europe, and the BBC. "The effectiveness of these broadcasts," analyst David Abshire writes, "became clear in December 1970."[62]

Not to mention in 1980. Like most people who want to overturn a government, the leaders of Solidarity recognized the primacy of information in producing change. By the summer of 1980, Lech Walesa and his fellow organizers had established reliable methods of spreading news across the country rapidly through Poland's telephone system. But they also knew that such use could be dangerous and might at any time be cut off by the government. Hence a major element of Solidarity's strategy during the critical early months was to set up an information railroad using foreign publications and foreign radio broadcasts. Solidarity knew, for example, that a fact delivered to a Western wire service or newspaper reporter would quickly find its way back into the country, sometimes in minutes, via the Western broadcasts. As the union managed to press the government into significant concessions, each development was fed to the Western radios, and regular listenership to Radio Free Europe soared near the 70 percent level.[63]

"If you would close your Radio Free Europe," communist spokesman Jerzy Urban later conceded, "the underground would completely cease to exist."[64] If they did nothing else as the Solidarity movement crested, our broadcasts served an enabling function, helping existing dissidents to organize peacefully a national movement for democracy. As Robert William Pirsein, who studied the formation and early programs of the Voice of America, wrote: "It cannot be said with certainty that the VOA was *the factor* that [drove] anyone to action as a result of a program. Certainly the Voice is *one* of the factors involved."[65]

And then there is the Soviet Union. It may be years or decades, of course, before a full account of *glasnost* can be written. Yet there is some evidence that Western broadcasting played an important role. Thanks to Chernobyl in particular, Soviet officials were keenly aware that the gray, sluggish, heavily censored gruel served up by their own media was ineffective. Party leaders said so openly in a number of Soviet journals and newspapers. Leonid Kravchenko, defending the expanded responsiveness of Soviet broadcasts, noted that previously television had been considered "the voice of the state," but that now the party recognized this approach as "futile," since the Soviet people manage to obtain information anyway—but from an external source.[66] Aleksandr Yakovlevitch, a principal architect of *glasnost,* articulated the new willingness to air unpleasant facts both within the Soviet Union and abroad. "Today's world is becoming ever smaller in the communications sense, ever more interconnected. To think it is possible in this world to create some sort of niche or cloister cut off from external influences and to sit it out there in timid resignation . . . is to indulge in illusions."[67]

In this sense, *glasnost* is simply the latest response to an inherent dilemma that has faced the Communist Party since U.S. broadcasts to Russia began after World War II.[68] Of course, the Soviets would like to speed up their media while retaining control of everything that is said, but this is impossible; choices must be made. On September 15, 1986, Ronald Reagan's adviser on Soviet affairs, Jack Matlock, appeared at a conference in the Soviet Union. Matlock proceeded to blast both the Soviet invasion of Afghanistan and its postwar annexation of the Baltic republics, declaring that the United States "has never recognized and will not recognize the legitimacy of the forcible incorporation of Latvia, Lithuania, and Estonia into the Soviet Union." Matlock cleverly began his speech, being broadcast live to parts of the Soviet Union, in Latvian—charming the Latvians, but also tripping up censors who were supposed to cut out anything questionable. His comments were broadcast at least twice on local television and spread like wildfire. In the days that followed, scores of Latvians braved Soviet secret police to stand outside the conference and shout, "You are our only hope!" A little *glasnost* can be a dangerous thing.[69]

Giving Truth More Consequences

As important as Western broadcasts have been, we can make them even more effective. One obvious yet neglected way is to get the truth to more people by strengthening our electronic signal itself. Unfortunately, by the early 1980s, much of the physical plant of the Voice and RFE-RL was ready for consignment to a radio history museum. Both the Voice of America and Radio Free Europe still used vacuum tubes, discarded by commercial stations decades ago. Some transmitters dated back to the 1930s. Spare parts had to be hand-tooled because much of the equipment is so obsolete. (Imagine the scandal that would result if one of America's poverty programs, or some Pentagon weapons bureaucrats, were found to be stuck with such tools.) Considering the financial commitment made to the broadcast services, it's not surprising. Measured in inflation-adjusted terms, spending on VOA and RFE-RL grew from $73 million in 1953 to $80 million in 1974 and $92 million in 1982. Thus, as a share of the federal budget or the U.S. economy, spending on the radio services declined substantially. The number of people working at the Radios fell from 5,000-plus in 1970 to fewer than 4,000 in 1982. The House Foreign Affairs Committee concluded in April 1982: "Though U.S. arsenals of defense are stocked with state-of-the-art weaponry, the United States has neglected the technology of broadcasting and has relayed the nation's messages on transmitters which were the state-of-the-art in 1938." After the Soviet crackdown in Poland, the Reagan administration vowed to correct the situation, calling in 1982 for a major rebuilding effort. Yet by the final year of Reagan's term, less than one-third of the $1 billion called for in 1982 had been spent. After the budget battles of the 1980s, it was far from clear whether the relatively small amount needed to beef up the radios would be spent in the 1990s.[70]

Technological advances expected in the 1990s could make possible a switch to direct satellite broadcasting, thwarting Soviet jamming efforts. International agreements regulating satellite communications would make permission difficult to obtain under present structures. But since the Soviets have repeatedly violated international law by jamming, a strong case can be made to allow such broadcasting under both the U.N. Charter and the Helsinki accords on human rights. Former Voice of America director Kenneth Tomlinson urges that the U.S. "go ahead and spend the research money to solve the technical problems. Then, if our diplomats made it a priority to work out arrangements, you could see a long period of virtually un-jammable broadcasting to Eastern Europe."[71] Unfortunately, negotiating even for badly needed new transmitters has seldom been a major concern of our State Department—not because of some evil conspiracy, but because a bureaucracy that focuses on elite agreements and negotiations simply isn't likely to be enthusiastic about what may seem to it a quixotic effort to reach the masses of foreign countries.

Of course, few would deny the proposition that if we are to have broadcast services, they should have decent equipment. The discussion heats up, however, when it turns to what material the services should broadcast, a matter worth some careful consideration.

In the late 1970s and early 1980s, one group of critics claimed that the Western services were bending over so far backward to seem objective that they were actually becoming anti-American in tone. Others responded that under the Reagan administration, the broadcasts became so blatantly pro-American that they lost their credibility. Thus, VOA official Phil Nicolaides complained that the mujahedin of Afghanistan were labeled "antigovernment rebels" rather than "freedom fighters." When the practice was changed, the *Columbia Journalism Review* groused that they were called "freedom fighters" rather than "antigovernment rebels." Reaganites objected to several minutes of uninterrupted airtime given to Soviet propagandist Georgi Arbatov and to a VOA broadcast that introduced Reagan simply as "a former movie actor and America's first divorced president." Anti-Reaganites objected to the Reaganites objecting. In the 1970s, readings of Aleksandr Solzhenitsyn's *Gulag Archipelago* were halted by U.S. officials, reportedly under the direction of Henry Kissinger, who argued such readings were inflammatory. The decision drew sharp attacks. In 1981, the new director of the agency that oversees the Voice, U.S. Information Agency director Charles Wick, ordered that the Solzhenitsyn readings be resumed, eliciting complaints that Solzhenitsyn's views are antidemocratic (they are), and were coming to dominate the Radios (they were not). At both the Voice and RFE-RL, different factions of the émigré populations have had repeated power struggles, often over issues that might seem obscure to Americans but to the émigrés were extremely urgent. One of the most bitter episodes involved charges early in the Reagan administration that the services had aired, repeatedly and systematically, anti-Semitic material. A special panel set up by the Board for International Broadcasting investigated, and, like such fair-minded observers as Ben Wattenberg and Martin Peretz, gave the Radios a clean bill of health. Several years later, on the other hand, a congressional study found that the Voice had helped finance numerous anti-American broadcasts produced by the United Nations Department of Public Affairs and aired at subsidized rates. Even the Reagan administration, while accused by some of trying to twist the Radios into brazen propaganda instruments, also stood charged of censoring broadcasts to further the détente that emerged in Reagan's second term. *Human Events* reported a number of instances in which Jack Matlock and Chester Crocker, Reagan advisers on the National Security Council and at the State Department, allegedly spiked material that might offend Soviet ears. Virtually every administration, in fact, has been attacked for what the Radios broadcast, often from both sides. McCarthy and others blasted Eisenhower for watering down the Voice too much, while Democrats said he had ordered it to stop airing criticism of his invasion of Lebanon. Barry Goldwater wanted more aggressive broadcasting, while some in Lyndon Johnson's own party accused him of abusing the VOA to propagandize in favor of his Vietnam policies.[72]

No doubt all these disputes harm our effort to spread the facts. If materials are aired that either unduly bash or extol America, it is a sign we aren't serious about the effort, and such broadcasts may positively confuse and discourage the very people we are trying to help. If racialist sentiments are aired, the culprits must be sought out and reprimanded or removed. Still, these debates are not the crux of the problem. No one is seriously suggesting that the stations should be uncritically pro-American or anti-American. The question is not so much whether Western broadcasts should be objective, but rather what they should be objective about. To someone living in Poland, neither an occasional barb against or for Ronald Reagan is of great interest. The typical East-bloc listener* is after a different sort of news. Like most people, they are most

---

*This chapter has focused almost exclusively on the impact of facts in the Soviet empire. There are some who argue that this is a mistake, that in fact U.S. public diplomacy should aim more at the peoples of Western Europe and the Third World who, because they live in freer societies, can more easily be reached and persuaded. One of the central points of this book is that our foreign policy toward all countries must pay much more attention to popular sentiment, carefully read. But it seems to me that the most important audience for our radio broadcasts in particular is precisely those who otherwise lack a free press. Western Europe, like the United States, is already surfeited with information. If Europeans don't like U.S. policy, it is generally not, as too many leaders assume, because they don't understand it, but rather because they understand it perfectly well and disagree. The noncommunist developing countries are not so sated, but neither are their limits on free speech nearly as severe as those of the Soviet Union and its empire. And while Third World countries are of course concerned with U.S. broadcasts, they are far more concerned with

interested in the things that affect their lives most directly: what their government is doing, how their countrymen are managing their lives, and what is going on in the world as it affects them. Whether our broadcasts are providing this sort of information ought to be the focus of the debate.[74]

One person who has thought a great deal about this question is Brigadier Maurice Tugwell, a retired Canadian military officer who is a frequent listener to international broadcasts. Tugwell's recipe for winning the "War of Ideas and Ideals" was delivered at a 1982 conference in Europe, excerpted here:

> Effective propaganda must be based on facts. It was the fact of Allied success in 1918 which enabled Anglo-American propaganda to influence the hitherto stoic German troops. The facts of economic and agricultural failures inside the Soviet empire today are what makes those populations susceptible.[75]

This has led many observers to conclude that what the West must broadcast is lots of statistics about the failure of this year's wheat crop in the Soviet Union and the corresponding abundance of food and other consumer goods in the West. According to this view, there should also be plenty of information about various policy disputes and congressional debates in the United States, showing how democracy and capitalism work and persuading listeners that our way is better. This war of facts about the systems, albeit more sophisticated than many other techniques, is still based on the old bullet theory. Tugwell argues against this approach and suggests an alternative strategy. It is excerpted here at some length:

> In my view we should not try to sell "democracy" or "freedom" or "free enterprise" or any of the concepts that we have found so valuable at our stage of development. In unraveling the Soviet web, our primary objective is [to enhance what is] a proven human preference anyway.
>
> The Soviets use a term "optimizing strategy," which describes graduated political initiatives which seek not one single objective but a set of graduated objectives. This is an important feature of all revolutionary conflict and one that the West has to adopt. Our ultimate objective . . . might be achieved by creating strains and conditions inside the Soviet Union and the bloc, and by world opinion and pressures, which force the Soviet regime, however unwillingly, to modify its present dangerous policies. This is coercion. A better answer may be to achieve real change within the existing regime, amounting to an evolution towards some kind of democratic socialism. This is conversion.
>
> Effective propaganda begins by accepting existing sociological beliefs and

---

U.S. economic policy, human rights commitments, aid to rebel movements, and so on. These issues are the subject of later chapters. Finally, the Soviet bloc is being examined with special care here because it presents the most difficult problem for a democratic foreign policy. Few Americans doubt that there is much we can do to help countries like Grenada or South Korea become democracies. But there is widespread doubt about our ability to promote greater democracy in Poland, Hungary, or Russia. We may as well spend most of our time discussing that which is in dispute.[73]

trends. We should not assume that all our audiences can comprehend real democracy or are longing for Western-style institutions. We should accept that, notwithstanding its distorted application, the principles of socialism are still respected, and are earnestly believed by many to be superior to capitalism. We must be aware of the Soviet people's fears of the West's degree of freedom which communist propaganda has taught them is synonymous with anarchy.

The same fear of anarchy can be used to justify the need for urgent political reform. An important task for the Russian soul in exile will be to inject ideas for evolution, to make Russians aware that there can be—must be—an alternative, and that they are capable of accomplishing it. One does not have to scrape the old paint off an automobile before spraying it another colour. The easiest course is to transfer these great men's heritage into the hands of the Russian people, out of the grasp of the CPSU which has betrayed them.

History, in this interpretation, will destroy the party. The silver bullet that is aimed at the heart of the CPSU is fashioned out of socialist principles. The divine right of the Party is punctured by the facts.[76]

Most scholars who have studied communications would agree with Tugwell's premises. While communism as it exists today is disliked by the people who live under it, for example, those same people admire many of the ideas they perceive as the core of communism. John Lenczowski, Ronald Reagan's adviser on Soviet affairs from 1983 to 1987, concedes that such concepts as equality remain very popular in the Soviet Union (as in the West) and are seen as a socialist ideal.[77] The facts we select, then, should not seek to debunk equality as an ideal, for it is a good one; or even necessarily to prove that capitalism produces less inequality than socialism, though it does. Rather, broadcasts should point out inequalities in the Soviet system and (more important) report on successful ideas and efforts to reduce them within the socialist world.

There is a utilitarian argument for the Tugwell approach as well. It does people living under communism little good to receive beautiful postcards showing how lovely things are in the distant capitalist West. They need do-it-yourself kits in Marxist repair and road maps to a more democratic socialism. "Public opinion is more likely to be moved," Sig Mickelson wrote, "if it is moved at all, at an almost imperceptible pace by a constant flow of information following a consistent pattern. Hopes for sudden shifts or cataclysmic results represent wishful thinking."[78] Since facts cannot produce massive shifts in opinion overnight, one of their most important functions is an enabling one. Facts can give the people of the communist bloc the tools they need to gradually reform the system.

The evidence suggests that the peoples of the communist bloc take exactly this pragmatic approach to change. When asked to name the "major problem facing your country," nearly two-thirds of Hungarians, Poles, and Czechs say "the economy," whereas less than a third say "political." When asked how to improve the economic situation, East Europeans give incrementalist answers—not explicit calls for greater capitalism. Pragmatism is also apparent in the careful distinction between the idea of communism, which has some support, and communism in practice, which has little. When Czechs were asked in 1979 and 1980 how socialism works in their country, 76 percent said "badly" or "very badly." Asked how they think democracy works in the West, 77 percent said "well" or "very well." Perhaps most important, East Europeans, while desiring more democracy, seem to feel that it can be attained best through evolution, agreeing in large numbers with the statement "One has to cooperate with the government under which one lives." Only 21 percent said the idea of Radio Free Europe is to "bring Western ideas to Hungary," while 56 percent said the primary purpose of the broadcasts is to "furnish information not easily available in Hungary."[79]

Do the Radios accomplish this? Unfortunately, despite the best efforts of dedicated and underfunded professionals at the Radios, the answer is, only somewhat. Solzhenitsyn, a great defender of the potential impact of broadcasts, offered this assessment of their content in 1982:

> The stations limit even simple information about current events. . . . Our people want to be told about our workers, how they fare in our country, but the broadcasts do not speak of that. What is the situation of the peasantry? There is never a broadcast on that subject. The situation in the provinces? The cruel conditions of service in the army? . . . Nothing is ever broadcast about any of these situations. Such information is widely available in the émigré press, and it could be broadcast to the USSR without much effort. But to do so would violate State Department policy. The Soviet rulers might get angry. . . .
>
> Instead, half-hour after half-hour is spent on interviews with recent émigrés: how they like America; how they have found work; how much they can earn; how they have furnished their houses. Not that there is anything wrong with this. But it is given disproportionate emphasis, and it replaces needed information about the situation within the Soviet Union. And what feeling does it arouse in the Soviet listener? Irritation. Most Soviet citizens cannot emigrate to the West. Why then boast about how well they are doing? It is tactless.[80]

Solzhenitsyn's impression fits the statistical facts, according to one study by the congressional General Accounting Office, which found that nonnews material on the Voice of America accounts for 44 percent of total airtime.[81] More disturbing is Solzhenitsyn's claim that when the services are airing newscasts and editorials, they fail to provide the kind of news needed to help promote democracy. Of course, there are no specific figures kept on the amount of information about reforms of communism. One way to get a good proxy estimate, however, is to look at the amount of "cross-reporting" that takes place on the different services. This occurs when a story developed by one service, say an experiment in private farming discovered by researchers in the

Polish bureau, is then broadcast over other services—so that people in Russia, Czechoslovakia, and Hungary, for example, will know about this important development and be better able to promote similar reforms at home. Because these stories may require more analysis and explanation, they are often run as features rather than as one of the short, fifteen-to-thirty-second headlines that appear in the newscasts. It was just such energetic cross-reporting, as we have seen, that provided critical aid to some of the major changes in communism since World War II. Yet of all feature programs broadcast over the RFE-RL services in 1985, cross-reporting took up only 5 to 10 percent of the total airtime. A three-page summary of "program highlights" provided in the report of the Board for International Broadcasting lists neither a single major story about communist reforms nor any serious effort to follow them in general, dwelling instead on such achievements as "an 18-minute interview" with a leading physicist defending the Reagan Star Wars program and "extensive coverage of the Academy Awards won by Czech-born Milos Forman."[82] There is nothing wrong with such broadcasts. They should not, however, be the main staple of the Voice or Radio Free Europe.

During 1983 and 1984, an assistant in the office of a U.S. congressman helped me to monitor Voice of America broadcasts. (This was necessary because the Voice of America is not allowed to send out transcripts of its material to Americans—even on request.) The scripts provided—mostly taken either from VOA editorials or from the longer "Focus" program of news analysis—were well written, objective in tone, and contained a good deal of interesting information. They did not, however, provide the kind of reporting suggested by Tugwell and Solzhenitsyn.

The "Focus" programs, for example, tended to concentrate on tales of misery from some of the most dismal totalitarian countries. There were numerous broadcasts about repression and poverty in Vietnam. VOA's Frank Ronalds put together an incisive program on "the frightful record of the Khomeini regime in Iran." He filed another good piece on Afghanistan, although it concentrated more on the Soviet Union's genocidal war tactics than on the brave resistance of the Afghan freedom fighters. The Voice also ran numerous solid reports on the West, such as a penetrating analysis of the politics of Hollywood films, from such movies as *Under Fire* and *Missing* to *Dirty Harry* and *The Green Berets*. Sam Iker filed a moving report on the Nazi Holocaust on the fortieth anniversary of its zenith, while VOA's Bob Blachly did an interesting story on Soviet "active measures" to plant false information in the West.[83] Out of more than twenty scripts, however, not one offered an analysis of such relevant political developments as the creeping economic reforms in Deng's China, or the proposed expansion of electoral choice in Hungary.

The same general observation was true of the Voice of America editorials, most of which fell into one of two categories. The first kind explained the virtues of capitalism, democracy, and republican government, with a particular emphasis on developments in the United States. Generally, these editorials used a particular news peg, such as the birthday of George Washington, or the rise of a particular black entrepreneur, or the naming of a Soviet émigré to the high school All-America basketball team, to make a more general point about the opportunities to succeed in a free society. Another discussed a National Inventors Day Exposition near Washington, describing what a "patent" is and noting how capitalism promotes innovation. Still another announced the release of Lenell Geter from a Texas prison, explaining that "in the United States . . . Mr. Geter could, and did, appeal his conviction." And an analysis of the virtues of the two-party system noted: "The Republicans emphasize the good that can be done by government policies that leave individuals and local communities free to make their own decisions about their lives. The Democrats emphasize the good that can be done by government policies that help people exercise the equal opportunities to which each is entitled."[84]

The second common type of editorial attacked the practices of communist governments. One blasted *Pravda* for criticizing the popularity of Western blue jeans. Several editorials pointed out the abuse of religious freedom in such countries as Nicaragua and Poland, noting that "communist doctrine obliges the state to promote atheism." The Voice also attacked terrorist attacks sponsored by the governments of Libya and Cuba, and explained in another broadcast that U.S. citizens taking part in a movement to "Ban the Soviets" from the Olympics were not agents of the government, but rather were "exercising an important right that is protected by our government: the right to express opinions freely. . . . It would be nice if the Soviet rulers' appreciation of competition in sports would allow them to see the value of competition in all the other human activities where excellence counts as well." A final editorial in this vein noted the frequent lies promulgated about Soviet output, an effort to cover up for the failures of communism. By contrast, the piece noted, "the free enterprise system has proved to be an unprecedented success in increasing and distributing wealth."[85]

All these, it should be stressed, were well-crafted pieces. Those promoting democratic capitalism were cogent, while those attacking communism were hard-hitting. Unfortunately, out of more than thirty VOA editorials reviewed, every one fell into one of these two molds. None offered any insight on *how* to get from communism to democracy.

Ludmilla Alexeyeva studied both RFE-RL and Voice of America broadcasts from 1980 to 1985 for the Helsinki Watch human rights group. She reached conclusions similar to my own—finding much excellent material, but also a shortage of the kind of material that is often of greatest use. A regular Radio Liberty program, "Russia Yesterday, Today, and Tomorrow," produced sixty-three scripts over the period she studied, of which a full forty-eight were devoted to the past. When the broadcasts turned to the present and future, Alexeyeva reports, they took little note of the lively debate on reforming the system going on in underground journals and organizations. "During all the review periods," she writes, "RYTT failed to use any of the very rich and unique material on discussions about the Soviet Union now going on inside Russia through the medium of *samizdat.*" Another important Radio Liberty program, "Problems of Communism," focused primarily on the affairs of foreign Communist parties, certainly a matter of interest, but hardly the top priority.[86] Those on domestic affairs and parties within the Soviet bloc contained very little information on efforts at democratic evolution. As Alexeyeva writes:

> Beyond the shadow of a doubt, change is today [1986] the chief subject of people's thoughts and private conversations in all strata of Soviet society . . . [including] Soviet bureaucrats in the RL audience. . . . They are professionals looking for practical ways to improve the system that is subject to them. "Problems of Communism" in its present form does not meet this need.[87]

The problem here is partly an institutional one. Bland broadcasts are less likely to ruffle the feathers of U.S. diplomats—who still play a dominant role in the operation of the stations—and are also easier to put together, and less controversial with the Congress. A simple lack of resources has been a critical factor, since the radios and other information programs of the USIA have had less money allocated for research. Naturally, as budgets are cut back, officials are loath to reduce broadcasting hours or eliminate whole language services. No one wants to reduce the output end of public diplomacy. Instead, it's often the input end that suffers, much as in the military, where the services try to preserve weapons systems by stretching out procurement over more years, neglecting to buy spare parts, and reducing spending on vital readiness measures such as training. Thus, from the mid-1950s to 1982, as the budgets of VOA and RFE-RL were declining slightly in real terms, the total hours of broadcasting more than doubled.[88] When funding increases came under the Reagan buildup, most of the monies were earmarked for new transmitters and other needed equipment, while the research staffs continued to shrink. From 1973 to 1983, the number of USIA personnel overseas declined by 27 percent, while research dwindled to only 3 percent of the budget, with a staff of forty-nine out of more than eight thousand employees. VOA and RFE personnel declined markedly in the 1960s and 1970s, recovering only part of the losses from 1981 to 1987. The effects were obvious. A 1982 study found that only about 22 percent of all news material broadcast by the Voice of America was generated by local bureaus.[89]

This is not meant as a criticism of those who were in charge of the broadcasts in recent years, many of whom—in particular Tomlinson, Pell, James Buckley, Frank Shakespeare, and the respective heads of the oversight boards for the radios and USIA, Steve Forbes and Edwin Feulner—worked hard to improve the stations. Reporting on these countries is hard work. Many of our finest print journalists go to Moscow as correspondents unable to speak Russian, and once there, do much of their reporting without even trying to venture outside the capital city.[90] Even the energetic reporters often fail to capture what is going on in the country, covering the activities of a few well-known dissenters but missing the strikes and the samizdats that rise up continually throughout the Soviet bloc. As a pair of East-bloc émigrés complained in *National Review* in 1983, many American journalists view the force of democracy in Russia through a lens that is "Moscow-centered to the extreme . . . celebrity-oriented . . . [viewing] the dissident movement as consisting primarily, if not exclusively, of those activists living in or with good access to the USSR's capital. . . . The press seems incapable of realizing that today's dissidents may not always be writers, artists, and scientists."[91]

Against this backdrop, both the Voice of America and Radio Free Europe have managed some impressive achievements given their meager resources. RFE's research reports were the single best source of information of *glasnost* in 1986 and 1987, regularly scooping the major print media in the West.[92]

With a small commitment of resources, and a shift in emphasis desired by many at the Radios themselves, then, the United States and its allies can greatly assist the force of democracy, even behind the Iron Curtain. Truth alone cannot stop armies. It can, however, strengthen our own forces while frustrating the impulses of totalitarianism. This is a great deal for such a little-noted lever of our foreign policy to accomplish.

6

THE CARROT AND THE STICK: USING ECONOMIC LEVERAGE

Eugene Rostow recited the conventional wisdom when he called sanctions "a fraud and a delusion. . . . They didn't work against Napoleon. They didn't work against Hitler. They didn't work against the Kaiser. . . ."[1]

Quite apart from their economic impact, however, it is generally acknowledged that sanctions can serve to give expression to outrage toward a given nation or practice. Israel, for example, does not sell oranges to Syria. Yet no one seriously thinks that Syrians are dying from scurvy as a result. Syrians get Vitamin C from someone else, and Israel must ship her oranges farther. The sanction, however, sends an important signal, indicating that Syria is an enemy of Israel, dealt with as little and as cautiously as possible. Consider the effect of not having such a sanction. This would tell people in Syria that Israelis may dislike their regime but don't consider it heinous. It would tell people in Israel that, while we may have differences with Syria, it is an acceptable nation and we have no objection to your dealing with them. Symbols matter, as Dartmouth professor David Baldwin points out in defending the Carter grain embargo in his seminal work on sanctions, *Economic Statecraft*:

The alternative to a grain embargo was "business as usual"—perhaps even better than usual—with respect to the grain trade. . . . The option to pull the economic lever existed in 1980, and, more importantly, the whole world knew it. Failure to impose a grain embargo might have been extremely damaging to America's image.[2]

In strictly economic terms, the question becomes more complicated. Consider the Arab oil embargo of the 1970s, directed against the United States and some of Europe. On one level, the embargo was a colossal failure. Billions of gallons of oil were indirectly shuffled to the United States from European countries the Arabs would sell to; actual consumption of oil in the United States fell by only a few percentage points. Nor did the embargo succeed in its professed objective of forcing Israel to withdraw from lands occupied in the 1967 War. One could even argue that the action was self-defeating, stirring up anti-Arab sentiment in the United States.

Yet the Arab oil embargo was a political and economic success. The fungible free market worked but, like all free markets, only by causing severe dislocations for many individuals and nations. In the United States, gas lines and unemployment fueled by the energy crisis helped bring down three consecutive presidents: Nixon, Ford, and Carter. Many European countries, more dependent on Arab oil than the United States, moved toward closer identification with the Arab cause, and some became stridently anti-Israeli in rhetoric and policy. In the following years, some thirty African nations severed relations with Israel. "The Arab oil embargo," wrote Fuad Itayim, editor of the *Middle East Economic Survey,* "was probably the major cause."[3] In the Middle East, PLO sympathizers such as Hafez el-Assad and Muammar Khadafy were strengthened by the demonstration of radical muscle, while moderate leaders faced greater pressures and saw a weaker United States and Western Europe available to help them resist. "In other words," concluded Margaret Doxey in a study of various sanctions for Oxford University Press, "economic pressure worked."[4]

Historically, the Arab embargo is no isolated example. Britain's sanction battle with France helped pave the way to Napoleon's final demise at Waterloo. Economic pressure against Germany and Japan first helped coax America into World War II—the "hinge of fate," as Churchill called it—and then helped win it. Indeed, the American oil embargo of Japan was the proximate cause of the desperate attack on Pearl Harbor that brought America into the war.[5] And though such countries as Switzerland continued trading with Nazi Germany well into 1945, Allied sanctions, coordinated by Dean Acheson, helped raise the cost to Hitler of supplies—petroleum, ball bearings, iron ore, and some industrial diamonds—that might have substantially lengthened the war. (When neutral countries wanted to sell vital materials to Hitler, for example, the Allies often bought them up.) "It was worth doing," Acheson concluded.[6] Historians still debate whether the impact of economic warfare was decisive or only marginal, with some pointing up the obvious fact that Germany still had bullets in May 1945. But W. N. Medlicott offered a fair assessment in his exhaustive study of the issue, *The Economic Blockade:*

> The fear of the consequences of blockade played a part in drawing Germany into the Russian adventure and the two-front war which ultimately proved so disastrous. . . . By the summer of 1944, the German economy was on the verge of decline both absolutely and relative to mounting Allied output. "Economic warfare" measures fulfilled their purpose, if we take this to be the weakening of the enemy's production for war purposes.[7]

In spite of these and other successes, "sanction" remains a dirty word, a foreign-policy lever regarded with suspicion by most democratic leaders. Perhaps the chief problem is the presence of some understandable, but damaging, conceptual errors. Two such errors are especially prevalent.

Sanction Bashing

The first error involves a misapplication of Adam Smith's classic free-trade theory, which argues, correctly in my view, that free trade enables all nations to become wealthier by concentrating on the production of goods in which they enjoy the greatest comparative advantage. What this theory does *not* argue is that all countries gain equally. Yet this is precisely what some analysts twist it to mean when they argue against a cutoff of, say, U.S. nuclear power technology, on the grounds that it will hurt the U.S. nuclear industry, or reduce our gross national product generally. Of course this is a cost of the sanction. The economic question is whether the United States will suffer more from this lost revenue than the country we wish to punish will suffer from losing our nuclear technology, or from buying less sophisticated technology from an alternative source. On these relative costs, free-trade theory is silent.

Consider a simple two-family economy involving Mr. and Mrs. Smith and Mr. and Mrs. Jones. Smith trades Jones bananas that grow in his backyard (bananas, by the way, are Jones's favorite fruit). In exchange, Jones gives Smith insulin, which Smith needs to survive. Both families gain; both are happy. One day Jones sees Mr. Smith beating Mrs. Smith. After repeated efforts to persuade Smith to cease this human rights violation, Jones decides to impose a sanction, cutting off all insulin trade to Smith. Smith retaliates by refusing to trade any bananas to Jones, forcing him to give up his favorite fruit and survive on wild nuts. Both families, in line with free-trade theory, will suffer. But Smith may die. The relative loss is not the same, and Mr. Jones's sanctions have a good chance of working.

Error two is the opposite notion that the fungible market will render any trade sanction useless: the someone-else-will-sell-it-to-them-anyway argument. Though this contradicts argument one, it is often raised in the same breath. In 1982, shortly after President Reagan announced the resumption of U.S.-subsidized grain sales to the Soviet Union, Agriculture Secretary John Block talked to editors of the *Washington Times* about the previous grain embargo.[8] His two-point argument for resumed sales: (1) the Soviets got all the grain they needed, buying from Argentina and other countries, and (2) we suffered, since our farmers lost vital sales to the Soviets. Yet both assertions cannot be true, and Block could not explain what happened to the countries that had planned to buy from Argentina. Why didn't they simply buy U.S. grain? And why were the Soviets so foolish as to resume buying grain from the United States in 1982 when continued purchase from Argentina could have inflicted great pain on U.S. farmers? Pushed to its logical extreme, the fungible-markets theory would mean, perversely, that trade barriers don't matter.

In practice, of course, even the most fungible commodities—including grain, oil, and gold—are often dominated by a small number of producers who can greatly influence price and production. Then, too, the notion of a fungible market is often based on a misunderstanding of the nature of a market, ignoring subtle costs and differences in production. To return to our Smith-and-Jones example, suppose Smith traded not only insulin but also cough drops, aspirin, and Q-tips. Smith can procure all these other items—but not insulin—from someone else. In this case, the world market for most "medical supplies" is fungible, and Smith will simply buy them elsewhere. The market, though, has been ill-defined: There remains one key medical supply Smith cannot buy.

Perhaps the critical confusion in the sanctions debate, however, is a political one. For even given that a sanction is effective, it is bound to inflict pain largely on the people of a country, and not, in an immediate sense, on its elites. Hence the complaint that sanctions will damage "the very people we want to help" in South Africa, as Ronald Reagan put it, or "hurt starving people in Poland," as Senator Patrick Leahy argued in questioning Reagan's effort to block Western credits and technology from flowing to the Soviet natural gas pipeline, a response to Soviet-planned martial law in Poland.[9] Whether a sanction really works may come down to whether this pain will cause the people to inflict pain on the government. Thus, politically, sanctions will tend to work best against governments that are responsive to the people, which might lead to the bizarre conclusion, as then-Harvard scholars Eric Breindell and Nick Eberstadt wryly observed, that "sanctions should be used only against democratic states."[10]

As we have seen, however, all countries must react to public sentiment to some extent. How a given sanction will operate, then, depends on the sanctionee. What sort of adversary is he? What sort of pressures is he subject to? Let us consider this problem in terms of several different targets.

Sanctions Against the Soviets

Probably the toughest sanction imposed against the Soviets in recent years was the Carter grain embargo. Launched in response to the Soviet invasion of Afghanistan, this sanction was removed by the Reagan administration on the grounds, as Mr. Block argued, that it was a "dismal failure." Careful examination by scholars, however, not to mention an Agriculture Department study praised by Block himself, suggests the Carter embargo had important effects. The Soviets were able to buy much more grain from Argentina and Canada, yet this effort cost money, and still left them millions of tons short. Most important, the Kremlin could not make up critical shortfalls in feed-quality grains. Meat supplies fell, sparking worker uprisings throughout the Soviet Union.[11] Similar meat shortages in Poland, a historically sensitive issue, also helped spur the Solidarity movement in 1980. As the Department of Agriculture noted, operations were thought-provoking.[12]

The Carter grain embargo, in fact, prompted a frightened Kremlin to discuss major reforms in Soviet agriculture at a meeting of the Central Committee on January 18, 1981.[13] Though Carter was to leave office in only a few days, the Soviets felt sufficient pressure to approve a decree abolishing existing limits on the use of private land for farming and not only legalizing the sell-off of state-owned livestock but encouraging it. The Central Committee even instructed the state bank to offer credits, at low interest rates, to interested private buyers. Here is an excerpt:

> The cattle on the private subsidiary plots of citizens are to be used according to the desires of their owners, for sale to consumer cooperative organizations at agreed on prices, for sale at markets, [or] for sale to state supply organizations, with the goal of raising the interest level of young families in the creation and development of private units. . . . It is important to create everywhere a social climate in which citizens will feel they are doing something of use to the state by raising livestock and poultry on their personal plots and engaging in vegetable gardening and fruit growing.[14]

Had these reforms been enacted, the cessation of U.S. grain sales might have produced what scholars Mikhail S. Bernstam and Seymour Martin Lipset called "the most dramatic move toward free-market policies since the death of Lenin." On April 1, 1981, however, Ronald Reagan revoked the Carter embargo, the pressure on Soviet granaries and livestock production eased, and the Central Committee's decree—drawn up by a relatively obscure operative named Mikhail Gorbachev—was canceled.[15]

The Reagan administration argued that grain sales rob the Soviets of hard currency, and thus are a good thing, weakening the Russian economy. This is an important question, since it has to do with the long-term economic relationship between the Soviets and the West, quite apart from the issue of whether various specific sanctions are effective. If the Soviet supply of hard currency were a static pool, this would be a compelling argument for U.S. grain sales, since it would leave less for the Soviets to buy other things, such as Western technology. But the Soviet supply of hard currency is not fixed. It changes in response to changes in national output, which grows and declines partly in response to the very kinds of transactions under discussion.

To determine the effects of a given transaction on Soviet revenues, we must think in terms of what economists call "opportunity cost" and ask, "What would it cost the Soviets to produce or purchase this much grain if we didn't sell it to them?" If it would cost the Soviets more to produce the grain themselves—by buying more tractors, applying extra fertilizers, paying farmers to work overtime, and so on, or by seeking out less reliable suppliers—then selling the Soviets grain does not "dry up" their supply of hard currency. To the contrary, it permits them to save an amount of hard currency equal to the difference between what they actually spent and what they would have had to spend to make that much more grain themselves or purchase it elsewhere. In the case at hand, the Soviets sell the West items they are efficient at producing, chiefly oil and other primary products, and buy grain and technology, which they aren't good at producing, in return. The relationship must be viewed as a series of flows and transactions, not a swap between static pools of wealth and capital.

Smaller sanctions, tied to smaller objectives, have a record of direct success against the Soviets. Throughout the Nixon presidency, the economic fruits of détente came with strings—specifically, our cooperation was linked to increasing emigration of Soviet Jews. Quiet pressure by Secretary of State Henry Kissinger was intensified by loud pressure from Senator Henry "Scoop" Jackson and much of the U.S. Senate, which called for Soviet emigration concessions before the Soviets could attain trading status as a most favored nation. On the face of it, something worked. From 1948 to 1967, a total of about 150 elderly pensioners a year had been allowed to leave the Soviet Union. From 1971 to 1973, the Soviets released an average of 33,000 people per year.[16] Paula Stern remarked that the Soviet Union was "operating as if in an incentive system—that is, if they cooperated, they would be rewarded."[17]

Kissinger argues that Jackson's effort was counterproductive, since by making the issue public, Jackson made it impossible for the Soviets to increase emigration without appearing to capitulate to U.S. pressure, thus losing face.[18] Soviet emigration totals did indeed decline in 1974 and 1975, although not for long: From 1976 to 1979, with the Jackson-Vanik Amendment in effect, Jewish emigration rose every year, and topped 50,000 in 1979.[19] The heart of the Kissinger problem, however, lies in taking the Jackson-Vanik Amendment too much at face value. The purpose of the amendment was not simply to increase emigration but rather to offer the Soviets a choice. Precisely by making it hard for the Soviets to hide, Jackson in effect upped the ante of détente. Only dramatic, public changes in the nature of the Soviet system would yield to the Kremlin leadership the most-favored-nation status it desired. By refusing, it made clear to the world that, at that time, it was not interested in significantly changing its ways.[20]

Another method of economic warfare against the Soviets should be mentioned because it has been applied with bipartisan determination since the 1940s: the denial of cutting-edge technologies to the Soviets. Many people see the cutoff of such technology, particularly where it has military applications, as a vital exercise. Moreover, the idea carries emotional punch. Technology obtained by the Soviets can often be traced to a specific weapon pointed at us, perhaps having passed through the hands of a particular country or corporation already unpopular with Americans. Since the Soviets rely so heavily on us for their own weapons development, and on weapons development for their own power, cutting off high technology would seem to be a way, to return to our Smith-and-Jones analogy, of denying the Soviets insulin.

As appealing as the notion is, much evidence suggests that the policy as applied has been counterproductive. The French air ministry calculated in 1979 that the annual value of illegal acquisitions from the West saved the Soviets perhaps $50 million. The U.S. Defense Department later estimated that expanded U.S. efforts to crack down on technology transfer cost the Soviets more than $5 billion a year. Its figure, however, was based on the questionable assumption that every export license the United States rejected resulted in the outright deprivation of a given technology to the Soviets. Wherever the truth lies, it seems clear that the clampdown effort costs the United States at least as much as it does the Soviets, tying up vital research and development in a Lilliputian web of paperwork and restrictions. Unlike cutting off grain sales or changing the policy of a finite number of U.S. bureaucracies and international agencies, restricting technology trade involved the regulation of a vast, complex network of private firms, investors, and scientists. In 1985, an export transaction that took an Asian firm one week to complete involved, for an American firm, an average of sixteen weeks of license applications and hearings with the government. Many promising branches of research are simply abandoned when they become classified; firms consider it unlikely they will ever reap substantial benefits once a given project is caught in the clutches of

Defense Department controls and scrutiny. Too much secrecy, then, as *The Economist* of London argued, "is to academic research as protectionism is to trade: self-mutilating." What is more, the Pentagon's share of government-backed research and development was rising through the Reagan years: it consumed about 74 percent of the total by 1987. The clampdown not only harms U.S. commerce but damages our military in precisely the area where we should be surging ahead of the Soviets. Many U.S. weapons scientists thus urge a drastic reduction in the amount of classified material and rapid declassification of all but the most precious secrets.[21]

By abolishing some of the limits on technology transfer, enforcement could focus more efficiently on curtailing truly criminal transactions and safeguarding the most vital secrets. "The good news," as George Gilder wrote, "is that the most critical sources of technology are forever beyond the Soviet reach. Technology is not a thing; it is chiefly a process, and the Soviet Union can never acquire it. Our only way to maintain leadership in the arms race is to accelerate technical progress far beyond the ability of the Soviets to absorb it."[22] Rather than seeking to thwart the progress of the tortoise, we should let the hare race ahead—a sanction, if you will, that might encourage the Kremlin to accelerate democratic development.

Even when we are not out to punish the Soviet leadership, however, there is no excuse for subsidizing it with artificially cheap credits. Subsidies weaken our own economy and finance transactions that the Soviets might not otherwise be able to afford. The Soviet economy enjoys only $20 billion to $30 billion in annual hard-currency earnings per year; the West provides an estimated $3 billion annually in direct and indirect trade and credit subsidies and in 1985 extended a total of $4.5 billion in credits. Of $29 billion in total Soviet debt as of 1984, $18 billion, or more than 60 percent of the total, was at subsidized rates.[23] The ironic result is to damage the prospects for Soviet democratization.

There are certain important political benefits that result from trade—we want to see our ideas and values penetrate the Iron Curtain—but those benefits stem only from trade that reflects a true market transaction, from the thousands of small exchanges between businessmen that represent real efficiencies. If the Soviet Union were to start importing on a large scale the products it truly needs from the West, such as computers and communications equipment, and open up its economy to Western visitors seeking markets, then there would assuredly be important benefits to democracy. Yet this is precisely the sort of trade that has not taken place between the Soviets and the West. In the 1970s, 70 percent of all U.S. exports to the USSR involved agricultural products, the majority of them subsidized. By 1984, the figure was up to 80 percent. Europeans dumped a shower of subsidized milk, butter, and vegetables on the Soviets over the same period. The bulk of the remaining trade involved large-scale projects such as the $20-billion-or-more gas pipeline. Bank loans for such projects would normally be granted only at high interest rates, but Western governments often intervened with loan guarantees or long-term purchase agreements: not quite as direct as handing the Soviets cash, but still a subsidy. The losers in this deal are the Russian people. "The Soviets," as Jude Wanniski writes, "reform only when the West is leaving them in the dust."[24] To subsidize trade is to deny the Kremlin the sting of its own failure, removing pressures for democratic change.

China Canards

With his return to power from 1976 to 1978, Deng Xiaoping, the jailed opponent of China's Cultural Revolution and numerous other excesses of Chairman Mao, amazed the Chinese people. Since then he has amazed the world, leading China farther down the road to economic and political freedom than any communist society has yet traveled. The question naturally arises: What role—if any—might a combination of U.S. economic carrots and sticks have played in the rise of Deng and the rise of Dengism?

It is satisfying and useful to recall now that reasonable and dispassionate experts viewing the situation in China have been misled often. In the 1950s and through most of the 1960s, America viewed with horror what seemed to be a monolithic communist empire stretching from Berlin to Moscow to Peking. We now know that the Sino-Soviet rift began as early as Eisenhower's first term and was relatively final before John Kennedy took office. Others, ranging from enthusiastic journalists to impressionable scholars, returned from China—as did others from Cuba—with new hope that a simplified, agrarian, Maoist model would revive the socialist ideal after its warping at the hands of Stalin.

In the evolution toward freedom that ensued after Mao's death, there has been space for equal confusion. One round of early reforms gave way to an apparent reversal in 1979. But the reversal was reversed with a new series of economic growth initiatives through the mid-1980s. Again in 1987, party bureaucrats struck back, forcing the removal of Deng's apparent choice for a successor, Hu Yaobang, and cracking down on academics and student protestors demanding even more rapid progress toward democracy. Yet a later party conference continued the process of democratization. Some delegates in attendance actually had been chosen in competitive elections, and they proceeded to criticize debate and vote—quite independently—on laws, appointments, and other measures. Still, the process was fragile, reversible, and questionable.

Whatever Deng's intent, China in the 1980s emerged as a source of wonder. Several years after dismissing Deng as "an orthodox and narrow Stalinist bureaucrat," and the various inevitable cycles of retrenchment from some of his changes as "heartbreaking," the respected China scholar Simon Leys conceded: "There has been a fairly spectacular relaxation" of socialism's "death grip."[25]

We may therefore be skeptical of claims made by a number of experts minimizing or denying that the United States helped bring about this transition from Maoism. China's great leap forward—the one that did not actually go backward—began, after all, in the years following the dramatic Nixon opening of 1971. Its acceleration coincided with an acceleration in popular contact, diplomatic and military cooperation, and economic integration with the West, particularly the United States. At the very least, this chronological correspondence suggests that the United States' policy was not retarding a natural process of Chinese resurgence. That alone would be no small accomplishment, given the hostility with which Washington had eyed Peking since the Truman administration—as Americans came to say, "lost China." Yet a review of U.S. policy and the Chinese reforms suggests more than a casual relationship.

Consider first the period of 1949 to 1969, the U.S.-China Cold War. U.S. troops fought directly against Chinese forces in bloody engagements of the Korean War, and indirectly against Chinese-backed forces, of course, in the longer and more tragic war in Vietnam. From the time Chiang Kai-shek's nationalists were expelled until a toast Nixon gave at a banquet in late 1970, no U.S. leader had used the term "People's Republic of China" in an official statement; "Communist China" or "Red China" was the accepted protocol.[26]

At the center of this was a U.S.-led economic embargo under which trade between China and most of the West almost ceased to exist. Now, most conventional analysis at the time maintained that this embargo was a failure. Noting that China's trade did not absolutely decline, John Garson concluded in 1970 that "the embargo has a very limited effect on the Chinese economy and on China's war-making potential." What his calculation left out, of course, was any comparison to a world in which most countries, enjoying the postwar boom, were experiencing a rapid growth in trade. As figure 6.1 shows, China's trade grew only gradually from 1950 to 1970, and not at all for about twelve years prior to the Nixon opening. In the twelve-year period between 1968 and 1980, by contrast, China's trade with the world grew by a factor of almost ten.[27]

Notice that when Chinese trade did surge, the bulk—more than 80 percent, in fact—was with noncommunist countries. In 1968, for example, the United States supplied virtually 0 percent of Chinese imports. This share grew to 2.8 percent in 1972, 13.0 percent in 1974, and 16 percent in 1985, even as China gobbled up factories and other capital goods from Europe and Japan.[28]

To an extent, the sluggish trade performance of the 1950s and 1960s was a reflection not just of U.S. policy but of China's own preference to live in "angry isolation," as Nixon wrote in *Foreign Affairs.*[29] (By the same token,

FIGURE 6.1

*Trade with Foreign Countries
by the People's Republic of China*

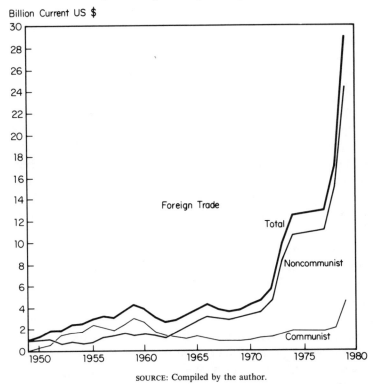

SOURCE: Compiled by the author.

later increases in trade were to some degree an effect of Chinese liberalization moves—not just their cause.) As figure 6.1 shows, though, the boom began well before the death of Mao in 1976 and the onset of rapid reform late in the decade.

U.S. sanctions, then, helped to heighten China's political, economic, diplomatic, and military crunch. To a degree few countries have known, China was isolated, threatened, and poor. Important domestic political consequences followed. "During Mao's last years, China was sinking," Leys writes. "There was a widespread realization that nothing could be worse, and in this feeling an odd comfort could be found—such demented policies simply could not last much longer; things *had* to change."[30]

It is often said that Nixon's *rapprochement* with China could not have been achieved by any Democratic president; only a man with solid credentials as an anticommunist hawk could explain and defend the maneuver to the American people. Yet there may have been a similar dynamic at work in Peking. "By legitimizing the Americans and the modest changes that came with them in the early seventies," notes Raimon Meyer, a Hoover Institution scholar on the Far East, "Mao legitimized Deng as well, to an extent. I think you can say that—that he did for Deng in China what Nixon did for China in America." If the opening to the United States removed some of the stench from ideas Western, so did the results. Even before Mao's death, rising trade had pumped new life into the moribund economy, and U.S. cooperation during the India-Pakistan war and the Soviet-border crises cemented a clear U.S. policy of building China as a bulwark against Soviet expansion.[31]

Mao's need for a counterweight to the Soviets, and the domestic decay induced by his own rule, thus made the U.S.-China détente possible. It was Nixon, however, who made it a fact. By the time he took office, Nixon had already concluded that "we simply cannot afford to leave China forever out-side the family of nations." Yet in the early months of his administration, Peking hardly seemed interested in becoming part of the family. The day after Nixon's inauguration, the New China News Agency denounced him as the new puppet chosen by the "monopoly bourgeois clique" to implement the "vicious ambitions of U.S. imperialism." The early steps in what Kissinger describes as an "intricate minuet" were almost all American. Where the John-son administration had often defined the Vietnam War as a response to Chi-nese-instigated aggression, Nixon never mentioned China in those terms; in fact, of course, he gained some Chinese leverage against Hanoi. In March 1969, Kissinger ordered a reexamination of U.S. trade policy toward China, and some limits on tourism were removed. In June, following the first major and public clashes on the Soviet-Chinese border, Kissinger reported to Nixon on Moscow's furious efforts to persuade Western European governments to with-hold recognition from Communist China. In a marginal note, Nixon suggested that the U.S. "subtly encourage" those countries to proceed in going against our previous wishes. In July—still without any serious response from Peking—Nixon ordered a modification of the embargo.[32] As Kissinger recalls:

> On July 21, 1969 . . . the State Department made a low-key, matter-of-fact announcement that eased (but did not eliminate) restrictions on trade and travel to the People's Republic. The announcement asked for no reciprocity; the Chinese could consider it without acting formally. On July 24, the Chinese released an American yachtsman [who had been held since his boat capsized and drifted into Chinese waters on July 16]. Chou En-lai, too, knew how to make moves that require no reciprocity. Peking had understood.[33]

Nixon's strategic—and unilateral—actions illustrate the importance not only of implementing sanctions well but of removing them skillfully. Crude analysts tend to think of the economic lever in stark, absolutist terms: We apply penalties; an opponent is forced to his knees; he agrees to hold free elections next Thursday. In fact, of course, they seldom work in this fashion.

THE CARROT AND THE STICK

The insight that both Nixon and Kissinger achieved in 1969 was that the sanctions on China might already have worked. The stick had helped punish the enemy; now, it could be used to probe for signs of a willingness to cooperate. In 1969, the United States could afford a certain generous unilateralism in dealing with Mao. Indeed, given the deep rift of the two countries over Taiwan, there was probably no other way to achieve a *deus ex machina.* If the Chinese simply pocketed the U.S. concessions, moreover, they could easily be withdrawn. Thus, the carrot could be dangled at little cost—nay, carrots could actually be passed out free for a limited time.

"Appeasement," writes Hendrik Hertzberg in *The New Republic,* "sometimes works quite satisfactorily, as it has in America's courting of China."[34] The point is well taken. Happily, in the case of China, the hard-headed geopolitical approach of Nixon-Kissinger intersects with the ambitious ideopolitical objective of building democracy. China in 1969 had been the object of U.S. pressures that few would seek to apply to a nuclear-armed Soviet Union, and that could not be sustained politically even if some leaders sought to do so.

In our relations with China after the Nixon opening, there may be a model for U.S. economic leverage. For in retrospect, U.S. economic diplomacy with Communist China was conducted with a remarkable restraint. Though America dropped many trade restrictions, U.S. policy and politics denied the Chinese entry into, and easy credits from, the large banks and international lending agencies that were sprinkling dollars on the Third World and Eastern Europe. Only a small portion of trade with the U.S. and Japan was subsidized, and that not until the late 1970s. China was not granted Most-Favored-Nation Trading status until 1980, gaining entry into the World Bank in the same year. Even then no gush of easy credit ensued. The World Bank projected its loans to China to run a mere $3 billion between 1986 and 1990. A flap arose as late as 1983 when Ronald Reagan proposed to allow China into the Asian development bank, expelling Taiwan.[35]

The result, quite simply, was that China could not seek economic growth by lobbying with Western bankers, governments, and corporate elites. "Commercial and trade relations," Heritage Foundation scholar John F. Copper noted in 1984, "are limited by the PRC's lack of foreign exchange and its inability to pay for [imported] products. The PRC, of course, can buy [imported] goods if foreign assistance is given, or if special access to the U.S. market is provided."[36] There was, however, another way for the Chinese to generate foreign exchange: reorganize the domestic economy around the principle of rewarding effort and efficiency, so that workers and farmers and entrepreneurs produce more. The generally unsubsidized U.S.-China trade, unlike much Western exchange with the Soviet Union, thus provided large incentives for a shift to private enterprise, for a Western factory or production technique planted in a socialist economy, after all, quickly ceases to produce fruit. Even in their initial effects, such a tapestry of real trades between businesses produces very different effects than the whopping, government-to-government grain deals that characterized so much of U.S.-Soviet exchange. Real trade encourages expanded popular contacts and builds mutual interests between institutions outside the state. By the 1980s, there were several Chinese students in the United States for every one from the Soviet Union; there were more business visas granted to U.S. businessmen bound for China than for Russia.[37]

America's use of the economic lever helped spark a continued Chinese drift from pro-Soviet alignment and socialism and toward economic and political liberalization. This was the result many observers hoped would follow expanded trade with Eastern Europe, and in fact, the steady vitality of Solidarity and similar movements suggests there was some success there as well. The irony here is that whatever dreamy notions of "differentiation" and "goulash communism" danced in the heads of Western leaders dealing with countries like Poland and Hungary, they had few such visions of a new China in 1971.

Well, they did and they didn't. "We must not only watch for changes," Nixon did say in one 1968 interview, "we must seek to make changes." Still, when asked (years later) to define the changes he had in mind, he said he was referring to "their external behavior. . . . They're always going to be communists and you can't change that." Actually, Nixon often held out the distant hope of American diplomacy promoting democratic capitalism by circuitous and indirect means. But this was couched in cloudy terms to communicate to most makers of policy that it was not to be taken too seriously. Kissinger defined the animating spirit of the Nixon gambit when he told reporters on December 18, 1969: "We have always made it clear that we have no permanent enemies and that we will judge other countries, including Communist countries—and specifically countries like Communist China—on the basis of their actions, and not on the basis of their domestic ideology."[38]

Nixon's modest denial of credit for his role in reshaping China is not a *pro forma* humility. It is sincerely felt, and springs from the very *weltanschauung*—"hard-headed," Nixon would call it—that prompted him to launch the Ping-Pong diplomacy. Something there is in both his and Kissinger's mind that sees more romance in a "triangular diplomacy" than a *novus ordo seclorum;* more charm in "balancing our geopolitical interests" than in assisting, even on the margin, in the most far-reaching reform of a communist society in seventy-five years. Yet the facts support a tentative hypothesis that Nixon and Kissinger, without even realizing it, have understated their own achievement.

THE CARROT AND THE STICK

Sanctions Against Major Allies

On occasion, the United States may decide to apply sanctions to one of its major allies, as we did to Western Europe during the 1956 Suez Crisis. One can argue about whether those sanctions had a sensible objective. One cannot argue about their impact: the British and French rapidly withdrew from the Sinai in response to U.S. restrictions on oil deliveries and trade credits to France and Britain. Western pressure on Turkey, the object of a series of U.S. and then European sanctions from 1974 to 1982, had equally clear results. Although our efforts did not appear to eradicate Turkey's continuing urge to intervene in Cyprus, Europe's 1981 cutoff of credits from the Organization for Economic Cooperation and Development and other assistance led to visible movement toward democracy. As a result, the West enjoyed a stronger, more stable ally.[39]

One of the most controversial sanctions involved the Reagan cutoff of U.S. technology for the Soviet-European gas pipeline. Nominally, the pipeline sanctions were directed at the Soviets and Poland, but when the allies refused to cooperate, and even did their best to circumvent the sanctions, the policy quickly became something more. George Ball denounced it as "a sanction against our allies," and, in truth, that is more or less the case.[40] This does not necessarily mean it was a bad policy.

Reagan sought, by denying export licenses, to block the transfer of critical turbines from General Electric and other high-technology items needed for the pipeline. When the allies pressured their own companies to ignore the ban, the United States threatened to revoke all such privileges for firms who disobeyed. There were significant economic results. The completion of the pipeline was delayed by at least one year, arguably two years. During that time, amid the general furor in Europe over whether the pipeline was a good idea even without U.S. sanctions, long-term purchase contracts were being negotiated. Some countries, notably the Netherlands, realized that Soviet demands for subsidized credit at about 8.67 percent, combined with a "floor price" for gas purchases in the midst of declining world energy prices, made the pipeline a poor deal anyway. Others were at least embarrassed as the details of their dealings became public. Axel Lebahn, until 1983 the Deutsche Bank's representative in Moscow, wrote an article in *Aussenpolitik* detailing the shrewd negotiating tactics used by the Soviets in cajoling the Europeans to both subsidize the pipeline's construction and guarantee an above-the-market price for the oil to finance it. These and similar embarrassments caused other countries, including France and Italy, to provide an escape clause allowing them to wriggle out of payment for 20 percent of the contracted shipments. Hence although the Soviets, with much bluster, announced in late 1983 that the pipeline had been completed, it began pumping only because the Soviets cannibalized valuable equipment from internal pipelines to save face, in effect causing a domestic energy crisis over at least two winters. U.S. sanctions drove up the construction costs. Original estimates for the pipeline were in the neighborhood of $10 billion; more recent guesses say the project cost $25 billion or more. And the sanctions drove down the benefits. The Soviets hoped for $10 billion a year in revenues; with smaller European purchases and lower oil prices, the best bet was $2.5 billion to $5 billion a year. Gordon Crovitz of the *Wall Street Journal* followed the deal closely, filing more than a dozen articles that make a strong collective case for the pipeline stick.[41]

The pipeline sanctions, of course, were only the most visible of several applied by the Reagan administration in the wake of Polish martial law. The United States also sought, with more cooperation from its allies, to frustrate Polish efforts to refinance the country's $25 billion debt. If the objective of these sanctions was to crush communist rule in Poland outright, they failed. They certainly did not fail to have an economic impact on Poland. The country's standard of living fell by more than 25 percent in 1981 and 1982.[42] The Polish government itself concluded that Western economic sanctions were a major cause of the contraction, costing $10 billion to $12 billion in lost output in 1982 and 1983 alone.[43] Interestingly enough, there was strong evidence that the Polish people themselves were happy to undergo this economic deprivation. In 1982, thousands of Poles took to the street to chant, "Down with Brezhnev, God bless Ronald Reagan." Solidarity leaders such as Lech Walesa cheered the imposition of sanctions, and actually thanked the administration for demonstrating America's commitment to Polish democracy. In short, Poland's economic travails focused anger not on the United States, but on the Jaruzelski government that the Polish people knew was the ultimate cause of their suffering.[44]

A well-designed sanction, then, can actually protect and nurture the third force for democracy within another country. By tailoring U.S. policy in part to the leadership of Solidarity and the Catholic Church, the Reagan sanctions gave Walesa and Cardinal Jozef Glemp the authority to distribute economic benefits to Poland—benefits Jaruzelski could not deliver by himself. The ability to pass out or withhold such rewards is almost a definition of political power. Hence economic sanctions empowered Solidarity and other democratic institutions in Poland, leading columnist Flora Lewis to conclude that "the sanctions did their specific job."[45]

There remains the questions of determining the cost of political and economic friction among the United States and its allies. "Americans may be standing tall these days," as Arthur Schlesinger noted during a low tide in NATO relations in 1984, "but it isn't going to help much if we stand tall all by ourselves."[46] Yet in the case of the Reagan pipeline sanctions, the allied governments' disagreement with us on this issue did not prevent them from supporting us elsewhere around the world. In the years that followed, the same presumably divided allies deployed controversial nuclear missiles in Europe; joined together in research on the equally divisive Strategic Defense Initiative; intervened jointly in Lebanon and the Persian Gulf; presented arms-control proposals to the Soviets with near-unanimous backing; and even cut back on subsidized credit to the Soviet bloc.

The Reagan administration's main failure in the pipeline episode, in fact, was in neglecting an opportunity for additive compromise to extend sanctions further. A strong theme in the allied criticism centered around Reagan's decision to lift the Russian grain embargo. While restricting a trade deal Europe feels to be in its best interest, the allies argued, America was busy selling wheat to the same enemy. A creative statesman might have taken the opportunity to reimpose the grain embargo in exchange for an agreement from our allies that they would help us pressure the Soviets to initiate democratic reforms.

Pest Control

Perhaps the most attractive targets for sanctions are small, pesky enemies: Cuba, Vietnam, Nicaragua. Most are weak economically, while tending to be heavily armed.[47] A stiff package of sanctions is often seen as the best way to keep the heat on.

Economically, such sanctions have a good record, provided we do not demand exorbitant results. Sanctions against Vietnam and North Korea, for example, raised the support costs of the Soviet Union significantly. Under Truman's sanctions, Korean trade fell from $180 million in 1949 to $68 million in 1954. National income dropped by 30 percent in the first year of the sanctions, at which time the North Korean government ceased keeping reliable statistics, a practice that lasted several years. Sanctions against the Vietnamese communists had a similar effect. Average annual Vietnamese trade, 1955 to 1961: $315 million. Average annual Vietnamese trade, 1975 to 1981: $226 million. Socialist economics and U.S. sanctions, one might say, were Vietnam's Vietnam.[48]

It is, of course, a bit discomfiting to take joy in America's success at damaging someone else's economy. If we consider what damage a strong North Korea or Vietnam might have done to many other free countries in turn, however, the exercise becomes a bit more enjoyable.

To work fully, of course, sanctions cannot simply be announced. They must be applied. In the case of U.S. sanctions against Nicaragua, for example, delays hampered effective execution. Outright U.S. aid continued into the fiscal year 1981. In the same year, trade with the United States accounted for more than one-third of Nicaragua's total trade. Even as the Reagan administration grew more hostile to the Sandinista dictators, seeking their virtual overthrow as early as 1982 and 1983, most trade continued. Not until 1985, when the Sandinistas had shifted toward dependence on Moscow and Europe, and America's share of Nicaraguan trade had declined to 14 percent, did the Reagan administration apply the basic economic sanction of cutting off trade.[49]

Too little, too late. But why? Part of the answer is that in 1981, major U.S. banana importers had not had time to pull back some of their thriving trade with Nicaragua. The leading importer of bananas—indeed, the sole importer in 1983—was Jack Pandol, a close friend of top Reagan aide Michael Deaver. Deaver not only helped convince the president not to apply stringent economic measures in 1981 and 1982. In 1984, he arranged for at least two meetings between Pandol and members of the National Security Council, then engaged in drawing up a list of options for increasing pressure on the Sandinistas. In the first six months of 1984—even as the administration was conducting covert operations in Nicaragua—U.S. banana imports from Nicaragua, according to the Department of Agriculture, increased by a factor of six over 1983. Thanks to his Deaver connection, Jack Pandol's business continued to boom, and the Nicaraguan government had an extra four years to solidify its revolution and adjust its trading patterns to isolate itself from the United States.[50]

In 1987, it struck me that it might be useful to find out, for one of my newspaper columns, how the sanctions were going. My fingers did the walking to various officials at the State Department's Latin America desk, former NSC aides, staffers of the Senate Foreign Relations Committee, White House public-affairs aides, sundry legislative assistants on Capitol Hill, and so on; out of more than a dozen officials deeply involved in aiding the contras, not a single one knew what persons or agency was in charge of enforcing the Nicaragua sanctions. (The job, it turns out, generally is carried out by an interagency task force.)

Small Allies and Large Injustices

Sanctions against small allies may offer the most potent opportunity to exercise a positive influence, since the small ally often relies on the United States for the economic or psychological equivalent of insulin. In the case of Nicaragua, for example, Jimmy Carter's withdrawal of U.S. support helped bring down an already rickety dictatorship in 1976. One can argue about the wisdom of these sanctions, since they brought to power a government no more humane, yet clearly they produced the immediate result Carter desired, the fall of Anastasio Somoza.[51] Far from worrying that sanctions against our allies will not work, U.S. leaders ought to recognize that they can often be very effective—and ask themselves if they really want success.

This was a particularly contentious issue for the West in its dealings with South Africa, one of the most sanctioned countries in history. In the early 1960s, Western sports associations began excluding South African athletes from their events, and John Kennedy embargoed the sale of military equipment in 1962. Several dozen nations cut economic and diplomatic ties with Pretoria in the 1970s. In 1975 and 1978, the United States applied sanctions nominally linked to South Africa's development of nuclear power but understood to be in the context of opposition to apartheid. The efforts were accelerated when Congress moved to apply much broader sanctions beginning in 1984, and by the fall of 1986, the United States and many allies had outlawed the purchase of South African gold Krugerrands, iron, steel, coal, textiles, and agricultural products; cut off air traffic; reduced international credits available to the regime; and prohibited all new investments in South Africa.[52]

Critics at first sneered that such actions would have no impact. "U.S. sanctions," argued columnist Suzanne Garment, were "just a sideshow."[53] The furious opposition of the Reagan administration and its supporters, of course, suggested otherwise, and soon the debate shifted from whether sanctions would be effective to the nature of their effect. Scholar Peter Duignan argued, for example, that pulling out of South Africa would "benefit white businessmen who could buy up U.S. plants cheaply,"[54] and indeed, the price of such assets did fall, although this simply reflected the market's judgment that a given piece of capital in South Africa could be expected to produce a smaller stream of revenues. Others noted that sanctions had not yet been applied by our allies, many of them much larger trading partners with South Africa. This oft-used argument about lack of unity in sanctions, however, begs the question of how unity is attained. In the case of South Africa, sanctions by college and union funds tended to spur sanctions by larger institutions and whole countries. French sanctions in 1985 put pressure on the U.S. Congress to pass its own sanctions, which in turn put pressure on the Reagan administration to abandon its "constructive engagement" policy and engage in rhetorical attacks on apartheid. By the fall of 1985, Reagan found himself signing an executive order outlawing Krugerrand sales in an effort to head off momentum for tougher measures. Congress steamrolled the president the next fall anyway, prompting many allies to join the ranks. Unity on sanctions, then, did not spring Athena-like from heads of state. It evolved.[55]

At times people were so busy shouting that they got their slogans crossed. So potent was the potential impact of sanctions, George Shultz argued, that they might produce a bloodbath "too terrible to contemplate."[56] In this model, put forth forcefully in an article for *Commentary* by Paul Johnson, sanctions retarded economic growth and thus the critical force for the emergence of democracy.[57] Yet six months after their imposition, sanctions opponent William Pascoe of the Heritage Foundation chirped that sanctions had "not damaged the economy severely," and in fact "have caused a short-term stimulus, as the economy moves to create its own substitutes for former imports."[58] (Pascoe nevertheless resisted the impulse to call for tougher sanctions yet, in order to provide "stimulus" to the South African economy and hasten the advent of democracy.)

In the event, of course, sanctions did not cause South Africa to collapse into chaos. Nor did they have no effect at all. National output declined 8 percent in 1985 and 2 percent in 1986 (the 1985 figure reflecting in part a falling world price for gold, South Africa's chief export). Of about three hundred American firms operating in South Africa in 1982, no more than eighty-five were left by the end of 1987. Blacks were hit hard, as every serious observer knew would happen: They suffered 30 percent unemployment in mid-1987. Confidence in South Africa's economy fell to its lowest level since World War II.[59] Sometimes nations put in this spot simply grit their teeth and dig their heels in. In South Africa, at least some actors realized that future prosperity might require tapping South Africa's greatest resource: the black people. Roger Thurow captured this development in a report for the the *Wall Street Journal:*

> JOHANNESBURG, South Africa—With international trade sanctions pinching it from all sides, South Africa is being forced to take a hard look inward in an attempt to achieve economic growth. . . .
> "Inward industrialization" is a hot new buzzword among corporate and government officials. . . . The main tenets call for developing labor-intensive manufacturing projects [and] promoting small businesses that would produce simple goods that have been imported, such as building materials, clothing, and household goods. Such efforts would be aimed at reducing black unemployment, thus increasing the consumer possibilities of the [black] market. . . .
> [S]ays David Mohr, an economist with the country's largest investment-fund manager, "A year ago, the government might have been reluctant to go to this area for demand for the economy. Now, they see this as an area for tremendous growth. This is the most important impact sanctions are having on economic thinking."[60]

The impact on South African politics seemed positive. Many had feared that sanctions would tend to radicalize blacks and destroy the white consensus for changing apartheid. In fact, however, sanctions coincided with moderate opinion. More clearly than ever, South Africans of all color could see change coming, and precisely because sanctions were applied in ratchet fashion, that reform could be orderly, gradual, and beneficial—if South Africa chose.

Some cited the South African elections of 1987 as proving the unwisdom of sanctions, on the ground that proapartheid parties gained a handful of seats in the parliament. It is important to note, however, that the winner in that postsanction election was Botha's National Party, which sanction opponents had claimed all along represented the force of gradual change in South Africa. Days before the vote, journalist William Rusher and other Americans met with Botha and proclaimed afterward that "far from refusing to abandon apartheid, the Botha government proclaimed its intention to do exactly that."[61] In national polls of party preference, the Progressive Federal Party, which urges faster change, actually rose to 35.4 percent, trailing the National Party's 35.9 percent only slightly, and running well ahead of the proapartheid groups.[62]

Blacks, of course, were not allowed a meaningful vote. Sanctions did, however, tend to strengthen the power of third-force leaders, and opponents of sanctions in the West feared the result. They worried that blacks would increasingly be led by men they regarded as irresponsible, such as Archbishop Desmond Tutu, Oliver Tambo of the Soviet-backed African National Congress,[63] and jailed ANC leader Nelson Mandela. Certainly, the sanctions raised the profile of those leaders: Botha met with Tutu to discuss apartheid reforms even as sanctions roared to approval in Congress, and representatives of the ANC were granted an audience with Western diplomats hoping to woo the group away from the communist leanings of some of its members.[64] Yet there is evidence that both the ANC and Tutu took the wrong message from their new opportunity, and that as a result blacks in South Africa viewed them with less enthusiasm.

Tutu, for example, engaged in increasingly inflammatory rhetoric. As Congress moved toward passage of a broad sanction bill in 1986, he said that the West could "go to hell" for its previous indifference to apartheid.[65] After the bill passed, he blasted America for having failed to stop apartheid when it was instituted, snapping, "Please spare us your new-found altruism."[66] Such frustration is of course understandable, but black leaders voiced dismay at Tutu's belligerence, while blacks continued flocking to various churches that had opposed sanctions.[67] The ANC, for its part, seemed determined to discredit anyone or anything—including my newspaper columns[68]—suggesting that the West at least test whether it favored true democracy or simply a dictatorship with darker faces. In October 1986, Congress asked the ANC to cooperate in a probe of its communist links, overstated or understated. Other third-force movements, such as the Nicaraguan contras, have wisely submitted to such scrutiny. Tambo refused.[69] A month later, he was in Moscow to discuss continued military aid with Mikhail Gorbachev. As a result, though, the ANC had persistent troubles attracting members and generating revolution in the wake of U.S. sanctions. Black unemployment focused anger on the leaders (such as Tutu and Tambo) who had advocated them in the first place.[70] By 1987, Tambo himself gave evidence of the antiradical tide among blacks, telling a conference of businessmen in London that sanctions were doing the ANC more harm than good.[71]

It may seem perverse to say sanctions worked because they convinced South African blacks they don't work. The point is, relatively limited Western sanctions gave South Africa a taste of what a complete embargo—nay, a complete race war—might be like. Blacks and whites alike hoped to avoid this more extreme hardship, and as a consequence there was less support for radicals and more for proponents of moderate change. The rising black stars in South Africa, therefore, were moderate voices such as Cyril Ramaphosa of the Mineworkers' Union, and Chief Mangosuthu Buthelezi, head of the Zulu nation that makes up 30 percent of South African blacks. Unions sought marginal economic changes and emphasized practical results—as against the utopian bloodbath sometimes espoused by the ANC. "We pride ourselves on being an organized workers movement," Ramaphosa said. "We pride ourselves on democratic organization."[72] Buthelezi, meanwhile, held an *indaba* (the Zulu word means "let us talk together") to draft a constitution for South Africa. For several months, members of Buthelezi's Inkatha group met in the City Hall of Durban, along with representatives of the Progressive Federal Party, union leaders, and more than thirty other organizations, to hammer out a document. In November 1986, they finished an impressive design for a constitution and bill of rights similar to our own. By 1987, the delegates could even point to a modest example of their plan's workability. Ciskei, a tiny and poor black homeland, adopted a local-autonomy scheme based on free enterprise and free movement. The result was 23,000 new jobs and a growth rate of 6 percent, even as the rest of the country stagnated.[73]

No one can say with certainty to what extent sanctions speeded or slowed this healthy evolution. It is clear, though, that some Western pressure on South Africa's government was an essential element. "As long as the U.S. appeared to side with Afrikaners against the blacks," William Pascoe of the Heritage Foundation conceded, "it had no credibility in opposition circles as honest brokers."[74]

One man who has studied South African society for many years is Dr. C. P. de Kock. He tracks public-opinion trends from his office at the Institute for Sociological and Demographic Research of Pretoria's Human Sciences Research Council, sort of the Ben Wattenberg or Norman Ornstein of South Africa. De Kock carefully tracked political attitudes among both whites and blacks during the key years from 1984 to 1987 when tougher sanctions were debated and then applied by the West. During those years, he found, almost every trend that a Western democrat would hope to see emerge in South Africa actually did emerge. Here come the numbers. The percentage of whites who thought reform was moving too fast, he found, declined: 33 percent in 1985, 24 percent in 1986. The share who thought it was moving too slow grew, to

28 percent in 1986 from 16 percent the year before. Whites favoring a law against mixed marriages stood at 61 percent in 1984, fell to 54 percent in 1985, and to 44 percent in 1986. At the beginning of the surveys, only 25 percent of all whites felt that the practice of excluding blacks from parliament "must be abolished," with 55 percent saying it "must be retained." By 1986, 43 percent said it "must be abolished," 38 percent said it "must be retained." De Kock concluded: "For Whites, reform is increasingly becoming the politics of survival. . . . Whites will be increasingly forced by their own self-interest to enter into wider alliances with other centrists—and the only other centrists remaining are on the other side of the historical color barrier." Sanctions, de Kock told a group of us at the Hoover Institution in October 1986, "have helped accelerate those attitudinal trends." Blacks, meanwhile, showed little interest in violence, despite years of oppression and major crackdowns in 1985 and 1986. Urban blacks polled in 1986 were asked what tactics would achieve more for them: 66 percent said "negotiation," 20 percent said "violence." The total favoring violence declined from 1985. A majority favored some sanctions but opposed a complete boycott by the West or the pullout of Western firms. Blacks also showed a sophistication that would confound many Western elites. As de Kock noted: "It is often said that blacks who support economic boycotts against South Africa appear to be unaware of the fact that such a measure could cost them their jobs. . . . [Yet when] those who were in favor of economic boycotts were asked whether they would still support such boycotts if it meant losing their jobs, approximately three-quarters (75.3 percent) answered in the affirmative."[75]

Perhaps most important, de Kock saw a growing political consensus in the sanction years, one that transcended race. "Many Blacks in the broad layers of the population regard a one-man–one-vote system in a unitary state as the ideal form of government, and would be willing to accept federalism as an alternative, provided it was seen as an honest attempt at replacing apartheid." Interestingly, when blacks were asked to identify what forms of government they would regard as "good to excellent," only 46 percent characterized a "black-dominated government" that way, but an overwhelming 74 percent applied that label to a "white, coloured, Indian, and black government without group dominance." The highest preference among whites was for a "white-dominated government," which 70 percent would find good to excellent. But a strong majority of 58 percent also found a government "without group dominance" acceptable. "A growing proportion of whites are convinced that reform is not only desirable, but that it can even be expanded and accelerated," de Kock concluded.[76]

Sanction opponents were not entirely unaware of these arguments. They simply feared that any genuinely democratic movement would be thwarted, as were similar trends in 1917 Russia, by a small group of armed revolutionaries.

The proponents of sanctions, for their part, were sometimes reluctant to take their own premises to their logical conclusion. If the ANC was a broad-based reform group, for example, why not seek to wean it away from the Marxists? Why not provide assistance? Here is how Congressman Stephen Solarz, a top Democratic spokesman on foreign affairs, responded:

> One could argue, for example, that the United States should aid the African National Congress. . . . Yet providing military support to the ANC is the wrong way to protect U.S. interests. Whatever its merits, this position would not be supported by the American public or by America's friends overseas. The United States should be aiming to minimize violence rather than increase it. . . .
>
> In the end, the descent into violence may be inevitable, bringing untold suffering. . . . Although it is important for the United States to promote democracy and stem the spread of communist ideology, ideological objectives must not be the primary, let alone sole, consideration behind U.S. insurgency policy.[77]

What the Solarz group seemed to be saying, to the alarm of sanction opponents, was that it was fine for the United States to exert a bland, generalized pressure that would tend to change things. We could even do this in such a way that the ANC might benefit. But having done so, the United States could not involve itself in shaping the outcome of that generic pressure. Such a policy seeks to avoid accountability for its effects, but it cannot. If the United States is to resort to such a potentially powerful foreign-policy tool as the economic carrot and stick, we cannot abdicate our responsibility for the consequences.

7

WHEN PUSH COMES TO SHOVE: ARMING GUERILLAS

> Any people anywhere, being inclined and having the power, have the right to rise up and shake off the existing government and form a new one that suits them. This is a most valuable and sacred right—a right which, we hope and believe, is to liberate the world.
> —ABRAHAM LINCOLN
> Speech on the Mexican-American War,
> 12 January 1848

DEMOCRATIC LEADERS are fortunate to have at their disposal many foreign-policy tools that are not violent and indeed involve only minimal risk of prompting violence from others. Naturally, tyrants would prefer that even these nonviolent methods not be used. So they blast Western radio broadcasts as "subversive" and trade limits as acts of "economic warfare." It is difficult to take such rhetoric seriously, though, so far out of proportion is it to the alleged offense.

But what if other countries began acting on their own bombast? What if the Soviet Union or Cuba or South Africa or any other country threatened actual war if the United States did not trade with them on certain terms, or stop criticizing human rights violations? In that case, the only choice for American foreign policy would be either to risk war on the one hand or, on the other, to renounce virtually all methods of influence, however benign.

To yield to such threats would be tantamount to surrender. Yet many respected leaders argue we should do just that when it comes to one particular lever of influence. They propose that the United States unilaterally forswear shipping arms to what we have called third-force movements (neither communist nor fascist) even when those movements face well-financed troops armed by undemocratic states. Still others would not completely rule out such assistance in principle. Yet they always seem to have a plausible argument, couched in pragmatic rhetoric, for opposing aid.

It is easy to understand the reluctance that some people feel toward assisting foreign guerillas. Guerillas, after all, kill people. Large numbers of guerillas kill large numbers of people. Not a pleasant subject, killing.

Inevitably, too, some weapons, if that is what we send, will go to people who will misuse the weapons—using them not to kill other soldiers but to steal property, rape women, or to wound or kill innocent civilians, even children. It would be nice to arm freedom fighters without arming, even inadvertently and incidentally, thugs.

Furthermore, though our leaders may promise that there will be "no U.S. combat troops," they have used similar words before, then withdrawn those words when they felt that U.S.-backed forces couldn't win on their own and determined we needed to help them more. So when a U.S. leader says he has "no plans" to send American forces to a country, voters are entitled to believe that whatever his "plans," there is a substantial risk of its happening anyway.

Finally, there is a large presumption in my own description of the people America sends arms to as a "third" or "democratic" force of "freedom fighters." Critics would dispute that characterization hotly, as applied to most of the rebel groups fighting tyrannous governments around the world. Many who joined the Nicaraguan contras in the 1980s, for instance, belonged to the fearsome National Guard of dictator Anastasio Somoza in the 1970s. Meanwhile, Jonas Savimbi—leader of the Unita rebels in Angola—was himself once a communist, and continued taking aid from the racist government of South Africa. The mujahedin of Afghanistan enjoyed wide support in the U.S. Congress, yet these Moslem fundamentalists—aided by, among others, Iran and Red China—hardly advocated a program of pure democracy.[1] Nor did the African National Congress (which unlike the others named has not, as far as we know, received U.S. aid) and some other groups engaged in armed struggle against Pretorian apartheid. In Cambodia, Laos, and Vietnam, guerillas took up arms against the communist governments that dominate Southeast Asia. Yet their ranks included the Khmer Rouge, which during a brief rule in the 1970s managed to slaughter perhaps a third of the nation's population.

The program and motives of any political group are often difficult to ascertain. In the United States, both the Republicans and the Democrats have claimed in repeated elections that their party would reduce the federal budget deficit; it's still not clear to many of us which one was right. The same uncertainty is doubly applicable to contentions about human rights between warring factions in a civil war.

Who's Guerilla Who

One way to tell if someone is a freedom fighter is to read what he writes and says. You would think that future despots would lie about their intentions, and often they do. Yet they also tell the truth now and then, laying out their actual plans in some detail. Hitler's *Mein Kampf* minced no words about his attitude toward Jews. Lenin often promised "democracy" but was undisguisedly contemptuous of "bourgeois democracy," which he characterized as the kind with elections and a free press and competing political parties.

Even Nicaragua's Sandinista leaders revealed their intentions to a surprising degree, though under a layer or two of prodemocracy slogans. In 1971, one of the founders of the Sandinista movement, Carlos Fonseca Amador, sent a message to the Soviet Communist Party declaring that "the ideals of the immortal Lenin are a guiding star in the struggle" and portraying the Sandinista front as "the successor of the Bolshevik October Revolution."[2] A scattered group of political journals such as *Human Events* issued warnings about the Sandinistas. They were of course dismissed as paranoid. As a contrite U.S. State Department report later put it, "Had the world been listening earlier, it might have anticipated the Sandinistas' intentions."[3]

It's possible, of course, that the predominantly pro-Western freedom fighters of the 1980s are being less frank than the mostly communist guerillas of the 1960s and 1970s. The world has little experience with democratic resistance movements defeating Soviet-aligned governments. So one must speculate about the sincerity of such groups as Angola's Unita or the Nicaraguan contras. Still, there are sound reasons for thinking that these military outfits are sincere in their commitment to democracy, as others have been in promising Marxist nondemocracy.

As we have seen, for example, more than a dozen military leaders in Latin America made good on announced plans to hold elections from 1978 to 1988. So did the generals of Turkey, Spain, and Portugal (see chapters 1, 4, and 6). Guerilla leaders have even more reason to make their oaths of democracy credible, for unlike established generals executing a coup d'état, the guerilla can gain power only by attracting volunteers to fight and popular support among the peasantry to secure food and shelter. That a substantial guerilla army even exists in a country indicates that the people have some genuine grievance and that those fighting enjoy at least some confidence.

In fact, a guerilla movement's popular support—both its magnitude and its character—is another means of judging the fit between statements and intentions. The background of its leaders is another. We might also consider a movement's present sources of aid, though this can be a highly fallible test: Guerillas can't be choosers, and the mere fact that a movement accepts arms from the Soviet Union or South Africa doesn't necessarily mean it wants to model its country after the donor's.

Where these standards give a clear indication of whether a particular force is democratic, our job is easy. Yet even where they don't—as will often be the case—the United States need not stand aside until the evidence is so clear that all but a handful of doubters are satisfied. We can ask opposition leaders what they stand for, probe their intentions, even force their hand to a certain extent. Support for certain groups can be made conditional on an adjustment of its personnel or policies.

As applied to the resistance groups established in the seventies and eighties, these tests show that there is indeed a democratic movement under way, with a number of revolutionaries who deserve U.S. help.

Afghanistan

The easiest case to settle, at least for the U.S. domestic debate, has been in Afghanistan. Rebels there began a tenacious resistance against a Marxist puppet regime even before the Soviet invasion of 1979. The mujahedin have enjoyed more support from the United States than all other such groups combined: about $500 million in 1986. The heavily Democratic House of Representatives, in fact, generally voted to provide more money than was requested by a Republican White House to implement its "Reagan Doctrine."

Still, many of the arguments used against arming other rebel groups could have been pointed at the mujahedin. They took aid from communist China and terrorist Iran. Among their ranks were supporters of the theocratic, oligarchic type of regime that existed before the Marxist takeover, and others who espouse what most Americans would consider undesirable forms of government. As in any army, there were some bad characters, and hence tales of occasional abuse of civilians by the rebels. Even the Heritage Foundation magazine *Policy Review* conceded, "There is little likelihood that if they came to power they would establish a democratic government respectful of civil liberties."⁴ Finally, while it is obviously in the U.S. interest for the Soviets to suffer bad consequences as a result of their invasion, Afghanistan is hardly what most Americans would consider a strategically important country.

One reason these imperfections didn't cripple widespread support for the Afghan rebels was the widespread support for the Afghan rebels. That is to say, the mujahedin were popular with both Republicans and Democrats from the start, which was during the presidency of Jimmy Carter. Carter wanted to do something to alter his image of softness-on-the-Soviets, and Republicans in Congress at the time obliged gladly. The main complaints from Capitol Hill, in fact, have come from members such as Senator Bill Bradley, Democrat from New Jersey, who argued that the Reagan administration was damaging the freedom-fighter cause by promoting peace talks at which the Afghan rebels weren't allowed to participate.[5]

The mujahedin were also fortunate, in a sense, in finding themselves up against actual Soviet troops. Many freedom fighters face only Soviet proxy forces: the estimated 20,000 Cuban troops in Ethiopia, the 40,000 Cubans in Angola, nearly 20,000 Soviet-bloc troops and advisers in Mozambique, and the troops of Vietnam occupying most of Cambodia and Laos.[6] By contrast, the spectacle of more than 100,000 Russian troops openly violating a national border riveted world attention, bringing little-known Afghanistan to the front pages of American newspapers. So did the continuing barbarities practiced by Soviet troops, including widespread use of chemical weapons and the planting of small toylike bombs designed to blow the limbs (and limbs only) off of children.[7] Despite such tactics, the Soviets continued to suffer heavy losses. An estimated 15,000 to 22,000 Soviet soldiers died in the war from 1979 through 1988; several times that number were wounded.[8]

It is wonderful, of course, to see tyranny pay such a price, and inspiring to see the Afghans fight so bravely. Still, it would be nice to see the same flexible thinking that allows U.S. leadership to back the mujahedin, despite their imperfections, applied to other worthy groups. If they may include former guardsmen from the previous government, why can't the Nicaraguan contras? If aid from a despotic power does not forever taint the Afghans, why so with Angola's Jonas Savimbi?

Angola

Savimbi, in fact, constituted what should have been a relatively easy case in meeting most of our standards for "freedom fighter." Far from being a puppet dependent on U.S. support, he and his Unita troops fought on for years, after the communist coup of 1975, without any direct American aid, which was banned under the Clark Ammendment. ("Unita" stands for the National Union for the Total Independence of Angola.) The rebels enjoyed broad support, and throughout the 1980s, Savimbi's forces generally controlled about one-third of the territory of Angola.[9]

Furthermore, Savimbi's commitment to actual democracy was as clear as, or clearer than, that of any other guerilla leader. Savimbi took back to the bush only after his party was cheated of an apparent election victory in 1975. In June of 1985, he and U.S. political activist Lewis Lehrman led a Democratic International in Jamba, Angola, with freedom fighters from several countries gathering to discuss how to make democracy triumph.[10] Although some members of Congress bitterly opposed aid to Savimbi when it was at last approved for 1986, the measure was proposed and pushed through by Democrats. Savimbi, then, seemed likely to enjoy steady bipartisan support from the United States, even though Unita, like the mujahedin, was a far cry from the League of Women Voters.

Cambodia

The Cambodian resistance posed a more complicated problem because it was really several resistance movements—including factions led by the murderous Khmer Rouge and the royal ruler who preceded them, Prince Sihanouk. A third army took root under the leadership of Son Sann, former prime minister of Cambodia and a charismatic democrat. The forces of the Khmer Rouge generally outnumbered the noncommunist armies of Sihanouk and Sann by a factor of three to two. Even so, according to one expert on the region, Al Santoli, the communists had "little political power and little control over the civilian camps [of Cambodian refugees]."[11] Sann was far more popular, by most accounts. Still, as of 1985, U.S. officials estimated, there were 30,000 men under arms fighting for the Chinese-backed Khmer Rouge, 10,000 fighting for Sihanouk, and another 12,000 to 14,000 fighting for Sann's Khmer People's National Liberation Front.[12]

There were, one might say, two struggles in Cambodia. One was between the government and the combined forces of the rebels. The other was within the rebel camp itself to see who would dominate the resistance.

It was mainly this latter struggle that Representative Stephen Solarz had in mind when he proposed providing the Sihanouk and Sann factions with $5 million in assistance, mostly for medical supplies and training, in 1985. Solarz was under no delusions that $5 million would actually tip the scales between the rebel forces of some 50,000 and the occupying Vietnamese army of more than 150,000. He did recognize that the resistance has a chance of achieving a military or political victory in the longer run (Vietnam has declared its intention of pulling out eventually), and that it was in our interests that the democrats predominate. Yet for several years, the United States, fearful of irritating Red China, actually leaned toward the communist Khmer Rouge and away from aiding Sihanouk and Sann. The Solarz Amendment providing assistance to the democrats was thus at once a skillful probe of the existing character of the resistance and a slight lift to the characteristics most Americans would favor. "The basic purpose," as Solarz aide Dawn Calabria put it, "was to strengthen the non-communist political forces within the resistance, so that it remains a strong presence in the field and in the political and diplomatic theatre."[13]

WHEN PUSH COMES TO SHOVE

Nicaragua

Of all the freedom-fighter groups that sought or received U.S. aid in the 1980s, the contras of Nicaragua stirred the most passion. In the interests of making a series of "freedom-fighter" tests seem objective and evenhanded, it would behoove one to say that the Nicaraguan resistance constituted a close call, a borderline case. Yet the contras, by the tests outlined, deserved help perhaps more clearly than the others.

That the contra debate proved so bitter in the United States was attributable chiefly to domestic politics, in particular the failure of the Reagan administration to devise a coherent policy and then talk and behave as if the policy made sense. It is quite understandable, given those errors, that the Nicaraguan resistance fomented such mutual frustration and resentment, with Democrats calling Republicans criminals and warmongers, and Republicans calling Democrats tools of world communism. But it would be posturing to suggest that the standards for judging resistance movements offer only ambiguous guidance concerning the contras. Indeed, if one judged the Nicaraguan guerillas in the same way America judged other, similar movements, they emerged as a deserving group of patriots.

Repeatedly, the contras promised rapid elections in the event they came to power. In 1987, the resistance leaders held a congress to set strategy and to draft a statement of the movement's purposes, goals, and philosophy, a sort of Declaration of Independence.[14] The contras also promised something which, to my knowledge, no comparable group, communist or democratic, had ever promised. The members of the contra directorate said that if their forces triumphed, they would all abstain from holding any government positions for one year, so that elections would be fair and a civilian leadership could emerge.

Again, all this could have been a clever and elaborate lie made in order to win U.S. assistance. Yet the one clear liar in the Nicaragua debate was the Sandinista government, which in 1979 promised pluralism and fair elections to the Organization of American States, and then proceeded to censor the press, jail dissenters, harass churches, and outlaw meaningful political parties.[15] Furthermore, the contra leaders met virtually every condition imposed on them by Congress and the Reagan administration as a price of U.S. support. They enacted specific changes in the structure of the resistance, spelled out detailed plans for a transition to democracy, and disciplined soldiers found guilty of reprisals or attacks on civilians. They agreed to intrusive monitoring by U.S. officials and private Western human rights groups and journalists. Thus, contra abuses could be seen, reported, and corrected. By contrast, the Sandinistas, an organized government with substantially greater resources, consistently rejected meaningful oversight by outside groups or peaceful internal opponents.

None of this rescued the Nicaraguan freedom fighters from a flurry of accusations. The contras were denounced for including numerous members of the Somoza regime in their ranks, the implication being that they would seek to establish a Somoza-style dictatorship once in power. Yet the political leadership of the resistance consisted wholly of active Somoza opponents, several of whom had been jailed by the ex-dictator and later served in the Sandinista government. The contra military leadership, as might be expected, included soldiers who had fought for the old regime: about 23 percent of the leaders had served in Somoza's National Guard. Yet 48 percent of the military leaders were former Sandinistas. The portrait of a force of Somocista mercenaries is even more absurd as applied to the young farmers and disgruntled Sandinista draftees that form the bulk of the contra army. Many fought for no money at all, while the typical pay for resistance members was $23 a month, or about 20 percent of the average monthly wage for a worker in Nicaragua.[16]

Journalist Fred Barnes camped out with the freedom fighters in 1986 and reported in *The New Republic:*

> The foot soldiers are exactly the stoical peasant fighters that 1960s radicals fantasized about in other contexts. . . .
> Why would thousands of men and boys gather along this remote, mountainous border of Nicaragua to fight the Sandinistas? It's not the money. They don't get any. I talked to scores of contras and got basically two answers.
> Most of the officers have ideological reasons. They hate communism. Or they love democracy.
> The common soldiers, the grunts, answer quite differently. Politics is meaningless to them, ideology even less so. They have specific grievances against the Sandinistas. Land was taken. Money was confiscated. A relative killed or jailed. A religious sect persecuted. Or, most common, conscription in the Sandinista army was imminent.[17]

So much for the background of the resistance members and their leaders. Did the contras enjoy popular support? Certainly they did among the 10 to 20 percent of Nicaragua's population that fled the country with the advent of Sandinista rule—an exodus on a scale with those of Cuba, Cambodia, and Afghanistan. If that many people have taken the painful step of leaving their homes, of course, then the level of discontent is much higher. Refugees interviewed by the human rights monitor Puebla Institute were by no means uniformly supportive of the contras. But nearly all opposed the Sandinistas, and reported many more abuses by government troops than by the guerillas. Within a few years, moreover, the resistance had recruited between two and four times as many volunteers as there were in the Sandinista Front at the time Somoza was ousted. They formed the largest guerilla resistance army in Central America.[18]

WHEN PUSH COMES TO SHOVE

Objective polls cannot be conducted in Nicaragua. When the Gallup organization asked people from neighboring countries about the struggle, however, the same pattern of support for the resistance emerged. In several polls conducted in Costa Rica, Honduras, El Salvador, and Guatemala, people were asked their attitudes about the contras and the Sandinistas. When asked "Which side in the conflict do you think the majority of the people of Nicaragua support?" Salvadorans estimated that Nicaraguans favored the contras by a plurality of 46 percent to 20 percent. In the other countries, the estimated margin for the resistance was larger: 72 percent to 12 percent in Costa Rica, 60 percent to 23 percent in Guatemala, and 75 percent to 14 percent in Honduras. Another question: "There are people living in the area of Nicaragua where there is armed conflict between the Sandinista government forces and the Contra opposition forces. Which of these two forces generally treats the people with more consideration?" Again, only in El Salvador was the margin less than 5 to 1, with 46 percent saying the contras treated people better, 10 percent saying the Sandinistas, in comparison with 72 to 6 percent in Costa Rica, 74 to 6 in Honduras, and 60 to 18 in Guatemala. In more than one poll, majorities of 3-to-1 to 4-to-1 indicated their support for U.S. aid to the contras and for similar aid from their own countries.[19]

Even many opponents of aid to the resistance said that they would support a U.S. invasion of Nicaragua if it attacked one of its neighbors. These critics questioned Reagan's methods of opposing communism in Nicaragua, but not the importance of such opposition. After all, Nicaragua is closer to our shores than other countries in which anticommunist civil war is being waged. And a Soviet base there, as in Cuba, would be within easy striking distance of the United States.

It was precisely Nicaragua's proximity that helped make for such a bitter debate. No one seriously thought a U.S. invasion of, say, Afghanistan, could happen. But many serious people—Alexander Haig, Robert Dole, Jeane Kirkpatrick, and others—proposed U.S. military action against Nicaragua. And U.S. forces did land to liberate the nearby island of Grenada in 1983. So it was one thing to vote a few million dollars in aid to Savimbi or the mujahedin. Central America is not so remote, and U.S. influence is such that a vote of Congress might actually determine the fate of a Nicaragua, El Salvador, or Guatemala.

At the least, though, the contras deserved support sufficient to keep their movement alive and allow them to demonstrate that their commitment to democracy, unlike that of the Sandinistas, was sincere. The *New York Times,* no enthusiast of the contra cause generally, put it well in an editorial on a congressional proposal to assist the guerillas—one that demanded increased sensitivity to human rights. "America's available choices," the editorial read, "depend on discernible facts. By giving the President some of what he asks, with the strings that he now offers to accept, Congress may actually get those facts."[20]

South Africa

Though it was never seriously proposed, the United States should have considered support for the African National Congress as early as 1983. Yes, the ANC includes among its leaders a number of Communist Party officials, and receives aid from the Soviet Union. Yet for years, the United States has pressured the country's apartheid government with sanctions and other human rights penalties. The ANC is likely to be a principal beneficiary of those pressures, perhaps playing a decisive role in the formation of a future government. So the character of the ANC is of paramount concern to American policy, just as the question of who would succeed Somoza or the shah was in the 1970s. Aid, at the least, might serve as a probe of the true intentions of the ANC. U.S. assistance could positively strengthen those elements of the ANC that want a true democracy, as opposed to the communist elements. It might serve to wean democrats away from the ANC if it clings to strong ties with the Soviets. Or, it might turn out that the ANC does not support democracy, in which case it would still be worth the price of aid to establish this fact clearly and publicly.

Time and new evidence may prove some of these tentative judgments about the merits of particular resistance groups wrong. The purpose of discussing them has not been to give an exhaustive defense of the contras or the mujahedin; volumes of studies and congressional hearings have been devoted to each. The reason, rather, has been chiefly illustrative: to show how the abstract tests tend to work in practice. Particular causes will come and go. My concern is with the standard by which we judge what groups to support.[21]

Even when Americans arrive at a broad agreement that particular freedom fighters deserve our help, difficult issues remain. What is it, for example, that we want to "help" them to do? Win a conventional military victory, taking over a progressively larger share of territory and eventually establishing a new government? Sustain sufficient pressure on the government to effect its collapse? Force the government not to outright capitulation, but to negotiate for a coalition government, with greater freedoms now and perhaps elections in the future? Raise the cost to tyrants of their own repressions, even with no hope of victory in sight? Or do we perhaps want our objective to be all of the above—that is, to simply assist various resistance groups without elaborate or precise expectations of a specific result? Finally, whatever outcomes we may wish to promote, the question arises: How to promote them?

Naturally, it's impossible to form an abstract model for aiding freedom fighters that would cover all possible cases. But the discussion is greatly simplified by two factors. The first factor flows from similarities between the resistance movements themselves. The second consists of limitations imposed by our own system, defining what democracies can and cannot do effectively.

Doctrinal Disputes

The freedom fighters that sparked such controversy in the seventies and eighties all shared important characteristics. They all professed to be democratic in nature, and they all shared a common strategy of warfare emphasizing mobile forces, quick strikes, and low-intensity struggle, summed up by the very term often used to describe them: guerillas.

What is the essence of guerilla warfare? T. E. Lawrence, a noted analyst of irregular warfare, defined the guerilla's objective as "the erosion of the will of the stronger." In the early and middle parts of the twentieth century, of course, much of the eroding was done by communists. Vietnamese general Vo Nguyen Giap, the victor at Dien Bien Phu, proclaimed: "Guerillas rely on heroic spirit to triumph over modern weapons." Mao Tse-tung, perhaps the century's foremost guerilla, emphasized the supremacy of spirit and will over the material, declaring: "It is people, not things, that are decisive in a war." Or, as a correspondent who followed Fidel Castro's triumph put it in a U.S. Marine publication: "Machinery does not win wars. Men do."[22]

If communists, who propound an analysis of human events based on dialectical materialism, understand this reality of ideopolitik, how much more should guerillas fighting for democracy. And they do. Nicaraguan Arturo Cruz, son of one of the founders of the contras, conceded in 1986 that "it may be unlikely that the resistance will win conventional military victories in the months ahead. But if it can sustain itself as an effective military presence inside the country, it can buy the time it needs to strengthen its political base. . . . As the costs increase and their own domestic pressures mount, Havana and Moscow will have to ask how great a commitment they are willing to make to sustain this highly vulnerable outpost in Central America."[23] The freedom fighters of Afghanistan and Angola, though they were better armed, and controlled some territories throughout the 1980s, applied much the same model. "We wage a protracted conflict," one mujahedin leader said at a meeting with editorial writers for the *Wall Street Journal* in 1984. "We will continue. That is what will finally show the Soviet Union that they might as well leave." Accordingly, the Afghans often practiced the same tactic of the "five-minute attack" preached by Mao.[24] So did Jonas Savimbi, who told journalist Fred Reed that his forces "spread all over the country and don't offer a target. . . . If we use regulars, we are giving a target to the enemy. They bring tanks and [fighter planes]. But when they think we are not there, that's when the guerillas are there." One Unita leader said, "We have the means to continue 20 years or more."[25]

This being the strategy of the guerillas, it is easy to identify the strategic hinge of their struggle: time. If freedom fighters and their democratic supporters can outlast totalitarian regimes, they can triumph. If the tyrants have more staying power, then guerilla struggle is futile, and the West must find other means to promote democracy.

It follows that meaningful U.S. efforts to aid freedom fighters must have as their animating goal sustainability. Policies must be devised that will not be overturned by the next public-opinion poll, the next Congress, or the next president. Perhaps the easiest way to describe what such a sustainable policy would look like is to ascertain what it would not look like.

The policy cannot be—if the public is to understand it and support it—covert. This is not, however, for the reasons some people advance. It isn't because covert acts are antithetical to democracy in and of themselves. Voters may decide that they want the country to do certain things in secret, or give a president or Congress power to take actions without telling anyone, even the voters. In one sense, ignorance is the essence of representative democracy, which enables us to have other people make decisions for us. The proceedings of the meetings that led to the framing of our Constitution remained secret for more than a generation, until Congress ordered the publication of James Madison's notes and other documents, locked in a State Department vault, in 1818. Thomas Jefferson launched a secret war against the Barbary Coast pirates, and American history offers plenty of examples right up into the 1980s of arms and even U.S. forces being used in secret.[26]

Nor is it true that democracies cannot keep any secrets. Though volumes have been written on the question, Americans still are not certain what actions Franklin Roosevelt did and did not authorize in transferring resources to Great Britain and readying the U.S. fleet at Pearl Harbor—actions and inactions that paved the country's way into World War II. Nor is it clear precisely what role the Central Intelligence Agency played in the revolt in Hungary: Author and journalist David Martin cites evidence that the agency was training an actual army of freedom fighters to liberate the country, but the revolution erupted in 1956 before it could be activated.[27] In democratic France, every year, the budget for whole weapons programs is prepared and approved without even the legislature being briefed, let alone the general public.[28] The U.S. Defense Department and Lockheed Aerospace spent years building a fighter plane with Stealth radar-evading technology that went unreported. We also managed to aid the mujahedin and other freedom fighters for some time until some (not all) of the facts came out.

Yet these particular covert operations are the exceptions that prove the rule. Each of these was either short-lived, or involved a relatively small number of people, or some operation confined to a limited space, or came at a time of great crisis, or all of these things. And aspects of each operation eventually did come out. A large enterprise—assisting guerillas in a de facto war—does not enjoy these aids to secrecy.

The key distinction to be made is between covert acts, which are part of a policy, and the policy itself. Acts can be covert in a democracy, and at times ought to be. Policies cannot be covert in a democracy, and never ought to be. Unfortunately, this distinction is often lost on particular officials in government. To cite just one example of that confusion, we have this statement by Robert C. McFarlane, Reagan's national security adviser during the launching of the arms sales to Iran:

> Do the American people really want their president, faced with the question of whether a friend like Salvador or Korea or Israel is being attacked, to have no other options than to go to war or to do nothing? I don't think so. . . . Should we not have some sort of intermediate option of policy, covert action?[29]

This notion of covert war as a kind of moderate's halfway house, between paralysis and send-in-the-marines, is not peculiar to Mr. McFarlane. It is not even especially debilitating in many areas where the distinction between single acts and a whole policy blurs, or when the policy undertaken is one which, if it were public, would not engender great controversy anyway. An example here would be the Nixon opening to China, established with the most elaborate secrecy, and in contradiction of some U.S. public pronouncements. Covertness is crippling, however, to an enterprise the essence of which is building solid, lasting public support.

Another requirement is that U.S. aid to a given guerilla group be substantial enough to have a material impact on the group's success. Token assistance, after all, will carry with it many of the risks of U.S. involvement, with none of the benefits. It may be sustained for a year or two if there is a plausible function—as in the case of the Solarz provision of funds for the Cambodian resistance. Or U.S. aid may persist if some other democracy is bearing the brunt of supporting the freedom fighters, as was the case in France's interventions in Chad in the 1980s, or in Israel's 1982 invasion of Lebanon, before U.S. marines rescued the terrorist Palestinian Liberation Organization. This is not to say that such tokenism cannot be attempted, and even survive as policy for a time, but it will rest on sandy ground.

As with secrecy, of course, tokenism poses a severe temptation to democratic elites. It seems to offer a way to punish enemies on the cheap, allowing a combination of high rhetoric and low budget figures. Alvin Bernstein, a thoughtful student of warfare at the U.S. Naval War College, advanced this rationale as well as anyone in an article for *Policy Review:*

> The United States is sending about $250 million a year to the Afghan *mujahideen,* $100 million to the contras of Nicaragua, $15 million to Jonas Savimbi's UNITA forces in Angola, and $3.5 million to two non-Communist guerilla organizations in Cambodia. In none of these countries is it likely that the resistance movements will achieve total victory. . . . But the Reagan Doctrine as the policy of supporting anti-Communist insurgencies has proved to be a highly cost-effective way of limiting the damage to American security interests.
>
> Some of the Reagan Doctrine's more romantic proponents conjure visions of a rollback of the Soviet empire. . . . In truth, [though,] the Reagan Doctrine is a doctrine of last resort . . . a defensive strategy for stopping the Soviet Union from taking full advantage of its territorial gains. Its purpose is to keep the Soviets from being in a geostrategic position where they can prevent the United States from honoring its commitments.[30]

Even Charles Krauthammer, who won a richly deserved Pulitzer Prize largely for his role as the Reagan Doctrine's muse, seemed to imply that hosannas to freedom were largely an opportunistic pretense. Describing the doctrine, he wrote: "The elements are simple: anti-communist revolution as a tactic. Containment as the strategy. And freedom as the rationale."[31]

This vision of freedom fighters as cost-effective bleeders for U.S. "geostrategic" designs has strong appeal to many U.S. intellectuals. It—and not the notion of helping freedom because it is a noble cause—was in fact the dominant line of thinking among elite supporters of freedom-fighter aid during the Reagan years.[32] Yet the cynicism it implies, if not intends, invites contempt from Americans and the world.

The first problem is that freedom fighters, and their potential recruits, aren't stupid. They are being asked to risk all they have, property and family and life itself, for a cause. The cause is their own freedom. To enlist them merely as low-cost mercenaries for the United States is not only contemptible, but self-defeating, because most people will not give away everything to support a cause that cannot succeed.

Another problem is that U.S. voters aren't stupid, either. However small the amounts involved, they know that they are being asked to support a policy that involves at least some risk to our own country. Opposition parties will demand to know why we are taking such risks for a policy that is unlikely to tip the struggle anyway.

To his credit, Ronald Reagan denied that the Reagan Doctrine matched the Bernstein description of it. "Some have argued that the regional wars in which the Soviet Union is embroiled provide an opportunity to 'bleed' the Soviets," he told the Congress in a 1986 message. "This is not our policy." The idea, he insisted, was no less than to secure "freedom."[33] Yet despite this and other denials, Bernstein and others were correct in a crucial sense. For the limited policy actions of the Reagan administration, both critics and supporters noted, often flatly contradicted its revolutionary rhetoric.

Another problem with the low-cost bleeder view of the freedom fighter is that it isn't accurate. It's true that supplying freedom fighters in their early stages is inexpensive, but that isn't the whole truth. The more successful the effort, the more costly it becomes. Guerillas are, as Krauthammer claimed in his eloquent propagation of the third-force doctrine, "astonishingly cheap" compared to opposing conventional armies—when the guerillas are in their initial stages.[34] But the costs rise as the guerillas gain recruits and effectiveness, and final victory is usually achieved not by guerillas as such, but by a guerilla movement that has evolved into something of a regular standing army. Aiding guerillas in South Vietnam was a low initial investment for the Soviets and the North Vietnamese. Yet the guerillas themselves never won; Saigon fell to a full-scale invasion by the North's conventional army. Soviet and Chinese aid to the North Vietnamese communists started at about $100 million in the mid-1950s, but grew to more than eight times that amount in 1966 and more than $1 billion by 1974.[35]

In the same way, the small sums of money sent by the United States to guerilla movements in the Reagan years (actually, the amount approached $1 billion in 1988) were best viewed as a mere down payment on a doctrine, not a doctrine itself. As Alan Tonelson, the editor of *Foreign Policy,* put it in one exchange:

> In his State of the Union speech, President Reagan explained why [Americans] can take no comfort from Krauthammer-like observations that today's skimpy U.S. aid for anticommunists is "astonishingly cheap." American aid, Reagan contended, must not permit these forces "just to fight and die for freedom, but to fight and win for freedom." Moreover, he seems to recognize that selling neo-interventionism by stressing how cheap it is is the perfect way to tell the Soviets that they can prevail simply by upping the ante.[36]

Tonelson points to another reason why democracies will find it difficult or impossible to build support for freedom fighters on the Bernstein model. We have been talking as if the cost of victory were a static calculation involving one variable. It is instead dynamic and involves at least one other variable, namely the country or countries backing totalitarian dictatorships: generally, the Soviet Union, Cuba, or one of their surrogates. A quick glance at the support offered by America to freedom fighters, and the comparable support provided by the Soviets to their allies, takes us into a more complex calculus. (See figure 7.1.)

In the post-Vietnam period, the Soviets repeatedly proved willing not only to apply increasing resources but to move to new levels of political and psycho-

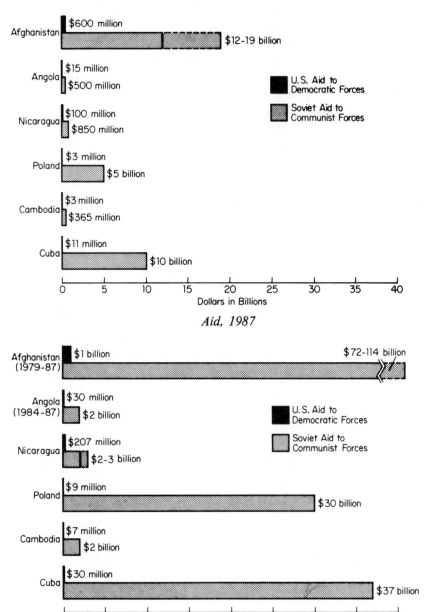

FIGURE 7.1

Doctrine or Down Payment? A Comparison

Aid, 1987

Cumulative Aid, 1981–87[a]

SOURCE: Compiled by the author and Adam Lieberman for the Alexis de Tocqueville Institution.
NOTE: Figures rounded. Though there was no substantial armed resistance in Cuba or Poland, figures on nonmilitary aid to various resistance forces—for example, spending on Radio Martí broadcasts to Cuba and aid to the Solidarity Union by the National Endowment for Democracy—may be of interest for comparison.[37]
[a]Unless otherwise indicated.

logical commitments if their clients needed help. What began simply with Soviet agents in Afghanistan grew into a full-fledged military invasion, backed with increasingly sophisticated weapons. Aid to proxy forces in Angola became Soviet and Cuban advisers, then thousands of Cuban troops, and finally, according to widespread reports in 1987, Soviet direction of the Luanda regime's war effort. Soviet forces occupied actual air-defense batteries in Cuba and Syria, a position that would have been unthinkable in the 1960s. Moscow also asserted increasing control over military operations in Ethiopia, sent armored helicopters to Nicaragua, and established forward naval and air bases in Vietnam to aid its continuing and expensive war against its neighbors.[38] Thus, Soviet aid to socialist forces not only typically dwarfed U.S. aid to freedom fighters; it rose in response to our efforts. For some years after Korea, the Soviets hesitated to make such massive, frontal commitments. Yet as author Bruce D. Porter has shown, they gradually overcame such apprehensions, building up to the use of Soviet advisers in war zones in Vietnam, actual Soviet commanders in the Ogaden war, and Soviet ground troops in Afghanistan.[39]

"The more you give the contras," Costa Rican President Oscar Arias told the *New York Times* in 1986, "the more Ortega gets from the Soviets. . . . You can't overthrow the Sandinistas."[40] This description, of a Soviet leadership willing and able to pay any price to secure socialism, is an accepted wisdom among Western elites, and is consistent with the statistics presented above. Still, that the Soviets were willing to up the ante for one or two hands does not mean they are able and willing to do so indefinitely. Soviet resources are finite; the Kremlin cannot spend more every year on everything. Hence, historically, Soviet leaders have often reduced and even eliminated commitment to some projects in order to redouble their efforts on others that are more promising or pressing.[41] America's experience at supporting guerilla movements is of course relatively limited. Yet what evidence there is undermines the view of the Soviet Union as monolithically determined and boundlessly committed to victory.

In 1987, for example, the Soviets refused a Nicaraguan request to increase the country's supply of free Russian oil, touching off an economic crisis. Partly as a result, the Sandinistas grudgingly acceded in the coming months to indirect talks with the contras and with other Nicaraguan opposition leaders. Similarly, in 1987 and 1988, Soviet television stations were airing stories on the agony of the Afghan war, even talking of plans to pull out.

Many of Bernstein's and Krauthammer's points are well taken. Freedom fighters, achieving liberation through their own exertions with U.S. aid, can achieve victory for less money, and without the potential loss of U.S. life and the risk of American prestige involved in direct uses of military force. This is obvious.[42] To make these undeniable advantages of aid to freedom fighters the principal rationale of a strategy for helping them, however, is to invite contempt from all concerned—the Soviets, the American voters, and the very people we are trying to help. It tells freedom fighters, and their potential recruits, that they are mere bleeding pawns in the service of a fickle U.S. It tells the voters that they, too, are being asked to take some risks—but for a cause that the government has undertaken in large part only because it costs little and can easily be abandoned. And it encourages our opponents to simply up the ante and hope to drive the U.S. out of the bidding.

Henry Kissinger saw just this dynamic at work in his efforts to conclude the Vietnam War. Here he writes perceptively of one proposal by Richard Nixon to escalate the war—a suggestion for massive strikes against the North and its sanctuaries in Cambodia that might create pressures for a final settlement:

> Nixon dropped the subject after ten minutes and never returned to it. But in retrospect I believe we should have taken it more seriously.
>
> The bane of our actions in Vietnam was their hesitancy; we were always trying to calculate with fine precision the absolute minimum of force or of time, leaving no margin for error or confusion, encouraging our adversaries to hold on until our doubts overrode our efforts.
>
> Perhaps the most difficult lesson for a national leader to learn is that with respect to the use of military force, his basic choice is to act or to refrain from acting. He will not be able to take away the moral curse of using force by employing it halfheartedly or incompetently. There are no rewards for exhibiting one's doubts in vacillation; statesmen get no prizes for failing with restraint. Once committed, they must prevail. If they are not prepared to prevail, they should not commit their nation's power.[43]

This maxim on the direct use of U.S. force, of course, does not apply fully to policies, such as aid to resistance groups, where there is only a risk of force. Democratic leaders, however, would be wise to keep Kissinger's general model in mind. In foreign policy, and particularly in wars, half a loaf is not necessarily better than none, and may be a disaster.

There is another argument for a sustainable policy of aiding freedom fighters, this one having to do with bureaucracy. U.S. leaders may be elected by, and answerable to, the people, but their policies must be carried out by agencies: the Defense Department, the Department of State, the Central Intelligence Agency, the U.S. Information Agency, the National Security Council, and others. These departments of government have vested interests of their own. They are filled with people who may not share the policy of the agency itself, or of the president above them. Even those who agree may have different views about how a policy should be implemented.

This reality was the cause of a good deal of confusion during the Reagan administration. Reagan supporters often accused the president of having the right ideas but failing to see that they were carried out. Opponents made a similar charge for different purposes, saying that Reagan's policies were not only wrong, but that the president himself was out of touch. To both sorts of attacks, Reagan or one of his press aides would reply that of course the president did not orchestrate or even know all of the "details" of a given policy, but was fully in charge of the general thrust of his administration while others performed the execution. Challenged about whether policies were actually carried out, the president noted that certain aides had never directly contradicted or ignored an explicit order.

All of which may be true, but irrelevant. An agile official seldom tries to undercut a policy by directly contravening a specific order. He does it by interpreting the order slightly differently than it was intended. "Find out whether this group needs Stinger missiles in order to win" becomes "Find out if they need them in order to produce a negotiated settlement." If an administration hasn't made clear what the goal is, this may be a perfectly legitimate reading. Or—without any subversive intent at all—a particular official can move in exactly the intended direction, but at a slower speed, with less urgency, than was intended by the policy. "Ship 500 rockets within the year" may result in all 500 being shipped at once—at the end of the year. Or they may be shipped only after the recipients have received extensive training in their use. Moreover, this is a rather simple order. A complex policy that involves supplying weapons, explaining goals, comparing different means, estimating the intentions of enemies—all this involves considerable nuance.

Divisions are a natural concomitant of government, and can give our leaders different options to choose from and different ways to evaluate whether or not policies are working. But diversity can only play this positive role if it is used properly. Real differences must be faced, not swept under the rug. Debates between the contending schools must be open and explicit, so that a leader knows what he is choosing and why, rather than choosing a particular course by bureaucratic default, when one agency or official more skillfully thwarts the ideas of another.

In short, if the natural divisions of bureaucracy make themselves felt at the top of government—if they bring the issues to the officials responsible to the electorate—then the result will be happy. If they do not, policymakers will not be able to learn from either victory or defeat.

The Doctrine in Practice

For an illustration of these maxims, one need look no farther than the 1980s, during which the policy of providing aid to freedom fighters, the "Reagan Doctrine," became a major theme. As it did, the agencies of government concerned with implementing the program fell into the alignment described by Dr. Angelo Codevilla, a Hoover Institution scholar and for many years a top staffer on the Senate Intelligence Committee:

> There is first of all the Department of State. Given the central place of diplomacy in that agency's mandate and functions, there has evolved . . . a disposition that assigns to negotiations the primary role in foreign policy. Short of being the instruments of "last resort," military power and armed force are seen as at best inputs into the negotiating process—as strengthening the bargaining hand. . . .
>
> The civilians in charge of the U.S. Defense Department's policy generally favor the liberation of . . . countries from communist control. They have pressed for formulation of national policy along these lines, but do not have a charter for dispensing aid. Moreover, they can count on resistance from the services to giving liberation movements . . . resources from their own hard-won shares of the budget.
>
> The Director of the Central Intelligence Agency, William Casey, [was] aligned with the officials in the Defense Department, and personally seem[ed] to favor the victory of liberation movements. His agency has the charter for dispensing the aid. But from among the CIA's senior personnel have come strong echoes of the State Department's view.[44]

Knowing that this was how the departments of government were divided, and given even broader cleavage in the Congress, it is easy to see why the system had a tendency toward chaos. Only repeated interventions from the White House to keep disparate officials in line, and clear and cogent statements describing what "the line" was, could bring order and unity to this departmental entropy. Unfortunately, such vigorous leadership was consistently lacking and, as a result, policy contradictions were pervasive.

Congress and the administration provided assistance to the Afghan mujahedin that was at once more substantial and more consistent than for any other freedom fighters. Yet even here, the agencies engaged in a guerilla war of their own. Years after the United States initiated assistance to undermine the Soviet-installed Kabul government, the regime continued to trade with the United States under most-favored-nation status. (MFN lets a country sell its goods here under lower tariffs and more favorable credit arrangements.) Aid, even when approved by Congress, moved glacially. When Congress approved a large aid package for 1985, the State Department took more than seven months to distribute a mere $6 million to relief agencies operating in Pakistan and Afghanistan. "The State Department has been cruelly slow in making funds available," complained Senator Gordon Humphrey, a leading proponent of Afghan aid in the Congress. This is not to say that U.S. officials disobeyed the letter of any particular instructions. Rather, they acted as they saw fit to interpret the ambiguous policy of the administration. Thus, when Congress appropriated $2 million for medical work by the International Medical Corps to treat "wounded Afghans," the State Department argued that this assistance applied only to wounded Afghans being treated in Pakistan refugee camps. If the aid actually went into Afghanistan, worried one State Department official, it might undermine America's slender claim to be taking no position in the struggle. "It [c]ould feed Soviet propaganda that it's Americans who are causing all the trouble in Afghanistan," the aide said. Hence only $650,000, or about one-third of the intended aid, was distributed—until members of Congress complained that their own will had been obstructed.[45]

As the Afghan war widened, U.S. officials weighed the possibility of sending weapons, such as shoulder-fired missiles useful in shooting down Soviet helicopters and aircraft. This time it was the CIA that played a dilatory role. Again, no specific commands were disobeyed. Deputy Director John Mac-Mahon reported in one briefing to Congress that the CIA opposed sending more useful weapons, such as the Stinger antiaircraft missile, because the Pakistanis had opposed providing such weapons to the mujahedin and threatened to confiscate them. Then a Senate fact-finding mission put the question to both President Zia and his top two military advisers. Both said the Pakistanis would welcome the shipment of more effective weapons to the freedom fighters; as it was, Pakistan bore the full burden of helping supply the mujahedin but enjoyed none of the fruits of an effective program. Disarmed of his first line of defense, MacMahon reportedly told Senators Helms, Wallop, and Humphrey that there was another problem: The Stinger and various other proposed weapons were too complicated for the inexpert Afghan troops to use. Stories peppered the U.S. press about the Stinger's alleged complexity and ineffectiveness. For more than two years, the Stingers sat.

While this debate simmered, through most of 1984 and 1985, the Reagan administration struggled with the question of the very purpose of Afghan aid. Was it merely to "keep the pressure on"? In 1984, the administration seemed to lean this way. Senator Paul Tsongas introduced a resolution calling on the U.S. to aid the mujahedin in amounts that would be "enough to win." Yet MacMahon and Secretary of State Shultz lobbied so hard against the wording that Tsongas agreed to change his resolution to one calling for the less concrete standard of "advancing freedom." Early in 1986, the administration made up its mind. President Reagan signed a National Security Decision Directive stating that henceforth the aim of U.S. policy was to drive the Soviets out of Afghanistan. Stinger missiles began to flow into Afghanistan, and with them came a rapid increase in Soviet losses and guerilla effectiveness.[46]

U.S. policy toward Jonas Savimbi mirrored the ambivalence over Afghanistan. When Congress proposed to repeal the Clark Amendment, a 1976 measure that outlawed assistance of any kind to Unita, Assistant Secretary of State Chester Crocker rushed to comment on the proposal in the *New York Times.* Crocker didn't take a position on repealing the measure; rather, he stressed that the Reagan administration had "no plans" to provide aid to Unita, undercutting proponents of the effort to repeal Clark.[47] Congress repealed the Clark Amendment anyway, after which different congressmen began proposing measures to initiate the aid.[48] Again, the State Department intervened. Secretary of State Shultz wrote an "eyes only" note to House Minority Leader Robert Michel asking him to "discourage" a bill to aid Savimbi, since negotiations between the United States, South Africa, and the Angolan government had reached a "delicate" stage, and a vote for U.S. assistance might disrupt them. Congress voted for aid, although the package was so small as to almost invite further foot-dragging by the opponents of the policy. Thus, even as Congress moved to repeal the Clark Amendment, State Department officials continued to stress that they would in no way involve the Angolan rebels, much less cede primary responsibility to it for negotiations. "U.S. officials," the *Washington Post* reported, "have made it clear that they consider Unita to be an internal Angolan problem and not part of the equation in seeking a southern African peace settlement."[49] At one point in the negotiations, the State Department even agreed to cut off any assistance to Savimbi and yet allow some 10,000 Cuban troops to remain in Angola until order was restored.[50]

This is not to suggest delinquency on the part of the U.S. diplomats. On the contrary, Crocker and the State Department were energetic in pursuing what they were told was U.S. policy: the removal of Cuban troops from Angola. Or at least this was one plausible interpretation of U.S. policy. To expect different results, the White House would perforce have had to clarify that Cuban withdrawal was only one U.S. aim, that democracy was another, and that diplomats were not to pursue the former in preference to the latter.[51]

The pitched bureaucratic battles over Afghanistan and Angola are but two prominent examples of the contradictory nature of the Reagan Doctrine.[52] At least these disputes, however, involved two guerilla groups that received broad bipartisan support in Congress, and, if they were not household words with American voters, they aroused little hostility, either. Not all freedom fighters were so uncontroversial. The story of the Nicaraguan contras contains all of the errors and missed opportunities of the Reagan Doctrine magnified several times over. Yet for that very reason, it offers hope.

Carter and the Contras

Not long after the Sandinista takeover, it became clear that the new rulers of Nicaragua had something other than pluralism in mind, a bitter pill for Jimmy Carter in several ways. Carter had for one thing operated a foreign policy predicated on the assumption that America had shed, and ought to have shed, what he called its "inordinate fear of communism." Furthermore, he had placed special hope in the Sandinistas, U.S. pressure having helped push Somoza out and Ortega into power. Finally, there was an election coming up, with many of Carter's Republican opponents proclaiming that the Carter administration had been sitting by and watching as the Soviets swept new countries into their empire.

Carter had to do something. Yet his noninterventionist assumptions, coupled with the general decline of U.S. intelligence, seemed to leave few options. Asked years later why he didn't take action to forestall the consolidation of Sandinista rule, Carter told me that he did "consult very closely" with U.S. allies in the region. He didn't specify any actions his administration took or considered, and has mentioned none elsewhere.[53] It is therefore fair to infer that none was taken except those measures known to the public, such as the cessation of U.S. aid to Managua and the issuance of mild statements of disappointment with the Sandinistas.

Or *is* it fair? To Carter's good fortune, at least one of his top aides had been seeking out information on the situation and looking for ways to shape events in a post-Somoza Nicaragua should the Sandinistas prove less democratic than their pronouncements.[54] Zbigniew Brzezinski, Carter's hawkish national security adviser, was suspicious of both Somoza and of many of his opponents, and chafed under a policy that promoted the rise to power of a group the United States knew little about and had no decisive leverage over.

Brzezinski had held several meetings in 1978 and 1979 with Nicaraguans opposed to Somoza but nervous about the nature of the Sandinistas as well. One such figure was Enrique Bermudez. A colonel in Somoza's National Guard, Bermudez had served as Nicaragua's defense attaché to the United States throughout the Carter years. However, he was quickly alienated by the growing brutality of Somoza and in fact had been so critical of Somoza in the years leading up to the revolution, both predicting and urging his fall, that he had special credibility with the Carter administration.

Working with Bermudez and other Nicaraguans—several of whom remain in Nicaragua as leaders of the unarmed opposition, and will therefore remain unnamed—Brzezinski put together a plan to provide aid to Nicaraguan democrats. Some already suffered police harassment, arbitrary seizure of property, and, in the case of Violeta Chamorro, widowed editor of *La Prensa,* a campaign of de facto censorship.

Bermudez drew up lists of key Nicaraguans who ought to receive aid. Most, like Chamorro, were involved in founding private political parties. Some, such as Pedro Gonzalez and resistance commanders "Douglas" and "Tigrillo" (code names) had obtained light arms and were fighting by as early as 1980, according to State Department documents.[55]

Brzezinski also sought help from U.S. experts outside the government. One source of advice was Constantine Menges, a former student of Brzezinski's and later Ronald Reagan's top Latin affairs specialist at the NSC. A frustrated Menges had briefed both NSC and CIA officials in January 1979, warning that the Nicaraguan revolution was in danger of becoming "another Cuba," in which communist forces joined with genuine democrats to achieve power, but then seized control of the revolution. "Everyone nodded and it was hard to take him very seriously at the time," said one Carter official who attended the Menges briefing. Later in the year it was hard not to. Hours after the Sandinistas took control on July 19, Brzezinski was on the phone to his old student: "Looks like you might have been right. Now what?"[56]

Menges responded with a two-page memorandum to Brzezinski, NSC aide William Odom, Michael Armacost, and Frank Carlucci, then serving as deputy director of the CIA. His proposal was binary. First, launch a "Portugal-type effort" to "strengthen the democratic forces" in Nicaragua. Second, move quickly and with force if needed "to ensure that there are *no* Cuban or Soviet military advisers" introduced. Brzezinski knew Carter would likely approve the first effort, the NED-style program also being urged by Bermudez. The second, which Menges argued later was critical "because it would have enabled the peaceful forces of resistance to build," was never adopted by Carter and, according to NSC aides at the time, was not given serious consideration.[57]

The plan finally submitted called for the United States to provide cash assistance—totaling about $5 million, according to reliable sources—to Bermudez, Mrs. Chamorro, and more than a dozen other democratic leaders, most of them connected with opposition parties and media outlets. Brzezinski presented a draft presidential finding to Carter in December of 1979 authorizing the plan. There was little dissension within the Carter national security team. Vance, who might have opposed, was swamped with crises on issues from the SALT II treaty to Afghanistan to Iran. Stansfield Turner, Carter's Director of Central Intelligence, another reluctant voice on covert action, could take comfort in the fact that the program would be largely under the CIA's control.

Besides—as Brzezinski stressed—the decision to send a few million dollars to mostly peaceful opposition factions hardly represented an irrevocable decision that the Sandinistas might not reform. The point of the program, he argued, was to "hedge our bets."[58] It was a policy designed to keep options open, or generate them later; not an irreversible choice to seek the overthrow of the Sandinistas. "They did something," Menges later said. "Not enough."[59]

Still, according to every source familiar with the Carter finding, it contained one remarkable phrase. The point of the program, the finding said, was to "change the emerging totalitarian nature of the Nicaraguan government." Not only, then, was the Carter administration prepared to recognize as early as 1979 that the character of the Sandinista revolution was not democratic. It at least implied that the United States found the emergence of a "totalitarian" and pro-Soviet regime in Managua unacceptable—else why the program?

In January of 1980, Turner briefed both the House and Senate Intelligence committees on the Nicaragua finding. He noted the existence of a similar program for aid to resistance groups in Afghanistan. One House member asked if this meant that the U.S. intended to provide aid to armed resistance movements. Turner: "The funds are not being provided for the purpose of assisting any armed forces or individuals." A House member: "Could you describe how you're going to know what they use it for?" Turner: "No. . . ."[60]

Turner's answer italicizes the ambiguous nature of the aid program, a sign of things to come as regards U.S. policy in the region. Nicaraguan democrats on the receiving end of this aid told me that most of the money was distributed either as cash payments delivered in Costa Rica or Honduras, or in the form of checks laundered through Mexican banks. Although the small amounts distributed in 1980 were hardly enough to supply armed resistance on a grand scale, there was enough to make a start. All the officials who commented on the program, including Turner and Robert Pastor, stressed that there "was never any finding allowing U.S. officials to support armed groups" in Nicaragua, as Turner put it.[61] Yet to provide cash to people setting up such groups and seeking arms is to do much the same thing. "You don't run a program like that without realizing, realistically, that you can't dictate how cash gets used," Hodding Carter recalled. "Money is fungible."[62]

It's anybody's guess what would have happened in, say, a second Carter administration. A Carter program with similarly limited objectives at the start—aid to the mujahedin of Afghanistan—evolved into the most ambitious, successful, and popular component of the Reagan Doctrine. In its essence, though, the Carter initiative focused on building a peaceful opposition. A number of Nicaraguans who spoke about the program said it was always made clear that the U.S.—at least as of Carter's finding—did not contemplate anything like the guerilla movement that emerged in the 1980s. In a sense, Carter's aid to the contras was what Reagan's often claimed to be: keeping pressure on the Sandinistas while testing their intentions, and preserving U.S. options for the future.

The Roads Not Taken

Ronald Reagan took office, then, with at least a fragile third-force movement beginning to stir in Nicaragua. With the Sandinistas by 1981 having discarded all but the "pretense of pluralism," as one member of the Sandinista directorate would later put it, the new president, it would seem, had two logical roads to take.

On the one hand, the Reagan administration could have decided that communist rule in Nicaragua was an acceptable thing. This would argue for a policy of leaving the Sandinistas alone. America could then concentrate on using its leverage to prevent the spread of Nicaraguan power elsewhere, rallying allies and the American people behind a policy of Sandinista containment. Swallowing this pill would have left a bitter taste in Ronald Reagan's mouth, of course. Yet the United States has lived with leaders such as Idi Amin, Muammar Khadafy, and, in our own hemisphere, Fidel Castro. Should Ortega begin to take over neighboring countries, that decision might have to be reevaluated. In the meantime, one could argue, there was prudence in keeping away from Managua altogether. If the communists there proved as bellicose as communists have elsewhere, Reagan would not have to wait long for a pretext to take strong action.

On the other hand, perhaps what Carter called an "emerging totalitarian" government in Nicaragua was not acceptable. In that case, we would want to consider ways to change that government so that it was not totalitarian. This might mean building on the Carter program to aid democrats inside Nicaragua. It might mean taking actions to remove the Soviet and Cuban advisers that Menges had suggested be kept out back in 1979. It might have meant arming the contras as a clear and explicit means of effecting the downfall of Ortega. It might even have meant a clear-cut invasion of Nicaragua, perhaps with token support from Latin allies, as in the invasion of Grenada, but no doubt chiefly dependent on U.S. ships, planes, and troops.

Ironically, the one agency that first sought to force these issues early in the administration was the State Department. Alexander Haig had been involved in some of the key decisions of the Nixon, Ford, and Carter administrations, from Vietnam to Iran. He therefore had a healthy disdain for issues deferred and measures halved. From everything Ronald Reagan had said in the campaign, Haig assumed that the president would not want to leave Nicaragua as a potential sanctuary for armed subversion in the Americas. So he proposed that the United States go "to the source" of the problem. His State Department counselor, Robert C. McFarlane—later Reagan's national security adviser and probably the key player in the Iran-contra scandal—drew up a policy report proposing U.S. attacks on Cuban aircraft and shipping, arming the contras, and instituting a naval blockade of Nicaragua and Cuba. "Taking the War to Nicaragua," the paper was called, and that about summed it up.[63]

Haig's plan would have been controversial and agonizing. It implied blood, sweat, and tears: a war with Cuba and Nicaragua, or a very high risk of such a war. If the U.S. really was unprepared to live with the Ortega dictatorship, it made sense. Yet even in the best of times, it is not the kind of plan Ronald Reagan would likely adopt.

And the spring of 1981 was hardly the best of times. The president spent much of those early months recuperating from John Hinckley's bullet. What energies the administration had were concentrated on winning passage of Reagan's economic program of tax cuts and budget cuts. Even on Reagan's directorate for foreign and defense policies, there was a strong inclination to rebuild capabilities now, use them later. Defense Secretary Caspar Weinberger, who remained a voice of caution when the use of force was contemplated, had little desire in 1981 to deflect interest from his Pentagon buildup plan. CIA Director William Casey, later a key proponent and executor of the Reagan Doctrine, wanted no less to rebuild the CIA before taking on an overt assault on communism in Central America. Thus, Casey was lukewarm; Weinberger opposed the plan; and top White House aides Michael Deaver and James Baker, along with Vice President George Bush, were strongly against it as an imprudent diversion of effort from other conflicts.[64]

This would seem to imply that the Reagan administration chose the other path, accepting at least temporarily that the Sandinistas would continue to solidify their rule unmolested by the United States. Yet Ronald Reagan didn't quite decide that, either. "If it is difficult for politicians to do bold things," Haig recalled in his memoirs, "it is almost impossible to do nothing."[65] And the United States, the administration believed, had to do something soon if it wanted to prevent the Sandinista revolution from washing over another American ally:

El Salvador.

In 1981, the Salvadoran guerillas, armed and directed by Managua, had proclaimed a "final offensive" against the fragile U.S.-backed government. Even Carter had resumed arms shipments to San Salvador in his final year in office, but the increased U.S. aid had not yet turned the tide. For Reagan, leaving a Nicaragua that was lost by Carter intact was one thing; losing El Salvador during his own presidency was another. The president pressed for something to be "done," and the departments went back to consider.

Against this backdrop, Haig dispatched Thomas Enders, assistant secretary of state for inter-American affairs, to Managua in August 1981. Enders offered the Sandinistas a deal the essence of which would have been to freeze the status quo in Latin America. Under his proposal, the Sandinistas would stop aiding the Salvadoran guerillas and scale back their own military buildup. In return, the United States would renew economic aid, crack down on Nicaraguan exiles training in Florida and the Western United States, and declare a policy of nonintervention in Nicaraguan affairs.[66] Enders left on an optimistic note, telling one colleague at the State Department, "We've got a better than 50-50 chance" of saving El Salvador.[67]

All this may seem a rapid retreat for the Reagan administration, even the Reagan State Department: from rescuing Nicaragua late in the Carter administration to merely plugging the dyke in El Salvador. In retrospect, it seems incredible.

Yet in retrospect, it is clear that the "final offensive" announced by Salvador's Nicaraguan-backed guerillas was either a complete bluff, to distract attention from Managua, or at best an optimistic boast. At the time, that wasn't clear—and the administration was obsessed with El Salvador.

William Casey, interviewed by *U.S. News & World Report* shortly after Reagan's first covert-aid decision with respect to the contras was taken, didn't mention the possibility of taking action against Nicaragua.[68] Yet he predicted that the Sandinistas would achieve "military dominance over the rest of Central America" by the fall of 1982. Never mentioning freedom fighters for the West, in Nicaragua or elsewhere, Casey ticked off Soviet insurgencies, implying that the Reagan administration's primary interest was in defending against these: "North Yemen . . . Chad . . . Morocco . . . El Salvador . . . Guatemala. . . . The Soviets work with Angola against Namibia and Zaire, with Ethiopia against Somalia, and with Libya and Ethiopia against the Sudan." Even Haig's memoir, published in 1984, begins a discussion of Central America policy with these revealing words: "To understand the circumstances of life in a nation like El Salvador . . ." The contras go virtually unmentioned.[69]

Once the expansion of Carter's initiative, or the Haig option of overt force, had been rejected, American diplomacy had no plausible choice but to seek a defensive option. The very nature of negotiations, as Henry Kissinger has noted, is that they tend to ratify the status quo. This is not so for any principled reason, such as that the status quo is always good. It is simply the likely outcome. Neither side, after all, has much incentive to give up what it has already gained. And even if a particular negotiator is willing to do so, he will not look very good to his superiors in the White House or the Kremlin if he suggests it. To propose that the other side give up what it has, however, is to ask for "unrealistic concessions." The search for an agreement, then, tends to be nothing more than the search for a common perception of what each side already has.

Even the refrigeration of the status quo, however, may not be achievable if one side feels it is likely to gain more over time. In that case, it pays to wait. And this is precisely the calculation that faced Enders. A confident Sandinista leadership felt no need to negotiate its own security, which at that point seemed unthreatened, in return for respecting the territory of El Salvador, which at that point seemed highly threatened.

Enders returned to Washington carrying only Sandinista promises to win the war.

Guerillas on Hold

Not long after Enders came back, in the fall of 1981, the State Department again renewed its request for some kind of action. This time, however, Haig had learned his lesson. If Reagan was reluctant to attack the communist source, perhaps he would be willing to contain it. And if not overt pressure, perhaps a covert plan would do the trick. Haig told McFarlane to collect options from the other departments.[70]

The program that emerged, worked out by mid-level officials at State, Defense, and the CIA, called for aid totaling $19.95 million to support about five hundred contras operating in Nicaragua. Their clear purpose, however, was limited. No evident thought was given to the future of the contras as potential liberators of Nicaragua. The chief aim of the assistance was to help interdict arms headed for El Salvador. A secondary purpose was to harass the Sandinista regime with attacks on key military and economic installations.

Yet there was still one glitch. Even this operation, Haig complained, was "too large to hide." If U.S. action was to be covert, Haig wanted to work through a third party to provide "plausible deniability" to the scheme. So the CIA shopped around for a proxy.

The natural answer seemed to be Argentina. Many of the contras in this early incarnation of the army were former National Guardsmen of Somoza. Many were products of the senior staff colleges in Argentina and still had friends there; in fact, there is some evidence that before the United States even launched its own plan, Argentina had gone ahead on its own and was providing assistance to the contras in Honduras. In November of 1981, Casey met with General Leopoldo F. Galtieri, then chief of staff of the Argentine armed forces and later the country's president. "The two hit it off very well," one unidentified source told the *Los Angeles Times*.

A few weeks later, President Reagan signed National Security Decision Directive 17, and at about the same time, he submitted a finding to Congress explaining the scope and purpose of the operation.[71] The plan approved by Reagan, which formed the basis of U.S. contra policy until at least 1984, was a compromise more reflective of bureaucratic and short-term political pressures than of sound strategic thinking. Any number of questions should have given the administration pause.

For example, if the operation was "too large" for U.S. officials to conduct and keep secret on their own, was it plausible that we could hide U.S. support merely by using Argentina? And if keeping arms out of El Salvador was the goal, why did this defensive aim require secrecy? Why not proclaim it publicly, and take measures, which certainly were available, to achieve this objective in rapid and decisive fashion?

On the more positive side, if there were contras willing to fight and die merely to interdict arms, why not consider having them fight and die to liberate their country—as rebels were already doing in Afghanistan and Angola?

On the skeptical side, was it believable that the contras shared Reagan's limited objective of shielding El Salvador?

In the years that followed, Reagan and his top aides were consistently pressed to answer questions like these, which point to the heart of the inconsistencies, confusions, and contradictions of the contra aid plan. From this, most observers concluded that the administration must have been dissembling. Ronald Reagan, they argue, could not possibly have intended what he said was intended by the early shipments of assistance. The irony, however, is that merely interdicting arms to El Salvador and frustrating Sandinista aggression—not establishing a democratic Nicaragua—really was the driving goal of the initial program. The Reagan administration wanted first and foremost to field an armed fighting force, any armed fighting force, and help the Salvadorans. As Arturo Cruz and foreign policy analyst Penn Kemble wrote:

> Most of the guerilla uprisings with which we are familiar actually began in political circles. . . . The heroism and pathos of the Nicaraguan resistance lie in its attempt to turn this experience around. *First* came the fighters. Only now [in late 1986] is this movement contending with the need for spokesmen and organizers who can help broaden it.[72]

Thus, with little thought, the Reagan administration had taken an important turn. From Carter's modest effort at long-term third-force building, U.S. policy toward the contras shifted its emphasis to producing military results for the relief of El Salvador. Political credibility and sustainability were sacrificed in favor of inflicting the most pain the fastest on Managua. Alas, even this was not so much a conscious decision, made with a clear understanding of the costs and benefits. Rather, important decisions were made by leaders who only dimly realized they were, in fact, making an important decision. The basic contradictions of contra policy were thus present and well established at its creation in 1981.

In the coming years, the administration's ambivalent attitude toward Nicaragua manifested itself repeatedly. Two examples suffice.

In 1983, the United States stationed warships off the coast of Nicaragua. Now, "the only sane reason to send such a show of force," as the *Wall Street*

Journal aptly editorialized, "is to remind our adversaries that we are capable of doing them a great deal of damage."[73] Yet at a news conference held shortly after the exercise began, President Reagan stressed that the United States was conducting only small maneuvers, had no intention of firing on any Nicaraguan vessels, and was making no plans for a larger U.S. presence in Central America. It may have been that all of those things were true, but to say so was to needlessly reveal our intention not to use force, thereby robbing the action of any impact. "You never say," Richard Nixon put it succinctly in one 1983 interview, "what you're *not* going to do."[74] By violating this never-say-never maxim, Reagan was left with all of the bad effects of a show of force, such as public concern and international tension, and almost none of the good ones.

The mining of Nicaragua's harbors, discovered by Congress in the spring of 1984, was executed and explained with similar hesitancy. In an effort to avoid confrontation with the Soviets, the United States used mines of relatively low effectiveness. The result was to create a hazard for small fishermen in the area, not all of them Nicaraguans, while posing only a minor threat to arms shipments coming in under escort from Cuba. Neither the United States nor El Salvador nor anyone else benefited much from the operation. Yet it carried all the moral stench of an undeclared act of war.

William Casey appeared before the Senate to explain the action as the Congress prepared for a critical vote on providing further funds for the contras. Howard Baker, the Senate majority leader, tossed Casey what he thought was a softball question: Was the mining important to the success of U.S. policy? Casey, however, swung and missed. "Not really," he said, listing it as simply one of a number of ways to apply pressure to the Sandinistas.[75] What Casey had just said, of course, was that the Reagan administration had committed what was arguably an act of war—yet for no clear reasons. It was at precisely that point, one senator friendly to the contras recalled, that the debate on the Senate floor began to turn and aid to the rebels was cut off decisively. Casey even went on to opine, according to published accounts, that there was "no chance" the resistance fighters would someday "overthrow" the Nicaraguan government. This remark, too, was intended to make the policy palatable to critics of administration policy. It didn't. But Casey's comments were played over and over on Managua radio in the coming days, as a proof to opponents of the regime that resistance was bootless.[76]

All these events, of course, were but symptoms of a deeper inability to decide on an objective and then correlate it to the means being used. Moreover, the aggressive pursuit of such objectives is a job that one cannot expect to be performed by the CIA, the Pentagon, the State Department, or any other agency. Bureaucracies by their very nature seek to avoid such clear-cut decisions, preferring open-ended instructions that allow them freedom to operate as they best see. Yet politics abhors a vacuum, and so when the Reagan administration's Nicaragua policy produced a vacuum, a Massachusetts congressman named Edward Boland countered it with an initiative.

Casey, Ron, and Ollie

Congress passed several of Boland's proposals, each with slightly different provisions, beginning with the first Boland Amendment in December of 1982. Various Boland amendments were in effect on and off for the next several years, with U.S. policy alternating between a ban on nearly all aid to the contras and the explicit provision of such aid by the Congress. The Boland Amendment was repealed in December of 1985 when Congress resumed more or less overt funding of the contras. Ironically, the repeal act expired in October 1986, just a few days before Attorney General Edwin Meese announced that NSC aide Oliver North had transferred monies from the Iran arms sales to the contras.

Whole books have been written, vast hearings held, and special prosecutors deployed to investigate Ronald Reagan's secret arms sales to Iran and the diversion of some of those funds to the contras. It is not my purpose to restate them here. There is one aspect, though, that seems to receive little attention.

To listen to the commotion during the congressional Iran-contra hearings, one would think many of the debaters were living on different planets. On the one hand, of course, were the outraged congressmen and their counsels, who strutted before the television cameras complaining that dirty tricksters had "violated the law." They grilled Oliver North for his alleged "contempt for democracy," and purred when George Shultz and Caspar Weinberger testified on the folly of arms sales to Iran. On the other hand, supporters of the Reagan policy rallied against the Boland amendments as a heinous abomination— vague and probably unconstitutional. Vice President Bush attacked the Boland amendments as a grotesque limitation on the president's authority, while Gordon Crovitz, writing for the *Wall Street Journal* editorial page, wrote piece after piece buttressing this legalistic defense. Patrick Buchanan, the president's communications director, accused Congress of selling out to communism. Congressman James Courter, a leading proponent of aid to the contras on Capitol Hill, ridiculed his feckless colleagues for passing nearly a dozen major changes in U.S. policy in half as many years.

What few people mentioned was that the Boland amendments themselves were in fact a compromise between the White House and the Congress. The deals that produced the amendments were crafted with advice from the White House, passed by Congress, and signed by the president. There certainly ought to have been some agreement about their meaning and their significance.

170

WHEN PUSH COMES TO SHOVE

The first Boland Amendment was passed during the lame-duck session of Congress in December 1982. At that time, Congressman Tom Harkin of Iowa introduced a measure prohibiting any U.S. expenditures for anyone seeking to overthrow the Nicaraguan government. Edward Kennedy introduced the identical amendment in the Senate. Both were defeated easily. Yet this—as McFarlane reportedly noted in a memorandum—created a problem, since it made it seem as if the "overthrow" of Nicaragua was a goal of the contras.[77]

Fortunately, in the view of some Reagan advisers, Boland had been working on a less restrictive amendment that simply barred various agencies of the United States government from expending any funds "for the purpose of overthrowing the Government of Nicaragua." Both the CIA and the State Department reportedly found the notion appealing. After all, administration spokesmen had consistently proclaimed that its intent was only to "change" or "democratize" the Nicaraguan government, something that theoretically could be accomplished without "overthrow." And whatever the hopes of the contras might be, we could maintain that our aid did not have as its "purpose" the goal of "overthrowing" the Sandinistas. Boland, in the eyes of the administration, protected contra aid from being attacked as a U.S. move to war. Yet it allowed contra aid to continue. It was, as McFarlane told one NSC staffer, a "blessing in disguise."[78]

It was certainly disguised. *The Almanac of American Politics* refers to this first version of Boland as "Delphic" in its ambiguity.[79] Yet that, in a sense, was its purpose, and it was a legitimate purpose considering the administration's own vagueness on the goal of its Central America policy. Boland, it seems to me, meant to force the issue one way or another. It put the onus on the White House, as Codevilla put it, "to prove by deeds that it was *not* working to overthrow the Sandinista regime."[80]

Of course, if Boland was a challenge, it was also an opportunity—a "blessing," though not for the reasons McFarlane thought. It was a sign that there was something askew with existing policy, and a chance to modify it.

Instead of rethinking its policy, however, the Reagan administration spent the next several years multiplying its assurances that no overthrow of the Nicaraguans was intended, no use of U.S. forces even remotely contemplated. Statements downplaying the program, of course, tended to dull public interest and support, so the administration coupled them with ever-shriller warnings about the threat from Central America. "Let me make this clear to you," Pentagon aide Fred Iklé declared one September. "We do not seek a military defeat for our friends. . . . We seek victory for the forces of democracy."[81] Yet this comment was sandwiched between the halfhearted fleet maneuvers of 1983 and the halfhearted mining of 1984. Still the danger-mongering continued. "Abrams Says Region's Future Depends on Contra Aid Vote," read one headline.[82] Simultaneously, of course, Congress was asked to approve piddling amounts of aid, and administration spokesmen were pledging never, never, never to dispatch U.S. troops.

One telling example of the confusion came in the early months of 1985. In February, the president held a press conference asserting that it was his goal to "remove" the communist structure of government from Nicaragua. Weeks later, he wrote to a member of Congress that his policy did not "seek the overthrow" of the Sandinistas.[83]

Of course, the administration built its case on more than just rhetoric. Throughout the Reagan administration, from a white paper by the Haig State Department right through Oliver North's slide show at the Iran-contra hearings, officials released a stream of documents, intelligence photos, and other evidence designed to offer final proof of Soviet involvement in the region. Yet the public seemed unmoved. In Nicaragua, voters were confronted by one group of politicians and experts who said the Sandinistas were not a threat. Another group, led by the Reagan administration, said they were a threat. The first group, however, acted in accord with its own argument; the Reagan administration did not. Henry Kissinger, the head of Reagan's Central America Commission, summed it up when he wrote: "The administration has put forth an analysis that logically implies the need to overthrow the Sandinistas. But the means it has requested . . . are clearly inadequate. And the repeated assertion that the use of American force is totally excluded underlines the incompatability between rhetoric and policy."[84]

These issues came to a head in 1984, as Ronald Reagan was nearing the zenith of his presidency, coasting along in opinion polls toward a landslide reelection. Aid to the contras had continued in a slow trickle despite the Boland Amendment, thanks in particular to private citizens donating their own money to the cause. In July, a housing bill popular with Democrats—who were running a campaign emphasizing their compassion—began to move through the Congress when Senator Malcolm Wallop managed to attach an amendment that would have made all forms of contra aid legal. Inexplicably, however, the senate majority leader, Howard Baker, allowed the amendment to be removed. Later in the same year, Baker himself put together a proposal to repeal the Boland Amendment, then abruptly withdrew it. Either initiative probably would have passed the Senate. What happened?

What happened is that in both cases McFarlane, then Reagan's national security adviser, convinced the senators to drop the effort. "We just don't want to have to make a big fight out of it right now," he reportedly told Wallop at one strategy meeting. According to a newspaper column at the time that was never rebutted by the White House, McFarlane acted on both occasions with the approval of top aides Michael Deaver and James Baker—who in turn had solicited legal advice on what could and could not be done under Boland from White House counsel Fred Fielding and presidential counselor Edwin Meese.[85]

Thus, for all the complaints later that the "pygmies" of Congress, as Pat Buchanan called them, had sold out the contras, it was the Reagan White House that decided not to raise the issue on Capitol Hill.[86]

The Next Contras

All the errors and missed opportunities of the Reagan Doctrine in Nicaragua, however, demonstrate one truth: The American people harbor a deep and abiding sympathy for those fighting tyranny, whether in Central America or South Africa or Eastern Europe. Time and again, the Reagan administration erred in its approach to the contra debate. And time and again, the administration went back to the Congress—and eventually won. "Every time the president asked for more money," Congressman Courter noted, "and every time someone, whether Ronald Reagan or Oliver North, explained the policy, proclaiming openly and publicly that the goal was freedom and democracy— every time this happened, public support for aid to the contras increased."[87]

There are other lessons to be learned from the contra experience as well. One is that the existence of such guerilla movements, even against communism, is not a historic aberration peculiar to the post-Vietnam era, as some seem to believe. "History and current events show that guerilla movements have always been [an] efficient military avenue for communist expansion," Jean-François Revel wrote in 1983. "After World War II, guerilla movements became a communist monopoly. . . . Today, however, a new phenomenon is taking place: For the first time, in various places, genuinely popular anti-communist movements are resorting to communist guerilla tactics."[88] Revel only repeats here what has been the conventional wisdom among many historians. Yet the facts do not bear it out. "Rebellions," historian Brian Crozier wrote back in 1960, "are not a monopoly of the Marxists."[89] Freedom fighters battled against the Soviet annexation of Lithuania and the Ukraine from 1944 to 1954, and were prepared to resume the fight in 1956 if the United States extended aid to the Hungarians.[90] The 1950s saw nearly as many democratic insurgencies against communism as the 1980s did, including major freedom-fighter uprisings in East Germany, Tibet, and North Vietnam.[91]

"The popular equation of guerilla fighters with fighters for socialist tyranny," Malcolm Wallop has written, "is historically false. In fact, whenever socialist tyrannies have taken hold, normal people who would otherwise have led peaceable lives, have become fighters. In some cases they have thrived. In most cases they have been defeated. But nowhere do socialist tyrants live without daily fear of violent resistance."[92]

Nor is there any reason why insurgents need to depend solely on the United

States. Usually clear-thinking people such as Elliott Abrams sometimes talk as if this were so, claiming that the "future of the region" hangs on a single vote by the U.S. Congress. Yet virtually every band of freedom fighters that enjoyed U.S. support during the 1980s was in the field before the U.S. support began. Virtually every one has occasionally had support from other countries, and some, such as Unita and Renamo, fought and thrived for years without American aid. "Military forces," Jeane Kirkpatrick wrote, "cannot be disbanded and re-created at the whim of legislators."[93] Indeed they cannot—which is why their sympathizers need not panic with the approach of each decision about U.S. assistance. As Professor Charles Moser of George Washington University observed in 1985:

> [M]any contemporary anti-communist insurgencies now exist almost or entirely independent of the United States. . . . Only in Nicaragua is American aid an important factor. In most other instances the insurgencies have developed quite independently of outside assistance and control. This very fact may account for their success. By its nature guerilla warfare should be spontaneous, whereas the recent tendency among the professional military has been toward ever more detailed control of hostilities. . . . The Nicaraguan insurgency might be doing better were it more independent of U.S. control.[94]

One of the best ways for America to support resistance groups is to get others to support them. More backers, more backing. And if guerillas have help from a variety of sources, insurgents needn't be so worried about one particular patron. The Reagan administration made a sincere and sometimes effective effort in this sphere. From 1985 to 1987, for example, the State Department convinced several European governments to halt or reduce direct subsidies to the Sandinistas.[95] Unfortunately, this success was balanced by a relatively heavy-handed effort to force governments in Latin America to help the cause. Countries refusing to assist the contras sometimes faced the threat of a U.S. aid cutoff. This might make sense as a means of quiet persuasion with a stable ally, but in the case of such countries as Guatemala and Honduras, which were themselves under internal pressure, it was out of line.

There are ways to sway such allies to back U.S. policy. Rethinking the policy a bit is one. Few Latin leaders failed to endorse U.S. contra aid on the ground that the overthrow of the Sandinistas would be a terrible thing. On the contrary, as James LeMoyne of the *New York Times* reported, they failed to back U.S. aid because they didn't think the program would lead to the overthrow of the Sandinistas: "The uncertainty about long-term United States aims and commitment may continue to make regional support for the rebel war less than whole-hearted."[96]

A populist focus suggests another strategy. Repeated polls, already cited, showed broad support for U.S. contra aid among Latin American voters. These should have been a cause for cheer in the Reagan administration.[97] They argued for patience; in time, if the people in a democratic country continue to support the United States, their leaders will respond. Instead, however, the administration remained hypnotized by elite reaction to every zig and zag in the region, with the predictable result that the Reagan policy toward Nicaragua persistently seemed to be the ball, not the bat, being shaped in foreign capitals rather than in the White House.

Then, too, there are direct diplomatic alternatives. Even as the Reagan administration was promoting the overthrow of the governments of Angola, Afghanistan, and Nicaragua, the United States continued to conduct normal diplomatic relations with these countries. This has important practical effects, such as permitting Daniel Ortega to roam about the United States collecting checks and winning supporters to his cause. By far the most important consequence, however, is political. To tell the American people that Ortega is a communist dictator, on the one hand, and then to treat him as if he were the ambassador to Sweden on the other, is to ask them to entertain two mutually exclusive ideas at the same time.

U.S. recognition of the foes of our friends not only confuses our people; it also harms our friends. The governments of Nicaragua and Afghanistan repeatedly reminded their peoples that even the United States viewed them as the true power ruling over the nation. As Malcolm Wallop argued:

> The central question at issue in these struggles [is this]: Who is the people's legitimate representative in countries like Afghanistan, Nicaragua, Poland, or Angola? . . . Perhaps the resistance would benefit more from clear statements by the Western world that the governments they fight are illegitimate than they do from halfhearted, ill-conceived aid.[98]

Many observers who have thought seriously about this issue nevertheless argue it is unwise to withdraw recognition. Some raise pragmatic arguments, noting that withdrawal would mean removing the American embassy, thereby depriving us of useful information. This was one of the Reagan administration's persistent arguments against withdrawing recognition from Managua. Yet there are ways to get information without having an embassy. And it is a curious reasoning that suggests that governments we are trying to overthrow allow us, out of generosity or stupidity, to maintain an embassy—even though it helps our cause more than theirs. If America's embassy in Kabul or Managua provided valuable information that could not otherwise be had, you can bet that those countries would order our diplomats to leave. Yet they do not, and for a good reason. One of the things undemocratic governments crave most is to be treated in the same way legitimate, democratic governments are. To treat them otherwise—to treat them as if our statements about them were true—is to deal them a severe blow.

Other opponents of a derecognition policy, such as Robert Kagan, Reagan's director of public diplomacy for Latin America, believe it is simply a bad precedent for the United States to withdraw recognition from governments for moral reasons. "Traditionally," Kagan notes, "when a group establishes sustained, serious control of a territory, we recognize it."[99] Yet such traditions, it seems to me, are made to be broken; they should bow to strategy, not the other way around. If the United States cannot adjust its policy on recognition to fit the modern reality of democratic insurgents fighting undemocratic governments, then the world may rightly wonder how serious we are about assisting democracy at all. Besides, since the presidency of Woodrow Wilson, there has evolved a tradition of not recognizing governments deemed to be especially corrupt—especially when we are sending arms to undermine them. The United States did not recognize the Soviet Union for more than a decade after the Bolshevik revolution. We ostracized the Red Chinese for a quarter century. We did not recognize the government of Angola for many years, and we did not, throughout the 1980s, recognize Savimbi's de facto government, which consistently controlled large portions of the territory of Angola. This precedent is not mere American moralism. Britain wisely recognized East European governments in exile during World War II. In the 1960s, every country in the Organization of American States except Mexico withdrew its recognition of Cuba in reaction to Cuba's efforts at subversion in Venezuela. In the 1980s, even the United Nations refused to legitimize the North Vietnamese puppet state that called itself the government of Kampuchea.[100]

There is, finally, a school of "neat-and-tidyists," as columnist William Safire has called them, which says: Well, if we remove recognition from Nicaragua, we would have to do so from the Soviet Union. There are several answers to that, among them: (1) Why so? Why can we not simply say that we find it in our interest to conduct formal relations with the Soviet Union, which has nuclear weapons, even though we view its government as no legitimate representative of the Russian will? In that case, the rule would be that America may refuse to recognize any undemocratic government, but chooses to recognize some when we deem it prudent. Alternatively: (2) Why not? This would not mean there would be no contact between the government of the United States and the government of the Soviet Union. We had contact with China for years before the full status of diplomatic recognition was extended. Perhaps a two-tiered system of recognition should be set up: one for more or less legitimate states, another for totalitarians. We would talk to all, but in appropriately different tones. It might be that our relationship with the Soviet Union would rest on a firmer foundation if there existed a constant reminder that the governments are not alike. The Soviets call democratic capitalism evil; we call communism evil. There would probably be better and more lasting agreements between the two countries if that ineradicable difference were kept in mind— until the day, long-delayed but still likely, the men in the Kremlin fully join the modern world, the world of democracies.

8

GROWTH AS DIPLOMACY: STABLE MONEY AND FREE TRADE

THE MODE OF PRODUCTION, Marxist doctrine holds, conditions and even governs a nation's political, social, and intellectual life. "With the change of the economic foundation," Karl Marx wrote, "the entire immense superstructure is more or less rapidly transformed." And while they would argue with the methodology of socialist production, many Western economists would agree with the important principle that economics is a powerful, perhaps decisive, factor in a society's politics.[1]

Few of us would take the relation so deterministically far. Such countries as Chile and South Africa, for example, have allowed a large and increasing degree of economic freedom for decades, yet both countries are far from free politically. Sweden curtails economic freedom yet has maintained a free and democratic political system.

Still, the connection between the two realms is strong. A strategy for building political democracy that does not include a strategy for economic freedom would, at best, omit an important tool.

For one thing, the elements of what used to be called "the political economy," are indivisible, almost by definition. A man who owns a farm capable of sustaining him and his family enjoys a greater degree of self-government, more "democracy" as we have used the term, than one who doesn't. And while terms like "economic freedom" and "political freedom" certainly have their valid uses, the distinction between them can be blurred and artificial. One can, for example, have the right to own a printing press—a "property right"—but without the right to use that press to publish a newspaper saying what you want to say—a "civil right" or "free speech"—the press may lose its value. As the earlier definition of the term "democracy" makes clear, these rights are best thought of as distinct but essential parts of a whole. The apposite metaphor for society and the state is not a building or a machine, but a living organism: the "body" politic.

Furthermore, even where clear distinctions can be drawn between political and economic activities, the two spheres clearly and importantly interact. Economic growth and economic freedom each encourage the formation and growth of free institutions: unions, commercial associations, communications networks, and eventually, political parties. With prosperity, too, comes rising aspirations for democratic rule, a trend clearly seen in such countries as Taiwan and South Korea, and even in Communist China during the 1980s. Yet people who are increasingly prosperous also tend to be satisfied with their political rulers. In economically free countries, this makes democracy less of a threat to ruling elites, as does the diffusion of economic power and social status that comes with economic growth. This diversity of interests and groupings forms a system of social and economic checks and balances that is analogous to, and supportive of, the checks and balances in successful, which is to say republican, democracies.

Development Mythology

If strategies for economic growth are important to democracy, however, so is democracy important to promoting healthy economic performance. One of the enduring fables that has debilitated development policy for decades has it that the people of Asia, Africa, and Latin America, while admiring Western ballots, are necessarily more concerned with getting their daily bread and butter. The conventional wisdom argues that people don't have time to worry about abstract rights of free speech and voting while they are hungry. It is only a small step to the conclusion that while democratic forms and political justice are fine things to develop for the future, they are a lower priority than the building of roads and factories.

This economic excuse for benign dictators was especially prevalent in the 1950s and 1960s, when an early wave of unrest and democracy hit Latin America. In those days, it was generally Republicans who stressed the iron laws of economics and order as superseding political justice. (Richard Nixon ably refuted the notion in his 1960 nomination speech and 1962 book, *Six Crises,* but it survived.) And this economics-über-alles theme persisted well beyond the 1960s. By the 1980s, the overemphasis on economic development was more popular with Democrats, who often moaned that even with free elections, such countries as El Salvador had no "real choice"—what they really needed was a good stiff dose of redistribution. The *New York Times* made this practically explicit in one 1987 editorial urging Philippine president Corazon Aquino to impose a vast program to seize lands from wealthy and not-so-wealthy landowners—an idea the legislature resisted, the paper suggested, only because "land barons" demanded no land reform at all. A 1984 *New Republic* cover featured a Yale professor sneering at the "Democratic Mystique," while an article months later in *Foreign Policy* called hopes for Latin pluralism a "pipe dream."[2]

In fact, economic prosperity rests on sand if it comes at the whim of an allegedly enlightened despot, whether a military dictator, as in Chile; or is the product of an autocracy, as in 1970s Korea, Chile, or Taiwan. And the global electorate understands this truth. Western elites continually stumble across this theme in their visits to the Third World, almost despite themselves. Consider this dispatch, filed by Alan Riding of the *New York Times* during Mexico's economic crisis of 1986:

> [T]he President has asserted that Mexico's troubles are not political but rather stem from the twin misfortunes of the earthquake that shattered the Mexico City area on 19 September 1985, and the near-collapse of oil revenues this year.
>
> In recent months, though, more and more Mexicans, inside and outside the Government, have begun to argue the opposite—that no solid economic recovery will be possible unless preceded by moves to modernize the political system. The resulting focus on the electoral system appears to have caught the regime by surprise.[3]

This sentiment is easy to miss, because the public, especially an impoverished one, cannot easily formulate its will in the explicit terminology of a Harvard-educated journalist. Naturally, a poor dirt farmer in Ecuador, who cannot read or write, is unlikely to quote Thomas Jefferson. Yet the interest is there, waiting to be noticed. In 1986 and 1987, the *Times* sent a number of reporters to Haiti to find out why the people of that country, despite wretched poverty, were so ignorantly blissful. Marlise Simons seemed genuinely mystified: "These people are far removed from the political debates now broadcast on Haitian radio and television on how new forms of capitalism or socialism might tackle extreme poverty. . . . Yet in the slum known as La Salin, just a step from disaster, people continued to talk with cheer about how life might change now."[4] The paper's Joseph Treaster wrote a similar article in 1987 entitled "Haiti a Year After Duvalier: Freedom Fills No Stomachs." An early paragraph reads: "Unemployment has increased, violent crime has soared, smuggled goods are flooding the country, and tourism is little more than a memory." Seething frustration, he worried, "threatens to explode at any time." Yet, he continued,

> no one would turn back the calendar. After nearly three decades under the heel of the Duvaliers, people are beginning to breathe free again.
>
> "For the first time, you are hearing people say whatever they want," said Louis Roy, who was the head of Haiti's Red Cross in 1959. A handful of newspapers and a dozen radio stations are churning out news reports and criticism. The capital is humming with debate over how to devise a form of democracy that can function in a land where the majority has always been poor [and] illiterate.[5]

The people of Haiti might not listen to the intricate details of every radio broadcast, or be able to cite the precise details of the emerging constitution, but this does not mean they are unconcerned about democracy. Quite the contrary: Their faith in democracy explains their optimism that economic problems can be worked out. It will one day be borne out. That this belief outlived not only the Duvalier dynasty but a subsequent succession of coups, upheavals, and retreats from the country's constitution testifies to the resilience of the democratic idea.

Even those who recognize the desire for democracy often argue that such political niceties must be held in abeyance, while the really critical work of promoting capitalism (or, for Democrats, social justice) speeds ahead. Democracy, this school argues, will eventually follow free markets or an end to maldistribution. Yet until the general population's material prosperity has been raised, this notion has it, the people lack the political instincts or education or institutions to make democracy flourish.

In fact, there is a "third force" for democracy in every country. Often it consists of the very people benefiting from economic freedom and clamoring for more, such as a rising business and labor class. Or the church members and intellectuals and would-be entrepreneurs whose persecution is cited as evidence that the government in question is unjust. In the Philippines, for example, Corazon Aquino said she probably would not have even run for the presidency had not thousands of committed Democrats stepped forward and convinced her that a race was winnable. Nevertheless, many Republicans continue to urge a policy of promoting capitalism first, democracy later, in such countries as South Africa, Chile, and Korea. At times, these Western capitalists sound almost Marxist in describing how the gradual erosion of socialism into capitalism will unfailingly produce democracy. Social welfarists, by contrast, seem to echo Adam Smith—or Edmund Burke's reflections on the influence of property on men's behavior—in their insistence that if land were properly distributed to peasants, democracy would flourish as a benign, invisible hand undermining oligarchs and death squads alike.

Those who remain skeptical about the prospects for democracy have certainly demonstrated mobility. When their argument doesn't fit one country, they simply move on to others. Early in 1986, a respected analyst of foreign affairs, writing in the *New York Times,* advised the United States to "keep Marcos," saying that we "should not bet" on Mrs. Aquino. In "virtually all" Asian countries, "most emphatically the Philippines, politics tends to be a winner-take-all business. . . . There is no consensus, no strong civic tradition," the author warned. "Neither are they hospitable to the emergence of a successful 'third force.' " A few months later, with Mrs. Aquino in power, the same writer argued in *The American Spectator* that the rest of Asia was no place to apply the "Philippines Corollary," contending: "It would be insanely dangerous and irresponsible for the United States to heed the advice of those who, in the name of democracy, now urge it to press change on the governments of the region."[6]

Often the proponents of this brand of cynicism are simply not looking hard enough at the world beyond supply curves and entitlements. Raul S. Manglapus, a leading adversary of Ferdinand Marcos in the Philippine Senate, has written an important refutation of the myth that despotism still dominates Oriental thinking entitled *Will of the People: Original Democracy in Non-Western Societies.* Manglapus convincingly demonstrates that democracy is deeply imbedded in the history of Asian thought and Asian practice, observing that the Filipinos practiced democracy "well before the advent of Western colonialism."[7] China scholar Simon Leys adds, "Human rights . . . are not a foreign notion in Chinese history." Kang Youwei, for example, made human freedom "a cornerstone" of his philosophy in the late nineteenth century. "Those who pretend that 'the Chinese are not interested in human rights' are blind and deaf."[8]

A more sophisticated variation on the economics-first model of democratic development holds that it is the direction of a country's economy, more so than its absolute position, that is critical to political liberalization. Here there are at least many cases that fit the theory. Numerous countries in economically stagnant Africa fell victim to coups during the turbulent eighties. Many of the countries cited as poor-man's democracies—such as China and India—may have started from a low base; yet at a time when the economies of many of their neighbors grew slowly or even shrank, both posted healthy growth rates.

Still, many countries managed the transition to elected government even during hard economic times. The gross national product per capita of Brazil, Peru, and Argentina actually shrank from 1980 to 1984, years in which all three countries shifted decisively toward democracy.[9] By contrast, Chile enjoyed relatively rapid growth, per capita income rising in real terms to $2,331 in 1980 from less than $1,700 in 1974. Supporters explained that at least Pinochet had stabilized the country, and brought about the prosperity from which democracy would surely flow. Yet these were the years in which Pinochet seized power, brutalized opponents, and solidified his dictatorial rule.

At the least, then, democracy is no hindrance to economic development: On the contrary, academic research suggests that the "poor, illiterate" masses, as the *Times* described the voters of Haiti,[10] are quite right to be so optimistic about democracy as an aid to economic growth. Atul Kohli, a political scientist at Princeton University, studied the economies of five democratic and five authoritarian regimes from 1960 to 1982, and determined that while countries ruled by benevolent dictatorships experienced economic growth in spurts, they trailed the democracies.[11] Notably, authoritarian regimes that did perform well—Brazil, Egypt, and South Korea—were well on their way to democratic rule in the 1970s and arguably had arrived in the late 1980s. The one democracy whose economy fared somewhat poorly, India, did so during the years when Mrs. Indira Gandhi undermined democratic rule. By the 1980s, Mrs. Gandhi's son Rajiv was an elected leader, and India was back on a growth track. Apologists for dictatorships, explains Paul Gigot, a columnist for the *Wall Street Journal,*

> often insist that democracy is bad for economic growth and free markets. Western nations cannot make the hard economic choices, they say, because democracies engage in self-destructive debate and must create welfare states to pay off political interests. . . . In my observation, however, the opposite is more nearly true in Asia. With the exception of Hong Kong, the region's authoritarian regimes are hardly the pristine models of unfettered capitalism. . . . Because they lack political legitimacy, authoritarians often attempt to buy their legitimacy by using state power to grant economic favors.[12]

Ironically, the one kind of advice many development officials are reluctant to give to struggling governments is to adopt greater democracy. This is deemed "interference" in the nation's affairs. Yet the same officials do not hesitate to impose economic policies in elaborate detail through the International Monetary Fund, the World Bank, the Agency for International Development (AID), and other institutions run or dominated by the United States. Harden Smith, a career foreign service officer assigned to several developing countries, chafed under such thinking. Here he exposes well its absurdity in a 1985 article for *The Washington Monthly:*

> The economic assistance we provide, the development projects we sponsor, and, above all, the military aid we give to Third World countries . . . inevitably affect the internal dynamics of a country, propping up the existing government or setting in motion political changes. . . . The real question is not whether we are interfering

in the political life of the Third World. Rather, it's whether our intervention is effective.

Why do we keep failing? I think a major reason is our failure to do *enough* meddling in these countries' internal affairs. Or, more precisely, we restrict our intervention to economic and social *programs,* hoping that well-fed people will not turn to the Soviets and that grassroots social programs will build responsive political institutions at the national level. But when such efforts go unaccompanied by the right kind of political action, they can produce results contrary to what we seek.[13]

Americans, unfortunately, tend to think of development in terms of specific programs, from the Peace Corps to AID to the IMF's bailout loans and restructuring programs. These in turn are seen and operated as transnational soup kitchens, analogous to our own domestic welfare system. At worst, they are carrots, handed out with little expectation that they will do anything more than keep the victim alive. At best, they involve telling people around the world how to grow carrots American-style.

Because we have our own domestic debates about what particular ideas are best to impose, these programs can appear to offer a diverse approach to foreign aid. Depending on ideological inclination, one Western development economist may recommend more spending on aid, another less. One may suggest we give aid only to countries that emphasize the redistribution of wealth; others may suggest that we demand recipients adopt lower tax rates or lesser subsidies for bread. Yet at the core, U.S. foreign-aid programs have essentially been the same, however differently they may be painted. All stem from an assumption that some "we"—Congress, the IMF, the *Washington Post* editorial page—understands what Paraguay really needs.

What would happen if we built foreign aid on a different assumption? Let us consider a program widely hailed as both an economic and a political success.

In the Beginning . . .

. . . was the Marshall Plan. Or at least that is where many accounts of the postwar recovery of Europe, and the world that resulted, begin. By the 1980s, for many politicians, to identify a troubled region in the world was to call for a Marshall Plan for it. Israeli Prime Minister Shimon Peres called for a Marshall Plan for the Middle East. Henry Kissinger, Jeane Kirkpatrick, and numerous neighbors to the south suggested a Latin American Marshall Plan. Jesse Jackson and Andrew Young proposed one for sub-Saharan Africa.[14]

If we compare Europe in 1945 to its condition a mere decade later, it's easy to understand these pleas. Of course, the situation of Third World nations in the 1970s and 1980s was hardly identical. Yet there are many parallels.

Even by 1947, two years after the war, European industrial production was below its 1938 levels. Total output over the same period had fallen by about 10 percent; agricultural production, by 17 percent. Many of these declines match those of the world's poorest nations after the inflation binge of the 1970s.[15]

Another measure of Europe's instability was its crushing war debt and trade shortfalls. Britain—one of the victors—had incurred lend-lease obligations to the United States alone of $25 billion, and a total war debt of $98 billion. The latter equaled almost two-thirds of the economic output of all of Europe in 1947, and was eight times total European exports for the same year. Britain, with less than $500 million in reserves at one point, expected to run an annual trade-deficit of between $5 billion and $10 billion for a minimum of several years.

Other countries—France, Greece, Italy—had smaller debts, having been occupied by the Germans for much of the war. Yet Europe's total reserves, including gold, totaled only $7.9 billion. Total European imports for the years 1945–50 amounted to between 150 percent and 350 percent of the exports they sold to pay for them.

All these figures are on a scale with those of the debt crises of the 1970s and 1980s. Indeed, many Third World countries, such as Mexico and Brazil, were running trade surpluses, though it was clear that what these countries truly needed was a massive program to import capital. At the end of 1986, both countries, according to a World Bank survey, had outstanding external debt of more than $100 billion. But both had annual exports of $20 billion to $30 billion, bank reserves of $5 billion to $10 billion, and total output of $150 billion to $250 billion.[16]

Indeed, a statistical comparison of the Bretton Woods situation with the debt crisis of the 1980s, provided in table 8.1, suggests some ways in which the former was more acute.

This is not to say that the overall situation of, say, France in 1948 was somehow worse than that of Brazil in 1984. France, along with the rest of Europe, was about to embark on a global boom of trade and growth unparalleled in two centuries. (From 1948 to 1971, world trade grew by an average of 7.3 percent per year; world industry, by 5.6 percent per year. In the entire history of growth cycles from 1720 to 1948, average growth in trade had never exceeded 4.9 percent, and growth in output never reached an annual average of 4 percent, for any twenty-year period.) And that, in a way, is the point. Huge debt figures, for a devastated continent, did not prevent an economic surge by Europe in the 1950s and 1960s. The main difference between the debtors of yesteryear and those of the 1980s is that the former generally paid off their

TABLE 8.1
A Tale of Two Debt Crises

	National Debt as Share of GNP (Percent)	External Debt (Public Only) as Share of GNP (Percent)
Bretton Woods Debtors		
France		
(1948)	51	14
(1950)	46	14
U.S.		
(1946)	125	n.a.
(1948)	96	n.a.
U.K.		
(1948)	210	13
(1950)	200	17
Third World Debtors		
Brazil		
(1984)	35	30
Mexico		
(1984)	48	44
Hungary		
(1985)	40	34
Nigeria		
(1984)	21	16
Total for 15 "troubled" IMF debtors		
(1985)	n.a.	46
Total for developing countries		
(1986)	50	35

SOURCE: National statistics compiled by the Alexis de Tocqueville Institution from annual reports by the International Monetary Fund, United Nations, Federal Reserve Bank of the U.S., British Treasury, and the World Bank.

loans at long maturities (five to thirty years) and low interest rates (1 to 4 percent) with very few conditions attached by the lender. That is a difference to which we shall return after we have analyzed the remarkable feat of Europe's revival from the debt.[17]

Of course, countries could print more of their own money to pay off the debt and, like contemporary Argentina, some tried to, with a predictable result: inflation. The French franc, valued at two cents at the time of the Normandy invasion, was worth about one-third of one penny by 1948. Hungary's currency nosedived until it took 11,000 trillion pengös to buy a single U.S. dollar. In February of 1946, *The New Republic* surveyed a group of leading university and business economists and found the majority "badly worried" about inflation. Most favored the indefinite continuation of price controls.[18]

Revisionists who have sought to put the success of postwar recovery into perspective point out that Europe—unlike many Third World countries in the

1980s—had railroads, telephone systems, and other infrastructure, as well as a highly skilled, well-educated work force. Fair enough. We should also remember, though, that much of the infrastructure had been blown up, and many of the skilled workers were dead. Britain lost almost half a million souls in the war. The wartime destruction of British productive capacity was more than seven times the total formation of productive capacity in 1938. In France, 500,000 buildings had been destroyed, another 500,000 seriously damaged. Half the country's cattle were gone, along with three out of every four railroad engines. Nine out of ten automobiles and trucks were inoperable, as were half the nation's roads and bridges. Germany was equally devastated; indeed, in the year after the war, German output was at one-third its 1936 level. Experts said it would take twenty years to rebuild.[19] "The skills and habits and arrangements of economic activity had been broken," writes historian Charles L. Mee. "Financial and political relationships were wrecked. The awesomeness of this act of self-destruction cannot easily be overstated. In short, the old empires left the world in a classical state of anarchy, or chaos."[20]

Even the arguments against helping were much the same. Many in the U.S. Congress urged against extending even $3.5 billion in emergency credits to Britain, much less aiding Greece and Turkey. Senator C. Wayland Brooks complained that the aid to Britain was "a gift, not a loan," while twenty-six governors wrote to Harry Truman urging him to achieve a balanced budget at least, a surplus if possible. Hysteria gripped many reporters and editorial writers. "U.S. in Role of Debtor Nation," blared a copy of the *United States News*. "Every American Owes $1,985," read a *New York Sun* headline. "Unless the budget is balanced," the National Association of Manufacturers warned, "it may never be until America goes over the precipice."[21]

This is the situation—no, the calamity—from which the United States and its major allies recovered and prospered; and the Marshall Plan is often credited with the result. From 1948 to 1971, world industrial production grew at a rate of 5.6 percent per year, exceeding the magnitude of increase for the entire "industrial revolution" from 1705 to 1948. Benefits were not limited to our allies; while European industrial production grew 76 percent from 1948 to 1955, the rest of the world's grew 74 percent. Even India outgrew the United States and Britain from 1950 to 1964. Japan outgrew just about everyone, its economy surging ahead with annual average rates of growth exceeding 10 percent through 1973.[22]*

---

*U.S. economists repeatedly warned that Japan's trade deficit, which reflected rapid importation of capital to expand production, would cause her to collapse or overheat. A 1957 report to the House Ways and Means Committee reported on a major "trade crisis," namely Japan's deficits. The next year Jerome Cohen wrote a book for the Rockefeller Foundation on the Japanese problem. He blasted Japan's "foolhardy" policy of large tax cuts, and asked: "How long can Japan continue to buy twice as much from us as it sells to us?" (*Japan's Postwar Economy* [Bloomington: University of Indiana Press, 1958]). The answer, apparently, was: for at least a generation, since Japan's large deficit with the United States was a permanent feature from 1945 to 1965.

Based on these extraordinary figures, the Marshall Plan has become a mantra for anyone seeking to revitalize the world economy. Tyler Cowen, a Harvard economist critical of the sometimes fustian claims made for its success, writes: "The success of the Marshall Plan is never questioned; the only issue is how to remodel the blueprint in order to suit the needs of the developing world."[23]

In popular legend, the Marshall Plan involved a sudden, spontaneous outpouring of U.S. generosity, in which we shipped dollars, food, and equipment in large amounts to countries that grew and prospered as a result. Generous the policies were. Yet the actual quantities were not astronomical. Marshall Plan shipments never represented more than 5 percent of the gross national product of the recipient countries, or more than 25 percent of their total imports.[24] As columnist Flora Lewis noted in the *New York Times:* "The real Marshall plan was not about pumping a large amount of money into distressed economies."[25]

If anything, the amount of aid, and its timing in relation to various recoveries, contradict causality. Britain received the most aid under the Marshall Plan and other forms of immediate postwar assistance; her anemic 2.8 percent annual growth through the mid-1970s, slowest in the industrial West, made her the laggard of modern Europe. France, too, received generous amounts of aid, but spent all of it and more maintaining an empire. In nine years, France spent 1.6 trillion francs in support of the Vietnam War—twice the amount of assistance received under the Marshall Plan.[26]*

Some observers focus intelligently on the conditions that came with U.S. help, some of which were constructive, others of which were not. Japan struggled through the early years of the recovery with industrial production at less than half its wartime levels. Not until she was permitted to ignore the cut-imports-and-raise-taxes advice of U.S. experts did Japan soar into the spectacular growth of 1955–71. Similarly, Austria's economy was stagnant during the early years of the Marshall Plan—despite $280 million in aid, the largest amount per capita going to any country. Tight wartime trade and production controls were kept intact by Allied occupation officials. Then aid was reduced: to $127 million in 1951 and $38.5 million in 1953. "The radical cuts," according to economist Franz Nemschak, compelled Austria "to make a basic change in its economic policy." By the end of 1953, inflation had been halted, the economy was growing, and Austria had a dollar surplus of $70 million.[27]

Germany labored under various restrictions into 1948, as the Allied Control Commission maintained Nazi-era price controls, rent control, and production quotas. Commissioners raised taxes by an average of 50 percent in the first two years after the war, and in 1945 and 1946, allowed no foreign trade.[28] The West

*Note that the "Marshall" Plan was in fact conceived in roughly equal parts by a number of Truman's top aides, including Marshall, Acheson, and Undersecretary of State Will Clayton.

GROWTH AS DIPLOMACY

German *Wirtschaftswunder* began in June 1948, when authorities allowed insistent local officials to stabilize the German mark against gold and other currencies. The economy improved within hours, as Germans began to accept money in exchange for goods and services. Weeks later, Ludwig Erhard, economic director of the British-American zone, embarked on a program of free trade and tax-rate cuts. One Sunday while the Allied officials were not in their offices, Erhard abolished rationing. When angry U.S. authorities confronted him the next day, something like the following dialogue took place:

> *U.S. official:* "How dare you relax our rationing system when there is a widespread food shortage!"
> *Erhard:* "But Herr Oberst, I have not relaxed rationing; I have abolished it! Henceforth the only rationing ticket the people will need will be the deutschmark. And they will work hard to get those deutschmarks, just wait and see. . . ."
> *General Clay:* "Herr Erhard, my advisers tell me you're making a terrible mistake."
> *Erhard:* "Don't worry, General; my advisers tell me the same."[29]

The Root of All Good

What happened becomes easy to understand if we look not at what Europe lacked in 1945, but at what it had, which was, despite erosion, a vast body of human capital—people capable of producing goods and services with the right tools. (The Third World has this today.) Europe had little money, and few immediate goods and services, to trade for things in the short term. (The Third World lacks all these things, too.) But Europe did have long-term potential. Europeans would gladly work hard, and promise to keep producing and sending goods and services in the years to come—in exchange for the goods they needed to survive, and for the industrial capacity they needed to produce efficiently.

America, meanwhile, had a healthy stock of existing capital capable of producing goods and services right now. Americans would gladly keep producing things today and shipping productive capital from a large existing pool—in return for promises to be rewarded later. What was needed was a mechanism to bring these two groups together.

Three years before the Marshall Plan, diplomats and economists and politicians meeting at a small resort in Bretton Woods, New Hampshire, hammered out the agreement that was the secret of the Marshall Plan's success. The pact, ratified by the U.S. Senate in 1945, promised:

1. To fix the values of all currencies to a set rate of exchange with the U.S. dollar; and to fix the dollar, in turn, to gold, at a price of $35 to the ounce.
2. To complete the settlement of postwar debts using this Bretton Woods system, and the IMF and World Bank it created, to finance loans at low rates of interest.
3. To stop erecting new trade barriers and begin dismantling the ones that existed.

Most notable of all, perhaps, the negotiators understood and agreed that these objectives were all connected. Stable money was the key to low interest rates on debt, reducing the premium that banks and nations demand when money is of uncertain future value. It was also a key to free trade, allowing businesses to plan, and making it harder for nations to engage in monetary warfare—inflating and deflating their money in an elusive attempt to gain a trading edge. "Trade restrictions," as the great French economist Jacques Rueff would write, "cannot be removed safely until a sound monetary system has been restored."[30] Lower trade barriers, meanwhile, were linked to debt: Growth in trade would promote growing production, which would pay off debts faster. And the reasonable rates of payment would help spur growth in and of themselves, as well as easing debtor resentments and nationalist sentiments. That made it easier to lower trade barriers.

One architect of the system, ironically, was John Maynard Keynes, who had once referred to gold-backing for currencies as a "barbarous relic." As early as 1933, though, Keynes had grown more concerned the Great Depression might precipitate a further deflationary "breakdown of the existing structure of contract and instruments of indebtedness, accompanied by the utter discredit of orthodox leadership." His remedy: Provide more credit that was simultaneously more creditworthy—instruments of debt in which lenders would have confidence. This, Keynes reasoned, meant a return to traditional financial instruments.

> It involves, that is to say, a qualified return to the gold standard. . . . It may seem odd that I, who have lately described gold as a "barbarous relic," should be discovered as an advocate of such a policy, at a time when the orthodox authorities of this country are laying down conditions for our return to gold which they must know to be impossible. . . . But I believe that gold has received such a gruelling that conditions might now be laid down for its future management.[31]

Bretton Woods worked well while it lasted. Prices and exchange rates were stable, with both severe inflations and deflations made impossible. Nations that could not maintain their currency had to repeg at a new rate. But the changes, as Keynes had advocated in his 1933 pamphlet, involved "small degrees" and took place only in "emergencies and exceptional cases."[32] With the future value of currencies far more secure, debt was manageable. Rates on short-term U.S.

Treasury bonds, at the height of the 1946 elite hysteria over America as a "debtor nation," were as low as 0.75 percent, and remained in the 2 to 4 percent range through the 1960s.[33] Trade liberalization followed, as Acheson and others had predicted. Economist Robert Triffin compiled an index of European trade barriers for the period, based on the percentage of imports covered by restrictions or tariffs. By 1950, the "average liberalization" of trade was 56 percent, growing to 65 percent in 1952, 83 percent in 1954, and 89 percent in 1956. In 1959, the Common Market was formed, and from 1963 to 1967, many restrictions on American trade fell as a result of the "Kennedy Round" of talks concerning the General Agreement on Tariffs and Trade, or GATT. From 1948 to 1971, world trade grew at an annual rate of more than 7 percent.[34]

Thus Charles L. Mee, despite giving short shrift to the role of Bretton Woods, concludes that it was the "enormously complex set of factors" behind what we call the "Marshall Plan" that made it work. "Monetary stabilization programs were enforced throughout Europe with particular strictness. . . . Tariff barriers were reduced. . . . [T]he plan contributed, more than dollars or credits or goods, the crucial element of confidence—for governments to reach across borders, for entrepreneurs to take new risks, for banks to extend credit."[35]

The years of Bretton Woods and the Marshall Plan, rightly understood, coincide with the solidification of democracy throughout much of the free world, most notably in Germany and Japan. The secret of this initiative, however, lay not in extensive micromanagement of national economies from Washington. Rather, America allowed countries to choose the national economic policies that seemed best to them. Successful experiments, such as Germany's, were quickly studied and emulated. Countries that floundered had no one to blame but themselves. At the same time, U.S. economic leadership created a general climate of economic growth based on stable money and increasingly free trade. In other words, America agreed to perform, and for twenty-five years did perform, the chore of maintaining the international price and trade system. This could only be done with U.S. leadership because only U.S. authorities controlled the supply and value of the dollar, the dominant currency in the world in 1945. World money needs a world banker, one willing to overlook narrow self-interest and act as the good shepherd for the system.

No one would say that the precise conditions of the Marshall Plan can be replicated in countries distant from Europe years after the war. For one thing, there is no occupying army to insist on fair, competitive elections. Yet to understand the urgent need for such a program, we might consider the problem in reverse. If even the democratization of Europe required an era of steady economic growth and liberalization, as many argue, how can we expect countries less well off, with even fewer material advantages than Europe in the forties, to thrive? If stable money and free trade were needed for powerful industrial countries to get back on their feet, don't poor nations need this solid foundation even more?

From the late 1960s on, however, the United States turned the development model of Bretton Woods and the Marshall Plan almost on its head. Whereas previously America had kept the dollar "as good as gold," as John Kennedy put it, it now gradually severed the link to gold, finally and formally smashing Bretton Woods in 1973. And where American aid programs, and American-dominated institutions such as the International Monetary Fund, had maintained a relaxed, hands-off approach toward imposing national economic policies, IMF and AID bureaucrats became ever more intrusive, often crafting specific budgets and austerity programs for entire countries.

Indeed, the two reversals were closely linked. The monetary chaos touched off when Richard Nixon first devalued the dollar in 1971 was a prime cause of much of the economic hardship that followed: the energy crisis, stagflation, Third World debt, trade and budget deficits, and the global stock market crash of 1987. Those crises, in turn, required crisis management. So experts from the IMF and Western banks dashed about the globe, recycling petrodollars from massive oil and commodity price inflations one year and patching together loans after drastic price deflations the next.

This monetary account of world instability since the 1970s strikes some economists as absurd, though scholars such as Robert Triffin, Robert Mundell, Arthur Laffer, Lewis Lehrman, and Alan Reynolds have published extensive documentation. Yet if we wish to account for the sea change from growth and relative stability, we must conclude that something fundamental changed in the economic system—something that undermined the efforts of workers, businessmen, and governments, even as they struggled to make the system work. (If not, then we must assume that leaders around the world simultaneously and inexplicably became incompetent around 1971—an assumption few Western leaders seem eager to make. By the end of the 1980s, having tried scheme after scheme to paper over the recurring crises, more and more politicians and economists were coming around to the systemic explanation.) This becomes quite understandable when one reviews the consequences of nearly two decades of a radical experiment with floating exchange rates and unbacked currencies.

Default American Style

Many economists and politicians reacted with glee when the postwar monetary order was dismantled. Milton Friedman foresaw an end to the periodic adjustments that took place when nations had to revalue their currencies. "Flexible exchange rates," he asserted, "are more stable." John Connally and George Shultz, two of Richard Nixon's top economic advisers, argued that America would now be free to promote a decline in the dollar. This, in turn, would make goods from Japan and Europe more expensive here, while making U.S. goods cheaper abroad: a trade surplus. Paul Volcker, then an aide in the Treasury Department, testified that fears of a resulting inflation were "greatly overstated," reassuring Congress that "our moves will yield major support to our balance of payments in the course of 1972 and 1973." As late as February of 1973, economist Alan Greenspan dismissed inflationary fears: "What we are observing currently," he said, "may well turn out to be a more fundamental disinflationary trend."[36]

Others demurred. Such then-obscure scholars as Arthur Laffer and Robert Mundell, members of what would later be called the supply-side school of economics—which focuses on the incentive effects of government policies, from tax rates to the value of the dollar—saw trouble. The combination of unbacked currencies and high tax-rate systems, Laffer said, would push countries throughout the West into an age of high inflation and slow growth. Mundell, speaking at a conference in Geneva in 1972, projected a dramatic increase in the price of oil, followed by other commodities. Add this dynamic to a world of steeply progressive tax structures, he said, and you would turn the Phillips curve inside out: High inflation and rising unemployment at the same time. Democrats railed against the illogic of both Volcker's inflation predictions and trade-deficit theory. "Making the dollar worth less," Senator Robert Byrd argued, "will make it worthless." Senator William Proxmire: "I would like to believe that there will be some decline in Japanese imports. . . . But I doubt it. I sure doubt it."[37]

There was excitement in the air one day early in the 1970s, as the American Enterprise Institute called together leading economists to speculate about the brave new world of floating. Triffin, however, rained on the AEI picnic, terming the idea of "institutionalizing daily fluctuations" in exchange rates "absurd." He noted:

> [F]loating rates might have the beneficial effects claimed for them only if nonintervention in the exchange markets could be made mandatory. . . . But giving up monetary union would also entail giving up economic union. . . . Neither the agricultural common market nor free trade in other goods would be able to survive free fluctuations of exchange rates within the community. Powerful lobbies would force governments to restore trade restrictions against what they would call—rightly or wrongly—unfair competition and exchange-rate dumping by the countries whose currency would depreciate in terms of their own.[38]

Triffin here underlines an important characteristic of fixed-rate systems: Whatever their direct benefits, they deprive protectionists of a monetary excuse for erecting tariffs and other barriers. And however often they may be violated by individual countries, they affix clear blame on the violator, who must revalue against the rest of the world.

Critics of Bretton Woods fondly made the following binary argument, paraphrased here but made commonly, even years later, by such economists as George Shultz: "If countries don't coordinate their policies to maintain a fixed rate system, it is of no benefit. Divergent fiscal and monetary policies cause fluctuations and undermine the system anyway. But if countries do coordinate their policies, they will produce stable exchange rates and honest currencies anyway. In that case, the system is unnecessary."[39] What this argument misses—as Triffin, Mundell, and the defenders of Bretton Woods saw—is that monetary agreements can build economic expectations and political coalitions, which in turn affect economic policies for the better. Consider how Shultz & Company might view, say, the schedule of the National Football League: "If all the players and fans don't show up at the right stadiums at the right time, there will be no games. The season is undermined anyway. But if everyone shows up at the right time and place, the season will go along nicely. In that case, the schedule is unnecessary."

Richard Nixon's decision had at least this virtue: Opponents of Bretton Woods would be offered a fair test of their theories that a free market for currencies—as they erroneously called it—would benefit American and international interests. An overview of the post-1971 era suggests that these benefits never materialized.

Under Bretton Woods, U.S. unemployment never rose above 7 percent. In the years that followed, it was considered a triumph when it dipped below 7 percent. The dollar exchange rate against twelve major currencies changed by an average of less than 1 percent for twenty-five years under Bretton Woods, with only an occasional devaluation by individual nations. After 1971, the U.S. exchangerate often varied more than 20 percent a year, and as much as several percentage points a day, against the yen, the mark, and the franc. Under Bretton Woods, interest rates on a ninety-day Treasury note ranged as low as 0.5 percent, never topping 5 percent until the system was half-destroyed in 1968. After Bretton Woods, interest rates never dipped below 7 percent. Yet these high rates didn't make banks rich; instead, they drove many of the loans the banks had made into the "nonperforming" category. From 1946 to 1970, there were never more than nine domestic bank failures in a single year. From 1971 to 1980, by contrast, a total of 83 banks failed; and then things got grim: The number of failures rose to 10 banks in 1981, 42 banks in 1982, 49 banks in 1983, 80 banks in 1984, and 120 banks in 1985. Ironically, the dismantling of Bretton Woods, undertaken partly for narrow nationalist reasons, didn't even improve America's trade position.[40]

The events following the dismantling of Bretton Woods, then, followed the

FIGURE 8.1

Before and After
Real Nonoil Commodity Prices, 1957–87

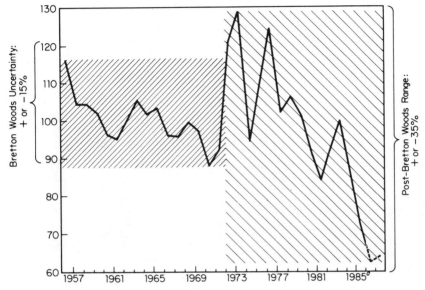

SOURCE: World Economy Survey (Washington, D.C.: International Monetary Fund, April 1988).
[a] Data after end-1986 are estimates.

pattern predicted by those who argued against such a policy. Unhitching currencies from one another and from gold, of course, produced many gyrations. But from 1971 through 1988, two distinct waves occurred. From 1971 through 1981, there was an inflationary wave; from 1981 through 1988, a deflationary wave. The sum was a large increase in uncertainty—a tendency for prices to move more sharply in both the inflationary and deflationary directions. In both cases, the impact on the economies of countries struggling to build democracy was unfortunate. Figure 8.1 provides an overview of those tides.

Let us consider first the wave to hit the international system, one of inflation. Within eighteen months of the decision to dismantle fixed exchange rates and the link to gold, the price of gold leaped as high as $170 from its initial $35, leveling off in the range of $120 until 1977. The clear implication—if the Bretton Woods model is correct, and gold is an accurate predictor of future price movements—was of a rapid rise in prices in the years ahead. And rise prices did, as we see in figure 8.2, bearing in mind that inflation rates for 1965 through 1970 already reflect the first deviations from Bretton Woods.

Among the first items to skyrocket—because like gold it reacts rapidly to changes in monetary policy—was oil. Between 1971 and 1974, oil prices

FIGURE 8.2

Exit Bretton Woods, Enter Inflation
Average Annual Percent Change in Consumer Prices

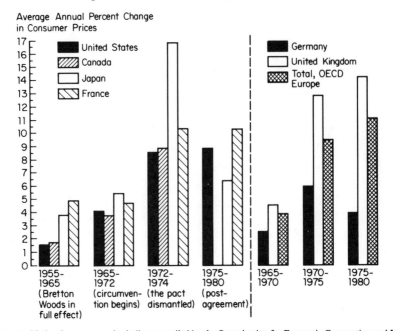

Average Annual Percent Change
in Consumer Prices

SOURCE: National consumer price indices compiled by the Organization for Economic Cooperation and Development, U.S. Commerce Department, and the Alexis de Tocqueville Institution. Figures compiled by John Mueller and Paul Craig Roberts from the annual *Economic Report of the President*, U.S. Department of the Treasury, Federal Reserve Board; and U.S. Department of Commerce, Bureau of the Census, *Historical Statistics of the United States . . . Colonial Times to 1970* (Washington, D.C.: Superintendent of Documents, 1975), and *Statistical Abstract of the United States* (Washington, D.C.: Superintendent of Documents, December 1986).

increased from $2.50 a barrel, a level from which they had not deviated substantially since the 1950s, to more than $12 a barrel. The rough quadrupling of the gold price coincides neatly with the quadrupling-plus of the oil price, suggesting that while OPEC certainly played an important role in the oil price rise, the primary factor was monetary.[41] Prices for other goods rose as well. Between 1966 and 1974, the price of oil rose 344 percent.[42] In the same period, the price of rice rose 375 percent, wheat rose 322 percent, and lead rose 233 percent. "The inflation had become worldwide," Mundell notes. "Currencies in general declined, and a shift out of money and financial assets commenced. A worldwide 'scarcity' of land and land-intensive products, including raw materials, emerged. Shortages of beef, sugar, and grains appeared, but gold and oil led to the most dramatic 'crises' and received the most attention."[43]

Most Americans will remember the strain placed on even their own relatively prosperous and stable country by these events. A vast library of books poured forth documenting a necessary *End of Affluence* and presaging the

GROWTH AS DIPLOMACY

Coming Oil War. Jimmy Carter declared a "national malaise," and many Americans tended to agree.

Now let us consider the impact on a country a fraction the size of the United States, with a less diverse economy: South Korea, Turkey, or Jamaica. Or one with a growing manufacturing sector, much of it energy-intensive: Thailand. Or a nation that imports not a quarter or half of its energy needs, but better than 80 percent: Taiwan. Or a farming country that's reliant on farm-export earnings, and may have to pump vast resources into fertilizers, machinery, and other oil-based products and operations: India, Peru, Brazil, or Argentina.

Each one of these countries suffered from sluggish growth in the 1970s. Those that could continue modest growth often found their products shunned in Europe and America, as Western farmers demanded import protection or production subsidies to beat back the foreign competition. The strain was sufficient to produce outright coups, or major crackdowns against democratic dissent, in every single one of the countries named during the great inflation of the 1970s. Many of these countries also received generous packages of foreign aid that helped patch over the crisis. Most survived and, with the end of the inflation binge in the 1980s, resumed a rapid path to democracy. They would have been far better off, however, without the gyrations in the world price and trade system.

Besides producing general discomfort, inflation and deflation cause a radical restructuring of many existing economic relationships, almost any relationships, such as loans or production contracts, that are denominated in terms of money. During an inflation, creditors suffer a windfall loss at the expense of debtors. Suppose the Topeka Savings and Loan has loaned Mike Tucker $100,000, which at present prices will buy one new home, or 20 new cars, or 200 ounces of gold. Then an inflation occurs in which prices double. Now the same home costs $200,000; or, to put it another way, the same $100,000 buys only half a home, or 10 new cars, or 100 ounces of gold. Yet Mr. Tucker still owes the bank only the original $100,000. When the bank gets its money, it will buy only half what it could have bought when the bank loaned it out. It suffers a windfall loss, while Tucker, who pays back money worth only half as much, enjoys a windfall gain of equal amount.

In a deflation, the roles are reversed. Suppose, for example, Mr. Tucker is a farmer. He borrows $100,000 for equipment to produce a field full of wheat, which at today's prices will fetch $130,000—enough to pay off the loan and feed his family. But a deflation occurs, driving the price of wheat down by 30 percent. Now the same field of wheat brings in only $91,000. Tucker can't even make enough to pay off the loan. What's more, if the falling price of wheat is part of a general deflation, he owes, in a sense, much more than what he borrowed. Dollars now buy more real goods and services in the world. Yet Tucker still owes the $100,000 set out in his contract. He must trade something that is far more valuable now than when he borrowed it in the first place.

In a country like the United States, with vast numbers of debtors and creditors, primary producers and finished manufacturers, inflation and deflation are bad enough. During the inflationary 1970s, for example, unemployment soared in New England, which tends to import oil and other commodities, while farm states like Iowa and Nebraska, commodity exporters, did well relative to the rest of the country. During the 1980s, the farm belt and oil states suffered from depressed prices for their products, while the Northeast thrived. At least in a large, industrialized, stable country, however, these winners and losers generally balance off.

Most countries in the world, by contrast, are smaller, less wealthy, and less diverse. Many rely on a single product or two, or a few closely related products, for most of their export earnings, tax revenues, and so on. With this in mind, the political unrest seen during the 1970s inflation surplus and energy shortage becomes understandable, if not predictable. The devastating effect of capricious price and exchange-rate fluctuations on these developing nations can be seen even more clearly in the second great wave of price manipulation of the post–Bretton Woods era, the deflation of the 1980s.

The Creditors Deflate

Something had to be done with all the unwanted liquidity floating through international banks. The dollars and other Western currencies shipped to Arab oil exporters and other commodity producers would do them no good sitting idly in accounts. Fortunately, the rising prices for most commodities made loans to many Third World countries a good bet. Indeed, loans to any sort of commodity producer made great sense. In the United States, farmers in the Midwest easily tapped banks for money to expand production of goods that seemed likely to rise in price for many years. A boom of new buildings scraped the sky in Dallas, Houston, and the oil patch. William J. Quirk, an economic analyst who followed the process closely, picks up the story in an analysis for *The New Republic:*

> The money transfer was tremendous. In 1972 the Arabs received $24 billion from the rest of the world. In 1982 they received $230 billion. . . . Poor countries, of course, could not pay. . . . The ingenious solution was "recycling."
> The banks loaned money to Zaire so it could pay the Arabs, who then deposited the collections back in the banks. The parties thought the merry-go-round could go on forever. In year one the banks loaned Zaire enough to pay its oil tax, say $1 billion. In year two the banks rolled over that billion and had to loan enough

new money to cover year two's oil tax, say another billion, plus the interest on the outstanding debt, say $200 million. [The result was] a geometric progression of compound interest.[44]

Thus, from 1973 to the peak of the recycling crisis in 1981, net international bank lending grew by more than a factor of five, cresting at $170 billion a year. Net lending by the International Monetary Fund moved from the minus column in 1973—meaning that nations were actually paying back more than they took out—to more than $6 billion at one peak in 1976, and another in 1981. Net IMF lending figures, of course, measure only a fraction of debtor distress, since the fund is supposed to function as a lender of last resort, stepping in when a country is already near bankruptcy and needs a "bridge loan" until it can get its economy in order.[45]

Now, many of these loans were justified, even needed. The only thing worse than recycling would have been not recycling. The debt of U.S. farmers, for example, more than doubled from 1970 to 1979, starting at $53 billion and ending at $136 billion. Yet the total value of farm output grew at about the same pace: $54.9 billion in 1970, it grew to $148.2 billion in 1979. Meanwhile, the value of farm assets, an estimated $314.9 billion in 1970, surged to $872 billion in 1979.[46]

Even Third World countries generally managed to stay afloat while the debt and inflation were building. Demand for the IMF's distress loans, in fact, fell steadily from 1975 on, and for most of 1977, 1978, and 1979 the IMF was still receiving more payments than it was lending out. As long as world trade was consistent—measured in nonadjusted dollars, world imports grew to $1.9 trillion in 1979 from $0.8 trillion in 1973, keeping ahead of inflation—most countries were able to make their payments easily, out of the expanded demand for their oil, or metals, or farm products. The balance on current account for developing countries moved from a onetime deficit of more than $20 billion to a positive balance of $20 billion by the end of 1979. In 1976, Mexico received an IMF stand-by loan of $1 billion. With prices for oil continuing to rise, Mexico paid the loan back early in 1978.[47]

A war merely to slow down and control inflation would have produced no disasters, either for those Western farmers and oilmen or for the debtor nations of the Third World. Unfortunately, when the U.S. Federal Reserve system finally set out to fight inflation late in the 1970s, it had not yet learned the full lesson of the decade of monetary instability. The Fed had learned about the ravages of inflation, and with the appointment of Volcker as chairman in October of 1979, the bank indiscriminately ravaged back. But the Fed was not prepared to handle a phenomenon Volcker would later describe as being equally destructive—deflation.

Since all prices are a ratio—say, dollars to oil or oil to dollars—the *rise* of the value of the dollar can be measured by the *decline* in the dollar price relative to other goods, gold being a good proxy for "other goods." At its peak, the price of gold stood at $800 the ounce—meaning the price of a dollar was ⅛₀₀th of an ounce of gold. Within three years, the Fed had clamped down on credit so hard that gold cost $300 the ounce. Dollars were so dear that it now took ⅓₀₀th of an ounce of gold to buy one dollar. The price had more than doubled. (This squeeze meant that the dollar was healthy indeed; not so healthy, however, were the millions of people around the world who needed dollars to exchange for goods and services, or counted on a steady currency to conduct business, write contracts, or store the value of their labor.)

Volcker was not alone in advocating this strategy, though as chairman of the Fed he played a major role.[48] When he abandoned supply targeting in 1982, allowing the price of gold to recover to the $450 range, there was a rash of protests from many economists, who argued that the resulting surge of money growth would revive stagflation. "We shall be fortunate indeed if we escape either a return to double-digit inflation rates or renewed recession in 1984," Milton Friedman wrote in *Newsweek,* predicting inflation of 12 percent or more in the *Wall Street Journal.*[49]

In the event, there was no hyperinflation and no U.S. recession after 1983. But the deep effects of the 1979–82 deflation were felt around the world. From 1979 to December 1982, unemployment in the United States surged to above 10 percent, a level not seen since the Great Depression. Given the implications such a price decline has for the condition of debtors, we should not be surprised at the crises that jolted the U.S. and world economies.

One debtor who suffers from a U.S. economic decline is the U.S. government. As the economy slows, businesses produce at a lower rate, and fewer people find work, causing revenues to decline. Meanwhile, as the ranks of the jobless swell, more and more families qualify and sign up for unemployment assistance, welfare, and food stamps, causing expenditures to rise. Moreover, when prices change rapidly and repeatedly, the premium needed to cover the true risks of lending increases. If interest rates rise—and they rose to drastically high levels throughout the 1980s—then the government must make much higher annual payments on its existing pool of debt. As Leonard Silk of the *New York Times* has observed:

> Every 1 percent drop in real gross national product . . . would increase the deficit by $6 billion in the first year and $21 billion in the second. . . . Thus, a recession that turned forecast growth of 2.6 percent in 1989 into negative growth of 2 percent would swell the projected deficit by $105 billion, to approximately $285 billion in the fiscal year 1990.[50]

From less than 2 percent of the gross national product in 1978, the U.S. budget deficit grew to more than 5 percent in 1983. Such was the impact of the Federal Reserve's deflation in the United States. There was a great deal of sermonizing in Congress and the press over deficits "out of control" as the GNP shrank by 2 percent for a year, and unemployment neared 11 percent. Yet in patches of the United States, the situation was much worse. In many states—West Virginia, for example, heavily dependent on steady prices for coal and other energy commodities—unemployment neared 20 percent. Whole towns and cities, some larger than whole nations in Africa, went belly-up. U.S. credit institutions with more assets than the gross national product of Ecuador, such as Penn Central, went broke.

Developing nations—most of them heavily in debt after the 1970s recycling—now also shared the brunt of the deflation. Following gold, the price of oil, a leading source of revenue for many debtor countries, fell to less than half its 1980 level by 1986. Nonoil commodities dropped almost as steeply. Various indices of prices for primary products plunged. See table 8.2.

The falling price of gold not only signaled a deflation that pulled down the income of Third World countries. It effectively reduced the world's monetary reserves by roughly one-half. This was a severe combination, leaving debtors less income precisely as banks began to demand repayment. All at a time when such countries were becoming an ever-worse credit risk. The value of having a Third World country owe you $1, as reflected by sales of such debts in secondary markets, was calculated not at $1, or even 75 cents, but at 12 cents for Bolivian debt, 16 cents for Peruvian debt, and 48 cents for Argentine debt. Regulators required that the banks reduce the share of their portfolios devoted to developing nations, and the squeeze grew tighter. Just when the Third World needed help, net bank lending to problem countries declined, from $56 billion in 1981 to a negative $1 billion in 1986 and 1987. Net transfers from the IMF to sub-Saharan Africa moved from an average of plus $1 billion a year

TABLE 8.2
Falling Return for Third World Exports:
IMF Price Index

Product	January 1980	November 1986	Percent Change, 1980 to 1986
Agricultural raw materials	104	80	−23
Beverages	114	92	−18
Food	94	62	−34
Metals	110	66	−40
IMF index for all commodities	103	71	−31
United Nations index: real price of nonoil commodities	100	62	−38

SOURCE: *World Economic Outlook* (Washington, D.C.: International Monetary Fund, April 1987), p. 94; United Nations index, cited in Victor Mallet, "African Economic Reform Fights 'Spirit of Despair,' " *Financial Times,* 5 March 1988.

from 1981 to 1983 to minus $0.4 billion in 1985 and minus $0.9 billion in 1986 and 1987.[51]

Consider the stress placed on a country like Nigeria. From 1980 to 1983, oil export earnings rose to $25 billion and then plunged to $10 billion. Debt, $9 billion in 1980, soared to $20 billion. A coup followed just days after the election of a new civilian government in 1983. Thus was the most populous country in Africa, a tenuous but rising democracy, brought to its knees— not willfully, but certainly carelessly—by a needless manipulation of the price level. "The coup in Nigeria," one central banker admonished colleagues at a 1984 conference, "was due to the impossibility" of Nigeria's financial situation.[52]

In the United States, great pain resulted when inflation-adjusted gross national product fell 2 percent and government revenues dropped by 2.8 percent, over one year, with the government's budget deficit reaching 5 percent of GNP. In El Salvador, real GNP fell by between 1 percent and 11 percent every year for seven years straight, forcing cuts in government spending (mostly from social programs) of 3 percent a year over the same period. It is hardly surprising that many such countries found it hard to sustain stability and democracy. What astonishes is that by the 1980s, popular interest in democracy was so strong that many countries throughout Asia and Latin America were able to overcome even these economic obstacles.[53]

The inflation of the 1970s tended to hit hardest those countries damaged by increasing prices for raw materials, such as the (now) newly industrialized nations of Asia and the nonoil-exporters of Latin America. Not surprisingly, the 1980s deflation, launched upon Volcker's 1979 appointment, tended to punish a different set of countries. "Beginning in mid-1979," the *Washington Post* later reported, "six coups and two coup attempts against the civilian governments of West Africa have reversed what was seen as a period of spreading political democratization in the region in the 1970s. . . . Nigeria and Guinea are the most recent additions to military councils. . . . The others are Mauritania, Mali, Niger, Upper Volta, Benin, Togo, Ghana, Liberia, and Guinea-Bissau."[54]

As the chart on pages 204–5 makes clear, there was a common thread linking these countries. Falling prices for the handful of goods their economies depend on made military takeovers, while hardly inevitable, far more likely.

African states that did tough out the deflation decade to remain significantly democratic often benefited from a diverse (though not necessarily prosperous) economy: Cameroon, Senegal, and Liberia, as described in the chart, all produce some finished or refined products, and accordingly their economic decline was not as severe as in many other countries. Indeed, Cameroon's per capita output rose to $1,300 in 1987 from $800 in 1983. Zimbabwe also benefited from what an administration human rights report called "the most complete economic infrastructure in black Africa—mineral resources, a strong agricultural base, and a diversified manufacturing sector." A one-party democracy, Zimbabwe held what the United States recognized as "largely free and fair" elections in 1985, with opposition candidates winning sixteen of eighty seats.[55]

Many African leaders undoubtedly made the problems of deflation worse by adopting ill-advised national economic policies of their own. The goal of U.S. policy, though, should not be to promote maximum suffering by every small country that bets wrong on the inflation-deflation roulette wheel, or fails to achieve the greatest possible efficiencies as its income sinks by 25 percent and more. Our goal should be to minimize such shocks in the first place. And to minimize the suffering when they happen.

Monetary Causes, Political Consequences

As damaging as monetary instability was in its direct effects, it had two important consequences. The first was an expansion of Western aid and lending programs—and with that expansion, growing power for the authorities who administer them. The State Department's Agency for International Development, which offers grants and loans for emergency relief and specific projects, has some influence, particularly over small countries in which the United States plays a large role: Jamaica, for example. The World Bank, which makes loans and gifts to the poorest of the poor at subsidized low rates, can have an important influence as well. Yet each has a focus and mandate, as well as funding limitations, that rule out a role for them as designers of whole national economic strategies. The institution with by far the most clout in deciding how to help whom, and for what price, is the International Monetary Fund.

Designed as part of the Bretton Woods order, the Fund was intended to function as something of a short-term crisis lender. It was to bridge the gap for countries with foreign exchange shortfalls while the country made adjustments to bring demand for its currency back in line with its pegged value against other currencies and gold. The vast dislocations of the seventies and eighties, however, impelled Western leaders to seek out a crisis management center and the IMF turned out to be a handy—and, in some ways, efficient—headquarters for patching up the frequent cracks in the international structure.

Western banks held and loaned much of the money. Yet their needs, too, helped buttress the IMF's power. Banks, as former Chase Manhattan chairman George Champion once observed, "don't have armies." Neither can individual houses of credit muster the clout, or authority, to insist that whole countries change policies in order to turn bad-risk operations into performing

Deflation Dénouement: Thwarting Democracy
GNP Growth Rates for Selected African States
and Related Political Chronology

Country	1980	1981	1982	1983	1984
MAURITANIA	11.0	1.3	3.3	−7.6	2.4

Efforts to form a civilian government in 1981 and 1983 founder among economic difficulties; early political reforms and a decaying economy helped produce another coup on December 12, 1984. Nominally democratic system, with elections in 1979 and 1985, hardened into one-party state by 1986. *Economy:* Mineral exports typically account for 85 percent of country's export earnings; agriculture accounts for half of all employment.

MALI	1.7	−1.3	−6.4	−5.4	−7.9

Student riots in 1981 seek to weaken military's hold but fail. Debate over country's 1985 economic restructuring plan is supposed to be widespread, but continuing deterioration convinces government to limit debate to meetings overseen by single ruling party. *Economy:* With 1984 per capita income of less than $200, Mali is an agrarian economy based on millet, rice, and peanuts; some gold, iron, and bauxite deposits contribute to exports. More than 70 percent of labor force is employed in agriculture.

LESOTHO

Accurate yearly figures not available, but per capita GNP was $538 in 1981, $460 in 1983, and $480 in 1985.

What would have been the first competitive elections in 15 years are scheduled for *1985. Sporadic violence breaks out* and the government cites this, and continuing economic malaise, as justification for severe curbs on participation by dissidents and opposition political parties, who ultimately do not field candidates. *Economy:* Citizens earning remittances for migrant labor in nearby South Africa account for about 50 percent of GNP. Designated by the U.N. as one of the world's "least developed countries," with 90 percent of the population dependent on subsistence agriculture and a 1983 per capita GNP of $460. Economy is "highly dependent" on weather, commodity prices, CIA report notes.

GAMBIA

Accurate yearly figures unavailable, but per capita GNP was $348 in 1981, $344 in 1983, and $230 in 1985.

The country's 300-man *parliament revolts in July 1981 over economic conditions,* following a bloody coup attempt. The blow to democracy is significant: Opposition parties were small but had served in parliament since the 1960s; Gambia had earned a "free" rating in the Freedom House surveys of the late 1970s. *Troops from next-door Senegal arrive to restore order* and limited democracy, but the country slips back to a "partly free" status. *Economy:* The State Department's 1986 human rights report notes: "Gambia depends on one major crop, groundnuts, for foreign exchange; this is subject to the vagaries of weather and world market conditions."

GHANA	−2.5	0.0	−3.4	−7.0	−4.8

Army officers wrest power from fragile (2-year-old) democratic government on December 31, 1981, amid economic turmoil. Popular uprisings and *several coup attempts in 1983 fail* to uproot the Marxist government, but do produce a rash of government reprisals, resulting in at least 100 civilian deaths. "Economic problems," the State Department's human rights report of 1984 notes, "have been partially responsible for the country's political instability." *Economy:* Cocoa and coffee account for more than 75 percent of exports.

NIGERIA	22.7	29.4	−10.2	−4.0	−11.7

Military officers seize power from a functioning democracy in Africa's most populous country on December 31, 1983. Economy: Earnings from oil, Nigeria's major export, fall by 50 percent over two years.

Country	1980	1981	1982	1983	1984

LIBERIA -6.3 -5.7 -1.0 -4.3 -1.2

Noncommissioned officers lead coup on April 12, 1980, toppling Africa's oldest republic and killing the president. They cite the country's economic distress and alleged inequities in distribution of wealth and power as a chief cause. An *attempt to hold free elections in 1984 results in widespread charges of corruption,* with the ruling party winning an alleged 50.9 percent of the vote and 80 percent of the seats in the legislature. In *1985, both a coup and an assassination attempt* are aimed at head of state Samuel Doe; they fail. Opposition parties do participate in parliament, and the country earns a Freedom House rating of "partly free" in 1987. *Economy:* Gross national product per capita is an estimated $480 in 1983, falling to $355 in 1987. But the economy does produce refined products for export such as iron, rubber, processed food, and timber, providing some stability.

NIGER   6.3   3.8 -1.6 -4.1 -7.2

Ruled by an authoritarian military regime since 1974, the government launches *efforts to allow greater private dissent and expand the private economy in the early 1980s. These are halted after 1983 coup attempts and popular uprisings in 1984 and 1985.* "The government," the annual U.S. human rights report for 1986 explains, "was preoccupied with the massive logistical effort required to distribute food aid to the many areas of Niger where people faced starvation." *Economy:* Chief exports are livestock and uranium; about 90 percent of the labor force is in agriculture.

GUINEA   (Not available)

The regime of longtime dictator Ahmed Sékou Touré suffers from economic breakdown, prompting a *smooth army takeover on April 3, 1984.* Respect for human rights actually improves in this case; deflation can hurt tyrants, too. The former socialist prime minister attempts his own coup in 1985, saying the government has failed to deal with the country's economic crisis. He fails. Guinea is listed as "partly free" in the Freedom House survey for 1987. *Economy:* One of the poorest countries in the world, with per capita income of $300 in 1983 and an agrarian economy that produces only 80 percent of the caloric requirements for its population.

BURKINA FASO (UPPER VOLTA)   Accurate yearly figures not available, but per capita GNP was $237 in 1981, $180 in 1983, and $140 in 1985.

Civilian government is toppled on November 24, 1980, following two years of multiparty democracy. In 1982, different officer factions conduct one coup and one coup attempt. An army-led attempt to return to civilian democracy is thwarted by another coup on August 4, 1983, this one led by radical leftists. In 1984, the country's rulers change its name to emphasize the new "revolutionary break with the past." *Economy:* "Highly vulnerable," a State Department analysis of 1985 human rights conditions concludes, "to fluctuations in rainfall" and commodity prices. Per capita income in 1983 stands at $180, roughly the mean between India and Ethiopia for that year. About 1 percent of the working-age population is employed in the monetized sector of the economy.

SOURCES: Adam Lieberman, "Debt, Deflation, and Democracy in Africa—Connections," research paper 87-1, Alexis de Tocqueville Institution, 1987. See also U.S. State Department, *Country Reports on Human Rights Practices* for 1983, 1984, 1985, and 1986 (Washington, D.C.: Superintendent of Documents, 1984, 1985, 1986, and 1987); *National Accounts Statistics: Main Aggregates & Detailed Tables* (New York: United Nations, 1984), pp. 1039–40, 1014–15, 117–18, 619–20, 957–58, 1554–55, and 1149–50; Victor Mallet, "Making the Medicine More Palatable," *Financial Times,* 9 May 1988; Leon Dash, "Gun Replaces Vote As Civilian Rule Fades in W. Africa," *Washington Post,* 8 April 1984; Gerard Alexander, "African Success Stories," *Policy Review,* Spring 1986; Raymond Gastil, "The Comparative Survey of Freedom," annual tables, *Freedom at Issue,* 1977–1987; and International Bank for Reconstruction and Development, *World Bank Atlas* (Washington, D.C.: World Bank, 1982, 1986, and 1987).

NOTE: Few governments are noted for keeping perfect statistics; but some African countries are, in this regard, particularly non-noted. Also, because most of these countries have rapidly growing populations, these figures—which reflect change in GNP not adjusted to population—tend to understate their economic distress.

assets. Yet banks do need some form of reassurance to offer shareholders reason to believe their money is being prudently managed. The IMF helped provide that psychological collateral at a time when international financial distress really did make massive lending by someone necessary. Bankers could tell themselves and those to whom they are responsible that they were lending money not simply to Country X, but to a country whose restructuring plan had been approved by the IMF: a body recognized as the prime catalyst of international lending and a reservoir of expertise. Once it gave a country the seal of approval, but no sooner, banks felt safe pouring in their resources as well. Many Western aid programs became linked to IMF planning too: The U.S. Agency for International Development often refused to fund projects in a country until it had won acceptance of its economic policies from the Fund. For at least two decades, then, there was a steady accumulation of greater and greater power in the hands of the IMF.

"The assistance that we provide ought to be provided in the context of a sound economic program," argued Carl Cunningham, the deputy director of the State Department's office of monetary affairs. "The one institution which is able to help countries in the development of such a program is the IMF." If this sounds unusually humble for a Foggy Bottom official, it is, but such deference toward the Fund was common. Nor are such sentiments wholly irrational. Many foreign-aid programs have had the historical effect of simply propping up and subsidizing corrupt governments, as economist Melvyn Krauss has recounted. The IMF seemed to offer hope that aid dollars would now be part of a "sound economic program." Then, too, the banks and the IMF were dealing with a full-fledged, multinational crisis. When currencies were unhinged, free trade and international banking itself were threatened. Nations were about to default. Politicians in Congress, the White House, and the State Department, thinking these issues technical and highly esoteric, deferred to technical esotericrats. Whereas low-conditionality funds made up 80 percent of IMF loans to African nations in 1975 and 1976, by 1980 about 70 percent of IMF lending to Africa involved higher conditionality. Thus, the West intervened "not through our foreign policy apparatus, seeking to foster democracy," as journalist Gordon Rayfield observed in *The Washington Monthly*. "Instead we've entrusted the job to private bankers [and the IMF]."[56]

Even if the IMF or some future aid body were to impose the best and wisest economic policies imaginable as a condition of Western aid, the political result would be far from optimal. The very operation of the program would send the message that while democracy is a fine idea, Western leaders do not trust it in practice. Have elections, Argentina, yes; but approval of really important decisions must come from an unelected cadre of alleged financial experts. ("Can you imagine the reaction," journalist John Eisendrath wrote, "if some obscure French financier told the American government it *must* balance its budget—or else?")

Repeatedly, of course, IMF officials denied their schemes represented austerity at all.[57] In practice, the IMF typically demands a combination of several policies aimed (the IMF thinks) at restoring economic growth. First, countries are urged to close budget deficits. This in itself, of course, involves a judgment about political and economic priorities. It also tends to promote, given the Fund's emphasis on short-term, static economic modeling, one of two solutions: a rise in already high tax rates, a cut in government subsidies on food or housing or other necessities—or both. Policies that might promote balanced budgets in the longer run, such as employment training or tax cuts to spur economic growth, simply do not fit into this model or, to the extent they do, will be discouraged. Second, in the same way, the Fund demands an improvement in a nation's trade deficit. Again, IMF negotiators profess not to care how this is done, but given the pressure for near-term statistical improvement, countries generally propose a program to restrict imports, or a devaluation of their own currencies, or both. Not only does the IMF thereby promote protectionism and retaliation from other countries—an irony, given that the Fund's two original purposes outlined in its charter were to *stabilize* exchange rates and *expand* free trade—but it arguably discourages some of the very measures developing countries need to improve their trade situation in the long run. For example, factory equipment that would produce a stream of exports over many years may be kept out of the country on the grounds it will show up this year as an import.

In isolation, of course, these policies are bad enough; in combination, they may be deadly. The currency devaluations drive up prices just as consumers are suffering reduced benefits and workers reduced wages. Resulting inflation creates Third World bracket gallop into high tax brackets that stifle entrepreneurship and growth. And the slowdown in economic activity deprives the government of revenues and exports, the provision of which the IMF sought in the first place. Any number of studies, including some by the IMF itself, have found that its programs tend to worsen, not improve, the national economies to which its mercantilist, budget-obsessed models are applied.[58]

Were there any evidence that the IMF policies worked even in the long run, nations would undoubtedly be more receptive to its guidelines. Stock and equity markets would react favorably to the announcement that a country has reached an IMF accord. The evidence, however, suggests that Third World voters and leaders were right to doubt the efficacy of IMF plans that predicate economic growth on years of austerity. Justin Zulu, the director of the IMF's own African department, studied the Fund's austerity programs for twenty-three African nations in 1983 and concluded that at least eighteen were failing. None were growing at healthy rates. At about the same time, the World Bank issued its own analysis of the debt crisis. "A number of major borrowers that are now experiencing difficulties," the study argued, "have (in the 1960s and 1970s) proved their ability to achieve high rates of export and income growth." Rather, the bank concluded, "austerity programs and attempts to achieve trade surpluses are exacting a heavy toll."[59]

All of which points to a second political effect of the end of Bretton Woods and international exchange-rate coordination: a rise in economic nationalism and protectionism.

Having severed the connection between national currencies and some common goal—price stability—monetary authorities were free to pursue narrow and secondary objectives. To a greater degree than before, pressure from particular interests would determine the conduct of monetary and other policies. If floating exchange rates did not make it inevitable that various industries and countries throughout the world would lobby successfully for deflation one year, inflation the next, they certainly made it more possible. What's more, the loss of price and exchange-rate stability encouraged the organization of vast economic interest groups.

Floating exchange rates in the 1970s and 1980s had the same effect they had in the 1930s, promoting beggar-thy-neighbor devaluations and mounting protectionism throughout the West. Not only did protectionists in various countries seek a cheaper or stronger dollar in pursuit of their perceived interests; they also sought further security through import quotas, tariffs, and the tacit protectionism of trade complaints and relief from unfair competition.

This was to be expected. "The danger that restrictive and discriminatory currency [and trade] practices will be resumed after the war," as Secretary of the Treasury Henry Morgenthau warned in *Foreign Affairs* in 1945, "makes international monetary cooperation essential." Many economists and journalists were stunned from 1984 to 1988, as Congress moved closer and closer toward passage of the most protectionist trade legislation since the Smoot-Hawley bill that ushered in the Great Depression. The trend had already been well established: By 1984, more than one-third of the U.S. market for manufactured goods was governed by some form of trade restrictions. "Floating exchange rates," as Lewis Lehrman noted in 1984, "become hidden proxies for the explicit tariffs, quotas, and export subsidies of the inter-war period. But we should not blame countries such as Japan, whose exports under the present system benefit at our expense. We must blame the true culprit—domestic and international monetary disorder . . . and the spectacle of ever more intensely gyrating currency values. Free trade will always remain a fantasy in the absence of a stable exchange rate system." While many believed a return of protectionism impossible—"protectionism is dead," proclaimed a February 1988 editorial in the *Wall Street Journal*—Lehrman continued to predict that it would remain a live issue until world leaders engineered a return to financial normalcy. As he warned in one January 1987 article, the choice was stark: "Trade War or Monetary Reform."[60]

Development Without Carrots

It's tempting, of course, to contemplate the establishment of a good system of foreign-aid handouts, one that would provide aid to needy Third World countries with conditions that would truly benefit their economies. Schemes to privatize fertilizer delivery and similar agrarian programs, for example, a pet AID idea in the 1980s, did some marginal good. In 1984, AID director Peter McPherson listed a number of countries that he said the *Wall Street Journal* editorial board should "keep an eye on" because they were following the privatization model. Sure enough, all the countries—Benin, Congo, the Ivory Coast, Nigeria, Togo, and Tanzania—enjoyed recoveries in 1985 and 1986. Then again, so did countries without privatization schemes across Africa. The primary cause for their 2 to 3 percent growth was the slow recovery of commodity prices. Land reform can also help—provided governments use it as a means to promote broader ownership and not class warfare. Successful land reforms in Japan and Taiwan were careful to reimburse owners, paying them shares of stock in privatized enterprises: sellable shares of real value. Unfortunately, U.S.-urged land-reform programs in Vietnam, El Salvador, and Brazil ignored this lesson, as old as the liberation of the serfs, and seized even medium-sized farms, compensating owners with worthless, and unsellable, paper bonds. "Reformed" farms were made into communes, not turned over to the poor. The predictable result: Landowners banded together to protect their holdings, fueling bitterness and violence. Farm output declined. Moreover, in a collapsing economy, little can be expected of either land-reform or sell-off programs. It does no good to turn over a public service to private cronies who happen to be friends of the government, or to sell the service to buyers at a bargain-basement price. The great tragedy of Western development policies since the 1960s was their failure to repair the high rates of taxation left over from the colonial era. Economist Alan Reynolds studied the nine major Latin American tax systems in 1988 and found that "in all but three . . . marginal tax rates are at least 50 percent on very modest incomes, around $5,000 a year, and rise as high as 79 to 95 percent on managerial, professional, and investor incomes." No wonder production, and with it, the value of land and all existing assets, sagged, with capital flowing abroad in a tidal wave of disinvestment.[61] Why not a Western aid program focusing on tax relief, balanced land reform, and free enterprise?

Alas, there is certainly no consensus in favor of such policies in the developed West—or even in the United States. Bitter debates rage about whether taxes should be cut or raised, social welfare programs slashed or expanded. This diversity of ideas and the debate over policies is healthy. Why, then, should we fear a similar outbreak of sovereignty and experimentation in other countries?

Good ideas will be adopted quite rapidly by governments if they are not forced to adhere to the strictures of the IMF or AID. Those who fear the prospect of unhitching the world's poor from our benign influence need not despair. Countries that received little Western aid and advice, in fact, tended to outperform all others: China, India, Taiwan, and Hong Kong among them. Others will naturally follow if only they are permitted the choice. The best development policy is democracy—a faith in the superior wisdom of people to run their own affairs. Thus, the first element in a foreign-aid policy for democracy should be broad reduction, if not outright elimination, of IMF and AID conditionality. Converting much aid into such a stark giveaway would no doubt produce a few examples of outrageous waste and fraud, and perhaps a gradual decline in public support for funding of such institutions as AID and the IMF. Yet this would not matter if, while ceasing to impose national economic policy on the Third World, America and the West resolve to create the one thing developing countries cannot provide themselves: free trade and stable prices.

From 1945 to 1985, the United States distributed more than $500 billion in various bilateral aid and multilateral lending programs. Add in Western Europe and the total comes to more than $1 trillion in inflation-adjusted dollars—roughly fifty Marshall Plans. Commercial credit brings the total to $1.5 trillion. Yet even these amounts are minuscule compared to the tidal waves of inflation and deflation, trade and debt, that have washed over the developing world in recent years. The interest rates of 1 to 4 percent that accompanied Bretton Woods would do far more for indebted countries—a savings of up to $50 billion a year—than temporary bridge loans, or forgiveness of a fraction of principal, or subsidized rates a point or two below what is charged to Exxon or Chase Manhattan. When James Baker, Bill Bradley, and even Third World debtor governments requested Marshall Plans or debt-reduction schemes, they spoke of amounts from $5 billion to $25 billion. Yet drastic price changes cost Nigeria $10 billion in foreign exchange in a single year, and the same deflation helped draw an estimated $8 billion to $11 billion out of Mexico in 1982 alone. Better policies by those governments would have helped, but so would U.S. monetary leadership. Seven percent real annual growth in world trade from 1980 through 1990 would have added more than $3 trillion to the world economy, triple the entire debt of the Third World.[62]

Increases of this magnitude have been realized in the past. Robert Pastor observes: "Trade has been the engine of growth in many small developing countries. Between 1950 and 1980, Central American trade increased eighteen-fold, stimulating the economies to an annual rate of growth of about five percent."[63] Expanding economies alone cannot solve the problems of development in the world. But can we solve the problems without them?

We might begin by listening to those whose countries we are trying to develop. If one looks closely at the statements and actions of Third World governments, one finds that they have repeatedly called not for more dollars, but for clearer thinking.

"The developed and prosperous democracies," Argentine President Raul Alfonsin said in 1986, "look at us with fondness but with no imagination," adding that he would trade a vast reduction of outright aid for stable prices and free trade "without hesitation." Pranay Gupte, a Kenyan economic development specialist, suggested priorities for Western dealings with the Third World in an article in the *New York Times:* "reducing bureaucratic meddling in third world development, providing fair agriculture prices, controlling currency fluctuations, curbing protectionism, instituting debt-readjustments, and eliminating wasteful subsidies."[64]

These comments are not mere isolated pleas from some developing country elites. Throughout the 1970s and 1980s, Third World producers of particular commodities banded together repeatedly in attempts to smooth out the wild price swings that battered their countries. There were efforts to form an "OPEC" for copper, coffee, sugar, tin, rubber, cocoa, and other products. In 1983, in a vast effort to achieve a nonmonetary, synthetic substitute for monetary, Bretton Woods stability, the Group of 77, a loose-knit alliance of developing countries, tried to form a stabilizing stockpile fund of some eighteen commodities. When this failed, countries tried to hedge against monetary manipulation through IMF negotiation. By the 1980s, debtor nations such as Mexico, Brazil, and Argentina demanded—and often won—IMF bailout loans that varied according to swings in the prices of their key exports. Latin debt, argued Peruvian President Alan Garcia, "should be valued at a market price . . . just like our copper and our wheat." Garcia's fellow Latin leaders agreed, urging stable prices, lower interest rates, and growing trade markets as the key to the world's debt woes at a 1987 conference.

Vast commodity stockpiles and indexed debt agreements are hardly the most efficient way to prevent inflation and deflation. That governments would strive to achieve them, however, suggests how strongly they wanted a return to monetary normalcy.[65]

The Burden and the Duty

From the start, the industrial countries looked for ways to ameliorate the chaos of floating monetary arrangements—at least for themselves. Europe held to pegged exchange rates in the wake of the Nixon devaluations of 1971 and 1973, and ultimately formed the European Monetary System within six years of the dismantling of Bretton Woods. The EMS required participants to maintain their own currency within a fixed band of purchasing power relative to the others. The system had many drawbacks, the chief one being that central banks had no real way of judging which particular currencies might actually be departing from price stability. Still, it was an attempt. In the 1980s, the Plaza and Louvre accords engineered by James Baker, along with a later agreement establishing a pair of commodities indexes as a (highly informal) guide to monetary policy, constituted several more steps in the same direction; they, too, however, lacked an explicit mechanism to monitor deviations.

As the calendar pushed toward the Nineties, all that seemed to hold some leaders back was the notion that fixed-rate, commodity-backed currencies were some kind of kooky notion out of a William Jennings Bryan speech. Yet the merit of a return to Bretton Woods was so compelling that it continued to gain support. At the depth of the 1982 recession, Treasury Secretary Donald Regan unwittingly touched off an avalanche of interest with a veiled suggestion for a "Bretton Woods–type conference." Weeks later, Henry Kissinger, one of the key international players in dismantling the old order, published a significant *mea culpa* in *Newsweek,* urging "fundamental reform" and pointing to what he later called a new "Bretton Woods" accord. Germany's Helmut Schmidt soon leaped on board, calling for "American leadership" toward "a stable world monetary system." Schmidt warned: "If governments do not find the strength to work together, they will inevitably repeat the mistakes of the 1930s: . . . devaluation races, protectionism, and breaks in the chain of international credit." Within the year, French president François Mitterrand, Walter Mondale, retired Federal Reserve Board Chairman Arthur Burns, and Nixon himself joined the parade. Nixon called the decision to sever the gold link and dismantle fixed rates one of his "greatest mistakes" in office. "Stable exchange rates, stable commodity prices, and stable governments," Nixon said. "If we have to convene 15 Bretton Woods conferences to do it, then let's do it." By decade's end the Bretton Woods train picked up friendly interest from such diverse corners as Vice President George Bush; Senators Robert Dole and Bill Bradley; the editorial pages of the *New York Times* and the *Wall Street Journal* and of Britain's *Financial Times* and *The Economist*; Gary Hart and Jack Kemp; the Republican platform; Federal Reservists Wayne Angell, Henry Wallich, Paul Volcker, Alan Greenspan, Martha Seger, and Manuel Johnson; and the heads of the German and French central banks. All supported fixed rates, a commodity price rule, or both, against the chaotic alternative.[66]

The West not only has the opportunity to rebuild what broke; we have a duty. We need only the will to help the world and ourselves.

III

THE HEARTS
AND MINDS

The cause of America is the cause of all
mankind.

—THOMAS PAINE

9

A DEMOCRATIC CENTURY

"**P**ROGRESS," C. S. Lewis wrote, "means motion towards a goal." It follows, as Lewis noted, that to judge whether a society or its policies have been making progress, we cannot simply ask whether they have been moving. One effort may have been advancing very fast—but in the wrong direction. Another initiative may be inching along; but if it appears to be headed down the right path, it is making far better progress, even if we judge it to be slow.[1]

What is the purpose of American foreign policy? What is our goal? Put the question to a dozen different leaders and you are likely to get widely differing replies.

Some would say our purpose is to defend and promote America's "interests." Yet this begs the question, "What are our interests?"

Some say it is defending ourselves and our allies. But how should we choose our allies? And why should we care about them? By what prior principle do we decide that, say, France should be supported and East Germany opposed? Or that our policy toward some other nation, say, Burma, should be one of relative indifference? Indeed, what do we mean when we say we support France?

Others might say America's purpose is, as the title of one book put it, "to promote peace."[2] Yet we can have peace—if it means merely not being directly engaged in war—at any time. We need only dismantle our armies and submit to superior forces. There must be some other goals for which we are willing, if need be, to sacrifice even peace.

Still others would respond, "human rights." But then we must ask: What rights? And which of these rights is at the core?

Many Americans would answer, "freedom."[3] But why should freedom be valued over other goals? Would we favor freedom, for example, if it meant the total annihilation of mankind in a nuclear war?

The purpose of American foreign policy, then, cannot be explained without first answering a prior question: What is the purpose of American government? To know what we are for in the world, we must know what we are for at home. Indeed, to know what American government is for, we must know why it is. If we can agree on this, then we may find the derivation of a distinctly American diplomacy rather easily; we may find that the goal of our foreign policy falls like a ripe apple from a branch.

"All men," our Declaration of Independence proclaims, "are created equal." Obviously this doesn't mean they are equal in the spurious sense of having the same color hair, the same size nose, or even the same merits and abilities. Yet they have been endowed, Jefferson and the Continental Congress declared, with certain rights fundamental to a just state and a just society. Because men are created with these equal rights, for example, no man or institution may justly rule over another without his enlightened consent. Abraham Lincoln argued: "As I would not be a slave, so I would not be a master. This expresses my idea of democracy. Whatever differs from this, to the extent it differs, is no democracy."[4] Now, it is possible to build arguments for democracy without admitting to any of these universal rights. Democracy is efficient and productive. People like it better than other systems. But democracy is only a process. The goal, as our framers put it, is to secure the rights of mankind.

What are those rights? Whole treatises by great philosophers—Locke, Rousseau, Hume, Jefferson, Mill, Strauss—have defended and defined them. It is beyond my scope to reconstruct here their elegant proofs. To most Americans, indeed to most people of the world, they are, in the Declaration's words, "self-evident." They flow from nature and from "Nature's god" itself. That is why all men, in all times, have had certain ideas about justice or fairness in relation to the state. They observe, for instance, that a just state, as Locke put it, rules by "promulgated, standing laws" applying to all.[5] Those laws, in turn, must be consented to by the ruled; for it would be contrary to nature for men to agree to an arrangement in which they give up their natural freedom to rule themselves in order to be ruled by an arbitrary force or will. This does not, of course, imply that, to be valid, every law must be the object of universal consent, but rather that the system must account for consent through a constitution that provides for that consent to be measured.

Even laws meeting all of these tests would trample on the higher, natural law if they tread into certain areas that, again, no man would reasonably agree to. A law allowing black men and women to be owned by white men and women as slaves, no matter how passed, would be an unjust extension of the state's power. As Rousseau observed, such laws would violate the general will of the people even if supported by a majority of particular wills.[6] For, to determine the general will, we would have to isolate each person in such a way that he would have to vote on such a law without knowing whether he would be a slave or a slaveowner, and none would give his enlightened consent to such an arrangement.

Similarly, a law that provided for Jews to be killed would be an unjust law, even if a majority of persons in a given country supported it. No reasonable person would agree to a law that one person in ten, possibly himself, should be killed. It is easy to see that, robbed of its application to a specific religious and ethnic group, the law on Jews would have the consent of almost no one.

In short: To imagine a society of men in which theft or slavery or *ex post facto* laws are right, we must imagine a society of men who are no longer men as we know them. Their very nature must change.

Hence, the Declaration speaks of "life, liberty, and the pursuit of happiness" (or "property," in Locke's formulation) as fundamental human rights. This book has described the arrangements that respect these rights as "constitutional, republican democracy"—a government of limited powers, respecting free speech and freedom from arbitrary trial or imprisonment or seizure of property, and providing for popular consent. It may be possible that other forms of government would satisfy the rights of man, but practical human experience suggests that certain institutions are needed for government to respect those rights consistently. Elections, mankind has found, are needed to renew the consent of the governed as new conditions arise, so that the officials making and executing new laws reflect the wisdom of the people. Constitutions, we have seen, are needed to define and limit what even those popularly selected officials can do. Locke goes further to suggest that a division of powers among different branches is needed to prevent the circumvention of the Constitution or of popular consent.[7]

It can fairly be said that in promoting democracy, America will promote the fundamental rights of mankind, those rights having been found to be unrealizable absent certain practical arrangements. It is important to note, however, that these rights—as Jefferson wrote in the Declaration—are prior to and higher than democracy itself, or any other form of government. That, as Lincoln observed, is the Declaration's great and radical principle. The rights of mankind are not good or just because they promote democracy, or any other form of government; rather, democracy exists to promote and protect those rights, and as soon as it ceases to do so, it ceases to act in accordance with the principles of just government, of natural law. To do this, however, democracy as defined would have to become undemocratic.

One can deny that these rights exist, but that would be denying the foundation of American democracy. To argue against a foreign policy to promote the rights of man, then, is to argue against the rights themselves, and thus against our own institutions. Truly, who gainsays human rights as the core goal of American diplomacy—leaving aside the issue of what prudent leaders will act on that principle—takes issue with far more than whether American foreign policy has a special mission. The man or woman who denies the rights of mankind may as well write a treatise on the imperfection and arbitrariness of American democracy in general, rather than quibbling with one member of it who advances, as a corollary, certain conclusions about diplomacy which seem to follow. If you find the whole sport of boxing to be corrupt, founded on a barbarous idea and tainted by venality, why take the trouble to analyze the style of Muhammed Ali, or the Tyson-Spinks title fight? If you believe a woman's cancer has also caused her vision to worsen, why begin her cure with a pair of eyeglasses?

Given that most people, in America and abroad, will agree with me that men have fundamental rights which it is the business of governments to promote—even the Soviet and South African constitutions say as much—my message on U.S. diplomacy is aimed at those who believe this. If the rights of man are the purpose of our government at home—"the animating and distinctive spirit which lies behind the laws and institutions" of America, as political scientist Charles Kesler has put it[8]—then it follows that the rights of man exist. And if a "right" to self-government is to have any meaning, it must mean the rights of all men and women everywhere and in all times and conditions. Whatever is peculiar to some is no right at all. Whatever is a "right" is universal. And what is universal certainly applies to American foreign policy.

There is no middle position to take in this matter; the rights of man are not a matter of multiple choice, but a true-or-false proposition. Without a universal right to self-government, republican democracy is merely a condition that happens to exist in some places and seems to have served some peoples well. It can claim no superiority in principle over communism, or fascism, or any other system. It may have produced better economic growth. It may enjoy more efficient trial procedures and fewer riots. Yet unless we start from some common notion of what is just and right, we cannot even say that economic growth is good or arbitrary trials bad. We are left with a sturdy vessel, but no direction to sail it in.

With the rights of man, however, there is a clear standard and a shining beacon to guide our diplomacy. Disparate efforts and random initiatives fall into place, and the thing is whole. If we accept the notion that American government is just because it accords with and promotes distinctive yet universal rights, then foreign policy ought to have as its central goal the promotion of those rights. And as it is my contention that men have a claim to those rights, it is my conclusion that the ends and means of a government based on them must be the rights of mankind themselves: rights embodied most faithfully in that form of government we call democracy.

"What great principle," Lincoln once asked, "has kept America so long together?" His answer: "The sentiment, in the declaration of independence, which gave liberty not alone to the people of this country, but hope to all the world, for all future time; the spirit which prized liberty as the heritage of all men, in all lands, everywhere."

"I would rather be assassinated on the spot," Lincoln said, "than surrender that principle."[9]

What fascinates is that most politicians would willingly admit to the universality of the rights in our Declaration; yet they steadily refuse to acknowledge that our foreign policy should be based on them. They would concede the design "in theory," but hasten to deny it in practice. This reluctance is grounded in political prudence, since any moral precept, particularly a powerful one, can be powerfully abused. Torches can be used not only to illuminate the high ideals of Athens but to burn down Troy. Yet the potential for great principles to be abused argues for caution in handling them, not for abstaining from handling them at all. Who fears handling the torch ought not aspire to a position of leadership. Who aspires to leadership should eagerly and reverently accept the torch, while recognizing that with sacred ideals come sacred duties.

For the most part, this book has focused on the particular components of diplomacy, using their tendency to promote or retard democracy as the proper standard of judging their efficacy. This chapter aims to sketch out what such an ambitious foreign policy might look like as a whole, when the parts are assembled and the thing is given life. Perhaps we will find that the obstacles to such an ambitious diplomacy—so widely perceived and bemoaned—can be overcome.

Voting for Democracy

Those who doubt democracy's strength are wont to cite the voters as a major restraint on what could otherwise be a foreign policy for democracy. Yet it is hard to find evidence that the electorate has held us back either from an assertive American foreign policy in general or from the particular acts embodied in it.

At regular intervals since 1947, the National Opinion Research Center has

FIGURE 9.1

Internationalist and Isolationist Trends, 1964–1980

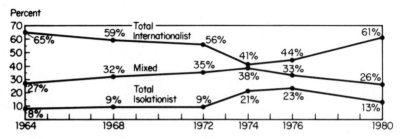

SOURCE: Lloyd Free and William Watts, "Internationalism Comes of Age . . . Again," *Public Opinion,* April–May 1980, pp. 48–49. Reprinted with permission of American Enterprise Institute for Public Policy Research.
NOTE: If anything, the Free-Watts index may overstate isolationist sentiment. For example, people disagreeing that the United States should "cooperate with other nations" are tagged "isolationist" on that issue. But some people want to stop cooperating with the U.N. because they are unilateralists, not isolationists, and want the United States to be more assertive and not so tied down by what other countries think. Others may simply feel that the U.N. is no longer an effective international entity.

put the following question to Americans: "Do you think it will be best for the future of this country if we take an active part in world affairs, or if we stay out of world affairs?" In more than twenty surveys, the percentage answering "active part" never fell below 61 percent, and was at least 70 percent more than a third of the time. Since 1964, Lloyd Free and William Watts have maintained an index of the public's general leanings on foreign policy, ranging from "total internationalist" to "total isolationist," based on their position on seven issues. Their data reveal a strong American tendency toward internationalism. Even at the nadir of American foreign policy, the abandonment of our democratic allies in Vietnam in 1974, the number of "total internationalists" was nearly double the number of "total isolationists." See figure 9.1.

Behind the general attitudes, of course, are a number of particular foreign-policy issues. Yet here, too, Americans consistently displayed a surprisingly high level of assertiveness. Here are some particularly revealing examples.

- "Do you agree or disagree with the following statement: The United States should come to the defense of Japan with military force if it is attacked by Soviet Russia or Communist China." Agree: 57 percent. Disagree: 24 percent. (1980)
- "Should the U.S. refuse to recognize communist Cuba until such time as it ends military alliance with the USSR and its military aid to communist insurgents in Latin America?" Yes: 72 percent. No: 27 percent. (1984)
- "Should the United States, in your opinion, encourage or support dissidents and ethnic minorities in Eastern Europe and in the USSR with the objective of bringing forth political liberalization in these countries?" Yes: 72 percent. No: 20 percent. (1984)

- Should the Central Intelligence Agency be "overhauling and stepping up" its activities, for example, working "to overthrow the Ayatollah Khomeini in Iran"? Yes: 79 percent. (1979)[10]

Polls are notoriously tricky. Change a phrase or two and you are likely to get what seem to be horribly contradictory opinions. Consider the particular case of Central America. As Ben Wattenberg, the editor of *Public Opinion* magazine, observed in 1986: "Americans say: do not give money to the Nicaraguan *contras,* but 62 percent also say that it is important to see that 'communism is eliminated from Latin America.' And 59 percent say, 'Nicaragua will provide bases for the Soviet Union.' Like most people, Americans would like to have their cake and eat it too."[11] One factor at work here is that Americans tend to react negatively when actual costs are mentioned. Then, too, it is always easier to endorse a general idea, such as "preventing communism," or "providing good health care," than some specific project that may or may not be related to that goal, such as "fighting a war" or "raising your taxes."

Furthermore, most Americans don't follow foreign affairs very closely, hence their opinions should not always be weighed equally. In 1983, two different polls asked Americans simply to identify the basic U.S. stand toward the Nicaragua government: pro or con. In both polls, about 25 percent of those sampled mistakenly stated that we backed the government, while about 45 percent admitted they didn't know.[12] When this generally uninformed sample was asked whether the United States should provide aid to the contras, a large majority said no. By contrast, when the Gallup poll put the question only to Americans who could identify current U.S. policy in the region, 50 percent of the refined sample supported aid to the rebels.[13]

This is not, properly understood, an argument for foreign-policy elitism. It is an argument for populism—as distinct from pollsterism. My guess is that if a pollster were to ask those who could not identify the U.S. position on Nicaragua, "How heavily should the government weigh your opinion on this matter?" many would answer, "Not very heavily." Americans not only don't follow foreign-affairs issues closely; they know they don't. They elect presidents and congressmen for the precise reason that they want their general inclinations followed—but not by constructing an elaborate grid of issues and taking a poll.

The Isoventionist American

When viewed in the context of hawkishness versus dovishness, or isolationism versus internationalism, public opinion can indeed seem schizophrenic. If we tune out the background noise, however, two rather consistent strains of American public opinion emerge.

First, as we observed on the question of Central America, the electorate expects its representatives to take the initiative on foreign policy. Thus, far more than on domestic policy, U.S. elected officials must rely on intuition and common sense.

For example, the invasion of communist Grenada in 1983 and the bombing of terrorist Libya in 1986 were popular in opinion polls taken after the events. Ronald Reagan used force decisively and the voters reacted favorably: better than 90 percent favoring the landing on Grenada, better than 65 percent the attack on Muammar Khadafy. Suppose, however, that a poll had been taken before the invasion of Grenada or the bombing of Libya. It's likely that a large majority of Americans, never having even heard of Grenada, would have opposed that operation. Even Khadafy, they might have felt, shouldn't be singled out for bombing.

This general inclination is not confined to obscure islands in the Caribbean. In July 1941, with the Nazis ensconced in Paris and U.S. convoys to Britain under attack by German U-boats, Gallup asked Americans how they would vote on the question of U.S. entry into the war against Germany; 79 percent said they would vote to stay out. As late as November, 63 percent said Congress should not pass a resolution declaring that a "state of war" existed between Germany and the United States.[14] Thus there is almost no escaping the foreign-policy rule; policy and action first, public approval, if it comes, afterward. "You conduct foreign policy by leadership," Irving Kristol argues. "If the president takes decisive action that makes sense, and if he can explain to the American people what he's doing and why, *then* they will mobilize behind him."[15]

A second, related rule of public opinion on foreign policy is that offering half a loaf provides no sure test of the popularity of a full loaf. This is not always the case in domestic policy, where differences can be split without grave damage. It is nearly always the rule on foreign policy. Suppose that the United States, rather than invading Grenada, had sent in thirty-five advisers. Or suppose the invasion force had consisted of a few thousand troops, but they were allowed only to occupy the medical school that housed several dozen Americans, and no more. In the first case, you would have had a situation remarkably similar to El Salvador, where a mere handful of advisers caused much more division and bitterness than the full-loaf invasion of Grenada. In the second case, you would have had something like the occupation of Lebanon in 1982—another use of U.S. force far less popular than the invasion of Grenada precisely because it was less successful.

Many of the foreign-policy errors made by U.S. leaders since World War II have resulted from a failure to recognize that Americans are prepared to make grand sacrifices, provided they are directed toward some good end. The consistent urge of the electorate on foreign policy is neither to get involved nor to stay aloof, but rather "in for a dime, in for a dollar." Columnist William Safire captured this truth artfully in an article for the *New York Times* extolling the virtues of what he called "isoventionism."

> This philosophy of selective involvement, of critical-mass commitment, may not seem consistent on the old hawk-dove scale. In Walt Whitman's words: Very well then, I am inconsistent. . . . We should fight the good fight and fight it to win; we should scrupulously avoid fighting any unnecessary fights at all.
> The symbol of isoventionism is the eagle's head on the long neck of the ostrich. It is capable of sticking its beak fiercely and decisively into those crises where it has the interest and power to shape events, and is also able, when its presence is unappreciated or redundant, to thrust its head determinedly into the sand.[16]

One sign of the public's isoventionism came in a poll conducted by the Chicago Council on Foreign Relations, which asked Americans how they would react to ten particular crises in the world: China invades Taiwan; North Korea invades South Korea; Arabs cut off oil to the United States; and several others. (Some of the other responses were cited earlier.) The poll compares how the American public would react to these events with how American leaders would react, but reveals no consistent distinction between leaders and the public in terms of their internationalism or isolationism. Leaders would be more willing than voters to use troops to meet a Soviet invasion of Japan, for example (78 percent to 50 percent), while voters, as we noted, would be more inclined than U.S. leaders to send troops to liberate Poland (31 percent to 6 percent). For every single issue, however, this striking general truth emerged: The voters were consistently unlikely to support intermediate measures, such as cutting off trade or sending military supplies. For every crisis in which there was a statistically significant difference, leaders were more inclined than voters were to react with trade sanctions or military supplies. In nine out of ten crises—a Soviet assault on NATO being the only exception—elites were also much more likely than the voters to favor negotiation as a solution. In only one theoretical situation did the public prefer negotiation over any other solution, that being a leftist takeover in El Salvador, where 29 percent said, "Negotiate," and 20 percent said, "Send troops." (By contrast, leaders favored negotiation by 10 percent.) And for every single crisis—bar none—the number of voters who favored sending U.S. troops outnumbered the sum of those who favored either trade sanctions or military supplies.[17]

For any given crisis, the public tended to see a stark choice between either getting involved or not. If they favored isolation, Americans favored a full-fledged isolation, ruling out U.S. troops and other options in large numbers. If they favored involvement, they still tended to rule out the intermediate choices—in a crisis—of trade sanctions or military supplies. The American approach, in a word: isoventionism.

"A decade after Vietnam," journalist David Ignatius wrote in 1985, "the war still hurts. The wound hasn't healed. 'No more Vietnams' has become a guiding principle—some would say a crippling obsession—of American foreign policy." Indeed, public reaction to Vietnam was interpreted by many U.S. leaders as a manifestation of America's irrefutable isolationism. Yet the Vietnam experience itself is offered no such instruction. American support for withdrawal never topped 20 percent until after the election of Richard Nixon, by which time withdrawal was a matter of U.S. policy. The approval ratings of both Lyndon Johnson and Richard Nixon tended to rise in the weeks following renewed U.S. bombing strikes against the North or its sanctuaries in Cambodia.[18] "It was not the American people which lost its stomach for the kind of sacrifices Kennedy had demanded," Paul Johnson writes. "It was the American leadership."[19]

This isoventionism makes it hard to intuit just how Americans will react to any particular foreign-policy initiative. Yet to intuit that reaction is the essence of democratic leadership, and those who find its limits capricious or arbitrary had best avoid positions of power. Americans may be tough judges, but they are hardly an obstacle to vigorous diplomacy. Indeed, as pollster Daniel Yankelovich wrote:

> On matters of foreign policy the public outlook is not at all volatile. In the post–World War II period it has enjoyed an orderliness, an inner logic and a grounding in principle that has been, if anything, more stable and consistent than American policy itself.[20]

The Energy Crisis

Some critics see the very structure of the American bureaucracy as frustrating an effective foreign policy. To look at the beast, in a sense, is to want to change it. One could tick off a number of proposals that might improve the system.

Richard Nixon suggested back in the 1950s that the Central Intelligence Agency be split into two parts: one an evaluation and intelligence arm, the other a covert-action arm. The reason—as the Reagan administration learned the hard way in the Iran-contra affair—is that it's dangerous to have the same group of people design a policy, carry it out, and judge its effectiveness.

The president's commission on public diplomacy, headed by Heritage Foundation chairman Edwin Feulner, recommended in 1983 that the head of the U.S. Information Agency sit on the National Security Council. It might sound like a bureaucratic chair shuffle, but given the damaging lack of attention to the populist aspects of foreign policy, this might be a useful one. Congress, many would argue, ought to play a different role in foreign policy. Even many leaders in the House and Senate, such as James Courter and Sam Nunn, say that the institution gets too involved in managing foreign policy down to its smallest details. But many officials from various administrations would like to see Congress have more say in designing basic strategies and policies, especially at the outset. It would have been nice, on the one hand, if the Reagan administration had requested a congressional resolution in favor of sending U.S. ships to the Persian Gulf in 1987—an idea proposed by Courter and pushed within the administration by Caspar Weinberger. On the other hand, it would be nice if Congress, having voted for ships in this region or freedom-fighter aid to that one, would sit back and let the executive branch execute.

Some of these changes might help. Some might be marginally damaging. Yet they are not, any more than the American voter, the crux of any major problem in U.S. foreign policy. The tools are there, and—when they are used properly by American leaders—the CIA and the Pentagon and the State Department have all performed their tasks well. Where errors are made, it is not because any of these agencies is too powerful or too weak. It is because they are used to do things they are not good at doing, as when the State Department is used as a body that strategizes, rather than as an agency that conducts negotiations as part of a strategy set by presidents and Congress, or when the CIA is used to avoid policy decisions and debates instead of being directed by them.

If there is one distinguishing flaw of American foreign policy, rather, it is a certain lack of vigor, and of creativity, at the top. It is frankly embarrassing, sometimes, to pick up a newspaper and flip through the pages comparing not who is winning more battles and who is losing, but simply the general level of initiative of America as against the Soviet Union. One particular day in 1987, one could read about the Soviet effort to gain entry to the International Monetary Fund on page 1; about promised Soviet withdrawals from Afghanistan on the same page; about talks pointing to increased Soviet trade credits with Europe on page 7; about the wide Soviet edge in space launches further inside; and on and on. Many of these initiatives flop, but the result is still to relegate the democracies to reacting and defending, trying to thwart the affirmative strategy of others.

There are some exceptions. The treaty on nuclear missiles in Europe, for example, signed in 1987, was the result of an American initiative of 1981: the zero option. Yet the zero option itself was a reaction to the vast buildup of Soviet missiles that took place in the 1970s. And no sooner was the pact's ink dry than American officials realized that it left unaltered a Soviet advantage in conventional forces that had been growing and festering for some twenty-five years.

Why is this? Democratic leaders have, if anything, less need to be defensive. The American official who can sit down over coffee and enjoy the *Wall Street Journal* or the *New York Times* has a much larger base of ideas to tap than the Soviet bureaucrat consigned to *Pravda*.

A far more important cause is the enduring schism between the Republican and Democratic parties, which sometimes seem more interested in taking credit or in laying blame on their opponents for particular policies than they are in creating new ones. It should be obvious that a general design for foreign policy, shared by both parties, would be stronger—at once more energetic and more durable. Yet the nature of the parties has made such a consensus difficult.

The Art of Additive Compromise

The Republicans, for historical reasons we need not detail, stood for most of the twentieth century as the party of commerce and anticommunism. Its general tendency was one of passive government, seeking no bold changes at home and, in the postwar period, concentrating on blocking communist advances abroad. On occasion, men of particular energy—Teddy Roosevelt, Ronald Reagan, Jack Kemp—advocated a policy of economic growth and opportunity and democracy at home, and of growth and democracy abroad: the "turbulent frontier" described by Frederick Jackson Turner and embodied in Roosevelt, or, as Kemp called it, *An American Renaissance.* Still this wing of Republicanism by no means represented the party's soul. The guiding spirit of the party was, in a sense, the rows of a neatly prepared ledger: balanced budgets at home, balanced budgets abroad, and a balance-of-power foreign policy. Roosevelt, Reagan, Kemp, and the charging horse were the exceptions. Hoover, Eisenhower, and the golf course were the rule.

It is not so much that this dominant strain of Republicanism has many bad qualities as that it lacks some essential good ones. Few people are against balanced budgets or a balance of power. But Americans are not strongly motivated by these things as ends in themselves. The highest goals of the orthodox Republican fail to tap the spirit, and leave the republic wanting *The Edge of the Sword.*

If Republicans tended toward mere anticommunism, the Democratic Party, at critical times, seemed moved chiefly by a kind of anti-anticommunism—not that it feared communism less, but that it feared crusades against communism more. Its domestic base, composed disproportionately of the needy and also the governing elite—legislators, journalists, intellectuals—tended to reinforce this orientation. Neither group is inclined to great exertions abroad, though the poor are probably less isolationist and more patriotic than most politicians estimate them to be. Still, a party that, tragically, spends so much energy promoting envy at home, in the form of schemes to tax and regulate The Rich or the Japanese, finds itself vulnerable to such attacks on America abroad. And a leadership class so ill-at-ease with the people's affection for God, country, and freedom tends to doubt the legitimacy of any effort that requires marshaling these forces.

In the middle of the century, three great Democratic presidents—Franklin Roosevelt, Harry Truman, and John F. Kennedy—broke and transcended the mold: Bretton Woods, the Marshall Plan, NATO, the Apollo program, the Alliance for Progress. Their successes, however, were hardly unbroken; there were also Yalta, Vietnam, the Bay of Pigs.

In the age that followed Vietnam, one could name a handful of Democratic leaders interested in a foreign policy of democratic expansion, such as Henry Jackson, Bill Bradley, Ernest Hollings, Richard Shelby, and Sam Nunn. Yet they by no means constituted the core of the party of Jefferson, Jackson, and Monroe.

There is no inherent reason why these two parties, individually and in concert, could not arrive at a foreign policy of democracy. The Democrats would prefer to spend their energies battling the dictators of Chile or South Africa; this may be a misplacement of emphasis, but it is by no means antidemocratic. Republicans struggle to contain communism, and although this strategy is incomplete by itself, it is part of a whole strategy for realizing the rights of man. Compromises could be struck, and have been struck, uniting the Democratic Party's emphasis on economic equality with the Republican emphasis on stability, joining anticommunism with antifascism in a dynamic and forward-looking diplomacy for democracy.

Unfortunately, there is a bias toward a different kind of compromise—let us call it "dilutive compromise"[21]—in which two parties approach an idea from different angles and agree, in a sense, to adopt a fraction of it. The Democrats want $10 billion for a jobs program that the Republicans oppose outright; $5 billion is spent. The Republicans want a 20 percent tax cut that the Democrats object to; taxes are cut by 10 percent. Such deals can be very productive, and are at times unavoidable, particularly in domestic policy. Yet they deliberately avoid a decision for the principles of either side. In effect, both parties have simply agreed to allow their difference in principle to stand until some future election determines which allows one or the other to gain the upper hand.

The problems with this type of compromise should be obvious, particularly in foreign policy, where half a policy may be no policy at all. There is no "half" of an effective economic sanction; effective ones are either applied or they aren't. Half of a policy to produce victory by a certain band of freedom fighters, as we observed, will not produce half a victory; it will likely lead to an entire defeat. Furthermore, dilutive compromise only serves to continue avoiding the question, What is the purpose of our foreign policy? Not until both parties have agreed on a principle will the American polity be able to unleash and focus energies that now lie dormant or spin off in contradictory directions.

There is another kind of compromise, however, which leads to a very different result. It is illustrated by a major domestic compromise that took place in 1986.

In the months following the 1984 election, Democrats were itching to close tax loopholes that allowed some wealthy Americans to avoid paying any taxes at all. Republicans left the same election determined to keep cutting tax rates. Now, one way to approach these initiatives would have been to treat them as separate issues with predictable results. Democrats, opposed by the White House and many congressional Republicans, at best would have achieved a dilutive compromise in which a few loopholes were halfheartedly narrowed. Republicans might well have run into a similar wall in the Democratic House, which had barely passed the first round of tax cuts back in 1981.

That is not, however, how these proposals were handled. Instead, they were grouped together under the banner of "tax reform." Democrats Bill Bradley and Richard Gephardt, and Republicans Jack Kemp and Robert Kasten, each fashioned very similar bills that showed how apparently conflicting objectives could coexist and even complement one another. Lower rates tended to pull rich people out of tax-avoidance schemes even as closed loopholes drove them out: Democrats happy. Driving people out of loopholes simply placed them where lower rates were drawing them anyway, spending more energy on generating income and less on hiding it: Republicans happy. The result was a simpler tax code, capable of collecting more revenue, yet posing fewer barriers to the creation of wealth and jobs than the old one.

The prime ingredient needed to make such an additive compromise work is the guarantee that each side can win what it wants on some principle, in return for which it gives up another principle, but one it perceives to be of lesser importance. The process is doubly beneficial if each side shares some higher principle that will be advanced by the deal, the presence of which made the great tax reform of 1986 such a triumph.

It seems to me that the same elements could contribute to a sweeping, additive compromise on American foreign policy. Neither party need surrender its most cherished goals. The Republican animus for communism, in this model, would simply be fused to the Democratic animus for fascism. Instead of weak sanctions against South Africa and weak sanctions against the Soviet Union, there would be strong sanctions against both. Rather than middling efforts to promote democracy in Chile and in Poland, strong efforts would be made in both countries.

There is, of course, no specific legislative vehicle that could be passed all at once to bring such a foreign policy, tax-reform-like, into effect. An additive compromise on foreign policy will take the form not of a single enactment but of a process. Republicans will have to extend their resistance to tyranny to include military dictators. Democrats will have to think of communists as military dictators, too—as they are. This will leave some members of each party a bit cranky, feeling that too much has been given away. When Ronald Reagan persuaded several key opposition members to support aid to the contras, many Democrats pounced, angrily denouncing any party member who would sell his antidictator soul to help the corrupt cause of Republican anticommunism. By the same token, when Jack Kemp supported a modest package of sanctions for South Africa—noting that he had resisted communist tyranny with a vigor equal to or even greater than that with which he resisted apartheid—many Republicans threw a tantrum, pronouncing any comparison of the two evils preposterous.

Nevertheless, my own reading is that most members of both parties would be delighted with additive compromises. If most Democrats had been offered a choice in 1983 between a victory by both the contras and the forces of democracy in South Africa, or by neither, most would have agreed to the former deal; most Republicans would have made the identical choice. It bears repeating that policy is seldom packaged in the form of such explicit deals. But an enlightened leadership can elicit the benefits of such an additive compromise without having a document that formally states the trade-offs. Thus, in 1986, the Reagan administration promoted the fall of Marcos in the Philippines—and found the effort gave added luster to its effort to promote democracy in Nicaragua as well. Democrats in the Congress, meanwhile, placed themselves ahead of the anticommunist administration in promoting aid to the freedom fighters of Cambodia—and thus could claim consistency in promoting more forceful support of hoped-for democracy in Haiti.

Perhaps the dynamic that is being proposed here would be best illustrated by a concrete example.

A More Perfect Union

It is difficult to name a tool of foreign policy that has been given as much lip service, and as little serious attention, as the matter of international law. True, the mere phrase itself is enough to elicit a snicker from some and a breathless respect from others. Yet despite the obvious limits of international law as demonstrated in the twentieth century—particularly in respect to war and peace—it is possible to discern some growth in both its range and its seriousness over a period of several centuries. The process in some ways parallels the gradual accretion of common law in England, as municipal courts and parliamentary law ever so gradually replaced the arbitrary rulings of the crown. In the 1980s, a much broader range of commercial and national disputes was prevented, or at least adjudicated, by international courts than at any time since popes rivaled kings as the center of political authority.

What is more, the United States can proudly claim, at least for much of its history, a large share of the credit for this benign evolution. In the development of judicial machinery for international settlements, as legal scholar Thomas Willing Balch noted many years ago, "the United States have played a leading role; indeed it may be said that they have been the leader."[22] The Jay Treaty of 1794 established mixed settlement commissions to rule on a number of international claims. It was only one of a number of agreements and actions by which the United States, in its first century, expanded and defined the rights of neutral nations under international law. U.S. instructions to federal troops in 1863, meanwhile—forbidding torture, poisoning of water and food supplies, and other acts of cruelty and mass population destruction, and drafted at the command of President Lincoln—formed the basis of international conventions on warfare in Brussels in 1874, in the Hague in 1899 and 1907, and in Geneva in 1925. Many of their limits, such as a ban on chemical warfare, were observed even by the Nazis. Both the League of Nations following World War I, and the United Nations after World War II, though of limited effectiveness, were efforts to extend these principles still farther. And both, like the 1975 Helsinki Human Rights Accords, were in large part American initiatives.[23]

In a sense, America is perhaps the first international nation. Our Declaration of Independence itself was a rather remarkable effort to explain to the world the causes of and justification for our revolt against the recognized sovereign power in the colonies, Great Britain, in terms of the law of nations. Our Constitution places international law not only close to, or equal to, the regular statutes passed by our own congress, but above them. "This constitution," Article VI reads, "and all Treaties made, or which shall be made, under the Authority of the United States, shall be the supreme law of the land." The laws of Congress, by contrast, are subordinate to the Constitution and international laws recognized by the United States, and are valid only where made "in Pursuance thereof."[24]

As the new millennium unfolds, America ought to take the lead in strengthening international law, for reasons as practical as they are idealistic. Democracies, built on the rule of law, have nothing to fear from it—provided, as should be implicit, that we are talking about serious international law, seriously enforced. And reducing the number of disputes that must be solved by national negotiation or a resort to force would be of obvious benefit to commerce and justice, not to mention peace.

Yet there has been little strategic effort to promote the extension of international law by any U.S. administration since the 1960s. Instead, as we saw in chapter 2, Republicans and Democrats have essentially used the notion of "international law" to wage domestic political war, seeing it as a useful slogan for embarrassing the opposition rather than as a good in itself. Democrats—Arthur Schlesinger, Mike Kinsley, and others—thus railed on the Reagan administration for mining the harbors of Nicaragua in 1983, allegedly in violation of international law. They raised no comparable fuss about Nicaraguan and Cuban subversion of El Salvador. Republicans—Jeane Kirkpatrick, Robert Dole—rightly pointed out this pattern of selectivity, and noted the impotence of international courts. Yet if Nicaragua's victory over the United States in the World Court was, as they said, a "propaganda device," they failed to explain why the United States had not used that device to draw attention to the violations of Cuba and Nicaragua. Even the Solidarity trade union, which repeatedly asked the U.S. mission to the United Nations to assist in its case against the government of Poland, reports that there was little interest. "We kept trying to get the administration to help us," a Solidarity spokesman in the United States told me, "but they just aren't interested."[25] For Reagan Era Republicans, international law was something to be constrained and defended against, not applied constructively in world politics. When, in 1988, the administration showed an interest in expanding the jurisdiction and sanctioning powers of the World Court, it was, like too many U.S. acts, a reaction to a Soviet proposal made some months before.

While its use as a domestic political tool is a constant, of course, international law has at least promoted a certain creativity. Thus, in the 1960 presidential debates, it was Richard Nixon who used the Rio Treaty and the Bogotá accords (which set up the Organization of American States) to argue against John F. Kennedy's calls for aid to the freedom fighters of Cuba. Such aid, which we now know was in fact being provided by the Eisenhower administration, would be illegal, Nixon implied, and would alienate our allies. "We would," Nixon said, "lose all of our friends in Latin America; we would probably be condemned in the United Nations." Kennedy correctly pointed out that Nixon was "misinformed," or, at least, misinforming. (The Rio Treaty provided for mutual assistance, while the agreement signed in Bogotá pledged to resist "the political activity of international Communism" which it said it would view as "an attack on democracy." The Bogotá agreement also contained a promise to fight attempts "by any foreign power," or even "any political organization serving the interests of a foreign power," to intervene in the Americas. Harry Truman, who signed the Rio pact, describes it in his memoirs as parallel to the treaty that created NATO: "With the North Atlantic Treaty and the corresponding Western Hemisphere arrangement concluded at Rio de Janeiro, we gave proof of our determination to stand by the free countries to resist armed aggression from any quarter.") By 1988, of course, the legal ledger had turned, and it was the Republican nominee for president, George Bush, who upheld the spirit of the Rio and Bogotá agreements in arguing for aid to the Nicaraguan contras. The Democratic nominee, Michael Dukakis, sanctimoniously declared aid to the Nicaraguan contras to be "illegal" and "unconstitutional."[26]

The point here is that even if one agrees with the Kinsley-Nixon-Dukakis view of the Rio treaty, there are infinite possibilities as to what policies should flow from it. One is that international law is weak and selectively applied; it must remain so; and we should work to minimize it: Foreign policy is a dirty business, and the Harvard Law School, as the *Wall Street Journal* editorialized in defending the invasion of Grenada, should "keep its mouth shut." Yet this frustrates the valid notion, generally advanced by the doves, that the United States must scrupulously obey the law. Another option is to pretend, as Kinsley does, that enforcement is not necessary, because it is "in the interest" of all countries generally to obey international law, and of any given nation to acquire a reputation for doing so.* Indeed it is; just as it is in the interest of thieves to be perceived as honest men, and to have laws protecting property enforced against others but not themselves.

Yet accepting international law as the status quo is only one possible response. There is, for example, John Kennedy's counterpoint in 1960: If law mandates enforcement, why not enforce it against the real aggressors in Cuba? And if Latin allies are not united behind present policy, why not toughen it and get them to unite behind an effective one? This proposal would incorporate

---

*Mr. Kinsley was kind enough to respond to my query about his international-law column asserting that enforcement does not matter. He cited several legal texts on the point. My own reading of those texts, however, leads me to conclude that the usually rigorous editor of *The New Republic* simply didn't read them closely enough. What the authors assert (with little documentation) is that international commercial law has been fairly well observed even by the Soviet Union. Yet both texts focus more than 80 percent of their discussion not on international law's regulation of war and peace but on such mundane matters as commercial agreements, fishing rights, and the like. This is an unfortunate way to defend Kinsley's thesis, since commercial agreements carry their own built-in enforcement mechanism: If you don't pay Exxon for its drilling equipment, Exxon won't deliver the goods. The texts, then, prove rather a different point: that the bulk of international law might be effective, but only if it had the automaticity of enforcement that is present in the body of international law most often respected and observed.[27]

both the dove's demand that things be done legally and the hawk's demand that things be done. In 1984, America could have taken its own complaints about Nicaraguan aggression before the OAS or the World Court, as some contra backers in fact suggested. We could have removed recognition of Nicaragua's military dictatorship. Any number of positive actions might have followed the World Court ruling against the United States. Instead, ironically, even such Reaganites as Michael Ledeen and Jeane Kirkpatrick seemed more interested in a debate they denigrated as "legalistic" than in forging a coherent and popular policy in the region.[28]

Unfortunately, in the quarter century following Kennedy's death, neither Republicans nor Democrats seemed interested in strengthening international law or the international bodies involved in its enforcement. In 1985, as the tenth anniversary of the Helsinki Accords approached, a broad and interesting debate about their utility was carried out in the popular press. Some U.S. officials, such as Max Kampelman, Michael Novak, and George Shultz, weighed in on behalf of continued U.S. observation of the pact, while arguing for continued verbal attacks from the West on the Soviet Union for failure to honor them. Others, such as Richard Pipes, argued ably that the pact, including the U.S. recognition of Kremlin hegemony in Eastern Europe that was traded for Soviet promises of freedom, should be renounced. What none of the assessors proposed, at least not in the many volumes and articles that crossed my desk, were any creative new ways to enforce the Helsinki Accords. The United States could, after all, have pressed for the creation of an impartial tribunal to weigh human rights cases and agreed to allow the referral of cases in U.S. law to the same tribunal. The Soviets, of course, would have rejected all such proposals. But that is partly the point: They would have had to reject them, with the world watching. And the heat on them would have been just one degree higher, while America's respect for the international law established at Helsinki, already sparkling in comparison to the Soviet record, would have shined even brighter.[29]

Similarly, throughout the decade, Republicans correctly assaulted the United Nations as a corrupted body, with the Heritage Foundation secreting a long stream of papers documenting the U.N.'s bias against the United States; its failure to act as a keeper of the peace; its wasteful and often counterproductive poverty programs; and on and on. Democrats generally defended continued U.S. participation in that body on pragmatic grounds, without explaining how it is pragmatic to do all the things attributed to the U.N. by the well-documented Heritage Foundation studies. But very few people, Republican or Democrat, proposed anything better. Even Charles Krauthammer, in issuing his verdict that the United States should "let it sink," floated no design for a superior international organization. Even Jeane Kirkpatrick, who weighed in on the side of the U.N. defenders, suggested no structural improvements, just more years of steely negotiation and lobbying to win an occasional vote or block a particularly noxious resolution.[30] The debate, in other words, was consistently and maniacally focused on whether to pull out of the U.N. or to accept the status quo—and not on whether and how to create an effective U.N., an international body true to the principles of the 1945 Charter.

Republicans who are seriously critical of the defects of international law and the U.N., and Democrats who are serious about the ideals behind those institutions, should unite to create one modest, but in the long run vital, institution: the League of Democracies. A League of Democracies would, if it filled its role well, gradually replace and absorb some of the functions now performed poorly by the United Nations, not to mention by the U.S. State Department. Yet it would replace them by doing the job better, rather than by abolishing the job altogether. For example, the League could help countries monitor their elections for fairness and accuracy; indeed, it should be a condition of membership that even the most powerful states, including the United States, submit to League volunteers assigned to the task. The advantages simply of being a member in the League of Democracies would be substantial, and therein, of course, would lie one of its most important, though subtle, influences. Nations that qualified for membership would be recognized as more solid and stable by international investors; nations that failed to live up to their obligations, by contrast, would suffer proportionately.

Human rights reports by the League of Democracies would enjoy a legitimacy and command an attention that too often eludes the United Nations. For they would be compiled solely by the representatives of governments who themselves maintain a general respect for fundamental rights. Votes condemning an aggressor nation in foreign conflicts would, unlike in the flawed League of Nations or the more modern Organization of American States, carry no automatic sanctions. Yet they would, unlike the U.N. assembly, which weighs the combined opinion of Zaire and Burma at double the level of the U.S. or Britain, at least represent the combined statement of a group of serious countries.

The one thing the League of Democracies clearly ought not to do, it seems to me, is engage in direct negotiations or other peace-keeping actions in the manner of the U.N. And the U.N. itself offers an excellent illustration of why the League should abstain from such a role, at least during the first century or two of its existence. The objective of a world government that is capable of keeping the peace, alas, is one beyond the means of mankind and the nation-states of today, not because nation-states are evil and arbitrary, but because they are essentially good, responding to real and healthy affections felt by men and women for other men and women of the same language, culture, experience, and geography. They will yield only very gradually to something better as it is built up.

A DEMOCRATIC CENTURY

What the League of Democracies can do, modestly and marginally, is to carry on the vital though arduous task of the gradual expansion and enforcement of international law between the member states. And here again, a nice synergism of expansion could be expected to occur. In place of attempting to apply human laws even to the brute, the League of Democracies would begin with the civilized, inculcating the notion that civilized nations are capable and worthy of receiving the law of nations. Every law applied to the member states, however modest, would be a true law. Every member state of the League would be, and would be seen as, law-abiding. This is in the nature of things, for all peoples aspire to the rule of law; and democracies, by definition, submit to aspirations of their peoples.

The solid gains for law and peace achieved by the League of Democracies would, on some time scales, seem remarkably slow. At least they would be solid, though, and they would be gains. If it takes us several centuries to reach the final goal, at least the goal will be defined, and our progress measurable. The design, moreover, is one that most Americans would share. Indeed, statements on behalf of such an institution were issued at a pair of bipartisan conferences of leaders held in 1986 and 1988 by former presidents Jimmy Carter and Gerald Ford. The League of Democracies would marry the most noble principles of Republican anticommunism and liberty with the highest Democratic ideals of peace and equality. As one paper advancing the concept of a League of Democracies argued: "The fundamental issue of the contemporary world is the political struggle between the democratic way of life and those who would deny human liberty and political freedom." It illustrates the wide appeal of those ideals that most readers probably would have some difficulty identifying whether that statement was made by a group of U.S. Republicans or Democrats.[31] Starting small, then building, the League of Democracies would make an important contribution to the right side in that momentous, twilight struggle.

The proposed fusing of such Republican and Democratic principles, in the League and other additive compromises, differs importantly from the usual design leaders have in mind when they implore one another to construct a "bipartisan foreign policy." Consider this passage from an article by one of the keenest observers of the Central American scene, Robert Leiken, in *The New Republic:*

> Armed resistance to the Sandinistas will necessarily take the form of a protracted struggle. This will require a sustained bipartisan policy of support. The administration and Congress must put aside narrow partisan interests to forge a national policy toward Nicaragua.[32]

Now, there is nothing exceptional in this formulation; it represents the normal understanding of bipartisanship. If we examine it carefully, though, we find that what the author extols is not bipartisan policy at all but, rather, nonpartisan policy. Professor Leiken asks the parties not to combine their particular impulses into a national program but to "put aside" those interests. To be Americans, in effect, Democrats must temporarily cease being Democrats, and Republicans must cease being Republicans.

This strikes me as simultaneously unlikely, unnecessary, and, worse, unproductive. Unlikely, because men form into parties precisely to promote ideas they consider vital; unnecessary, because the highest principles of both parties in no way rule out aid to the contras; unproductive, because far from wanting Democrats and Republicans to relinquish those principles, we ought to encourage their extension.

A nonpartisan foreign policy, then, seeks to smash or suspend the ideals that divide the parties. Even if it were to succeed, there would be something lacking. The achievement of nonpartisanship would eliminate divisions, but it could not create unity. A bipartisan foreign policy, by contrast, seeks not to suspend ideals and divisions but to harness them—in the direction of a still higher purpose than mere Republican anticommunism or Democratic antifascism.

That higher purpose is a diplomacy of democracy, by democracy, for democracy: a foreign policy for securing the rights of man.

A Flame Eternal

The history of America is the history of the gradual realization of that Jeffersonian ideal. It gave life to all of America's greatest achievements: the forming of the Constitution and subsequent drafting of the Bill of Rights; the abolition of slavery; the extension of the franchise; the protection and gradual expansion of civil rights. Prudence has guided its application, making progress seem unduly slow. Hence the founders, rightly or wrongly, compromised with slavery; and even Abraham Lincoln stopped short of recommending its immediate abolition. Yet Lincoln persistently reminded Americans that a nation half-free, half-slave, could not long endure, and left no doubt that an America true to its own principles must abolish it.

That same realism tells us that a world half-democratic, half-totalitarian, is a world that must change in one direction or the other. Communism, eventually, must either perish or rule the globe. It is possible to envision a world with one government; or a world composed of nation-states, all democratic; or a world of nation-states, all communist; or a world in which some new systems have swept these alternatives from the globe. It is not plausible to posit a world forever suspended on one side or the other of a vast Iron Curtain. Either the democracies will take the democratic idea to its conclusion or we will fail.

Either America will help secure the rights of man for all, everywhere, or America itself, as a free and democratic state, will perish.

Let us be specific; let us say the great unsayable. "Everywhere" includes the Soviet Union. To say that we must help achieve democracy in Russia is not to say that we must achieve it by war; it is assumed, on the contrary, that such a war would likely bring the end of democracy as well. Nor must we complete our task in a fortnight. To say that our goal must be a democratic world does not mean we must achieve it in the next year, the next decade, or the next generation.

Indeed, History and Reality, though often called to the stand by self-proclaimed pragmatists, have stubbornly refused to testify against democracy, and the general tide of history points not toward Russian despotism but toward freedom. George Kennan, the noted scholar of Russian history, writes:

> When the Revolution [of 1917] occurred, Russia already was, and had been for some three or four decades, in a process of quite rapid evolution . . . in the direction of the modern liberal state. The development of a firm judicial system was far advanced; a beginning had been made toward the development of local government; public opinion was a force to be reckoned with. While the long-term trend of Russian society was interrupted by the Revolution and its consequences, I can see no reason to doubt that it still represents the direction in which, in the long run, Russia must move.[33]

Can America actually assist in such a vast undertaking—the conversion of Russia and other great empires to the principles of our own declaration? It has been the burden of this book to demonstrate that we can and, indeed, already have made great progress. That we have done so almost unconsciously, by a kind of benign and invisible hand—even as the leaders of the free nations proclaim over and over again that such grand tasks are beyond our scope— only gives evidence of the power of the idea and the achievability of the goal. Imagine how effective we will be when the goal is proclaimed and the means orchestrated to the end. "France," wrote Charles de Gaulle, "is only her true self" when engaged in some great enterprise, for "France is not France without greatness."[34] What is true and obvious of that great republic is truer and more obvious of America, perhaps the first nation since the New Ilium to be founded on an idea.

It is true, as historians as diverse as Paul Johnson and Paul Kennedy have noted, that America can no longer achieve great things merely by the mindless application of overwhelming resources. In fact, as our study of the Marshall Plan and other distinguished endeavors of American policy has suggested, we never did. Our enterprises have been large and they have been great; but they were great not because they were large but because they were wise.

It is ironic to hear so many leaders speak in terms of American limits.

America cannot be "the world's policeman," they say. She has neither right nor might to "impose our system." Few would disagree. If so, however, it would seem all the more urgent to debate the means by which our (admittedly finite) power can be used more efficaciously; to determine how our foreign policy can be smaller, but smarter. Instead, the chanting of platitudes about limits seems to be an end in itself, a pretext, frankly, for inaction. Our leaders too often seem more concerned with talking about what cannot be done than with what we may still accomplish.

It is obvious, for example, that America's economy, as a share of the world economy, may well shrink. With it, in all likelihood, will shrink the preponderance of American arms—if not relative to the Soviet Union, then certainly relative to such countries as Japan and West Germany, whose rearmament it should be our design to promote. Yet in this sense, it may be a measure of our success if the U.S. role does shrink—provided the "decline" is a reflection not of stagnation here but of even more rapid growth in the surging democracies of Asia, Latin America, and Africa, and of a recrudescent pride on the part of Europeans in the heritage of civilization they have shared with the world. What we cannot do alone, we can do in concert with a growing orchestra of proud and prosperous democracies. In this sense, the decline of American material hegemony should be a primary goal of American foreign policy.

"We cannot," said a writer in the London *Economist* of Britain's growing dependence on America in 1941, "resent this historical development. We may rather feel proud that the cycle of dependence, enmity, and independence is coming full circle."[35] What was true for Britain in the middle of the twentieth century is true for America in the twenty-first. It is only by the extension of the democratic idea, after all, that our sisters of the world will become great nations. And the extension of the democratic idea is, far from a fearsome trend, the essence and the raison d'être of America itself.

If there was an American Century—as Henry Luce both urged and prophesied in his essay of that title—it is, in the narrow and ethnocentric sense, already over. Yet to reread his urgent essay almost fifty years later is to realize that Luce had something much bigger in mind. In a way, his label did not do justice to his idea. For the age of American dominance did not begin in the 1940s; it was nearing its end. What did begin, as Luce in some passages intimated, was something grander and nobler still: a Democratic Century. As America remains the most revered and daunting of the democracies, and will for some time, this may seem like a caviling distinction. Yet in its nuance, it is as important as the difference between self-interest and charity; between pride and humility. And truly, it is the promotion of a thing much broader than mere Americanism the author of "The American Century" had in mind: "a love of freedom, a feeling for the equality of opportunity, a tradition of self-reliance and independence and also of cooperation."[36] It is fair to say that

A DEMOCRATIC CENTURY

America has been especially blessed with these; it is wrong to think of the ideas themselves as peculiarly American, for as ideas, they are as old as man.

The Democratic Century, in this sense, is not an assertion of fact, or even a prediction, but a possibility. This Democratic Century was foreshadowed, perhaps, in those ships that carried the Lincoln Brigades and other volunteers to the Spanish Civil War. It was half-born after the war, when America helped rebuild half a continent ill-fed, ill-housed, and, more important, somewhat ill-led, threatened by a communist empire that had swallowed much of the world and still seemed unsated.

The Democratic Century is still, in its essence, waiting to be completed. Too often, our leaders have feared or rejected such grand notions. Yet the soul of the Democratic Century is the soul of our nation. Reviving, or, more precisely, rediscovering that spirit, then, is a vital task for America. For as Luce wrote:

> Other nations can survive simply because they have endured so long. . . . But this nation, conceived in adventure and dedicated to the progress of man—this nation cannot truly endure unless there courses strongly through its veins from Maine to California the blood of purpose and enterprise and high resolve. . . .
>
> Ours cannot come out of the vision of any one man. It must be the vision of many. It must be a sharing with all peoples our Bill of Rights, our Declaration, our Constitution. . . . It must be an internationalism of the people, by the people, and for the people. . . .
>
> For the moment, it may be enough to be the sanctuary of these ideals. But not for long. It now becomes our time to be the powerhouse from which the ideals spread throughout the world.[37]

A half-century after Luce penned those words, America still stands at the head of the democratic revolution. This is not to say that America is morally or culturally superior. On the contrary, the democratic idea is a gift we happened to receive; a sign of our fortune, not our intrinsic merit. It is better because it is better, not because it is ours.

What is ours, nevertheless, is a unique responsibility. Some Americans will shrink from this challenge. But the American spirit will welcome it.

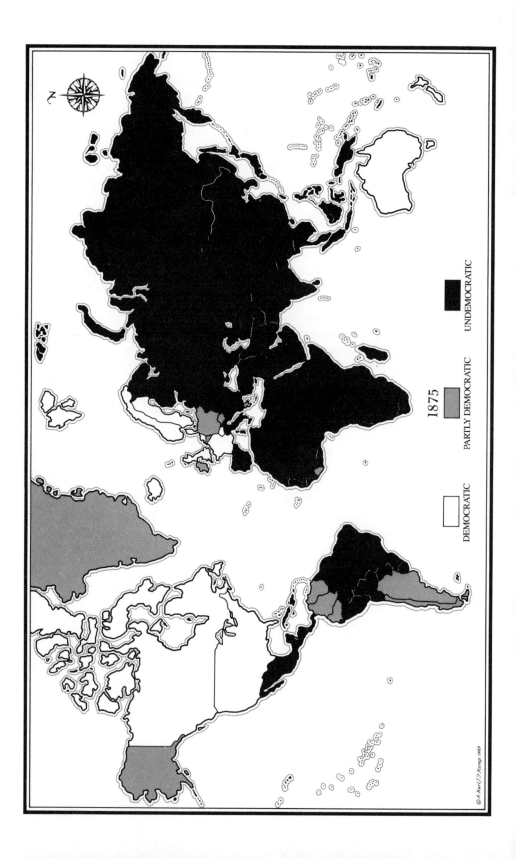

1875

DEMOCRATIC

PARTLY DEMOCRATIC

UNDEMOCRATIC

©A.Karl/J.Kemp 1989

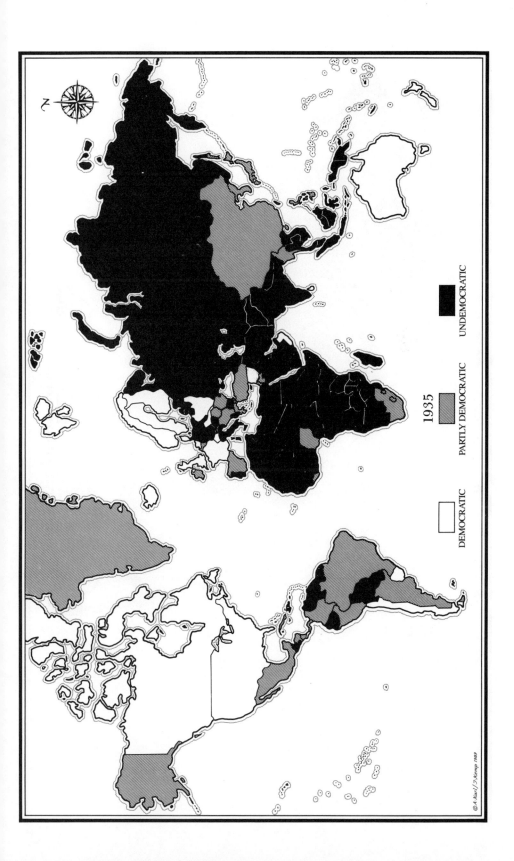

1935

DEMOCRATIC

PARTLY DEMOCRATIC

UNDEMOCRATIC

© A. Karl / J. Kemp 1989

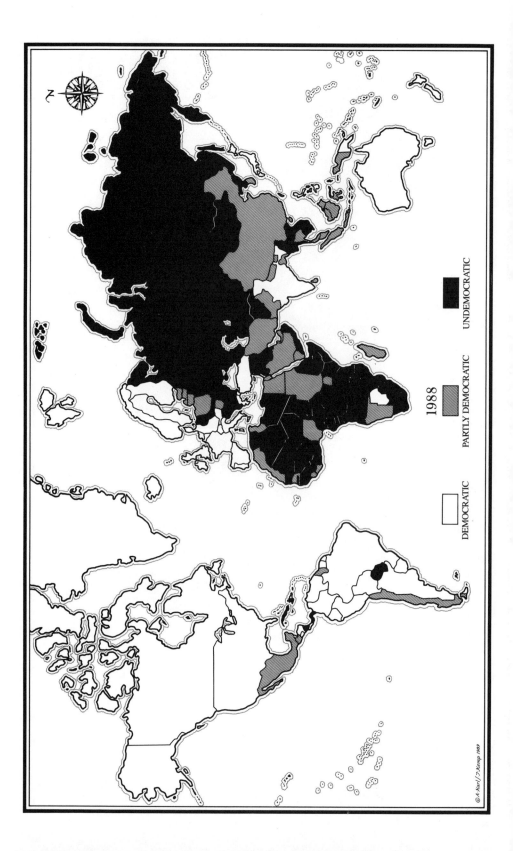

1988

DEMOCRATIC

PARTLY DEMOCRATIC

UNDEMOCRATIC

© A. Karl / J. Kemp 1989

Democratic: Australia, Canada, Denmark, France, Iceland, Netherlands, New Zealand, Norway, Sweden, Switzerland, United Kingdom, United States.

Partly Democratic: Alaska, Argentina, Austria, Belgium, British Honduras, Chile, Colombia, Ecuador, Germany, Greece, Greenland, Ireland, Liberia, Venezuela.

Undemocratic: Afghanistan, Algeria, Bolivia, Brazil, British Guiana, Cape Colony, Ceylon, China, Cochin China, Continental Africa (pre-colonization), Costa Rica, Cuba, Dominican Republic, Egypt, El Salvador, French Guiana, Gabon, Gambia, Guatemala, Haiti, Honduras, India, Indonesia, Iran, Italy, Japan, Libya, Madagascar, Malaysia, Mexico, Morocco, Mozambique, Natal, Nicaragua, Obock, Ottoman Empire, Panama, Paraguay, Peru, Philippines, Portugal, Portuguese Guinea, Russian Empire, Saudi Arabia, Senegal, Siam, Sierra Leone, Spain, Spanish Guinea, Sudan, Suriname, Uruguay, Yugoslavia.

Democratic: Australia, Canada, Ceylon, Chile, Costa Rica, Czechoslovakia, Denmark, Finland, France, Iceland, Levant States, Netherlands, New Zealand, Norway, Oman, Poland, Sweden, Switzerland, United States, Uruguay.

Partly Democratic: Alaska, Argentina, Belgium, Brazil, Burma, China, Colombia, Cuba, Greece, Greenland, Hawaii, Honduras, Hong Kong, Hungary, Ireland, Japan, Korea, Liberia, Macao, Mexico, Nicaragua, Nigeria, Palestine, Panama, Peru, Philippines, Puerto Rico, Romania, South Africa, Spain, Taiwan, Transjordan, Turkey, Yugoslavia.

Undemocratic: Afghanistan, Albania, Algeria, Angola, Austria, Bechuanaland, Belgian Congo, Bhutan, Bolivia, British Guiana, British Honduras, British Somaliland, Bulgaria, Dominican Republic, Ecuador, Egypt, El Salvador, Eritrea, Estonia, Ethiopia, French Equatorial Guinea, French Guiana, French Somaliland, French West Africa, Gambia, Germany, Gold Coast, Guatemala, Haiti, India, Indochina, Iran, Iraq, Italian Somaliland, Italy, Jamaica, Kenya, Latvia, Libya, Lithuania, Madagascar, Malay States, Morocco, Mozambique, Nepal, Netherlands Indies, New Guinea, Nyasaland, Paraguay, Portugal, Portuguese Guinea, Rhodesia, Saudi Arabia, Senegal, Siam, Sierra Leone, Southwest Africa, Sudan, Suriname, Tanganyika, Tunisia, USSR, Venezuela, Yemen.

Democratic: Argentina, Australia, Austria, Belgium, Belize, Bolivia, Botswana, Brazil, Canada, Colombia, Costa Rica, Denmark, Dominican Republic, Ecuador, El Salvador, Falkland Islands, Finland, France, French Guiana, Germany (W), Greece, Greenland, Grenada, Honduras, Iceland, India, Ireland, Israel, Italy, Jamaica, Japan, Netherlands, New Zealand, Norway, Papua New Guinea, Peru, Philippines, Portugal, Puerto Rico, Spain, Suriname, Sweden, Switzerland, Turkey, United Kingdom, United States, Uruguay, Venezuela.

Partly Democratic: Bahrain, Bangladesh, Bhutan, Chile, China, Egypt, Estonia, Gambia, Guatemala, Guiana, Hong Kong, Hungary, Indonesia, Iran, Korea (S), Latvia, Liberia, Lithuania, Macao, Madagascar, Malaysia, Mexico, Morocco, Namibia, Nepal, Nigeria, Pakistan, Poland, Saudi Arabia, Senegal, Sierra Leone, Singapore, Sri Lanka, Sudan, Taiwan, Thailand, Tunisia, Uganda, United Arab Emirates, Yemen (N).

Undemocratic: Afghanistan, Albania, Algeria, Angola, Benin, Brunei, Bulgaria, Burkina Faso, Burma, Burundi, Cambodia, Cameroon, Central African Republic, Chad, Comoros, Congo, Cuba, Czechoslovakia, Djibouti, Equatorial Guinea, Ethiopia, Gabon, Germany (E), Ghana, Guinea, Guinea-Bissau, Haiti, Iraq, Ivory Coast, Jordan, Kenya, Korea (N), Kuwait, Laos, Lebanon, Lesotho, Libya, Malawi, Mali, Mauritania, Mongolia, Mozambique, Nicaragua, Niger, Oman, Panama, Paraguay, Romania, Rwanda, Somalia, South Africa, Swaziland, Syria, Tanzania, Togo, USSR, Vietnam, Yemen (S), Yugoslavia, Zaire, Zambia, Zimbabwe.

SOURCE: Gregory Fossedal and Adam Lieberman, "An Historical Survey of World Democracy," Alexis de Tocqueville Institution, 1989. Our primary sources of information were as follows: For the year 1988, Raymond D. Gastil, "The Comparative Survey of Freedom," Freedom at Issue, January 1988 and January 1989; idem, "The Comparative Survey," chap. 1 of Freedom in the World, 1986–87 (Westport, Conn.: Greenwood Press, 1987); and idem, "The Comparative Survey of Freedom: Experiences and Suggestions," address delivered at the Hoover Institution, 1988; for the year 1935, Council on Foreign Relations, The Political Handbook of the World (New York: Simon & Schuster, 1936), and from more recent editions of the Handbook, where detailed histories provided background information not always available in earlier editions (since 1986, published by CSA Publications, State University of New York at Binghamton); for the year 1875, all of the above, as well as the annual The Statesman's Yearbook (London: Macmillan Press, 1874–1876 editions). Final judgments, however, are those of the author. In particular, our rankings place relatively greater emphasis than Gastil's on the following factors: 1.) the legal status and strength of competing political parties, including the peaceful transfer of power among them, which in our system is almost a guarantee of "democratic" ranking; and 2.) freedom to emigrate, to dissent publicly even from a single ruling party, and to own property, form free civic organizations, and so on. (Gastil places some emphasis on competition, little emphasis on emigration rights, and more emphasis on such rights as the freedom from torture, invasion of privacy, and so on. Our system tends to lift such states as China and Saudi Arabia up from his "not free" category to our "partly democratic," while pushing Nicaragua by a nose into the "not democratic" section.)

For purposes of the two-color, three-category, limited-size maps in this book, we have had to make some rather sweeping generalizations, as in classifying most of the African continent as "not democratic" when in fact many tribes were partly democratic in character. Along with ignoring such important tribe-by-tribe distinctions, we have similarly left out such countries as Vatican City, whose addition would simply clutter the graphic without significantly altering its composition.

ACKNOWLEDGMENTS

THE INITIAL INSPIRATION for this work came from three men who have offered me critical support since the early 1980s. Their acts and words have also been a vital force, to my mind, in shaping many of the good things that have happened in the world in the last twenty-five years.

First came Jude Wanniski, an economic consultant, former editorial writer for the *Wall Street Journal,* and author of *The Way the World Works,* the initial and widely praised book setting forth the tenets of supply-side economics. But to describe Wanniski as a supply-side economist is about as adequate as calling Benjamin Franklin a politician. Wanniski, a joyous tinkerer in things disparate, is better regarded as a sort of populist Lord Keynes, a self-described radical and wild man whose thinking is always fresh and whose insights span every field of activity.

On my first day at the *Journal,* Wanniski advised me to take on some long-range project that went beyond my duties at the paper, and his enthusiasm at my response—"already have one"—encouraged me to forge ahead.

A few weeks later, Richard Nixon agreed to let me interview him about foreign policy generally and his own book, *Real Peace,* in particular. At the close of the interview he asked about my own projects and seemed enthusiastic about the book idea. The trouble with American diplomacy, he said, is that it has been carried out by people "who only know how not to do it."

He agreed to keep in touch, and ever since has favored me—along with a number of other authors, politicians, and journalists—with helpful ideas, useful bits of information, and intelligent questions.

The third *homme d'influence,* Martin Peretz, became an acquaintance at around the same time. Peretz and his magazine, *The New Republic,* were already busily engaged in the business of remaking the Democratic Party. He agreed that the foreign-policy debate, in both parties, had grown stale, and urged me to write about the subject. My first effort, an article about economic sanctions, appeared in the magazine in 1985;* a few sections of it are reprinted

*"Sanctions for Beginners," 21 October 1985. Reprinted by permission of *The New Republic,* © 1985, The New Republic, Inc.

247

in chapter 6 of this book. When the search for a publisher began, Peretz was an early thought. Fortunately, he and the New Republic Books editor at the time, Steve Wasserman, liked the project, which has also benefited from guidance by Wasserman's successors, Robert Wright and Bill Newlin, as well as by Martin Kessler, Linda Carbone, and the rest of the fine staff at Basic Books.

In addition, my efforts have been strongly influenced by several writers who, whether they know it or not, are chief sources of information and inspiration. My colleagues David Asman, John Fund, Tim Ferguson, Dan Henninger, Paul Gigot, George Melloan, and Robert Bartley at the *Wall Street Journal* aren't cited as often as they might have been in these pages, because much of what they write appears under the byline "Review & Outlook" that runs above the paper's editorials. But it was the *Journal*'s focus on democracy, beginning in the 1970s, along with Ronald Reagan's critique of U.S. foreign policy in the 1976 campaign, the precursor of Jimmy Carter's similar theme, that shifted national debate on foreign policy decisively toward human rights. Then there are Irving Kristol, Michael Kinsley, Tom Bethell, Alexander Cockburn, and Jonathan Schell. These fellows have about as much in common as the members of the firm of Wanniski, Nixon, and Peretz mentioned above. Yet their flexibility of mind, their disdain for the hackneyed, and their energy in finding a synthesis transcending conventional wisdom unite them. So, while it isn't my privilege to know well any of the names dropped in this paragraph, they were in a sense contributing editors of this book. Here's hoping their role doesn't embarrass.

Too many people helped in the actual research, writing, typing, editing, reviewing, and production to explain their precise contributions. But here are some who deserve thanks: researchers Joe Anderson, Gerald Hughes, Adam Lieberman, Brad Mehl, Zelda Novak, Debbie Stone, and Fareed Zakaria; and secretaries and administrative assistants Betty Oates, Marsha Green, Pam Lover, Anne Robertson, Kate Power, and Wendy Minkin. Todd Lindsay at the *Washington Times* library, and the fine reference librarians here at Hoover, were especially kind in chasing down last-minute footnotes. Others provided assistance of a different sort. Ideas and guidance on the model: above all, Merrick Carey and Dennis Teti. Proofreading: my mother, Mrs. Stanley Smith. Agenting: Carol Mann. And then, there's that critical form of assistance, money. This came from the Hoover Institution, the think tank W. Glenn Campbell built; Paul Hexter, Frank Miele, Chen Wang, Bruce Thompson, Eugene Ravizza, and Terry Rose, who generously donated the funds that began the Alexis de Tocqueville Institution, which will carry on the work of this book until the entire world is a free-enterprise democracy; and George Champion, the former chairman of Chase Manhattan bank, who helped raise funds from others eager to support the de Tocqueville Institution's work.

One person provided all of these things and, in addition, put up with a fanatically obsessed man during what became several years of research and

ACKNOWLEDGMENTS

writing: my wife, Elizabeth. Her nudges got me up at 5 A.M. day after day; her coffee kept me awake on too little sleep; the look of delight on her face at night made me eager to come home with "another chapter finished."

If my efforts are half as fruitful as hers, then this volume cannot fail, for by the end of the process we had not only a book but a fine addition to the family as well, Christopher Felix Fossedal.

May God, whose all-seeing eye every act of tyranny offends, grant that both these pages and my son will advance the cause of freedom and democracy; yet let it be as His will, not mine, would have it.

—Stanford, California

NOTES

Chapter 1 Opportunity

1. Arthur H. Landis, *The Abraham Lincoln Brigade* (New York: The Citadel Press, 1967), p. xvii. Volunteers from America formed a number of units to fight in the war as part of the International Brigades. Among them were the Abraham Lincoln Batallion, the George Washington Batallion, and the American-dominated Mackenzie-Papineau Batallion. I have adopted the nomenclature of most U.S. journals at the time of the conflict, as described by Landis: "In all areas of combat the men were referred to as the *Abraham Lincoln Batallion;* where American volunteers in general were being dealt with they were referred to as the *Abraham Lincoln Brigade*" (italics in original).

2. Robert A. Rosenstone, "Abraham Lincoln Battalion," in *Historical Dictionary of the Spanish Civil War,* ed. James W. Cortada (Westport, Conn.: Greenwood Press, 1982), pp. 5–7. Unless otherwise indicated, statistics on the composition of the Abraham Lincoln Brigade are taken from this volume.

3. Hugh Thomas, *The Spanish Civil War* (New York: Harper & Row, 1977), p. 533.

4. Ibid., pp. 646–68. See also Jesus Hernandez Tomas, *La grande trahison* (Paris: Fasquelle, 1953), p. 66; Indalecio Prieto, *Convulsiones de España,* vol. 3 (Mexico: Ediciones Oasis, 1967), p. 220.

5. For detailed accounts of the purges, see Alexander Orlov, testifying before the Senate Subcommittee to Investigate the Administration of the Internal Security Act and Other Internal Security Laws, in "Scope of Soviet Activity in the U.S.," part 51, 85th cong., 1st sess., 14 and 15 February 1957 (Washington, D.C.: 85th cong., 1957); and Walter Krivitsky, *I Was Stalin's Agent* (London: Right Book Club, 1940). Thomas, *The Spanish Civil War,* summarizes with supporting footnotes on pp. 703, 766.

6. George Orwell, *New English Weekly,* 29 July 1937 and 2 September 1937; Ronald Radosh, "My Uncle Died in Vain Fighting the Good Fight," *Washington Post,* 6 April 1986; and Bernard Knox, "The Spanish Tragedy," *New York Review of Books,* 26 March 1987.

7. Rosenstone, in *Historical Dictionary,* ed. Cortada, p. 6.

8. See, for example, "President Aquino," Review & Outlook, *Wall Street Journal,* 26 February 1986.

9. See, for example, Eric Schwartz and Holly Burkhalter, "Press Seoul for Democracy, Too," *New York Times,* 24 February 1986; Edward Neilan, "Korea's Opposition Leaders Quit Talks on Constitution," *Washington Times,* 30 September 1986; Bernard Wysocki, Jr., "Could Korea Go Way of the Philippines?" *Wall Street Journal,* 7 March 1986.

10. *New York Times,* 7 March 1986. Such pledges and U.S. debate over their value were frequent. See, for example, from combined dispatches, "U.S. Envoy, S. Korea Opposition Leader Talk," *Washington Times,* 22 April 1986; Kwan Ha Vim, "Reform in South Korea Off to a Poor Start," letter to *New York Times,* 4 September 1986; and editorial, "The Real Danger in Seoul," *New York Times,* 30 September 1986.

11. *New York Times,* 30 September 1986.

12. June Kronholz, "Political Change Inches Ahead in Taiwan," *Wall Street Journal,* 18 June 1986.

13. Martin L. Lasater, "New Challenges Confront Fifteen Years of U.S.-China Ties," Backgrounder No. 58 (Washington, D.C.: Asian Studies Center, Heritage Foundation), 27 February 1987.

14. Quoted in Georgie Anne Geyer, "Change in the Two Chinas," *Washington Times,* 16 March 1987.

15. Georgie Anne Geyer, "China and the Road not Taken," *Washington Times,* 19 March 1987.

16. See Steven R. Weisman, "Struggle in Pakistan," *New York Times Magazine,* 21 September 1986.

17. Mahnaz Ispahani, "Perils of Pakistan," *The New Republic,* 16 March 1987. See also

Theodore L. Eliot and Robert L. Pfaltzgraff, Jr., "The Red Army on Pakistan's Border," special report of the Center for Asian Political Affairs, The Asia Foundation, and the Institute for Foreign Policy Analysis (McLean, Va.: Pergamon-Brassey's, 1986).

18. Bradley Graham, "U.S. Increases Support for Opposition in Chile," *Washington Post,* 17 January 1986.

19. In Bernard Weinraub, "Chile's Leader Reported to Reject U.S. Calls for Democratic Change," *New York Times,* 18 August 1986.

20. Clyde Farnsworth, "New Pressures Against Chile," *New York Times,* 10 November 1986.

21. Reuters dispatch from Santiago, 15 January 1986.

22. See, for example, Associated Press report from Santiago, 3 September 1986; "Pinochet Berates U.S. and Church," *Washington Times,* 12 September 1986; Bill Gertz, "Helms Charges CIA, State Trying to Destabilize Chile," *Washington Times,* 8 August 1986; and Bernard Gwertzman, "U.S., in Reversal, Faults Chileans over Rights Issue," *New York Times,* 13 March 1986.

23. Chronology taken from chart, "Changing South Africa," *New York Times,* 27 April 1986; and "South Africa Chronology," White House Issue Brief, Office of Public Affairs, 22 July 1986.

24. Quoted in "South Africa Chronology," White House Issue Brief.

25. Comparisons in this paragraph taken from Raymond D. Gastil, "The Map of Freedom," *Freedom at Issue,* January–February 1977 and January–February 1987.

26. Quoted in the forum, "Why Are We in Central America?" *Harper's* magazine, June 1984.

27. "Remarks by the President at Human Rights Day Event," The White House, Office of the Press Secretary, 10 December 1986.

28. Adam Meyerson, "Brave New Hemisphere," *Policy Review,* Fall 1985, pp. 24–25.

29. Alan Riding, "Mexicans, Hurt in the Oil Crisis, Turn Their Anger on de la Madrid," *New York Times,* 25 June 1986. As a sample of U.S. editorial concern, see "Mexico: Policy Priority," *Washington Times,* 12 August 1986.

30. David Gardner, "Cardenas Puts Mexican Discontent in Focus," *Financial Times,* 19 March 1987.

31. Jonathan Kwitny, *Endless Enemies* (New York: Congdon and Weed, 1984), p. 418.

32. Quoted in Gerard Alexander, "African Success Stories," *Policy Review,* Summer 1985.

33. Stephen R. Lewis, Jr., "Democracy Enables Botswana to Cope with Drought," *Wall Street Journal,* 28 August 1985, p. 19.

34. Gastil, "Map of Freedom."

35. Robert Low, "The Battle for Greece," *Time,* 17 November 1947.

36. Quoted in *The Pursuit of Happiness and Other Sobering Thoughts* (New York: Harper & Row, 1979), p. 41.

37. Xan Smiley, "Hungary's Appetites," *The New Republic,* 20 December 1982.

38. Michael Dobbs, "Experiments Make Hungary Pacesetter for Soviet Bloc Economic Reforms," *Washington Post,* 25 October 1982.

39. Smiley, *The New Republic.*

40. Margaret van Hatten, "Reforming Stalin's Machine," *Financial Times,* 12 January 1987.

41. Sophie Kujda, "Hungary Introduces Some Choice into Elections," *Christian Science Monitor,* 22 July 1983.

42. Paul Lewis, "Recession in Eastern Europe Forces Reappraisals of Policy," *New York Times,* 27 November 1982.

43. Van Hatten, "Reforming Stalin's Machine."

44. Smiley, *The New Republic.*

45. Lewis, "Recession in Eastern Europe."

46. Information obtained in an interview with underground Solidarity leaders now in Poland, who cannot be identified. Comments were reviewed by other members of the union and cleared as a statement of the union. The interview was conducted in New York City in October 1985; excerpts were published in the *San Diego Union* on 1 December 1985. A more complete transcript is available through the Alexis de Tocqueville Institution in California. For an excellent analysis of how the Solidarity union survived underground into the 1980s, see Cord Meyer, "Poland's Thriving Underground," *Washington Times,* 23 May 1986.

47. David Buchan, "Hungary's Reformers Turn to Politics," *Financial Times,* 16 February 1983; Kujda, "Hungary Introduces Some Choice."

48. Barry Newman, "Budapest Embraces a Democratic Device: The Survey of Opinion," *Wall Street Journal,* 8 January 1987.

49. Interview with Eugene Pell, director of Radio Free Europe, in Washington, D.C., 18 August 1986.

50. Strobe Talbott, telephone interview with the author, 19 March 1987.

51. Patrick Cockburn, "Wages and Prices Attract Gorbachev Scrutiny," *Financial Times,* 29 October 1986.

52. Patrick Cockburn, "Moscow Legalizes Private Enterprise in Service Sector," *Financial Times,* 20 November 1986; news story, "Moscow Approves a Bit of Enterprise," *New York Times,* 23 November 1986.

53. Cockburn, "Wages and Prices Attract Gorbachev Scrutiny."

54. Philip Taubman, "Sakharov Publicly Calls for More Rights," *New York Times,* 15 February 1987.

55. Richard Pipes, "The Glasnost Test," *The New Republic,* 2 February 1987.

56. Combined dispatches, "Gorbachev Was Prepared to Quit," *Washington Times,* 20 February 1987; and Philip Taubman, "Gorbachev Candid About Opposition," *New York Times,* 25 February 1987.

57. Bill Keller, "Moscow Says Changes in Voting Usher in Many New Local Leaders," *New York Times,* 21 September 1988; news story, "Gorbachev Shies Away from Attacks on Critics," *Financial Times,* 12 May 1988; Arnold Beichman, "Candor Creeps into Soviet Journals," *Washington Times,* 19 February 1987.

58. On the inherent contradictions between capitalism and authoritarian rule in China, see Eileen Chamberlain, "China's Quest for Modernization: The Dilemma of Communist Party Authority vs. Economic Performance," thesis paper submitted to Professor Landesat, Harvard University, 16 January 1984.

59. Quoted in *Korea Times,* 2 August 1986.

60. Gastil, "Map of Freedom."

61. See, for example, his interview with Martin Andersen and Barry Came, *Newsweek,* 19 March 1984. Alfonsin repeated his thanks at a conference in the fall of 1986 in Atlanta, Georgia, attended by the author.

62. Alan Riding, "A Latin Spring: Democracy in Flower," *New York Times,* 29 November 1984.

63. Michael Novak, talk given at Union League Club, Institute for Educational Affairs, New York City, 27 October 1983.

Chapter 2   Skepticism

1. Jean-François Revel, *How Democracies Perish,* trans. William Byron (New York: Doubleday, 1984), pp. 3–6.

2. Paul Johnson, *Modern Times* (New York: Harper & Row, 1983), pp. 671–72; and Henry Luce, "The American Century," *Life,* 17 February 1941. Interestingly, classmates of Luce say he gave a talk on the American century at Yale several years before, or about the time of the Lincoln Brigades.

3. George F. Will, *The Pursuit of Happiness and Other Sobering Thoughts* (New York: Harper & Row, 1979), p. 5.

4. George F. Will, *Statecraft as Soulcraft* (New York: Simon & Schuster, 1983), pp. 18, 24.

5. George F. Will, *The Pursuit of Virtue and Other Tory Notions* (New York: Simon & Schuster, 1982), pp. 54, 213, 290, 291.

6. See Plato, *The Republic,* trans. B. Jowett, esp. Book VIII (Roslyn, N.Y.: Walter J. Black, 1969); Aristotle, *Politics,* ed. Louise Ropes Loomis, esp. pp. 288–410, (Roslyn, N.Y.: Walter J. Black, Classics Club, 1943); Thomas Hobbes, *The Leviathan,* in *French and English Philosophers,* ed. Charles W. Eliot (New York: Collier, 1910); John Locke, in *The Second Treatise on Government,* ed. Thomas P. Peardon, esp. chap. 19, "On the Dissolution of Government" (Indianapolis: Bobbs-Merrill, 1952, reprinted 1979); and Jean-Jacques Rousseau, *Of the Social Contract,* trans. Charles M. Sherover (New York: Harper & Row, 1984), p. 64.

7. See Harry V. Jaffa, "The American Founding as the Best Regime," lecture delivered in Claremont, Calif., on 17 September 1987, publication forthcoming, Claremont Institute. Available from Gregory A. Fossedal, Alexis de Tocqueville Institution.

8. Jeffrey Bell, from unpublished correspondence with the author, abstract "On the Origin and Development of Modern Democracy." Available from Gregory A. Fossedal, Alexis de Tocqueville Institution.

9. H. G. Wells, *The Outline of History* (New York: Macmillan, 1924), pp. 259, 262.

NOTES

10. Aristotle, *Politics*, pp. 320–36; Rousseau, *Social Contract*, p. 65; Plato, *Republic*, p. 433.

11. Publius, presumably James Madison, in Federalist no. 14, *The Federalist Papers*, ed. Clinton Rossiter (New York: Times Mirror, 1961), p. 100.

12. Plato, *Republic*, Book VIII, p. 443.

13. The author is aware that statements about the diffusion of wealth are controversial. Only if we look at misleading snapshots of "quintile" divisions of income, however, is this diffusion obscured. The author is relying on a view of wealth and its diffusion as expressed in the findings of the Michigan University panel on income dynamics. See Greg J. Duncan, *Years of Poverty, Years of Plenty* (Ann Arbor: Institute for Social Research, University of Michigan, 1984). See also "Rich Man, Poor Man," Review & Outlook, *Wall Street Journal*, 28 November 1984; Mark Lilla, "Why the 'Income Distribution' Is So Misleading," *The Public Interest*, Fall 1984; Warren Brookes, "Sorry, Wrong Numbers on Jobs and Poverty," *Washington Times*, 20 April 1987; idem, chart, "Family Net Worth Distribution," *Washington Times*, 27 August 1986; Gregory A. Fossedal, "The Second War on Poverty," *The American Spectator*, February 1986; Editorial, "Das Kapital (Revised Ed.)," Review & Outlook, *Wall Street Journal*, 7 October 1986.

14. Alexis de Tocqueville, *Democracy in America*, vol. 1, trans. and ed. Henry Reeve and Francis Bowen (New York: Random House, 1945). Citations from "Why the Federal System Is Not Practicable for All Nations," chap. 8, and "Respect for Law in the United States," chap. 14, pp. 170 and 258.

15. Rousseau, *Social Contract*.

16. Doris Kearns, *Lyndon Johnson and the American Dream* (New York: Harper & Row, 1976), pp. 395–400.

17. George F. Will, "The Madison Legacy," *Newsweek*, 7 December 1981. For a more extensive discussion of the interesting politics of the tax reform, see Gregory A. Fossedal, "The Art of Additive Compromise," *The American Spectator*, October 1985, and idem, "Kemp-Bradley-Packwood," *The American Spectator*, August 1986.

18. George F. Kennan, "The Sources of Soviet Conduct," *Foreign Affairs*, July 1947, p. 582.

19. Zbigniew Brzezinski, *Game Plan* (Boston: Atlantic Monthly Press, 1986), p. xiv.

20. David K. Shipler, "Brzezinski Offers a New Strategy Toward Soviet," *New York Times*, 17 June 1986.

21. Ibid.

22. Ibid.

23. Jonathan Kwitny, *Endless Enemies* (New York: Congdon & Weed, 1984).

24. Richard Barnet and Ronald E. Müller, *Global Reach* (New York: Simon & Schuster, 1974).

25. Jimmy Carter, *Keeping Faith* (New York: Bantam Books, 1982), pp. 142–43.

26. Joshua Muravchik, *The Uncertain Crusade* (Lanham, Md.: Hamilton Press, 1986); Jeane J. Kirkpatrick, *Dictatorships and Double Standards* (New York: Simon & Schuster, 1983).

27. Paul Kennedy, *The Rise and Fall of the Great Powers* (New York: Random House, 1988); and James Chace, *Endless War* (New York: Vintage Books/Random House, 1984).

28. Hodding Carter, telephone interview with the author, 18 July 1986; Leslie Gelb, "A Winning Style," *New York Times Magazine*, 30 March 1986; Editorial, "No Corys in Karachi," Review & Outlook, *Wall Street Journal*, 20 August 1986; Editorial, "Meeting, or Beating, the Russians," *New York Times*, 6 September 1986; Stephen J. Solarz, "When to Intervene," *Foreign Policy*, Summer 1986, p. 38; Ronald Reagan, remarks to the Foreign Policy Association, New York City, 9 June 1977, reprinted in "United States Foreign Policy and World Realities" (Berkeley: Hoover Institution), reprint no. 104, pp. 4–5.

29. Paul Johnson, *Modern Times* (New York: Harper & Row, 1983), p. 320; Suzanne Garment, "U.S. Sanctions Just a Sideshow in African Drama," *Wall Street Journal*, 16 August 1985; editorial, "They Shoot Airplanes, Don't They?" *The New Republic*, 3 October 1983; Richard M. Nixon, *RN: The Memoirs of Richard Nixon* (New York: Grosset & Dunlap, 1978), p. 876; Jack Kemp, personal interview with the author, 22 July 1982.

30. Johnson, *Modern Times*, pp. 320–21.

31. Nick Eberstadt, "The Perversion of Foreign Aid," *Commentary*, June 1985, p. 33.

32. Doug Bandow, ed., "U.S. Aid to the Developing World" (Washington, D.C.: Heritage Foundation, 1985), pp. xii, xix.

33. Melvyn Krauss, *Development Without Aid* (New York: McGraw-Hill, 1983), pp. 157–59.

34. Phil Gramm, press release by the National Republican Congressional Committee, quoted in Anatole Kaletsky, "Anti-Communist Jibe by Republicans Puts IMF Bill at Risk," *Financial Times*, 17 August 1983.

NOTES

35. Krauss, *Development Without Aid,* p. 190; Bandow, "U.S. Aid to the Developing World," pp. xxxii, xvii; World Bank, *World Development Report* for 1984 (New York: Oxford University Press, 1984), p. 41.

36. Aleksandr Solzhenitsyn, "The Soft Voice of America," *National Review,* 30 April 1982, p. 478.

37. This comment was attributed to Mr. Weinberger by someone present at a conversation he had with Mr. Poindexter at the White House on the afternoon of 24 September 1986. Weinberger finally relented, according to that source, and allowed the transfer, as a column by the author for Copley News Service reported in October 1986. Weinberger and Poindexter would not comment. A copy of the column, "Unsafe for Democracy," as it appeared in the *Cumberland News* (Maryland) and numerous other newspapers, was sent to Weinberger, again asking for his comment. There was no reply. A spokesman at Radio Liberty said the report was "accurate."

38. Max Kampelman, personal interview with the author at the U.S. State Department, 25 August 1985.

39. Symposium, "Human Rights and American Foreign Policy," *Commentary,* November 1981, pp. 25–63.

40. Brzezinski, cited in ibid., p. 30.

41. Richard Falk, in "Human Rights," *Commentary.* p. 35.

42. Carter, *Keeping Faith,* pp. 149–50.

43. Daniel P. Moynihan, quoted in Jane Perlez, "Latin Panel's Soviet Finding Is Challenged by Moynihan," *New York Times,* 13 January 1984.

44. Les Aspin and Stephen J. Solarz, *Securing Freedom: Principles for a Democratic Foreign Policy,* The Report of the Task Force on Foreign Policy to the Committee on Defense and Foreign Policy (Washington, D.C.: Democratic Policy Commission, 26 June 1986), p. 16.

45. Victor Fazio, *Congressional Record,* 19 March 1986, p. H1401.

46. "Dancing to a Tin Drummer," *Time,* 29 September 1986, p. 23.

47. Stephen J. Solarz, *Congressional Record,* 17 September 1986, p. H7028.

48. Reports of those assessments first appeared in David Ottaway and Patrick Tyler, "DOD Alone in Optimism for Savimbi," *Washington Post,* 7 February 1986. Some months later a source who prefers to remain anonymous sent the author a series of memoranda, some confidential and some for the record, which tended to confirm the Ottaway-Tyler story. The memoranda, by Jim Phillips, Elizabeth Arens, and Mike Pillsbury, were written between March 1986 and February 1987 and concerned various aspects of U.S. efforts to aid freedom fighters. A two-part memorandum by Arens credited Tyler with this and a number of other accurate disclosures of U.S. covert operations. The first part of the Arens memorandum, for example, concluded that "Tyler has a network of sources in the intelligence community. He quotes NSC minutes, a senior administration official present at NSC discussions, NSC records, CIA officials, internal administration documents, one of Casey's aides, a House Intelligence Committee memo, and House and Senate Intelligence Committee members, often by name."

49. Adam Lieberman, "Reagan Doctrine, Brezhnev Doctrine," *DTI Brief* no. 87-02, published under grants from the Hoover Institution on War, Revolution, and Peace and the Alexis de Tocqueville Institution, 27 April 1987.

50. Solarz, "When to Intervene," pp. 28–29.

51. See Anthony Lewis, "The Rambo Doctrine," *New York Times,* 10 October 1985; Arthur Schlesinger, Jr., "Grenada Again: Living Within the Law," *Wall Street Journal,* 14 December 1983, and "Bay of Pigs Again—Only Worse," *Wall Street Journal,* 17 April 1986; Alexander Cockburn, "U.S. Ignores International Law on Two Continents," *Wall Street Journal,* 27 March 1986; and Michael Kinsley, "Reagan Doctrine Is an International Lawbreaker," *Wall Street Journal,* 26 June 1986.

52. A copy of Weinberger's memorandum was sent to the editorial page of the *Wall Street Journal* in 1985 and distributed to the author. Weinberger's memo was widely reported in the press.

53. Quoted in Judith Miller, " 'Sometimes I Say Things Differently,' " *New York Times,* 13 March 1987.

54. Burton Yale Pines, interview with the author, November 1985.

55. John McLaughlin didn't think so, but he noted that many U.S. leaders did, in "Is America Going to the Dogs?" *National Review,* 31 July 1987.

56. Robert W. Tucker, *The Purposes of American Power* (New York: Praeger Publications for the Lehrman Institute, 1981), pp. 3–4.

57. Editorial, "Angola: Stay on Track," *Christian Science Monitor,* 13 December 1985.

58. George Ball, "The Case Against Sanctions," *New York Times Magazine,* 12 September 1982, pp. 118–19.

59. Editorial item in "The Week," *National Review,* 31 January 1986, p. 20.

60. Editorial, "The Central America Debate," *Washington Post,* 12 January 1984.

61. Christopher Dickey, "Behind the Death Squads," *The New Republic,* 26 December 1983.

62. Editorial, "Trial by Ballot," Review & Outlook, *Wall Street Journal,* 1 February 1984. That editorial was drafted by this author, reviewed by editors David Asman, Robert Bartley, and George Melloan, and then published (unsigned) in the paper's "Review & Outlook" column. Hence it represented the editorial position of the *Journal,* and should be considered as such. Since the bulk of the research and writing was mine, readers of this book should know it is my own work being cited, not that of an independent reporter. Readers should credit the editors cited for any achievements in style, and blame me for any errors in research.

Chapter 3   Ideopolitik

1. Title of a 1904 paper by Halford J. Mackinder, cited in the preface to his *Democratic Ideals and Reality* (1919; rep. 1947 [New York: Holt] with introduction by Edward Mead Earle), p. v; and ibid., rev. ed., ed. Anthony J. Pearce (New York: Norton, 1962) (see pp. 268, 242, and 150).

2. Alfred Thayer Mahan, *The Influence of Sea Power upon History,* 12th ed. (Boston: Little, Brown, 1890), p. iii.

3. Giulio Douhet, *The Command of the Air,* 2d ed., trans. Dino Ferrari (London: Faber and Faber, 1927), p. 204. See also Alexander P. De Seversky, *Victory Through Air Power* (New York: Simon & Schuster, 1942), and Louis A. Sigaud, *Air Power and Unification* (Harrisburg, Pa: Telegraph Press, 1949).

4. The economic theory of geopolitics pervades the speeches of postwar presidents, but perhaps the best specimen, and one that should be read half as often as it is quoted, is Eisenhower's farewell address, reprinted in the *Washington Post* and the *New York Times* on 18 January 1961. On the emphasis of Ike, Churchill, and also de Gaulle on technology, see Gregory A. Fossedal, "S.D.I. Deployment and History," *The American Spectator,* December 1986. For Graham's geopolitics of space-cum-technology, see, for example, Daniel O. Graham, *High Frontier: A New National Strategy* (Washington, D.C.: Heritage Foundation, 1982). Quotations from Frank Barnett and Helmut Schmidt from Barnett's introduction to Colin S. Gray, *Geopolitics of the Nuclear Era,* sponsored by the National Strategy Information Center (New York: Crane, Russak, 1977), p. vii. Gray himself seems an exponent of the "resource war" theory. Safire's gem is from William Safire, "Gorbachev's Global Respite," *New York Times,* 20 October 1986.

5. Mackinder, *Democratic Ideals and Reality* (Holt ed.), pp. 148–200; extended quotation on p. 8.

6. Alfred Thayer Mahan, *The Problem of Asia* (Boston: Little, Brown, 1900), p. 7.

7. Mahan, *Influence of Sea Power,* pp. 52–54.

8. Ibid., pp. 54–57, 58.

9. De Seversky, *Victory Through Air Power,* pp. 6–7, 334, 350–52.

10. Paul Johnson, *Modern Times* (New York: Harper & Row, 1983), pp. 687, 688.

11. "A World at War," in *Defense Monitor* (Washington, D.C.: Center for Defense Information, 1986); see also Juan J. Walte, "Little Wars Have Deadly Potential," *USA Today,* 22 March 1983. U.S. combat statistics from Pentagon report cited by David Broder, "Deadly 'Twilight Struggle' with Communism," *New York Post,* 27 May 1987, p. 23, copyright Washington Post news service.

12. Richard Nixon, *The Real War* (New York: Warner Books, 1980), p. 313.

13. Henry Kissinger, *White House Years* (Boston: Little, Brown, 1979), pp. 118–19.

14. Phil Nicolaides, quoted in Gregory A. Fossedal and Daniel O. Graham, *A Defense That Defends* (Greenwich, Conn.: Devin-Adair Books, 1984), p. 105.

15. Irving Kristol, quoted in "Beyond Containment?" symposium in *Policy Review,* Winter 1985, p. 21; Jean-François Revel, *How Democracies Perish,* trans. William Byron (New York: Doubleday, 1984), p. 59; George Bush, interview with the author, July 1979. Excerpts, but not this particular quotation, were printed in Gregory Fossedal, "Bush Attacks Energy Dept.," *The Daily Dartmouth,* 13 July 1979.

16. Kenneth Waltz, "Another Gap?" in *Containment, Soviet Behavior, and Global Strategy,* ed. Robert E. Osgood, Policy Papers in International Affairs, no. 16 (Berkeley: Institute of International Studies, University of California, 1981), p. 80.

17. Jeffrey Bell's comments come from a chapter in an uncompleted book on democracy,

drafted while he was a fellow at the American Enterprise Institute. Bell generously provided the drafts of several chapters to this author. Copies can be obtained from the Alexis de Tocqueville Institution.

18. Statistics on Asian television ownership are from Ralph de Toledano, "Miracle on Taiwan," *National Review,* 19 August 1983; East German viewing of Western television is cited in William Drozdiak, "East Germany Shows Greater Independence," *Washington Post,* 27 February 1984; on circulation of Soviet samizdat literature, see Vladimir Bukovsky, "Critical Masses: The Soviet Union's Dissident Many," *The American Spectator,* August 1980, pp. 7–10; and estimate of popular impact of factory samizdats and word-of-mouth in Poland is taken from an interview the author conducted with a member of the Solidarity directorate in the fall of 1985. The latter cannot be named, but transcripts of the interview are available from the Alexis de Tocqueville Institution. On the "electronic Peace Corps," see David H. Rothman, "On-Line Diplomacy," *National Review,* 27 March 1987.

19. James V. Ogle, "Will Computers Destroy the Soviet System?" *Washington Post,* 1 November 1981.

20. Irving Kristol, "Socialism: Obituary for an Idea," *The Alternative: An American Spectator* (now *The American Spectator*), October 1976.

21. Michael T. Kaufman, "Moscow Said to Lose Sway Among Africans," *New York Times,* 22 November 1983.

22. Leslie H. Gelb, "U.S. Power in Asia Has Grown Since Vietnam," *New York Times,* 18 April 1985; and Geoffrey Walker, "Saigon's Fall Masked a U.S. Victory in Vietnam," *Wall Street Journal,* 28 April 1983.

23. Johnson, *Modern Times,* p. 698.

24. On the relationship between Islam, communism, and democracy, see Daniel Pipes, "Fundamentalist Muslims Between America and Russia," *Foreign Affairs,* Spring 1986. On the real, though not limitless, diversity of political views within Iran, see, for example, "Democracy Among the Mullahs," editorial, *The Economist,* reprinted in *Washington Times,* 14 July 1987; Ihsan A. Hijazi, "Rift Among Iran's Leaders Appears to Widen," *New York Times,* 7 November 1986; and Elaine Sciolino, "Khomeini Deputies Differ in Outlook," *New York Times,* 8 November 1986. On Egypt, see, for example, Judith Miller, "Viable Opposition Parties Are Emerging in Egypt," *New York Times,* 8 January 1984.

25. Statistics from: Nicholas Daniloff, "In Russia, Shortage of Workers Is the Problem," *U.S. News & World Report,* 18 July 1983; chart, "The Numbers from Moscow," *New York Times,* 12 November 1986; David Satter, "Soviet Death Rates Rising, Report Says; Trend Is Unique in Developed World," *Wall Street Journal,* 18 October 1982; Nicholas Eberstadt, "A Pattern of Soviet Bloc Health Reversals," *Wall Street Journal,* 30 April 1986; and Stanley S. Henshaw, "Induced Abortion: A Worldwide Perspective," *Family Planning Perspectives,* November–December 1986, p. 252.

26. Ben J. Wattenberg, *The Birth Dearth* (New York: Pharos Books, 1987).

27. See, for example, Mikhail Bernstam et al., eds., *Below-Replacement Fertility Rates in Industrial Societies* (New York: Cambridge University Press, 1987), and Michael S. Teitelbaum and Jay M. Winter, *The Fear of Population Decline* (Orlando: Academic Press, 1985).

28. Gregory A. Fossedal, "To Win Yuppies, Democrats Must Learn to Pipe a New Tune," *Peninsula Times-Tribune* (Palo Alto, Calif.), 25 September 1986, copyright Copley News Service, 21 September 1986; John Wilke, "Total of Unmarried Couples Has Tripled," *Washington Post,* 1 July 1983; Claudia Bowe, "The Rush to Maternity—Why Everybody Suddenly Wants a Baby," *Cosmopolitan,* September 1986; and editorial, Review & Outlook, "Love American Style," *Wall Street Journal,* 6 July 1987.

29. Wattenberg, *The Birth Dearth,* pp. 174–75.

30. Ibid., p. 171; and Neal Peirce, "The Fearsome Long-Term Implications of One Million Immigrants a Year," *Washington Post,* 15 November 1981.

31. Wattenberg, *The Birth Dearth,* pp. 134, 22.

32. Robert Reinhold, "New U.S. Law Appears to Deter Illegal Aliens," *New York Times,* 20 February 1987. Deter, yes, but not by much: According to the statistical chart that runs with the article, the number of illegal aliens apprehended along the U.S.-Mexican border was about the same over two periods: (a) from October 1985 to January 1986, without the anti-immigration law in effect, and (b) from October 1986 to January 1987, with the new law in effect. And such arrests were rising steadily from 1970 (less than 400,000 arrests) to 1985 (more than 1,200,000) due to increased border patrols. See Ellen Hume and Dianna Solis, "Immigration-Control Measures Spawn Alliances That Encompass Diverse Political, Social Camps," *Wall Street Journal,* 28 August 1985. Indeed, as this writer and others predicted, the 1986 immigration bill may ultimately

produce (perversely, but happily) a surge in immigration from foreigners seeking to take advantage of the first amnesty, which may of course be followed by others. See, for instance, John Gonzalez, "Amnesty Plan Luring Aliens, U.S. Agents Say," *Dallas Morning News,* 29 August 1982.

33. For a moving and fact-chocked account of the economic, cultural, and demographic rise of the Asians, see Robert Lindsey, "The New Asian Immigrants," *New York Times Magazine,* 9 May 1982. Statistics are from pp. 22 and 25.

34. Calculation by Leon Bouvier for the Population Reference Bureau, cited by Peirce, "Fearsome Long-Term Implications."

35. Bill Keller, "Demographics Put Strain on Soviet Ethnic Seams," *New York Times,* 28 December 1986.

36. For a succinct guide to the statistical Everest showing immigration to be a boon to the United States—not an economic or environmental drag—see Julian Simon, "Nine Myths About Immigration," Heritage Foundation Backgrounder 326, 1 February 1984; also Simon and Roger Conner, in debate, "How Immigrants Affect Americans' Living Standard," Heritage Lectures, no. 39, 30 May 1984. See also Lindsey, "The New Asian Immigrants."

37. See Ben J. Wattenberg, "Bad Marx: How the World Sees the Soviets," *Public Opinion,* March–April 1987.

38. For examples of the impact of East-bloc popular dissent on East-bloc policies, see: Steven R. Reed, "Soviet Allies Suffering Rift," Associated Press, 29 June 1983; Robert S. Greenberger and Roger Thurow, "East Europe Leery of Soviet Missile Policy," *Wall Street Journal,* 29 November 1983; Adam Hochschild, "East German Dissent," *New York Times,* 29 September 1982; and Frederick Kempe, "Losing Sway . . . Fortieth Anniversary of Yalta Conference Finds Soviets Uneasy," *Wall Street Journal,* 8 February 1985.

39. Richard Pipes, "The Soviet Union in Crisis," Speech to the *Institut pour Relations Internationales,* 16 October 1982, printed in French in *Politiques Etrangères,* no. 4, pp. 867–80. Transcript of the English translation available through the Alexis de Tocqueville Institution.

40. Mikhail Gorbachev, address to the Central Committee of the Communist Party of the Soviet Union, *Pravda,* 14 February 1987, and *Izvestia,* 15 February 1987.

41. See, for example, V. I. Lenin and Josef Stalin, quoted in Leon Trotsky, *The Revolution Betrayed,* trans. Max Eastman (New York: Pathfinder Press, 1972), pp. 50, 257.

42. Bell [see note 17], p. 5.

43. Jeffrey Bell, "The Elites and Reagan's Populist Agenda," *Wall Street Journal,* 4 May 1981.

44. Ibid.

45. Eduardo Ulibarri, interview with the author and research assistant Joseph Anderson, June 1987, one of a series of interviews with Latin American leaders on how the U.S. can spread democracy. The interviews included government officials and private citizens from Argentina, Brazil, El Salvador, Chile, Costa Rica, Panama, Guatemala, and Mexico. They were sponsored by the Hoover Institution and the Alexis de Tocqueville Institution, through which transcripts are available.

46. Jonathan Kwitny, *Endless Enemies* (New York: Congdon and Weed, 1984), p. 403.

47. Seymour Martin Lipset, Speech to the Commonwealth Club of California, 24 July 1987. Excerpts appeared in Ronald J. Getz, "Democracy Gaining, Says Hoover Fellow," *Campus Report,* Stanford University, 12 August 1987.

48. Jan T. Gross, "Rights as *Realpolitik,*" *New York Times,* 19 April 1979.

49. Aaron Wildavsky, *Beyond Containment* (San Francisco: Institute for Contemporary Studies, 1983), p. 17.

Chapter 4   Words into Deeds: The Evolution of Human Rights

1. Patricia Derian, "Face the Nation," CBS-TV, 25 December 1977, p. 16 of transcript.

2. Jo Marie Griesgraber, "Implementation by the Carter Administration of Human Rights Legislation Affecting Latin America," Ph.D. diss., Georgetown University, 1984, p. 65.

3. Joshua Muravchik, *The Uncertain Crusade* (New York: Hamilton Press, 1986), pp. 176–77, 240.

4. Stanley Heginbotham, testimony before the Senate Foreign Relations Committee, in *FY 1980 International Security Assistance Program* (Washington, D.C.: Government Printing Office, 1979), p. 75.

5. Interview with the author, 17 November 1986.

NOTES

6. Computed by the author based on Muravchik, *Uncertain Crusade,* p. 2, and Raymond Gastil, "Freedom House Survey," *Freedom at Issue,* January 1984 and January 1987.

7. Adam Meyerson, "Brave New Hemisphere," *Policy Review,* Summer 1984.

8. Jeane Kirkpatrick, "Dictatorships and Double Standards," *Commentary,* November 1979, and "Human Rights and American Foreign Policy," symposium in *Commentary,* November 1981; Sidney Blumenthal, "An Ideology That Didn't Match Reality," *Washington Post,* 2 March 1986; and Jeane Kirkpatrick, "Philippine Exception," *Washington Post,* 3 March 1986 (Los Angeles Times syndicate).

9. Jeane Kirkpatrick, "Crediting Jimmy Carter for Reagan's Foreign Policies," *San Francisco Chronicle,* 30 July 1986 (Los Angeles Times syndicate).

10. Paul Gigot, "Cory Hallelujah . . . The Democratic Revolution Spreads to Asia," *Policy Review,* Spring 1987.

11. Quoted in *The Security of Korea: U.S. and Japanese Perspectives in the 1980s,* ed. Fuji Kamiya and Franklin B. Weinstein (Boulder, Col.: Westview Press, 1980), pp. 2, 3.

12. Kirkpatrick, "Philippine Exception"; and Gigot, "Cory Hallelujah."

13. Jeane Kirkpatrick, "Magellan's Fate in the Philippines," *Washington Post,* 10 February 1986 (Los Angeles Times syndicate). *The Wall Street Journal,* like Kirkpatrick, was critical of the pressures, but did credit (or blame) them for the outcome in the Philippines. See Editorial, "World Policeman," Review & Outlook, 25 February 1986.

14. Jeane Kirkpatrick, "U.S. Security & Latin America," *Commentary,* January 1981.

15. Jimmy Carter, *Keeping Faith* (New York: Bantam Books, 1982), p. 144.

16. Quoted in Carl Gershman, "The Rise & Fall of the New Foreign-Policy Establishment," *Commentary,* July 1980, and from Brzezinski's own memoirs, *Power and Principle* (New York: Farrar, Straus & Giroux, 1983), p. 543. Cyrus Vance, *Hard Choices* (New York: Simon & Schuster, 1982). Stanley Hoffman quoted in Gershman, "Rise & Fall."

17. Patricia Derian, testimony before the House Committee on Foreign Affairs, *Human Rights and the Phenomenon of Disappearances, Hearings Before the Subcommittee on International Organizations* (Washington, D.C.: U.S. Government Printing Office, 1979), p. 330.

18. Walter Mondale, "Address to the World Affairs Council of Northern California," *Department of State Bulletin,* July 1977, p. 42.

19. Quoted in forum on covert action, "Should the U.S. Fight Secret Wars?" *Harper's,* September 1985.

20. U.S. State Department, "U.S.-Soviet Relations," *Department of State Bulletin,* 12 September 1977, p. 356.

21. Vance, *Hard Choices,* p. 31.

22. Carter, *Keeping Faith,* p. 143.

23. Ibid., p. 21.

24. Kirkpatrick, "Crediting Jimmy Carter."

25. Alexander Haig, quoted in Tamar Jacoby, "The Reagan Turnaround on Human Rights," *Foreign Affairs,* Summer 1986, p. 1080.

26. Elliott Abrams, State Department memorandum he drafted for William Clark, Richard Kennedy, and Alexander Haig, quoted in "Excerpts from State Department Memo on Human Rights," *New York Times,* 5 November 1981.

27. Elliott Abrams, "Promoting Free Elections," U.S. State Department, Bureau of Public Affairs, Current Policy no. 433, November 1982, p. 4.

28. Kirkpatrick, "Human Rights and American Foreign Policy," p. 44.

29. Jacoby, "The Reagan Turnaround on Human Rights."

30. Ibid.

31. Abrams, "Excerpts from State Department Memo."

32. U.S. State Department, *Country Reports on Human Rights Practices for 1982,* Report to the House Committee on Foreign Affairs and the Senate Foreign Relations Committee (Washington, D.C.: U.S. Government Printing Office, 1983).

33. Lucy Martinez-Mont, then named Lucy Schwank, telephone interview with the author and research assistant Joseph Anderson, July 1987. (Transcripts of this and other interviews are available through the Alexis de Tocqueville Institution.)

34. Everett G. Martin, "Democracy Spreads in South America," *Wall Street Journal,* 16 March 1984.

35. Michael Posner, "Reagan Becomes a Force for Rights," *New York Times,* 16 March 1986.

36. Leslie H. Gelb, "U.S. Vows to Resist Despots of Right as Well as of Left . . . Major Shift in Emphasis Seen," *New York Times,* 14 March 1986.

37. Ibid.

38. Posner, "Reagan Becomes a Force for Rights."

39. Abrams, "Promoting Free Elections."

40. White House release, 4 November 1982, Office of the Press Secretary. For information on the conference on supporting democratic institutions in communist countries, see Arch Puddington, "A New Plan for Eastern Europe," *The American Spectator,* March 1983.

41. See National Endowment for Democracy, "Annual Report" (Washington, D.C.: National Endowment for Democracy, 1984, 1985, 1986, and 1987).

42. Ibid.

43. Information from author's telephone interview with Barbara Haig of the National Republican Institute of the NED, 18 June 1986; and Associated Press dispatch, "11 Parties in Political Accord in Chile," *Washington Post,* 27 August 1985.

44. J. Brian Atwood of the NED's National Democratic Institute, telephone interview with the author, 18 June 1986.

45. Clifford Krauss, "Labor Activists: Aided by Washington, AFL-CIO Unit Backs Latin Goals of U.S.," *Wall Street Journal,* 31 December 1985.

46. Atwood, interview with the author, as well as testimony before the House Foreign Affairs Subcommittee on International Operations, 11 June 1986.

47. See David K. Shipler, "Missionaries for Democracy: U.S. Aid for Global Pluralism," *New York Times,* 1 June 1986.

48. Ibid.

49. Carter, *Keeping Faith,* p. 578.

50. Robert Pastor, conversation with the author in Atlanta, Georgia, 17 November 1986.

51. Jose Zalaquette, telephone interview with the author and research assistant Joseph Anderson, June 1987; and Muravchik, *Uncertain Crusade,* pp. 175, 103.

52. Griesgraber, "Human Rights Legislation Affecting Latin America."

53. Frank Ranew, Jr., and Brenda Crayton-Pitches, "Democracy in Latin America Consultation Set," press release of 20 October 1986, from the Carter Presidential Center, Atlanta, Georgia. See also Gregory A. Fossedal, "Democracy in Latin America," *Detroit News,* 4 December 1986.

54. Raymond Bonner, "The Salvador Strategy," *The New Republic,* 7 October 1985.

55. Jeff Gerth and Joel Brinkley, "Marcos's Wartime Role Discredited in U.S. Files," *New York Times,* 23 January 1986; and Joel Brinkley, "U.S. Voices Fears Fraud Could Mar Philippine Voting," *New York Times,* 24 January 1986.

56. Shirley Christian, *Nicaragua: Revolution in the Family* (New York: Vintage Books, 1986).

57. William H. Sullivan, "Living Without Marcos," *Foreign Policy,* Winter 1983, pp. 150–56.

58. Quoted in "Can the U.S. Live with Latin Revolution?" forum in *Harper's,* June 1984.

59. Jimmy Carter, in answer to a question from the author posed at a press conference, Atlanta, 18 November 1986.

60. Sullivan, "Living Without Marcos," pp. 152–53.

61. Charles Krauthammer, "Bringing a Third Force to Bear," *Time,* 10 March 1986, p. 84.

62. See, for example, William H. Sullivan, "Dateline Iran: The Road Not Taken," *Foreign Policy,* Fall 1980; Carter, *Keeping Faith,* pp. 433–518, esp. 436, 439, 441, and 443; Vance, *Hard Choices,* p. 331; and Brzezinski, *Power and Principle,* pp. 354–98, esp. 354, 356–58, 360, 365–68, 371–74, 377–79, and 393–98.

63. Michael A. Ledeen and William H. Lewis, "Carter and the Fall of the Shah: The Inside Story," *The Washington Quarterly,* Spring 1980, esp. pp. 38–40. On the same theme, see also William H. Forbis, *Fall of the Peacock Throne: The Story of Iran* (New York: Harper & Row, 1980); Barry Rubin, *Paved with Good Intentions* (New York: Oxford University Press, 1980); Grace Goodell, "How the Shah De-Stabilized Himself," *Policy Review,* Spring 1981; and Max Lerner, in "Human Rights and American Foreign Policy," symposium for *Commentary,* November 1981. Gary Sick, another principal in the Carter administration's Iran policy, seems to take issue with the notion that there was a choice other than the shah and Khomeini in his book *All Fall Down* (New York: Random House, 1985). "The question that will occupy future historians is whether such an outcome"—that is, a noncommunist, nonfanatic, democratic republic—"was ever feasible" (p. 83). He seems to answer in the negative (pp. 84–86, 161–73). Yet his qualified conclusion is only that such an outcome was unlikely as of November 1978—given U.S. intelligence capabilities, the anti-interventionist leanings of the Carter administration, the historical focus on the shah as an "island of stability," and the unfortunate ways in which these realities reinforced one another, all militating against strong U.S. action. Things might, however, have been different, had these factors been different, and that is the question that most concerns us as regards

NOTES

American policy facing similar choices in the future. (See Sick's sharp description of the revolution, pp. 22–156.)

64. Jimmy Carter, quoted in "Tehran, Iran," *Weekly Compilation of Presidential Documents,* 2 January 1978, p. 1975; Ledeen and Lewis, "Carter and the Fall of the Shah," p. 15; Rubin, *Paved with Good Intentions,* p. 227; and Muravchik, *Uncertain Crusade,* pp. 210–11.

65. Forbis, *Fall of the Peacock Throne,* pp. 237–41.

66. In Goodell, "How the Shah De-Stabilized Himself"; Forbis, *Fall of the Peacock Throne,* pp. 259–61.

67. Sick, *All Fall Down,* p. 24.

68. Ledeen and Lewis, "Carter and the Fall of the Shah," pp. 10, 15.

69. Carter, *Keeping Faith,* p. 438.

70. Brzezinski, *Power and Principle,* p. 357.

71. Sick, *All Fall Down,* pp. 30–31, 344–45. Extended quote is on p. 32.

72. In Ledeen and Lewis, "Carter and the Fall of the Shah," p. 11.

73. Sullivan, "Living Without Marcos" and "Dateline: Iran."

74. Ibid.

75. Brzezinski, *Power and Principle,* pp. 354–98.

76. See Carter, *Keeping Faith,* pp. 441–42; Sick, *All Fall Down,* pp. 107–16; and Brzezinski, *Power and Principle,* pp. 370–73.

77. See Sick, *All Fall Down,* p. 121.

78. Vance, *Hard Choices,* pp. 327–31.

79. Sick, *All Fall Down,* pp. 69, 119–21.

80. Sullivan, "Living Without Marcos" and "Dateline: Iran"; Carter, *Keeping Faith,* pp. 438–46.

81. Carter, *Keeping Faith,* pp. 442, 447–51, 453–54, 497–505. Sick, *All Fall Down,* pp. 113–18.

82. Sick, *All Fall Down,* pp. 66–67.

83. Quoted in Brzezinski, *Power and Principle,* p. 354.

84. Quoted in Sick, *All Fall Down,* p. 110.

85. Carter, *Keeping Faith,* p. 433.

86. Larry Diamond, "Nigeria in Search of Democracy," *Foreign Affairs,* Spring 1984; and Larry Diamond and Seymour Martin Lipset, "Ensuring Free, Fair, and Peaceful Electoral Competition," workshop memorandum submitted to "Democracy in Latin America Consultation Set," p. 3.

87. David K. Shipler, "Shultz Raises Heroin Issue in Nigeria," *New York Times,* 13 January 1987.

88. Bob Woodward and Michael Dobbs, *Washington Post,* 4 June 1986; and Eric Chenoweth and Jerzy B. Warman, "Solidarity Abandoned," *The New Republic,* 14 July 1986.

89. Woodward and Dobbs, *Washington Post;* Chenoweth and Warman, "Solidarity Abandoned." See also Gregory Fossedal and Angelo Codevilla, "Mission Invisible," *The New Republic,* 3 October 1988.

90. Ibid.; Alexander Haig, *Caveat* (New York: Macmillan, 1984), p. 246, and letter to the author, 13 August 1987; and Richard V. Allen, letter to the author, 18 August 1987.

Chapter 5   Tuning in to Glasnost: America's Radio Voices

1. Julian Hale, *Radio Power* (Philadelphia: Temple University Press, 1975), p. 109.

2. Allan A. Michie, *Voices Through the Iron Curtain* (New York: Dodd, Mead, 1963), p. 238.

3. Dwight D. Eisenhower, *The White House Years... Waging Peace... 1956–1961* (New York: Doubleday, 1965), pp. 88–89.

4. Michael Kinsley, "The Grenada Illusion: War Can Look Easy in Hindsight," *Wall Street Journal,* 13 March 1986.

5. See John Malcolm Mackintosh, *Strategy and Tactics of Soviet Foreign Policy* (London: Oxford University Press, 1962), pp. 177–78.

6. Eisenhower, *The White House Years,* p. 82.

7. Audience Analysis Section, Radio Free Europe, "The Hungarian Listeners of Western Broadcasts" (Munich, October 1957), p. 77.

8. Bennett Kovrig, "Rolling Back Liberation: The United States and the Hungarian Revolution," in *The First War Between Socialist States: The Hungarian Revolution of 1956 and Its Impact,*

ed. Bela K. Kiraly, Barbara Lotze, and Nandor F. Dreisziger (New York: Columbia University Press, 1984), pp. 286–88.

9. Jiri Valenta, "Soviet Decision Making and the Hungarian Revolution," in *The First War Between Socialist States,* pp. 268, 273, 277.

10. Eisenhower, *The White House Years,* pp. 70–71.

11. Committee on Foreign Affairs, U.S. House of Representatives, *Report of the Special Study Mission to Europe on Policy Toward the Soviet Satellite Nations* (Washington, D.C., 4 June 1957), p. 4.

12. In Eisenhower, *The White House Years,* pp. 59–60.

13. For specific scripts of Voice of America broadcasts, see Voice of America, "VOA Briefing Paper, Subject: Examples of Voice of America Hungarian Programming Prior to and During the Hungarian Revolt" (Washington, D.C., 20 November 1956), pp. 1–4; for an analysis of overall VOA content, see Robert William Pirsein, *The Voice of America: A History of the International Broadcasting Activities of the United States Government, 1940–1962,* Ph.D. diss., Northwestern University, June 1970, esp. pp. 345–78; for examples of Radio Free Europe broadcasting, see "Report by the Special Committee on the Problem of Hungary," General Assembly of the United Nations (New York, 1957), and Robert T. Holt, *Radio Free Europe* (Minneapolis: University of Minnesota Press, 1958); for an assessment of the overall aims and strategy of Radio Free Europe broadcasts, see Michie, *Voices Through the Iron Curtain,* pp. 153–241.

14. For more information on this fascinating program, "Operation Veto," see Michie, *Voices Through the Iron Curtain,* pp. 143–54.

15. Ibid.

16. For an excellent collection of original materials, see Melvin J. Lasky, *The Hungarian Revolution* (New York: Praeger, 1957); the banners and slogans cited here from pp. 43–57.

17. Quoted in *New York Times,* 23 October 1956.

18. Michie, *Voices Through the Iron Curtain,* pp. 149–52, 178–88, 221–31, 272, 172.

19. Audience Analysis Section, Radio Free Europe, "Hungarian Listeners," pp. 3, 7, 71.

20. Michie, *Voices Through the Iron Curtain,* p. 222.

21. Ibid., p. 145.

22. Ibid., pp. 226–41. See also Holt, *Radio Free Europe,* pp. 185–99; and Sig Mickelson, *America's Other Voice* (New York: Praeger, 1983), pp. 97–102.

23. Katrina Vanden Heuvel, "No Free Speech at Radio Liberty," *The Nation,* 7 December 1985.

24. Richard Holbrooke, in symposium, "Can We Win the War of Ideas?" ed. Ben Wattenberg, *Public Opinion,* February–March 1982, p. 9.

25. In Michie, *Voices Through the Iron Curtain,* p. 257.

26. "Report by the Special Committee," to the United Nations; and Pirsein, *The Voice of America,* pp. 361–67.

27. Michie, *Voices Through the Iron Curtain,* pp. 260–66. Mickelson *(America's Other Voice)* is largely dependent on Michie as an original source, but his perspective of the same set of facts is also worth reading, esp. pp. 97–102.

28. Michie, *Voices Through the Iron Curtain,* pp. 296–97.

29. For an insightful account of the bullet theory and its flaws, see John Spicer Nichols, "Wasting the Propaganda Dollar," *Foreign Policy,* Fall 1984; quotation in text is from pp. 85–86. The letters in the following issue of *Foreign Policy* make up a useful point/counterpoint on Nichols's ideas about effective public diplomacy.

30. Frank Altschul, status report to the Free Europe Committee, housed in the Lehman Collection, Columbia University Library, New York.

31. Michie, *Voices Through the Iron Curtain,* pp. 12–16.

32. See U.S. Senate, *Final Report of the Select Committee to Study Government Operations with Respect to Intelligence Activities,* vol. 4 (Washington, D.C.: U.S. Government Printing Office, 1976), p. 32.

33. Mickelson, *America's Other Voice,* pp. 32, 35.

34. Pirsein, *The Voice of America,* pp. 2–23.

35. Wallace Carroll, *Persuade or Perish* (New York: Cambridge University Press, 1948), p. 5.

36. James L. Tyson, *U.S. International Broadcasting and National Security,* study for the National Strategy Information Center (New York: Ramapo Press, 1983), pp. 34–42, 149; Hale, *Radio Power,* pp. 34–35; and Pirsein, *The Voice of America,* pp. 273–360.

37. On VOA's gradual shift to the objectivity emphasis, see Pirsein, *The Voice of America,* pp. 273–360; on the similar shift at RFE, see John Robert Price, *Radio Free Europe: A Survey and Analysis* (Washington, D.C.: Congressional Research Service, 29 February 1972), pp. 22–23.

38. See Tyson, *U.S. International Broadcasting,* pp. 47–52, 124.

NOTES

39. Robert Kagan and Phil Peters of the U.S. State Department, interviews with the author, March and July 1987.

40. Editorial from *The Economist,* quoted in Michie, *Voices Through the Iron Curtain,* p. 19.

41. United States Advisory Commission on Public Diplomacy, annual reports for 1985 and 1986 (Washington, D.C., 1985 and 1986); National Endowment for Democracy, annual reports for 1985 and 1986 (Washington, D.C.: National Endowment for Democracy, 1985 and 1986); Soviet figures calculated by author from figures in Richard Staar, *USSR Foreign Policies After Détente,* (Stanford: Hoover Institution Press, 1985). Naturally, there are widely differing estimates. The United States Information Agency calculates Soviet expenditures of $700 million on broadcasting alone for 1980; see Sen. Charles Percy, *Congressional Record,* 16 December 1982, p. S15103.

42. Estimate by the British Broadcasting Corporation, cited in Richard Evans, "Jamming 'Costs Russians £500m,' " *The Times,* 31 October 1985, and Board for International Broadcasting, *1987 Annual Report to the President* (Washington, D.C.: BIB, 31 January 1987), p. 29. Again, estimates vary. See also Sen. Percy, *Congressional Record;* Jonathan Eyal, "Recent Developments in the Jamming of Western Radio Stations Broadcasting to the USSR and Eastern Europe," Radio Liberty Research, RL 419/86, 7 November 1986; Stanley Leinwoll, "Jamming—Past, Present, and Future," *World Radio TV Handbook;* James P. McGregor, "Jamming of Western Radio Broadcasts to the Soviet Union and Eastern Europe," Research Report R-4-83, Office of Research, U.S. Information Agency, April 1983.

43. Board for International Broadcasting, *1987 Annual Report,* p. 30.

44. Eyal, "Jamming of Western Radio Stations," p. 4. Some reports are considerably less sanguine; see, for example, the other papers cited in note 41, as well as M. Rhodes, "The Impact of Soviet Jamming on Western Broadcasts to the Soviet Union," Soviet Area Audience and Opinion Research, Radio Free Europe–Radio Liberty, AR 10–81, December 1981.

45. For samples and figures on communist denunciation of Western broadcasts, see, for example, Radio Liberty Committee, *Annual Report, 1972* (Washington, D.C.: Radio Liberty Committee, 1972); and Alex Inkeles, "The Soviet Attack on the Voice of America: A Case Study in Propaganda Warfare," *American Slavic and East European Review,* no. 12, 1953.

46. Hale, *Radio Power,* pp. 28–31.

47. Gerhard Wettig, *Broadcasting and Détente* (New York: St. Martin's Press, 1977), pp. 12–35.

48. *Davar,* Tel Aviv, 6 February 1985.

49. Rowland Evans and Robert Novak, "Don't Cripple Radio Liberty," *Washington Post,* 25 March 1987.

50. Not all of the following were needed for the table, but here are the surveys that went into the compilation, and then some (they will be cited hereafter by letter):

a.) Board for International Broadcasting, *1986 Annual Report* (Washington, D.C.: 31 January 1986), pp. 17–21.

b.) Idem, *1987 Annual Report* (Washington, D.C., 31 January 1987), pp. 21–25.

c.) East European Area Audience and Opinion Research, "Political Legitimacy in Eastern Europe—A Comparative Study," Radio Free Europe, no. 738 (Munich, March 1987).

d.) Idem, "East Europeans and the Chernobyl Events," Radio Free Europe, no. 732, (Munich, December 1986).

e.) Idem, "The Political Self-Assessment of East European Respondents in Terms of a Left-Right Continuum," Radio Free Europe, no. 731 (Munich, December 1986).

f.) Idem, "Czechoslovak, Hungarian, and Polish Expectations Concerning Domestic Developments," Radio Free Europe, no. 712 (Munich, October 1985).

g.) Idem, "Support for Polish Solidarity Among Polish, Czechoslovak, and Hungarian Respondents," Radio Free Europe, no. 710 (Munich, September 1985).

h.) Idem, "Perception of, and Attitudes Toward, Bias in RFE Broadcasts," Radio Free Europe (Munich, March 1982).

i.) Idem, "Listeners Assess RFE's Influence on Themselves, on Public Opinion, and on the Government of Their Country," Radio Free Europe (Munich, October 1981).

j.) Idem, "Eastern Socialism–Western Democracy and the Functioning of the Two Systems" (Munich, November 1981).

k.) Audience and Public Opinion Research Department, "Attitudes Toward Key Political Concepts in East Europe," Radio Free Europe (Munich, December 1969).

l.) Idem, "Listening to Western Broadcasts in Czechoslovakia Before and After the Invasion," and "Listening to RFE in Czechoslovakia Before and After August 21," Radio Free Europe (Munich, 1969).

m.) Idem, "What Is the Most Important Problem Facing Your Country Today?" Radio Free Europe (Munich, January 1967).

n.) Idem, "The Attitudes of Czechoslovak, Hungarian, and Polish Respondents Toward Cooperation with the Government," Radio Free Europe, (Munich, January 1966).

o.) Idem, "The Effectiveness of Radio Free Europe," Radio Free Europe (Munich, December 1965), pp. 9–10.

p.) Audience Analysis Section, "The Hungarian Listeners of Western Broadcasts," Radio Free Europe (Munich, October 1957).

q.) Burton Paulu, *Radio and Television Broadcasting in Eastern Europe* (Minneapolis: University of Minnesota Press, 1974), pp. 355–56.

51. Survey cited in note 50(o), pp. 10–11.

52. Cited in note 50(q), p. 220.

53. Cited in note 50(b), p. 22–23.

54. Pavel Gurevich, "Soviet TV and Radio: Foreign News and Audience Reaction," *Zhurnalist,* August 1968, p. 61–62.

55. *Party Life,* May 1965.

56. Quoted in Mickelson, *America's Other Voice,* p. 212.

57. Confidential interview between the author and a spokesman for Solidarity, November 1985. Partial transcript available to researchers through the Alexis de Tocqueville Institution. Also cited: Ludmilla Alexeyeva, *U.S. Broadcasting to the Soviet Union* (New York: Helsinki Watch Committee, September 1986), pp. 1–2.

58. Tyson, *U.S. International Broadcasting,* pp. 47–52, 124; and Pirsein, *The Voice of America,* pp. 421–26.

59. Michie, *Voices Through the Iron Curtain,* p. 81.

60. Surveys cited in note 50(l), pp. 1–5, 14 ("Listening to Western Broadcasts . . ."), pp. 6–14 ("Listening to Radio Free Europe . . .").

61. Hale, *Radio Power,* p. 43; see also RFE survey figures cited in note 50(q), p. 309.

62. David M. Abshire, *International Broadcasting: A New Dimension of Western Diplomacy,* The Washington Papers of the Center for Strategic and International Studies, Georgetown University, vol. 4 (Beverly Hills/London: Sage Publications, 1976), pp. 69–70.

63. Confidential interview (see note 57); Mickelson, *America's Other Voice,* pp. 212–13.

64. Quoted in *Wall Street Journal,* 14 August 1984.

65. Pirsein, *The Voice of America,* p. 429.

66. Leonid Kravchenko, *Argumenty i Fakty,* no. 45, 1986.

67. Aleksandr Yakovlevitch, quoted in *Pravda,* 22 October 1986.

68. "Radio Moscow's Blooper," *Newsweek,* 6 June 1983.

69. Based on author's interview with Ben Wattenberg, a participant at the Latvia conference, and a pair of wire service stories, as printed in "U.S. Aide Smites the Soviets on Their Turf," *Washington Times,* 16 September 1986, and "Latvians Hail U.S. as Nation's Only Hope," *Washington Times,* 19 September 1986.

70. Author's interviews with Pat Sowick of Radio Free Europe (13 August 1986) and Kenneth Tomlinson, former director of the Voice of America (22 July 1987); Tyson, *U.S. International Broadcasting,* pp. 82–86, 149–50; Board for International Broadcasting, cited in notes 50(a) and (b); Voice of America fact sheet, "The Voice of America Modernization Program," January 1985; Kenneth Y. Tomlinson, "America's Stifled Voice," *Washington Post,* 20 February 1983; and Congressman Jack F. Kemp, "VOA's Broadcast Burial Ground," *Congressional Record,* 22 February 1984, pp. E542–43.

71. Kenneth Tomlinson, telephone interview with author, October 1987; W. J. Howell, *World Broadcasting in the Age of the Satellite* (Norwood, N.J.: Ablex Publishing, 1986); John B. Whitton, "Hostile International Propaganda and International Law," in *National Sovereignty and International Communications,* ed. Herbert I. Schiller and Kaarle Nordenstreng (Norwood, N.J.: Ablex Publishing, 1979).

72. See Tedd Knapp, "VOA 'Unbalanced,' USIA Boss Maintains," Scripps-Howard dispatch, 1 October 1981; *Source,* a publication of the Republican National Committee, 30 November 1981; Aleksandr Solzhenitsyn, interview with Congressman John LeBoutillier taped for NBC's "Tomorrow" show, reprinted in *National Review,* 10 May 1982; Tom Bethell, "Propaganda Warts," *Harper's,* May 1982; Leonard J. Thelberge et al., "Voice of America at the Crossroads," panel discussion (Washington, D.C.: Media Institute, 24 July 1982), pp. 41–48; Robin Grey, "Inside the Voice of America," *Columbia Journalism Review,* May–June 1982, pp. 23–30; Tyson, *U.S. International Broadcasting,* pp. 43, 58–60, 99–101; Sally Greenway, "America's Constricted Voice," *New*

York Times, 19 March 1984, and response by Kenneth Y. Tomlinson, Letter to the Editor, " 'Accurate, Comprehensive, and Objective' Voice of America," *New York Times,* 23 March 1984; Geryld B. Christianson, "New Management at Radio Free Europe–Radio Liberty and the Pell Amendment," Staff Report to the Senate Committee on Foreign Relations (Washington, D.C., 1984); John O'Sullivan, "Czarists and Pink Leather Boots," *The American Spectator,* July 1985; Lars-Erik Nelson, "Dateline Washington: Anti-Semitism and the Airwaves," *Foreign Policy,* Summer 1986; John M. Goshko, "Waves of Dissension Said to Weaken Radio Liberty," *Washington Post,* 12 July 1986; Dmitri K. Simes, "Getting America's Overseas Broadcasts Back on Track," *Christian Science Monitor,* 11 September 1986; Nicholas P. Vaslef et al., "Report of the Task Force of the Board for International Broadcasting to the Jewish Population of the Soviet Union," in response to PL 99-33, sec. 306 (Washington, D.C., 1986); *Newsweek,* 5 May 1972, as cited in Hale, *Radio Power,* p. 31; John Elvin, "Censoring Marti," *Washington Times,* 25 June 1987; Joseph Sobran, "America's Muted 'Voice,' " *New York Post,* 4 February 1982; Russ Braley, "The Assault on Radio Liberty," *Human Events,* 22 June 1985; Capitol Briefs, *Human Events,* 27 September 1986; John Tagliabue, "At U.S. Radio for East Bloc, Time of Flux," *New York Times,* 27 July 1986; and Arnold Beichman, "A Lapse at Radio Liberty?" *Washington Times,* 24 February 1987.

73. For more discussion of these points, see Nichols, "Wasting the Propaganda Dollar," and Kenneth Adelman, "Speaking of America: Public Diplomacy in Our Time," *Foreign Affairs,* Spring 1981.

74. Carnes Lord, "In Defense of Public Diplomacy," *Commentary,* April 1984; Wattenberg, ed., "Can We Win the War of Ideas?" *Public Opinion.*

75. Brigadier Maurice Tugwell, "The War of Ideas and Ideals," in *Global Collective Security in the 1980s,* ed. Geoffrey Stewart-Smith (London: Foreign Affairs Research Institute, 1982), pp. 111–23.

76. Ibid., pp. 111–23.

77. See Hale, Radio Power, p. 177; John Lenczowski, *Soviet Perceptions of U.S. Foreign Policy* (Ithaca, N.Y.: Cornell University Press, 1982), pp. 27–30; Tyson, *U.S. International Broadcasting,* p. 124.

78. Mickelson, *America's Other Voice,* p. 203.

79. See note 50(o). On perceptions of RFE objectivity, see note 50(h).

80. Solzhenitsyn, interview with LeBoutillier (see note 72).

81. General Accounting Office study, "A Look at America's Voice to the World" (Washington, D.C., 1982), p. 12.

82. See note 50(a), pp. 10, 11–13.

83. Transcripts from Voice of America broadcasts cited in text: "Focus: Vietnam Today," Special Report 4-0638, 14 March 1983 and 27 March 1983; Frank Ronalds, "Focus: Fanaticism in Iran," Special Report 4-0724, 15 May 1984; Rory Eriksen, "Focus: Political Movies," Special Report 4-0670, 5 April 1984; Sam Iker, "Focus: Remembering the Holocaust," Special Report 4-0737, 23 May 1984; Frank Ronalds, "Focus: The Afghans Fight On," Special Report 4-0663, 2 April 1984; and Bob Blachly, "Focus: Active Measures," Special Report 4-0676, 11 April 1984.

84. Voice of America editorials cited in text: Editorial 0-0865, "A More Perfect Union," 22 February 1984; Editorial 0-0773, "R*E*S*P*E*C*T (OUS89)," 21 November 1983; Editorial 0-0871, "Freedom to the Max!" 28 February 1984; Editorial 0-0859, "Genius and Ingenious (OUS60)," 16 February 1984; Editorial 0-0905, "Righting the Wrong (OUS40)," 2 April 1984; and Editorial 0-0912, "You Can't Have One Without the Other," 9 April 1984.

85. Voice of America editorials cited in text: Editorial 0-0764, "Love Those Levi's (2UR39)," 12 November 1983; Editorial 0-0337, "Nicaragua and the Free Exercise of Religion (0NU42)," 19 August 1982; Editorial 0-0887, "Crosspurposes (2PL80)," 15 March 1984; Editorial 0-0922, "In Cold Blood (4LY17)," 19 April 1984; Editorial 0-0927, "Terminological Inexactitudes (1CU42)," 24 April 1984; Editorial 0-0915, "First Place in Grousing (80175)," 12 April 1984; and Editorial 0-0933, "Don't Confuse Me with the Facts (2UR30)," 30 April 1984.

86. Alexeyeva, *U.S. Broadcasting to the Soviet Union,* pp. 17–37, 54–58.

87. Ibid., pp. 56–57.

88. Figures from Tyson, *U.S. International Broadcasting,* pp. 149–51; BBC statistics cited Paulu, note 50(q), p. 205; Board for International Broadcasting cited in note 50(a) and (b).

89. Ibid.; also General Accounting Office, "A Look at America's Voice."

90. See, for example, Andrew Nagorski, *Reluctant Farewell* (New York: New Republic Books, 1985), introduction and chap. 1.

91. Alexander J. Motyl and Adrian Karatnycky, "All Quiet on the Pro-Western Front?" *National Review,* 18 February 1983.

92. Edwin J. Feulner et al., U.S. Advisory Commission on Public Diplomacy, Report to the

President for 1983, 1984, and 1985 (Washington, D.C.: 1983, 1984, 1985). See also Review & Outlook, "Beyond Wickgate," *Wall Street Journal,* 26 January 1984.

Chapter 6   The Carrot and the Stick: Using Economic Leverage

1. Eugene V. Rostow, in symposium on foreign policy, "Beyond Containment?" *Policy Review,* Winter 1985, p. 27.

2. David A. Baldwin, *Economic Statecraft* (Princeton, N.J.: Princeton University Press, 1985), p. 273.

3. Fuad Itayim, in Adelphi Paper no. 115, "Security and the Energy Crisis," *The Middle East and the International System; Part II* (London: International Institute for Strategic Studies, 1975), p. 4.

4. Margaret P. Doxey, *Economic Sanctions and International Enforcement* (New York: Oxford University Press, 1980), p. 28.

5. See Nobutaka Ike, ed., *Japan's Decision for War: Records of the 1941 Policy Conferences* (Stanford: Stanford University Press, 1967), esp. p. 188.

6. Dean Acheson, *Present at the Creation* (New York: Norton, 1969), pp. 58–62.

7. W. N. Medlicott, *The Economic Blockade,* vol. 2 (London: Longmans, Green, 1952), p. 647.

8. John Block, editorial luncheon, 24 August 1982. Transcript was made available to the author by the *Washington Times* and its excellent librarian, Todd Lindsay. Let us not pick on the former Secretary of Agriculture, though, for Mr. Block is hardly alone in such illogic. In the fall of 1982, Senator Daniel Patrick Moynihan urged the U.S. to cease its policy of extending bailout loans to Poland and declare that nation in default for its failure to meet scheduled payments of its huge debt to the West. Secretary of State George P. Shultz wrote Moynihan to argue that this action would help Poland, allowing it to cease all payments to the West. Of course, it might, but then, virtually all trade with Poland would have ceased, as banks refused to extend further credits and Poland's economy shrank. By Shultz's logic, the right policy for the Polish government would have been to declare itself bankrupt. After all, this would have allowed it to repudiate all such payments. The Jaruzelski regime, according to Shultznomics, was stupidly allowing the clever government of the United States to pay off $1.6 billion of its debt. See the *New York Times,* 1 September 1982.

9. Patrick Leahy, quoted by David Goeller, Associated Press, 30 December 1981.

10. Nick Eberstadt and Eric M. Breindell, "Western Europe's Use of Economic Sanctions," *Wall Street Journal,* 16 November 1982.

11. See the *Financial Times* of London, as usual unsurpassed in its coverage of events behind the Iron Curtain, 13 June 1980 and 23 June 1980.

12. Angel O. Byrne and Anton F. Malish, *The U.S. Sales Suspension and Soviet Agriculture* (Washington, D.C.: U.S. Department of Agriculture, 1980), p. 21.

13. Reagan attacked the Carter grain embargo during the campaign, but on the grounds that it called for unequal sacrifice from U.S. farmers. Farmers thought this meant the boycott would be undone under Reagan, foreign policy hardliners hoped this meant that the embargo on grain exports would be expanded to cover other items, spreading the sacrifice. The farmers had it right; indeed, by 1986, the Reagan administration extended an estimated $52 million in subsidies in an effort to encourage Soviet purchase of U.S. grain. (The Soviets then reneged on their agreement to buy in 1985 and 1986; see Dennis D. Miller, "Seeds of Suspicion over the Wheat Deal," *Wall Street Journal,* 22 July 1986.) The idea was to swing the farm vote in several key Midwestern states and thus retain Republican control of the U.S. Senate. (See Rowland Evans and Robert Novak, "Reagan's Grain Retreat," *Washington Post,* 4 August 1986.) But the brazen bribe backfired, undercutting one of Ronald Reagan's strongest sources of appeal—his image as a principled man—and the GOP was swept out of the Senate.

14. Central Committee of the Communist Party, "Additional Measures for Increasing the Amount of Agricultural Production in the Private Subsidiary Plots of Citizens," quoted in Mikhail S. Bernstam and Seymour Martin Lipset, "Punishing Russia," *The New Republic,* 5 August 1985.

15. Ibid.

16. Statistics from Gary Clyde Hufbauer, Jeffrey J. Schott, and Kimberly Ann Elliot, *Economic Sanctions Reconsidered* (Washington, D.C.: Institute for International Economics, 1985), p. 514.

17. Paula Stern, *Water's Edge: Domestic Politics and the Making of American Foreign Policy* (Westport, Conn.: Greenwood Press, 1979), pp. 201–2.

18. Henry Kissinger, *Years of Upheaval* (Boston: Little, Brown, 1982), pp. 985–98.

NOTES

19. William Korey, "Jackson-Vanik: It Has Worked Well," *Christian Science Monitor*, 20 October 1983.

20. Korey, "Jackson-Vanik."

21. Richard Bernstein, "Soviet Data from West Detailed in French Press," *New York Times*, 2 April 1985; Lawrence J. Brady, "Technology Transfers: Do Crackdowns Work? . . . They Deny a Sword to the Soviets," and George Gilder, "Secrecy Manias Only Backfire," *Wall Street Journal*, 1 October 1985; Editorial, "The Military-Industrial Complex," *The Economist*, 12 August 1987; and Edward Teller, interview with the author, the Cosmos Club, 10 March 1987. The baseball bat vignette originated in an oft-cited bit of testimony by McGeorge Bundy before a Senate committee on Trade and Technology.

22. Gilder, "Secrecy Manias Only Backfire."

23. Rand Corporation Report cited in Stephen Woolcock, *Western Policies on East-West Trade* (London: Royal Institute of International Affairs, 1982). Daniel F. Kohler, *Economic Cost and Benefits of Subsidizing Western Credits to the East* (Santa Monica, Calif.: Rand Corporation, July 1984), pp. 5–14; James Hackett, "Financing the Soviet Empire," *National Security Record*, Heritage Foundation, April 1986; and *Wall Street Journal*, 14 May 1984.

24. Jude Wanniski, *Recommended Reading*, April 1983.

25. Simon Leys, "The Path of an Empty Boat: Zhou Enlai," *The Times Literary Supplement*, 26 October 1984, reprinted in *The Burning Forest* (New York: New Republic Books, 1985), pp. 159–69.

26. Rowland Evans and Robert D. Novak, *Nixon in the White House* (New York: Random House, 1972), pp. 403–4.

27. Central Intelligence Agency, *People's Republic of China: International Trade Handbook* (Washington, D.C., October 1976), and Citibank, N.A., Hong Kong, *China Business Review*, March–April 1981; *1981 Yearbook, Far Eastern Economic Review;* and the Joint Economic Committee of Congress, *People's Republic of China . . . Economic Assessment*, and *China: Economic Performance in 1985* (Superintendent of Documents, Washington, D.C., 1972 and 1985); see also Robert Thompson, "China Battles to Get Out of the Red," *Financial Times*, 17 January 1987; William Proxmire, quoted in Robert D. Hershey, Jr., "China's Economic Ills Are Many, C.I.A. Says," *New York Times*, 27 April 1988; and editorial, "Peasants Rising," *The Economist*, 2 February 1985.

28. Ibid.

29. Richard Nixon, "Asia After Viet Nam," *Foreign Affairs* 46, no. 1 (October 1967).

30. Leys, *The Burning Forest*, p. 163.

31. Raimon Meyer, telephone interview with the author, 10 September 1987; see also Peter J. Moody, *Chinese Politics After Mao* (New York: Praeger, 1983); and Michael Yahuda, *Towards the End of Isolationism: Chinese Foreign Policy After Mao* (London: Macmillan, 1983).

32. Richard Nixon, *RN: The Memoirs of Richard Nixon* (New York: Doubleday, 1978).

33. Henry A. Kissinger, *White House Years* (Boston: Little, Brown, 1979), p. 180.

34. Hendrik Hertzberg, "Chicken McMencken," *The New Republic*, 8 April 1985.

35. See sources in note 27; see also Cheah Cheng Hye, "China Finally May Borrow More Abroad," *Wall Street Journal*, 19 November 1986; and Thomas D. Brandt, "Asian Bank Issue Seen as Next Strain on Sino-U.S. Relations," *Washington Times*, 25 April 1983.

36. John F. Copper, *Briefing Book . . . President Reagan's Trip to Asia . . . Part II* (Washington, D.C.: Heritage Foundation, April 1984), p. 17.

37. Figures on students and business visas are an estimate based on applications for March 1987, from the author's interview with a U.S. State Department official, January 1988.

38. Richard Nixon, interview with *U.S. News & World Report*, 16 September 1968, p. 48; Richard Nixon, interview with the author, December 1983; Kissinger, *White House Years*, p. 192.

39. Robert R. Bowie, *Suez 1956: International Crisis and the Role of the Law* (New York: Oxford University Press, 1974), pp. 75–76.

40. George Ball, "The Case Against Sanctions," *New York Times Magazine*, 12 September 1982.

41. See the following editorials from the *Wall Street Journal*, Review & Outlook: "Politicizing Politics," 12 July 1982; "Breach of Contract," 25 July 1982; "Deflating Pipeline Bluster," 30 July 1982; "Cash on the Barrelhead," 4 August 1982; "Pipeline Basics," 11 August 1982; "The Four-Letter Pipeline," 6 October 1982; "The Pipeline Episode," 16 November 1982; "Pipeline Pains," 15 March 1983; "Europe's Pipeline Folly," 28 April 1983; "Paying the Pipeliner," 30 September 1983; "Can Italy Bend the Piper?" 16 December 1983; "Hard Pipeline Facts," 12 January 1984; and "The Europolitics of Gas," 5 October 1984. See also Gordon Crovitz, "The Soviet Gas Pipeline: A Bad Idea Made Worse," *World Economy*, December 1982, and "Europe Pays for Its Soviet Pipe Dream," *Wall Street Journal*, 8 December 1983; Wilfried Prewo, "The

Pipeline: White Elephant or Trojan Horse?" *Wall Street Journal,* 28 September 1982; Michael Dobbs, "Soviet Pipeline Reportedly Hit by Serious Fire . . . Western Experts Doubt Upbeat Progress Reports," *Washington Post,* 11 January 1984; John F. Burns, "Doubts on Soviet Gas Line's Start," *New York Times,* 11 January 1984; Ed Rogers, "Soviet Pipeline Pumps Clout to Europe, Pentagon Warns," *Washington Times,* 13 February 1986; and Hackett, "Financing the Soviet Empire."

42. Roger Thurow, "Poland Will Seek Over $1 Billion in New Credits from West in '86," *Wall Street Journal,* 7 February 1986.

43. Associated Press Report, "Polish Leaders Concede Economy Is in 'Unprecedented Breakdown,' " *New York Times,* 28 October 1982; Dan Fisher, "West's Sanctions Cost Poland $12 Billion," *Los Angeles Times,* 14 June 1983; and Bradley Graham, "U.S.-Polish Relations Mired in Antagonism," *Washington Post,* 10 April 1984.

44. Michael Ledeen, "Reagan's Surrender on the Sanctions," *Los Angeles Times,* 18 November 1982; Peter Osnos, "Walesa's Nobel Talk Calls for a Dialogue with Polish Regime," *Washington Post,* 12 December 1983; John H. Cushman, "Reagan Lifts Polish Trade Curbs, Citing Progress on Human Rights," *New York Times,* 20 February 1987.

45. Flora Lewis, "Time to End Sanctions," *New York Times,* 5 December 1986.

46. Arthur Schlesinger, Jr., "NATO: Time for a Divorce?" *Wall Street Journal,* 5 March 1984.

47. For a comparison of the armed force ratios that characterize different types of regimes, see James L. Payne, "Marx's Heirs Belie the Pacifist Promise," *Wall Street Journal,* 5 April 1985.

48. Joseph Sang-hoon Chung, *The North Korean Economy: Structure and Development* (Stanford, Calif.: Hoover Institution Press, 1974), pp. 105, 109, 146–47; Vietnamese trade statistics are from the *International Financial Statistics Yearbook* (Washington, D.C.: International Monetary Fund, 1980).

49. Gary C. Hufbauer and Jeffrey J. Schott, "Nicaragua Sanctions: Too Little, Too Late," *Christian Science Monitor,* 28 May 1985.

50. James Clarity and Warren Weaver, Washington Briefing Column, *New York Times,* 29 September 1984. Two sources at the NSC confirmed Weaver's account and added that Michael Deaver, not just his brother, had been influential in arranging at least two meetings with NSC officials, including Lieutenant Colonel Oliver North.

51. Observers as diverse as William Bundy and Jeane Kirkpatrick agree that U.S. sanctions toppled Somoza. For a good summary of the evidence, see Joshua Muravchik, *The Uncertain Crusade* (New York: Hamilton Press, 1986), pp. 205–9.

52. Steven Roberts, "Senate, 78 to 21, Overrides Reagan's Veto and Imposes Sanctions on South Africa," *New York Times,* 3 October 1986.

53. Suzanne Garment, "U.S. Sanctions Just a Sideshow in African Drama," *Wall Street Journal,* 16 August 1985.

54. Peter J. Duignan, "It Would Be Wrong to Impose Sanctions," *USA Today,* 24 July 1986.

55. Gary C. Hufbauer and Jeffrey J. Schott, *Newsday,* 19 June 1985; Ellen Hume, "Continuing Anti-Apartheid Protests Hasten Pace of Exits by U.S. Companies from South Africa," *Wall Street Journal,* 27 February 1986; Frederick Kempe, "Sanctions Bill Puts Pressure on Thatcher," *Wall Street Journal,* 4 August 1986; Peter Almond, "Thatcher Averts Major Split by Giving on Sanctions Issue," *Washington Times,* 5 August 1986; Karen DeYoung, "Europeans Vote Weakened Sanctions," *Washington Post,* 17 September 1986; "Japan's Cabinet Approves More Sanctions on Pretoria," *Wall Street Journal,* 22 September 1986; Frederick Kempe, "Reagan Panel Said to Urge New Sanctions If South Africa Doesn't End Apartheid," *Wall Street Journal,* 10 February 1987; Eric Pace, "Pretoria Sanctions at U.N. Vetoed by U.S. and Britain," *New York Times,* 21 February 1987; "Shultz Denounces Apartheid, Saying: 'It Must Go Soon,' " *New York Times,* 3 June 1986; "Shultz Calls U.S. United in Opposing Apartheid," *New York Times,* 3 October 1986; Alan Cowell, "Botha Declares Sanctions Will Retard Radical Change," *New York Times,* 10 September 1985.

56. Quoted in "Sanctions Would Set the Stage for Bloodshed, Shultz Warns," *Washington Times,* 24 July 1986.

57. Paul Johnson, "The Race for South Africa," *Commentary,* September 1985.

58. William W. Pascoe, "U.S. Sanctions on South Africa: The Results Are In," *Heritage Foundation Backgrounder* no. 584, 5 June 1987.

59. South African government statistics on GNP are from a telephone interview with Heyn Van Rooyen, 26 August 1987; those on withdrawal of U.S. firms are in Hume, "Continuing Anti-Apartheid Protests," Harry Anderson et al., "Big Business Pulls Out," *Newsweek,* 3 November 1986, and Alan Cowell, "Leaving South Africa Increasingly Alone with Its Troubles, *New York Times,* 26 October 1986; low confidence seen in "Faith in Pretoria Economy at Lowest Level Since

NOTES

1940s," *Wall Street Journal,* 6 August 1986; black boycotts of white stores reported in Steve Mufson, "South African Blacks Mount Successful Boycott," *Wall Street Journal,* 30 July 1985.

60. Roger Thurow, "Sanctions Force South Africa to Rely on Itself to Achieve Economic Growth," *Wall Street Journal,* 18 September 1986.

61. Peter Younghusband, "Botha Wants End of Apartheid Put to Vote," *Washington Times,* 10 September 1986; William Rusher, "Botha's Election Mandate," *Washington Times,* 14 May 1987. My own sources, including Hoover Institution scholar Peter Duignan and two other persons at the meeting, dispute Rusher's account of the March 3 session. They quote Botha as saying: "The reforms have ended." (See Gregory A. Fossedal, "Botha's Candid Concessions," Copley News Service release, 8 April 1987.) This would weaken an attempt to read the election of May as a vote for continued democratization—except that the meeting was (a.) secret, and (b.) prior to the surge of forces that sought an even faster demise for apartheid. Whatever Botha's motives and whatever his private statements, Rusher is correct that the public Botha adopted a strong pro-reform stance in the weeks before the election.

62. Anthony Robinson, "S. Africa Poll a Boost for Opposition," *Financial Times,* 16 March 1987.

63. That the ANC receives Soviet assistance, and has numerous contacts with and leaders from the African Communist Party, is not open to serious dispute. Whether it is dominated by these elements, and whether it need be, are different and debatable questions. For a fair-minded summary of the evidence, see Nathan Perlmutter and David Evanier, "The African National Congress . . . A Closer Look," *ADL Bulletin,* the magazine of the Anti-Defamation League of B'nai B'rith, May 1986. On Soviet aid, see "Gorbachev Vows to Aid ANC," *Washington Times,* 5 November 1986; "Soviet Military Pledge to ANC, Claims Tambo," *Financial Times,* 7 November 1986; and James Morrison, "ANC's Communist Ties Big Issue as Tambo Makes Political Rounds," *Washington Times,* 29 January 1987.

64. Alan Cowell, "Tutu and Botha Hold a Rare Talk on Nation's Crisis," *New York Times,* 14 June 1986; Reuters dispatch, "U.S. Envoy Holds Talks with 3 ANC Leaders," 31 July 1986; "South African Rebel Has London Talks," *New York Times,* 21 September 1986; Rita McWilliams, "U.S. Extends a Hand to ANC in a Test of Communist Ties," *Washington Times,* 21 October 1986.

65. Peter Younghusband, "Tutu Outburst Stuns Diplomats," *Washington Times,* 24 July 1986, and "Tutu Sets Terms for Switching on Sanctions," 8 September 1986; and "South African Group Rejects Boycott," *New York Times,* 18 January 1987.

66. Quoted in John D. Battersby, "Tutu Has Meeting with Rebel Group," *New York Times,* 22 March 1987.

67. Peter Younghusband, "Tutu Outburst Stuns Diplomats," and "International Role Costly to S. African Anglicans," *Washington Times,* 8 September 1986, "Tutu Policies Drive Blacks and Whites from his Church," 5 January 1987.

68. See Gregory A. Fossedal, "A Morality Test for South Africa's Opposition," *New York Times,* 4 February 1986, and "The Case for U.S. Sanctions on S. Africa," *New York Post,* 9 April 1987.

69. Peter Younghusband, "ANC Won't Aid Hill Probe of Its Communist Connections," *Washington Times,* 7 October 1986.

70. Peter Younghusband, "Black Miners Dread Sanctions," *Washington Times,* 10 September 1986, and "Sanctions Devour Non-White Jobs, Weaken Militant Leaders' Support," 17 November 1986.

71. Peter Younghusband, "South African Rebels Back Off on Sanctions," *Washington Times,* 2 June 1987.

72. In Alan Cowell, "The Struggle . . . Power and Politics in South Africa's Black Trade Unions," *New York Times Magazine,* 15 June 1986.

73. Copies of the Indaba bill of rights and constitution are available from P.O. Box 2925, Durban 4000, Republic of South Africa, telephone 031-301-5998, and from the Alexis de Tocqueville Institution in the United States. See also Mangosuthu G. Buthelezi, "The Future of South Africa: Violent Radicalism or Negotiated Settlement?" address to the Heritage Foundation of 24 November 1986, *Heritage Lectures* series no. 81; Peter Younghusband, "Durban Talks Are 'Island of Sanity' in Troubled South Africa," *Washington Times,* 5 August 1986; William Pascoe III, "Indaba We Trust: South Africa's Last Best Hope for Racial Peace," *Heritage Today,* January 1987; and Editorial, "After Apartheid," Review & Outlook, *Wall Street Journal,* 11 March 1987.

74. Nic J. Rhoodie, C. P. de Kock, and M. P. Couper, "Black/White Perceptions of Major Sociopolitical Issues in South Africa," and "Division for Group Interaction," (Pretoria, South Africa; Human Sciences Research Council, 1986).

75. Ibid.
76. Ibid.
77. Stephen J. Solarz, "When to Intervene," *Foreign Policy,* Summer 1986, pp. 37–38.

Chapter 7   When Push Comes to Shove: Arming Guerillas

1. See, for example, Nasir Shansab, "The Struggle for Afghanistan," in *Combat on Communist Territory,* ed. Charles Moser (Lake Bluff, Ill.: Regnery-Gateway, 1985), pp. 124–25.

2. Carlos Fonseca Amador, quoted in Martin Arostegui, "Central America's Guerillas Aren't 'Robin Hoods,' " *Human Events,* 31 March 1979, pp. 10–16.

3. See "Background Paper: Nicaragua's Military Build-Up and Support for Central American Subversion" (Washington, D.C.: U.S. Department of State and U.S. Department of Defense, 18 July 1984), p. 5.

4. Michael Johns, "The Lessons of Afghanistan," *Policy Review,* Spring 1987, p. 35.

5. Senator Bill Bradley, Hearing of the Congressional Task Force on Afghanistan, 30 April 1986, quoted in Reuters News Agency dispatch of that day, published in *Washington Times,* 1 May 1986.

6. U.S. estimates cited in Jeane J. Kirkpatrick, speech to the National Press Club, 30 May 1985, Washington, D.C. Reprinted in "Anti-Communist Insurgency and American Policy," *The National Interest,* Fall 1985.

7. Information from interviews at *Wall Street Journal,* with Afghan resistance leaders, 1983 and 1985. Of particular allegations of Soviet brutality there has been much debate, particularly the charge that forces in Afghanistan used chemical weapons. Of the general pattern there can be little doubt. See, for example, "Afghanistan: This Is Genocide," Editorial, *Washington Post,* 15 December 1985.

8. Estimates by European diplomats and U.S. officials cited in Bill Keller, "Soviet Afghanistan Veterans Call for End of Neglect and for Honor," *New York Times,* 22 November 1987; and Johns, "The Lessons of Afghanistan," p. 33.

9. Widely cited estimate claimed by Savimbi and Western intelligence services. See, for example, the floor debate on aid to Unita, *Congressional Record,* House of Representatives, 17 September 1986, pp. H7008–H7042. For various other estimates of Unita strength, see, for example, "Advantage Unita," *The Economist,* 26 November 1983; David B. Ottaway and Patrick Tyler, "DOD Alone in Optimism for Savimbi," *Washington Post,* 7 February 1986; Eugene Tarne, "The State Department v. the Freedom Fighters," *National Review,* 29 August 1986; Neil A. Lewis, "Angola Rebels Say They'll Allow Vital Rail Link to Sea to Reopen," *New York Times,* 27 March 1987; Bernard E. Trainor, "Angola Drive on the Rebels Is Said to Fail," *New York Times,* 22 November 1987.

10. "Lehrman's Contra Conclave," *Newsweek,* 17 June 1985.

11. Al Santoli, "The New Indochina War," *The New Republic,* 30 May 1983, p. 19. See also Elizabeth Becker, "The Quiet Cambodian," *The New Republic,* 20 January 1982.

12. Estimates cited in Benjamin Hart, "Rhetoric vs. Reality: How the State Department Betrays the Reagan Vision," *Heritage Foundation Backgrounder,* no. 484, 31 January 1986.

13. Dawn Calabria, interviews with the author and with Hoover Institution research assistant Adam Lieberman, 31 March 1987 and 2 December 1987; Morton Kondracke, "Making Amends in Cambodia," *Chicago Sun-Times,* 23 September 1983; House debate on aid to the Cambodian resistance, *Congressional Record,* 9 July 1985, pp. H5294ff; Santoli, "The New Indochina War"; and Becker, "The Quiet Cambodian."

14. Declaration of the Nicaraguan Resistance, April 1987. Copies available through the U.S. State Department, Office of the United Nicaraguan Opposition in Washington, D.C., and the Alexis de Tocqueville Institution. See also Timothy Ashby, "Nicaragua: A Blueprint for Democracy," *Heritage Foundation Backgrounder,* no. 558, 20 January 1987, and Joanne Omang, "Shultz Meets with Contras . . . Leaders Deliver Set of Principles," *Washington Post,* 29 January 1986.

15. It is not my purpose to prove either that the Sandinista regime is totalitarian or that the contras are essentially democratic. My concern here is with the standard of judgment we apply to all self-described "freedom-fighter" movements. The contras and other specific groups have been used to illustrate how these tests work when applied to actual groups, for it cannot be denied that they have implications regarding whom we would and would not assist.

For fine summaries of the Sandinista human rights record, the following sources are recom-

NOTES

mended: the 1980–87 human rights reports published by the Department of State (Washington, D.C.: U.S. Government Printing Office); Barry Rubin and Robert S. Leiken, eds., *The Central American Crisis Reader* (New York: Summit Books, 1987); Ronald Radosh, "Nicaragua Revisited," *The New Republic,* 3 August 1987; Nina Shea et al., report to the Puebla Institute on interviews with Nicaraguan refugees (Washington, D.C.: Puebla Institute, 1987); Permanent Commission on Human Rights, *CPDH Report on the Situation of Human Rights in Nicaragua* (Washington, D.C.: Puebla Institute, 1987); Shirley Christian, *Nicaragua: Revolution in the Family* (New York: Random House, 1985); U.S. Department of State, "Sandinista Elections in Nicaragua," Resource Book (Washington, D.C.: Department of State, Office of Public Diplomacy for Latin America and the Caribbean, October 1984); Bayardo Arce, speech before the Nicaraguan Socialist Party, May 1984, published in Barcelona newspaper *La Vanguardia,* translations available from the U.S. Department of State, Publication 9422, Inter-American Series 118, released March 1985; Robert S. Leiken, "Nicaragua's Untold Stories," *The New Republic,* 8 October 1984; W. Bruce Weinrod, "Thirty Myths About Nicaragua," Remarks to the Washington and Lee School of Law, 11 March 1986, reprinted in *The Heritage Lectures,* no. 54 (Washington, D.C.: Heritage Foundation, 1986); International League of Human Rights, *Nicaragua's Human Rights Record—Working Paper* (Washington, D.C., March 1983); and Richard Araujo, "The Sandinista War on Human Rights," *Heritage Foundation Backgrounder,* no. 277, 19 July 1983.

16. Cited in Weinrod, "Thirty Myths About Nicaragua."

17. Fred Barnes, "Contra for a Day," *The New Republic,* 7 April 1986.

18. Nina Shea et al., report to Puebla Institute; Weinrod, "Thirty Myths About Nicaragua"; Timothy Ashby, "The Road to Managua . . . How the *Contras* Can Win," *Policy Review,* Winter 1987, pp. 10–16.

19. U.S. Information Agency, Office of Research, Research Memorandum, 5 March 1987, pp. 6–7. For information on previous polls, see *La Nación,* 2 March 1986; and Glenn Garvin, "Sandinista Regime Is Threat, Say Neighbors," *Washington Times,* 25 March 1986; and John Chamberlain, "A Poll in Central America," *Washington Times,* 17 June 1986.

20. Editorial, "Finally, a Standard for the 'Contras,' " *New York Times,* 25 June 1986.

21. Gregory A. Fossedal, "A Morality Test for South Africa's Opposition," *New York Times,* 4 February 1986.

22. T. E. Lawrence, from *Seven Pillars of Wisdom,* quoted in J. Bower Bell, *The Myth of the Guerilla: Revolutionary Theory and Malpractice* (New York: Alfred A. Knopf, 1971), p. 6; General Giap, quoted in Robert Taber, *The War of the Flea: A Study of Guerilla Theory and Practice* (New York: Lyle Stewart, 1965), p. 63; Mao Tse-tung, in Jay Mallin, ed., *Strategy for Conquest: Communist Doctrines on Guerilla Warfare* (Coral Gables, Fla.: University of Miami Press, 1970), p. 327; and Dickey Chapelle, "How Castro Won," essay reprinted in Franklin Osanka, ed., *Modern Guerilla Warfare: Fighting Communist Guerilla Movements, 1941–1961* (New York: Free Press, 1962), p. 335.

23. Penn Kemble and Arturo J. Cruz, Jr., "How the Nicaraguan Resistance Can Win," *Commentary,* December 1986, pp. 27–28.

24. Interview with Afghan resistance leaders, held at the offices of the *Wall Street Journal* in 1984; see also Moser, ed., *Combat on Communist Territory,* pp. 205–6.

25. Fred Reed, "Savimbi Outlines UNITA's Strategy," the *Washington Times,* 2 December 1982; and Georgie Anne Geyer, "Odds Tilting Toward Savimbi's UNITA," *Washington Times,* 7 January 1987.

26. Max Farrand, ed. *The Records of the Federal Convention of 1787,* (New Haven, Conn. and London: Yale University Press, 1966), pp. xi–xxv; L. Gordon Crovitz, "Presidents Have a History of Unilateral Moves," *Wall Street Journal,* 15 January 1987; and J. S. Sorkin, "Jefferson, Madison, and the Colonel North of 1805," *Wall Street Journal,* 6 July 1987.

27. See David Martin, *Wilderness of Mirrors* (New York: Harper & Row, 1980), p. 90.

28. See the author's editorial, "Packard and the Complex," Review & Outlook, *Wall Street Journal,* 25 November 1985; also, "U.S. Urged to Emulate Others in Arms Buying," *New York Times,* 8 October 1986; and Robert A. Magnan, "In Search of the 'End Game . . .' A Comparison of U.S. and Foreign Weapons Acquisition Systems," Study under the DCI (Department of Central Intelligence) Exceptional Intelligence Analyst Program, 1985.

29. Robert C. McFarlane, appearing on "Meet the Press," 13 May 1984, and reprinted in Daniel Patrick Moynihan, moderator, "Should the U.S. Fight Secret Wars?" *Harper's,* September 1985, p. 35.

30. Alvin H. Bernstein, "Insurgents Against Moscow," *Policy Review,* Summer 1987, p. 26.

31. Charles Krauthammer, "The Poverty of Realism," *The New Republic,* 12 February 1986.

32. Roger D. Hansen, "The Reagan Doctrine and Global Containment: Revival or Recession," *SAIS Review,* a publication of the Johns Hopkins School of Advanced International Studies, Winter–Spring 1987, pp. 39–66.

33. Ronald Reagan, "Freedom, Regional Security, and Global Peace," Message to the Congress of the United States, Office of the Press Secretary, 14 March 1986.

34. Krauthammer, "The Poverty of Realism."

35. Figures on aid to North Vietnam taken from Jon M. Van Dyke, *North Vietnam's Strategy for Survival* (Palo Alto, Calif.: Pacific Books, 1972), and Arnold R. Isaacs, *Without Honor* (Baltimore: Johns Hopkins University Press, 1983).

36. Alan Tonelson, "The Real National Interest," *Foreign Policy,* Winter 1986.

37. Adam Lieberman, "Brezhnev Doctrine, Reagan Doctrine: A Comparison of U.S. Aid to Democratic Forces and Soviet Aid to Communist Forces in the 1980s," *DTI Brief* no. 87-02 (Redwood City, Calif.: Alexis de Tocqueville Institution, 1987). Research for the paper was supported in part by grants from the Hoover Institution on War, Revolution, and Peace; Stanford University; the Alexis de Tocqueville Institution; and Mr. Paul Hexter.

38. Ibid.

39. For general news stories on the same theme, see, for example, David B. Ottaway, "U.S. and Rebel Sources See Soviets Bolstering Support for Third World," *Washington Post,* 11 June 1986; and Cord Meyer, "Consolidating Every Advance," *Washington Times,* 7 February 1986. On the history of Soviet Third World military involvement, see Bruce D. Porter, *The USSR in Third World Conflicts* (Cambridge: Cambridge University Press, 1984), pp. 242–43.

40. Oscar Arias Sanchez, quoted in Stephen Kinzer, "Costa Rica Gets Tougher on Contras," *New York Times,* 10 September 1986.

41. On the Sandinista energy crisis, see Stephen Kinzer, "For Nicaragua, Soviet Frugality Starts to Pinch," *New York Times,* 20 August 1987.

42. See Jeffrey Record, "Sending Aid Instead of Troops," *Baltimore Sun,* 22 August 1986.

43. Henry Kissinger, *White House Years* (Boston: Little, Brown, 1979), pp. 497–98.

44. Angelo Codevilla, "The Reagan Doctrine—(As Yet) a Declaratory Policy," *Strategic Review,* Summer 1986, pp. 18–19.

45. Hart, "Rhetoric vs. Reality"; and Codevilla, "The Reagan Doctrine," pp. 24–25.

46. Ibid.; also, Interviews with officials at the CIA, State Department, and a Senator on the Intelligence Committee; see also Codevilla, "The Reagan Doctrine."

47. See Bernard Gwertzman, "Angola, Angry over Rebel Aid Issue, Ends U.S. Talks," *New York Times,* 14 July 1985.

48. Ibid.

49. See Peter Wise, "Disagreement About Strategy Surfaces Among Angolan Rebels," *Washington Post,* 22 February 1985.

50. Codevilla, "The Reagan Doctrine," p. 23.

51. Ibid.

52. See Hart, "Rhetoric vs. Reality," p. 14.

53. Jimmy Carter, in answer to a question from the author posed at a press conference, Atlanta, 18 November 1986.

54. In the course of researching the evolution of the covert action plan that follows, the author spoke to more than a dozen Carter and career officials in the U.S. State Department, National Security Council, Defense Department, White House staff, and Congress and its committee staffs, as well as several of the principal founders and leaders of the Nicaraguan democratic resistance, armed and unarmed. Where those officials made pertinent comments on the record, they are individually cited. Others, of course, preferred to speak on background or on the condition that their names not be used in relation to particular quotes. Their wishes are respected. Of those interviewed, several confirmed the existence of the Carter program as described, provided their names not be used. Some would not comment or said they did not know. But none of the following officials, all contacted by the author, said either on or off the record that there was any flaw in the story in its general outlines. Those interviewed by the author included: Zbigniew Brzezinski, Carter's national security adviser; Robert Pastor, Brzezinski's top aide on Latin American affairs and later a scholar at the Carter Center at Emory University; Stansfield Turner, director of Central Intelligence during the Carter administration; William Casey, CIA director under Ronald Reagan; Angelo Codevilla, a Senate Intelligence Committee aide; Peter Tarnoff, undersecretary of state under Cyrus Vance; Phil Peters and Robert Kagan, Reagan administration aides at the State Department specializing in Latin America; Constantine Menges, an NSC specialist in Central America during the Reagan administration; Nicaraguan resistance leaders and press spokesmen Arturo Cruz, Adolfo Calero, and Boscoe Matamaros; State Department aide Mike Fitzpatrick;

NOTES

Mike Pillsbury, an aide in the Reagan Pentagon and to several Republican senators; Hodding Carter, spokesman for the Carter State Department; and former President Jimmy Carter. Again, several of these officials confirmed that the Carter administration provided aid to Nicaraguan democrats. None denied it.

55. In 1987, officials at the State Department, under instructions from Elliot Abrams, drew up a series of biographies of the key figures in Nicaragua, from resistance leaders to members of the Sandinista government. No author or editor is listed on this document, which was obtained by the author from a reliable State Department source. A table of contents carries the title, "Nicaraguan Biographies," along with a serial number, SEARAPPC318. Various section headings inside carry the date December 14.

56. See note 54. For further details of Menges's role, see Constantine Menges, *Inside the National Security Council* (New York: Simon & Schuster, 1988).

57. Ibid. Quotation is from Constantine Menges, interview with the author, 16 January 1988.

58. Brzezinski neither confirmed nor denied this account when he spoke with me on 17 December 1987 about the initiative.

59. Menges, *Inside the National Security Council.*

60. Stansfield Turner, quoted in notes by a staff member of the House Intelligence Committee, January 1980. Turner did not confirm or deny making those remarks when we spoke on 11 December 1987 and 15 December 1987.

61. Ibid.

62. Hodding Carter, interview with the author, 10 December 1987.

63. The following account of Reagan administration policy is based on a number of sources. Where possible, particular facts are attributed to the public record or to on-the-record statements made in interviews. Naturally, however, some parts of the narrative came out in discussions in which sources preferred not to be identified. Among the major sources of information for the author's account are: many of the officials cited in note 54; Henry A. Kissinger, interview with the author, June 1984; Congressman Jack Kemp, a member of Kissinger's Central America Commission, interviews with the author, 1985, 1986, and 1988; Fred C. Iklé and Michael Pillsbury, leading Pentagon officials with oversight responsibilities for arms transfers, interviews with author; and Martin Anderson, Reagan's chief domestic policy adviser and later a member of the President's Foreign Intelligence Advisory Board, in numerous interviews with the author, 1985–88, and from advance excerpts from his book, *Revolution* (New York: Harcourt, Brace, Jovanovich, 1988). Major published sources include Alexander Haig, *Caveat: Reaganism, Realism, and Foreign Policy* (New York: Macmillan, 1984), esp. pp. 117–40; David Ignatius and David Rogers, "Why the Covert War in Nicaragua Evolved and Hasn't Succeeded," *Wall Street Journal,* 5 March 1985; "How CIA Aided Raids in Nicaragua in '84 Led Congress to End Funds," *Wall Street Journal,* 6 March 1985; and Robert C. Toth and Doyle McManus, " 'Cowboy' in Control; Contras and CIA: A Plan Gone Awry," *Los Angeles Times,* 3 March 1985.

64. Ibid.

65. Haig, *Caveat,* p. 128.

66. Toth and McManus, " 'Cowboy' in Control."

67. Interviews with Reagan officials; see note 63.

68. William J. Casey, quoted in interview with *U.S. News & World Report,* 8 March 1982.

69. Haig, *Caveat,* pp. 117–40.

70. See note 63.

71. Ignatius and Rogers, "Covert War in Nicaragua"; Toth and McManus, " 'Cowboy' in Control."

72. Kemble and Cruz, Jr., "How the Nicaraguan Resistance Can Win."

73. Editorial, "Uncertain Trumpet," Review & Outlook, *Wall Street Journal,* 28 July 1983.

74. Richard M. Nixon, interview with the author, December 1983.

75. William Casey, cited by a U.S. Senator who was present during the exchange. A second source confirmed the account.

76. William Casey, quoted in Philip Taubman, "How Congress Was Informed of Mining of Nicaragua Ports," *New York Times,* 16 April 1984; and Angelo Codevilla, "The Reagan Doctrine: It Awaits Implementation," in *Central America and the Reagan Doctrine,* ed. Walter F. Hahn (Boston and London: University Press of America, 1987), p. 287.

77. For the legal analysis of the Boland amendment here and in the paragraphs that follow, the author is indebted to John Schmitz and Boydon Gray, who served, respectively, as deputy counsel and counsel to Vice President George Bush, and their paper on "The Boland Amendment and Its Repeal," sent to me in 1987.

78. On the narrative portions of this and following paragraphs particularly dealings within the administration, see note 63.

79. Michael Barone and Grant Ujifusa, *The Almanac of American Politics 1986* (Washington, D.C.: National Journal, 1985), p. 622.

80. Codevilla, "Reagan Doctrine," in Hahn, ed., *Central America*, p. 287.

81. Fred C. Iklé, quoted in Fred Hiatt, "Central America Military Victory Called Necessity," *Washington Post,* 13 September 1983.

82. *Washington Times,* 10 July 1986; *New York Times,* 20 August 1986.

83. Ronald Reagan, quoted in Hedrick Smith, "President Asserts Goal Is to Remove Sandinista Regime," *New York Times,* 22 February 1985; Ronald Reagan, June 1985 letter to Congressman Dave McCurdy, quoted in Robert Leiken, "Reform the Contras," *The New Republic,* 31 March 1986.

84. Henry A. Kissinger, "Nicaragua: Pressure Sensitive," *Los Angeles Times,* 13 April 1986.

85. See note 63. The column referred to was mine, put on the Associated Press wire by Copley News Service in December 1986, as appearing, for example, in "Leadership, Then Mandate," *San Diego Union,* 27 December 1986.

86. Ibid.

87. Congressman James Courter, telephone interview with the author, March 1987.

88. Jean-François Revel and Branko Lazitch, "The West Learns the Art of Guerilla Warfare," *Wall Street Journal,* 11 May 1983.

89. Brian Crozier, *The Rebels* (London: Chatto and Windus, 1960), p. 89.

90. Frederic Smith, "The War in Lithuania and the Ukraine Against Soviet Power," in Moser, ed. *Combat on Communist Territory,* pp. 2–21.

91. Crozier, *The Rebels,* pp. 89–104.

92. Malcolm Wallop, introduction to *Combat on Communist Territory,* p. v.

93. Jeane Kirkpatrick, article for the Los Angeles Times Syndicate, July 1987, as published in *San Diego Union,* 31 July 1987.

94. Moser, ed., *Combat on Communist Territory,* p. 212.

95. Gregory A. Fossedal, "Nicaragua Scandal: Policygate," column for Copley News Service, published as "Sandinistas Getting Mixed Signals from All Directions," *Washington Times,* 16 June 1987.

96. James LeMoyne, "Central America Asks How Far U.S. Will Go," *New York Times,* 2 November 1986.

97. U.S. Information Agency, Research Memorandum, 5 March 1987, *La Nación,* 2 March 1986; Garvin, "Sandinista Regime Is Threat"; Chamberlain, "Poll in Central America."

98. Wallop, introduction to *Combat on Communist Territory,* p. vi.

99. Robert Kagan, interview with the author, June 1987.

100. For an excellent list of arguments in favor of a derecognition policy, see Samuel T. Dickens, "21 Reasons to Break Relations with the Sandinistas," *West Watch,* May 1986, p. 3.

Chapter 8   Growth as Diplomacy: Stable Money and Free Trade

1. See Karl Marx, "Historical Materialism," in *Marx and the Marxists,* trans. Sidney Hook (Princeton, N.J.: Van Nostrand Reinhold, 1955), p. 141; and Friedrich A. Hayek, *The Road to Serfdom* (Chicago: University of Chicago Press, 1944), pp. 69–70.

2. Richard Nixon, *Six Crises* (New York: Doubleday, 1962); Editorial, "Mrs. Aquino's Oft-Promised Land," *New York Times,* 29 July 1987; Robert A. Dahl, "The Democratic Mystique," *The New Republic,* 2 April 1984.

3. Alan Riding, "Mexico's Embattled Ruling Party: The Calls for Change Grow Loud," *New York Times,* 22 October 1986.

4. Marlise Simons, "In Haiti, Hopes Are Named 'Freedom,' " *New York Times,* 27 April 1986.

5. Joseph B. Treaster, "Haiti a Year After Duvalier: Freedom Fills No Stomachs," *New York Times,* 7 February 1987.

6. Owen Harries, "Keep Marcos—For Now," *New York Times,* 23 February 1986, and "There Are Limits to the Reagan Doctrine," *The American Spectator,* June 1986.

7. Raul S. Manglapus, *Will of the People: Original Democracy in Non-Western Societies* (New York: Freedom House, 1987).

8. Simon Leys, *The Burning Forest* (New York: New Republic Books, 1986), excerpted in *The*

NOTES

New Republic, 7 October 1985; and Tom Bethell, "Confucius Says," *National Review,* 7 November 1986.

9. World Bank, *World Development Report 1987* (New York: Oxford University Press, 1987), p. 270.

10. A. M. Rosenthal, "Journey Among Tyrants," *New York Times Magazine,* 23 March 1986.

11. Atul Kohli, "Democracy and Development," in *Development Strategies Reconsidered,* ed. Lewis and Valeriana Kalleb (Washington, D.C.: Overseas Development Council, 1986).

12. Paul Gigot, "Cory Hallelujah," *Policy Review,* Spring 1987.

13. Harden Smith, "Exporting Idealism: The Right Kind of Intervention," *The Washington Monthly,* April 1985.

14. See, for example, Jeane Kirkpatrick, as quoted in *New York Times,* 6 March 1983; Latin leaders cited in Robert Alexander, "Diminishing U.S. Aid in Latin America," *Current History,* July–August 1979; Bill Kritzberg, "Economics a Focus of Peres's Visit," *Washington Times,* 1 April 1986, and "Support Grows for Peres's Mideast Aid Plan," *Washington Times,* 7 April 1986; Rita McWilliams, "Jackson Proposes South African Airlift," *Washington Times,* 20 June 1986, and "Jackson Sees Sanctions' Ill Consequences," *Washington Times,* 4 September 1986; Flora Lewis, "Help for Pretoria's Neighbors," *New York Times,* 16 January 1987, and "Remember Mr. Marshall," *New York Times,* 1 May 1987; and editorial, "The Marshall Plan's Legacy," *Detroit News,* 7 June 1987.

15. Robert Triffin, *Europe and the Money Muddle* (New Haven, Conn.: Yale University Press, 1957), pp. 19, 46, 87.

16. *Congressional Record,* 16 January 1946, pp. A59–60, and 5 March 1946, pp. 1946–47; Triffin, *Europe and the Money Muddle,* pp. 1, 31, 87, 316, 324; Robert Triffin, *Gold and the Dollar Crisis* (New Haven, Conn.: Yale University Press, 1960), pp. 71–72. See also Dean Acheson, *Present at the Creation* (New York: Norton 1969), pp. 216–17, and Charles L. Mee, Jr., *The Marshall Plan* (New York: Simon & Schuster, 1984), pp. 20–21. Latin debt and output figures from U.S. Commerce Department and World Bank published surveys, cited by officials in a telephone interview with the author.

17. W. W. Rostow, *The World Economy . . . History and Prospect* (Austin: University of Texas Press, 1978), table II-7.

18. H. Stuart Hughes, *Contemporary Europe: A History* (Englewood Cliffs, N.J.: Prentice-Hall, 1981), p. 408; survey cited in Walter Spahr, ed., *Monetary Notes,* monthly publication of the Economist's National Committee on Monetary Policy, New York, January–March 1945; and Mee, *The Marshall Plan,* p. 17; *New York Times,* 17 January 1946.

19. For summaries of the revision, see Lewis, "Help for Pretoria's Neighbors," and Tyler Cowen, "The Marshall Plan: Myths and Realities," in *U.S. Aid to the Developing World: A Free Market Agenda,* ed. Doug Bandow (Washington, D.C.: Heritage Foundation, 1985), pp. 61–74. Other figures are from Hughes, *Contemporary Europe,* pp. 406–7; and Mee, *The Marshall Plan,* pp. 16–20, quotation from p. 57; and Edwin S. Shaw, *Money, Income, and Monetary Policy* (Chicago: Richard D. Irwin, 1950), p. 612.

20. Mee, *The Marshall Plan,* pp. 17–18.

21. Senator C. Wayland Brooks, speech summarized in *The Commercial and Financial Chronicle,* 17 January 1946; Representative Jones, quoted in *Wall Street Journal,* 22 December 1945; *United States News,* 13 April 1945, p. 45; "Every American Owes $1,985," *New York Sun,* 21 January 1946; National Association of Manufacturers release quoted in *New York Times,* 8 February 1946.

22. Rostow, *The World Economy,* p. 49, Triffin, *Europe and the Money Muddle,* p. 19; and various sources quoted in Alan Reynolds, "Growing Away from Large Deficits," *Wall Street Journal,* 5 March 1987.

23. Cowen, "The Marshall Plan," p. 62.

24. George F. Kennan, quoted in Mee, *The Marshall Plan,* p. 262; Hadley Arkes, *Bureaucracy, the Marshall Plan, and the National Interest* (Princeton, N.J.: Princeton University Press, 1972), p. 3; and Triffin, *Europe and the Money Muddle,* p. 317.

25. Lewis, "Help for Pretoria's Neighbors."

26. Scheiber, Vatter, and Faulkner, *American Economic History,* p. 425; Cowen, "The Marshall Plan," p. 62; Joseph Buttinger, *Vietnam: A Dragon Embattled,* vol. 2 (New York: Praeger Press, 1967), p. 780; Warren C. Baum, *The French Economy and the State* (Princeton, N.J.: Princeton University Press, 1958), p. 121; and Karl Hardach, *The Political Economy of Germany in the Twentieth Century* (Berkeley, Calif.: University of California Press, 1963), p. 163.

27. Reynolds, "Growing Away from Large Deficits"; Melchoir Palyi, *The Dollar Dilemma*

(Chicago: Regnery, 1954), p. 59; L. S. Stavrianos, *Greece: American Dilemma and Opportunity* (Chicago: Regnery, 1952), p. 195; K. W. Rothschild, *The Austrian Economy Since 1945* (London and New York: Royal Institute for International Affairs, 1950), pp. 67–71; and Franz Nemschak, *Ten Years of Austrian Economic Development: 1945–1955* (Vienna: Association of Austrian Industrialists, 1955), pp. 13–28.

28. Nicholas Balabkinds, *Germany Under Direct Controls* (New Brunswick, N.J.: Rutgers University Press, 1964), pp. 169, 185; Gustav Stolper, Karl Hauser, and Knut Borchardt, *The German Economy: 1870 to the Present* (New York: Harcourt, Brace, 1967), p. 183; Edwin Hartrich, *The Fourth and Richest Reich* (New York: Macmillan, 1980), p. 131.

29. See Hartrich, *Fourth and Richest Reich,* p. 145.

30. Jacques Rueff, from an essay in *Synthèses,* no. 45, 1950, later reprinted in *The Age of Inflation* (Chicago: Regnery, 1964). Rueff was critical of Bretton Woods because he thought its link to gold would be too weak to prevent monetary authorities from gradually undermining and severing it—a correct prediction.

Dean Acheson had to defend Bretton Woods against attacks not only from this direction but from early monetarists and libertarians who said Bretton Woods established too great a link to gold, undermining U.S. authority to run its own policy. Acheson told the Economic Club of New York City on 16 April 1945: "It has been said in England that it is not the gold standard. It has been said in the United States that it resembles the gold standard. I think it doesn't make much difference what we call it. It is an agreement to provide stable and orderly exchange rates. We can leave the selection of the names to scholars to work out at their leisure." (Excerpts appeared in Spahr, ed., *Monetary Notes,* May 1945.)

31. John Maynard Keynes, *The Means to Prosperity* (London: Macmillan, 1933). For more detailed analyses of the flaws in and eventual breakdown of Bretton Woods, see Lewis Lehrman, "Monetary Policy, the Federal Reserve System, and Gold," paper for Morgan Stanley Investment Research, 25 January 1980, and Lewis Lehrman, with John Mueller and Gregory Fossedal, in "Protectionism, Inflation, or Monetary Reform," published by Morgan-Stanley, November 1985; Lewis Lehrman and Ron Paul, *The Case for Gold,* minority report of the U.S. Gold Commission (Washington, D.C.: Cato Institute, 1982), pp. 131–37; respective testimony of Roy Jastram and Alan Reynolds before the U.S. Gold Commission, Washington, D.C., 13 November 1981; Rueff, *Synthèses;* Triffin, *Europe and the Money Muddle;* assorted papers at the 1983 conference on monetary reform, published in Jack Kemp and Robert Mundell, eds., *A Monetary Agenda for World Growth* (Boston: Quantum, 1983); and John Mueller, "The Reserve Currency Curse," *Wall Street Journal,* 4 September 1986.

32. Keynes, *The Means to Prosperity.*

33. Federal Reserve Bank of New York, *Monthly Review of the Federal Reserve Bank of New York* (New York, August 1946; U.S. Commerce Department, *Statistical Abstract of the United States Since 1900* (Washington, D.C.: Department of Commerce, 1976).

34. Triffin, *Europe and the Money Muddle,* p. 208; Rostow, *World Economy,* p. 68.

35. Mee, *The Marshall Plan,* pp. 261–62.

36. See Milton Friedman, *Newsweek,* 20 December 1971; Paul Volcker, cited from congressional testimony in Gregory A. Fossedal, "Paul Volcker, Man of the Year," *The American Spectator,* December 1984; Alan Greenspan, quoted in *Barron's* magazine, 5 February 1973.

37. Robert Mundell, 1972 paper delivered in Geneva, cited in Jude Wanniski, *The Way the World Works* (New York: Simon & Schuster, 1978), p. 235 (1983 paperback ed.); Robert Mundell, *The International Monetary Reform and Development Finance,* University of Waterloo Economic Series, no. 67 (Ontario, 1972); Robert Mundell, "Inflation from an International Viewpoint," in *The Phenomenon of Worldwide Inflation,* ed. David Meiselman and Arthur B. Laffer (Washington, D.C.: American Enterprise Institute, 1975); Jude Wanniski, "The Mundell-Laffer Hypothesis—A New View of the World Economy," *The Public Interest,* Spring 1975; Robert Byrd and William Proxmire, comments at congressional hearings, quoted in Fossedal, "Paul Volcker, Man of the Year."

38. Robert Triffin, in Fritz Machlup, Armin Gutowski, and Friedrich A. Lutz, major participants, *International Monetary Problems* (Washington, D.C.: American Enterprise Institute, 1971), p. 126.

39. See, for example, George Shultz, paper delivered at Kemp-Mundell conference, published in *A Monetary Agenda for World Growth.*

40. See U.S. Department of Commerce, Bureau of the Census, *Historical Statistics of the United States . . . Colonial Times to 1970* (Washington, D.C.: Superintendent of Documents, 1975), p. 211; "Reserve Board Finds Action Unnecessary," *New York Times,* 30 October 1929; U.S.

NOTES

Treasury Department, *Charts Relating to the Bretton Woods Proposals,* pamphlet dated 30 April 1945; Leonard Silk, "Why Markets Are Confident," *New York Times,* 18 March 1987; Gregory A. Fossedal, "The Right Price of Gold," *The American Spectator,* July 1984; and Lehrman, with Mueller and Fossedal, "Protectionism, Inflation, or Monetary Reform."

41. Robert L. Bartley, speech to the Oil Producers Association, excerpted in "The Monetary Source of Oil Boom and Bust," *Wall Street Journal,* 29 December 1986; see also Alan Reynolds, "Decisions On Oil and Gas" (Morristown, N.J.: Polyconomics, Inc., 14 February 1983), "Debt Deflation, Part Two" (Morristown, N.J.: Polyconomics, Inc., 31 July 1984), and "Oil, Gold, and Potential Growth" (Morristown, N.J.: Polyconomics, Inc., 2 November 1984).

42. In Wanniski, *The Way the World Works,* p. 235.

43. Mundell, "Inflation from an International Viewpoint," p. 144.

44. William J. Quirk, "The Big Bank Bailout," *The New Republic,* 21 February 1983, p. 18.

45. Net lending figures by Morgan Grenfell & Co., cited in Susan Dentzer et al., "Birth of a Borrowers' Cartel?" *Newsweek,* 5 September 1983; fund statistics from the IMF as cited in *New York Times,* 9 January 1983.

46. Commerce Department, *Statistical Abstract of the United States,* 1981, pp. 670–75.

47. Wharton Econometrics estimate of world trade; information on Mexico loans taken from chronology of Mexican debt problem in Melanie Tammen, "Déjà Vu of Policy Failure: The New $14 Billion Mexican Debt Bailout," *Heritage Foundation Backgrounder,* no. 588, 25 June 1987, p. 12; balance on current account figures from International Monetary Fund, *World Economic Outlook,* one in series of World Economic and Financial Surveys (Washington, D.C., April 1987), p. 105.

48. On the dismal forecasting record of demand-only models after Bretton Woods dismantling, see Melville J. Ulmer, "Economics in Decline," *Commentary,* November 1984. On the contrasting record of models accounting for tax incentives, and judging monetary policy by the behavior of sensitive commodity prices, see, for example, Gregory A. Fossedal, excerpt of letter responding to Ulmer, *Commentary,* April 1985; editorial, "Voodoo's Revenge," Review & Outlook, *Wall Street Journal,* 4 January 1984; and Gregory A. Fossedal, "This Voodoo Is Great Stuff," *San Diego Union,* 4 September 1983.

49. Milton Friedman, "The Needle Got Stuck," *Newsweek,* 25 July 1983; and "Why a Surge of Inflation Is Likely Next Year," *Wall Street Journal,* 1 September 1983.

50. Leonard Silk, "Budget Gap Still at Top of Agenda," *New York Times,* 4 March 1988.

51. Leonard Silk, "Gold, Inflation, and Deflation," *New York Times,* 2 March 1983; David R. Obey and Paul S. Sarbanes, " 'Recycling' Surpluses to the Third World," *New York Times,* 9 November 1986; IMF figures cited in Michael Prowse, "When Forgiveness Could Pay Off," *Financial Times,* 27 July 1987; and Victor Mallet, "African Economic Reform Fights 'Spirit of Despair,' " *Financial Times,* 5 March 1988.

52. James Brooke, "Nigeria Trying to Start Over Amid Recession and Turmoil," *New York Times,* 23 November 1987; James Buxton, "Change in Handling Debt Crisis Urged," *Financial Times,* 12 April 1984.

53. *The World Almanac and Book of Facts 1988* (New York: Pharos Books, 1988), p. 94; U.S. Department of Commerce, Bureau of the Census, *Statistical Abstract of the United States* (Washington, D.C.: Superintendent of Documents, December 1986), p. 483; and James W. Wilkie, David E. Lovey, and Enrique Ochoa, eds., *Statistical Abstract of Latin America* (Los Angeles: University of California, Latin America Center Publications, 1988), p. 237.

54. Leon Dash, "Gun Replaces Vote as Civilian Rule Fades in W. Africa," *Washington Post,* 8 April 1984.

55. Adam Lieberman, "Debt, Deflation, and Democracy in Africa—Connections," research paper 87-1, Alexis de Tocqueville Institution, 1987. See also U.S. State Department, *Country Reports on Human Rights Practices* for 1983, 1984, 1985, and 1986 (Washington, D.C.: Superintendent of Documents, 1984, 1985, 1986, and 1987); and *National Accounts Statistics: Main Aggregates & Detailed Tables* (New York: United Nations, 1984), pp. 1039–40, 1014–15, 117–18, 619–20, 957–58, 1554–55, and 1149–50; Victor Mallet, "Making the Medicine More Palatable," *Financial Times,* 9 May 1988; Gerard Alexander, "African Success Stories," *Policy Review,* Spring 1986; Raymond Gastil, "The Comparative Survey of Freedom," annual tables, *Freedom at Issue,* 1977–1987; and International Bank for Reconstruction and Development, *World Bank Atlas* (Washington, D.C.: World Bank, 1982, 1986, and 1987).

56. Carl Cunningham, quoted in Mary Ann Sieghart, "Proposal Would Cut Foreign Aid Policy From IMF Decisions," *Washington Post,* 10 July 1984; Gordon Rayfield, "Strangling Debtor Democracies," *The Washington Monthly,* April 1985; Melvyn Krauss, *Development Without Aid*

(New York: New Press, 1983); and Robert S. Browne, "The IMF in Africa," in *The Political Morality of the International Monetary Fund,* ed. Robert J. Myers (New Brunswick, N.J.: Transaction Books, 1987), p. 68.

57. See John Eisendrath, "How the IMF Makes the World Safe for Depression," *The Washington Monthly,* February 1983; and Azizali F. Mohammed's letter of protestation, "The IMF Seeks to Stimulate Growth," *Wall Street Journal,* 21 June 1984.

58. See, for example, the fine volume *IMF Conditionality,* ed. John Williamson (Washington, D.C.: Institute for International Economics, 1983), esp. essays by Williamson, "The Lending Policies of the International Monetary Fund," and "On Judging the Success of IMF Policy Advice," as well as by C. David Finch, "Adjustment Policies and Conditionality," Sidney Dell, "Stabilization: The Political Economy of Overkill," and Samuel Lichtensztejn, "IMF Developing Countries: Conditionality and Strategy"; International Monetary Fund, "Fund Study Examines the Causes of Success in Economic Adjustment Programs in Africa," *IMF Survey,* 15 April 1985; Clyde Farnsworth, "The IMF's Help Can Sometimes Hurt," *New York Times,* 14 April 1985; J. de Larosiere, *Does the Fund Impose Austerity?* (Washington, D.C.: International Monetary Fund, June 1984); Henry R. Nau, "Where Reaganomics Works," *Foreign Policy,* Winter 1984–85; World Bank, *World Development Report 1984* (Washington, D.C.: World Bank, 1984) and *Sub-Saharan Africa: Progress Report on Development Prospects in Programmes* (Washington, D.C.: World Bank, 1983); Justin B. Zulu and Sahel M. Nsouli, *Adjustment Programs in Africa: The Recent Experience,* Occasional paper no. 34 (Washington, D.C.: International Monetary Fund, 1985); and, finally, the survey volume edited by Robert J. Myers, *The Political Morality of the International Monetary Fund* (New Brunswick, N.J.: Transaction Books, 1987), esp. essays by Henry B. Schlecter, "IMF Conditionality and the International Economy," and Alvin Rabushka, "From Austerity to Growth: A New Role for the IMF."

59. Zulu and Nsouli, *Adjustment Programs in Africa;* International Bank for Reconstruction and Development, *Annual Report* (Washington, D.C.: World Bank, September 1983); and Martin Tolchin, "House Panel Votes to Curb Aid Agency's Powers," *New York Times,* 8 June 1984.

60. See Henry Morgenthau, *Charts Relating to . . . the Bretton Woods Proposal* (Washington, D.C.: United States Treasury, 30 April 1945); and Lehrman, "Protectionism, Inflation, or Monetary Reform"; idem, "Protectionism or Monetary Reform," 22 December 1984, draft article available through the author; idem, "Trade War or Monetary Reform," *Wall Street Journal,* 28 January 1987; and idem "An Exorbitant Privilege," *National Review,* 21 November 1986.

61. Peter McPherson, interview with the author and Jonathan Fund of the *Wall Street Journal,* April 1984; growth rates from Sylvia Quick, U.S. Commerce Department, unpublished data provided in interview with Hoover Institution research assistant Adam Lieberman; Ralph de Toledano, "Miracle on Taiwan," *National Review,* 19 August 1983; Tom Bethell, "Riches of the Orient," *National Review,* 7 November 1986; and Alan Reynolds, "The Urgency of International Tax Relief" (Morristown, N.J.: Polyconomics, Inc., 2 April 1985), and "Latin American Debt: The Case for Radical Tax Reform" (Morristown, N.J.: Polyconomics, Inc., 2 February 1988).

62. Figures from the Agency for International Development, Organization for Economic Cooperation and Development, and World Bank, cited in Doug Bandow, "Foreign Aid Prescriptions," *The American Spectator,* September 1986; Pranay Gupte, "The Haves Can Help the Have-Nots," *New York Times,* 28 September 1986; Barnaby J. Feder, "New Report Offers a Plan to Rescue Latin Economies," *New York Times,* 28 September 1986; Brooke, "Nigeria Trying to Start Over," and William R. Cline, *International Debt and the Stability of the World Economy* (Washington, D.C.: Institute for International Economics, September 1983).

63. Robert Pastor, "Sinking in the Caribbean Basin," *Foreign Affairs* 60, no. 5 (Summer 1982); and Peter Kenen, quoted in Lawrence Rout, "New Study Indicates World Debt Crisis May Be Solved as Global Economy Spurts," *Wall Street Journal,* 26 May 1983. See also Cline, *International Debt;* and C. Fred Bergsten, William R. Cline, and John Williamson, *Bank Lending to Developing Countries: The Policy Alternatives* (Washington, D.C.: Institute for International Economics, April 1985).

64. Raul Alfonsin, address to the Carter-Ford conference on democracy in Latin America, Emory University, Atlanta, 17 November 1986; and Gupte, "The Haves Can Help the Have-Nots."

65. Paul Lewis, "Commodity Stockpile Fund," *New York Times,* 27 June 1983; Mary Helen Spooner, "Chile and IMF Reach Agreement," *Financial Times,* 21 November 1986; Clyde Farnsworth, "Argentina Seeks IMF Loan Tied to Crop Prices," *New York Times,* 5 September 1986; Tim Coone and Stewart Fleming, "Argentina Says $1.2bn IMF Loan Agreed," *Financial Times,* 12 January 1987; Michael R. Sesit and S. Karene Witcher, "Mexico Signals It Wants Debt

NOTES

Concessions," *Wall Street Journal,* 6 October 1986; and Larry Rohter, "Latin Chiefs Urge Overhaul of Debt and of O.A.S. Too," *New York Times,* 30 November 1987.

66. Henry Kissinger, in his modestly entitled, "Saving the World Economy," *Newsweek,* 24 January 1983, and also at Kemp-Mundell conference, published in *A Monetary Agenda for World Growth;* Helmut Schmidt, "The World Economy at Stake," *The Economist,* 26 February 1983; John Vinocur, "Mitterrand Seeks Parley to Revamp Monetary System," *New York Times,* 10 May 1983; Shlomo Maital, "Knowledge and Opinions . . . Arthur Burns Still Has Plenty of Both," *Barron's,* 19 December 1983; Richard M. Nixon, quoted in Gregory A. Fossedal, "What the Real Nixon's Saying," *Wall Street Journal,* 22 December 1983, and Fossedal, "Volcker, Man of the Year"; Leonard Silk, "Gold, Inflation, and Deflation," *New York Times,* 2 March 1983, "Fixed Rates May Be Better," *New York Times,* 23 March 1983, and "Global Debate on Currency," *New York Times,* 30 March 1983; Peter T. Kilborn, "Fed Alters Economic Monitoring," *New York Times,* 26 February 1988; Walter Mondale, quoted in Kenneth Bacon, "Mondale Backs Plan for Major Overhaul of the System of Taxing Personal Income," *Wall Street Journal,* 10 May 1983; George Bush and Robert Dole, quoted in interviews with *Conservative Digest,* January 1986; Karl Otto Poehl, quoted in Seth Lipsky, "Bundesbank's Mr. Poehl Awaits the Americans," *Wall Street Journal,* 3 February 1988; Eduard Balladur, quoted in Ian Davidson, "Europe Pressed to Create Common Currency," *Financial Times,* 20 January 1988, and Editorial, "Good as Gold," Review & Outlook, *Wall Street Journal,* 5 February 1988; and Editorial, "Get Ready for the Phoenix," *The Economist,* 9 January 1988.

Chapter 9   A Democratic Century

1. C. S. Lewis, *Mere Christianity* (New York: Macmillan, 1975), p. 1.

2. Dennis L. Bark, ed., *To Promote Peace* (Stanford, Calif.: Hoover Institution Press, 1984).

3. See, for example, R. W. Apple, Jr., "New Stirrings of Patriotism," and Adam Clymer, "The Nation's Mood," both in *New York Times Magazine,* 11 December 1983.

4. Abraham Lincoln, in *The Collected Works of Abraham Lincoln,* vol. 2, ed. Roy P. Basler (New Brunswick, N.J.: Rutgers University Press, 1953), p. 532.

5. John Locke, *The Second Treatise of Government* (Indianapolis: Bobbs-Merrill, 1979), pp. 77–78.

6. Jean-Jacques Rousseau, *Of the Social Contract,* trans. Charles M. Sherover (New York: Harper & Row, 1984), pp. 26–27, 62–67.

7. John Locke, *Second Treatise of Government,* pp. 70–91.

8. Charles Kesler, "Jeane Kirkpatrick . . . Not Quite Right," *National Review,* 29 October 1982. For another fine essay on natural rights by the clear-thinking Kesler, see "A Tribute to Harry V. Jaffa . . . A Special Meaning of the Declaration of Independence," *National Review,* 6 July 1983.

9. Abraham Lincoln, Speech at Independence Hall, Philadelphia, 22 February 1861. See Basler, ed., *Collected Works.*

10. From Lloyd Free and William Watts, "Internationalism Comes of Age . . . Again," *Public Opinion,* April–May 1980.

11. Ben J. Wattenberg, speech to a 1986 human rights conference in Latvia; unpublished text, provided to the author by Mr. Wattenberg, is available through the American Enterprise Institute in Washington, D.C.

12. See "Central America . . . How Informed Are We?" in "Opinion Roundup," *Public Opinion,* August–September 1983, p. 21; and Adam Clymer, "Poll Finds Americans Don't Know U.S. Positions on Central America," *New York Times,* 1 July 1983.

13. George Gallup, Jr., "Americans Leery About Further U.S. Intervention in Nicaragua," *Gallup Poll,* 31 March 1985.

14. Figures cited in Karlyn Keene and Victoria Sackett, "El Salvador: What the Polls Said," *Wall Street Journal,* 23 April 1982.

15. Irving Kristol, quoted in interview with Charles E. Wheeler, "Foreign Policy by Leadership, Not by Argument," *Washington Times,* 20 June 1984.

16. William Safire, "The Isoventionists," *New York Times,* 28 May 1984.

17. John E. Rielly, "American Opinion: Continuity, Not Reaganism," *Foreign Policy,* Spring 1983, p. 99.

18. See David Ignatius, "Vietnam's Legacy . . . A Decade After War, U.S. Leaders Still Feel

Effects of the Defeat," *Wall Street Journal,* 14 January 1985, along with accompanying chart of Gallup poll, "Presidential Performance and Conduct of the War—What Americans Said," p. 8; William Lunch and Peter Sperlich, "American Public Opinion and the War in Vietnam," *Western Political Quarterly,* Spring 1979; and John E. Mueller, *War, Presidents, and Public Opinion* (New York: Wiley, 1973).

19. Paul Johnson, *Modern Times* (New York: Harper & Row, 1983), p. 637.

20. Daniel Yankelovich and Larry Kaagan, "Assertive America," *Foreign Affairs,* special issue, "America and the World" 59, no. 3 (February 1981): 696–713.

21. For further exploration of the distinction between "dilutive compromise" and "additive compromise," see Gregory A. Fossedal, "The Art of Additive Compromise," *The American Spectator,* October 1985, and "Shanty Talk," *The American Spectator,* May 1986.

22. Thomas Willing Balch, "The United States and the Expansion of the Law Between Nations," *University of Pennsylvania Law Review* 64 (December 1915).

23. Percy E. Corbett, *Law in Diplomacy* (Princeton: Princeton University Press, 1959), esp. chap. 2, "Enter the United States."

24. Thomas James Norton, *The Constitution of the United States . . . Its Sources and Its Application* (New York: Committee for Constitutional Government, 1922); see esp. pp. 176–81 of the 1945 ed. with a preface by Samuel B. Pettengill.

25. Eric Chenoweth, interview with the author, July 1986.

26. In a 1949 survey of U.S. foreign policy, the U.S. Council on Foreign Relations described the Rio Treaty as follows: "This country . . . was obligated to assist any American state subjected to armed attack, but retained the right to decide whether or not to employ armed forces. . . . Any armed attack within this area was to be considered an attack against all the American states, requiring them to take specific measures as prescribed by the treaty." This section would certainly seem to apply to Nicaragua, whose officials have admitted to launching subversion efforts against El Salvador, and probably are involved in Cuban efforts in Costa Rica, Guatemala, and Colombia as well. On the meaning of the Rio and Bogotá pacts, and for the quotations cited in the text and this note, see John C. Campbell, ed., *The United States in World Affairs, 1948–1949* (New York: published for the Council on Foreign Relations for Harper & Bros., 1949), pp. 12–13, 352–69; U.S. Department of State, *Ninth International Conference of American States: Report of the Delegation of the United States of America* (Superintendent of Documents, Washington, D.C., 1948); and Harry S. Truman, *Years of Trial and Hope* (Garden City, N.Y.: Doubleday, 1956), p. 250. On the Kennedy-Nixon debate, see Tad Szulc and Karl E. Meyer, *The Cuban Invasion* (New York: Ballantine Books, 1962), pp. 65–71. On Nicaraguan subversion efforts in the 1980s, see, for instance, Alan Riding, "Salvador Rebels: Five-Sided Alliance Searching for New, Moderate Image," *New York Times,* 18 March 1982; Sam Dillon, "Base for Ferrying Arms to El Salvador Found in Nicaragua," *Washington Post,* 21 September 1983; and U.S. House of Representatives, Permanent Select Committee on Intelligence, Report 98–112, pt. 1, 13 May 1983. On the World Court case, see Robert F. Turner, *Nicaragua v. United States: A Look at the Facts* (Washington, D.C., published for the Institute for Foreign Policy Analysis by Pergamon-Brassey's, 1987); and Gregory A. Fossedal, syndicated column, as published in "Would Dukakis Cut Off the Contras? Blame It on Rio," *Orange County Register,* 5 July 1988.

27. One of the texts Kinsley recommended, it should be noted, does assert that nations generally obey international law, and for the reasons cited. See Michael Akehurst, *A Modern Introduction to International Law* (London: Allen and Unwin, 1977). But none of the paragraphs making these assertions, mostly from chap. 1, "Is International Law Really Law?" is footnoted, nor is mention made, in a brief recommended reading section at the end, of a single serious historical study backing Akehurst's large assertion that "states do accept that international law is law; and, what is more, they usually obey it." Furthermore, the qualifiers Akehurst heaps on this statement make it essentially meaningless as a statement about international law in the field in which Kinsley applies it—the use of force. For most of the last few decades, as was noted in chap. 3, anywhere between a tenth and a third of the countries of the world have been at war. Given that most people assume one country must be at fault for such conflicts, this fact, as Akehurst notes, helps produce the popular notion that international law is routinely violated. Now, as Akehurst writes, this may not be so: A large number of international wars may not even be covered by international law, even as a large number of quarrels between Mrs. Smith and the baker may not be covered by U.S. criminal or even civil statutes. But to say this is simply making a point that most people understand to begin with: International law poses no serious check on the major international disputes, such as wars, that the public sees as central to foreign relations. We might as well observe that Adolf Hitler "generally" observed international law, for example, in thousands of matters from fishing rights to currency exchange—

violating it in only a handful of cases, such as the invasion of Poland, which were never even taken before an international tribunal; or in the slaughter of some 7 million Jewish and Christian souls, who the Nazis might claim were a matter of purely domestic concern.

And it is precisely those states who most need to be restrained by international law who will not hesitate to observe its words but not its spirit or intent. As George Kennan noted:

> The American concept of world law ignores those means of international offense, those means of the projection of power and coercion over other peoples, which bypass institutional forms entirely or even exploit them against themselves. Such things as ideological attacks, intimidation, penetration, and disguised seizure of the institutional paraphernalia of national sovereignty. It ignores, in other words, the device of the puppet state and the set of techniques by which states can be converted into puppets with no formal violation of, or challenge to, the outward attributes of their sovereignty and their independence ("Diplomacy in the Modern World," one of six Charles R. Walgreen Foundation lectures delivered at the University of Chicago, later reprinted in *American Diplomacy 1900–1950* [Chicago: University of Chicago Press, 1951], pp. 91–103).

More careful and historical texts than Akehurst's, meanwhile, bear out the common-sense assertion that laws without courts and police are not laws. "In a very general sense," writes Percy E. Corbett, "it can be said even of the strongest legal systems that their subjects bow to legal regulation only when they perceive a coincidence of interest and legality. In that context the prospect of coercion figures prominently in the calculation of interest"—so that, while the Soviets may fear being censured by the U.N. if they invade Afghanistan, this fear may be overwhelmed by the perception of more vital interests. "However eloquent and sincere their appeals to the general interest of the 'family of nations,' governments demonstrate in action the conviction that this individualism is their bounden duty to their people" (Corbett, *Law in Diplomacy* [Princeton: Princeton University Press, 1959], pp. 276–77).

By seeking, in contrast, to establish that nations obey international law by explaining that it is in their interest to do so, Kinsley and Akehurst thus put the cart several leagues before the horse. Why not simply cite the examples of important treaties, and establish that they have been observed? Answer: Because a comprehensive look at the record reveals numerous breaches of international law; simply to state that nations "generally" obey is to say that the law always protects us except when it does not protect us, or when it is not in fact even relevant. This logic fails to explain what we do at precisely the critical moment of law: the moment when someone, considering an invasion of Afghanistan, or, by analogy, the murder of another human being, contemplates its circumvention. (Note that in 1929, forty-five nations, including Germany, Italy, and Japan, unaware of Kinsley's law, signed a treaty outlawing war.) It fails even to explain why the U.S., in the view of Kinsley and others, violated international law and mined the harbors of Nicaragua. If this simply shows that nations may stupidly ignore their own interest, Americans may rightly ask, "How are we to trust international law to shield us from Soviet leaders who may also miscalculate the Soviet interest?"

Civil laws, in fact, even in the Soviet Union, generally protect citizens from what they would consider the most important threats: murder, robbery, and so on. Yet it is precisely the use of force, and other supreme matters, that international law *sans* police fails to thwart. "International law," as two scholars highly desirous of its perfection write, "has lacked the sanctions which, in the last resort, compel obedience to State-law. However much such a system might have been tolerable in the past, it is to-day increasingly an anachronism" (George W. Keeton and Georg Schwarzenberger, *Making International Law Work* [London: Sevens & Sons, 1946], p. 133). Nations, as even James Leslie Brierly, another rather bullish proponent of international law, put it, "do not allow the law, or at any rate it is not their settled practice to allow it, to have the final word in issues which affect their so-called 'vital interests,' and as they reserve the right to decide which of their interests are vital, that means that in the last resort they regard the observance of law as optional" (Address given at Chatham House, 15 January 1946, as published in Sir Hersch Lauterpacht, ed., *The Basis of Obligation in International Law* [Oxford: Oxford University Press, 1958], p. 328).

It is true, as Mr. Kinsley and most of those cited above note, that national laws are violated too. Yet the common assumption is that we need police to deal with those violations, both because it is just to punish the criminal and to deter other potential criminals. Would Mr. Kinsley, who avers that we do not need international sanctions to make international law effective, care to apply that theory to, say, the five-block area of Washington, D.C., where *The New Republic* has its offices? Let us hope not, for the country would eventually lose a great editor and a great magazine.

28. See Michael A. Ledeen, "When Security Pre-empts the Rule of Law," *New York Times,* 16 April 1984; and Jeane Kirkpatrick, address to the American Society of International Law, 12 April 1984.

29. See, for example, Bernard Gwertzman, "Shultz Supporting Compromise Terms at East-West Talk"—a dog-bites-man headline if ever one was written—*New York Times,* 12 July 1983; François de Rose, "Rights Charade in Madrid," *New York Times,* 17 August 1983; Editorial, "Helsinki in the Victims' View," *New York Times,* 2 August 1985; Editorial, Review & Outlook, "Bitter Anniversary," *Wall Street Journal,* 30 July 1985; Richard Pipes, "A Loss for the West," *New York Times,* 1 August 1985; and Roger Reed, "Soviets Score 'Human Rights' Propaganda Victory," *Human Events,* 16 August 1986. Typical of the progressive recommendations in this literature is the bold suggestion advanced by a former member of the National Security Council Staff in one *Times* opinion piece: "The United States should build on what has already been achieved and continue to press for improvements in those areas where compliance has been faulty" (Op-Ed page, *New York Times,* 1 August 1985).

30. For a representative and well-edited collection of these essays, see Burton Yale Pines, *A World Without a U.N.* (Washington, D.C.: Heritage Foundation, 1984). See also Charles Krauthammer's well-reasoned article, "Let It Sink," *The New Republic,* 24 August 1987. While silent on the matter of a League of Democracies in that particular article, Krauthammer and his *TNR* colleagues have not, as noted later in the text, by any means been silent on the proposed League of Democracies. See, for instance, Editorial, "Bad Ideas and Good," *The New Republic,* 3 December 1984.

31. It so happens that the answer to our puzzle is . . . the Democrats. See the Advisory Task Force, Coalition for a Democratic Majority, *Democratic Solidarity . . . Proposals for the 1984 Democratic Party Platform on Foreign Policy and National Defense* (Washington, D.C., 1984), pp. 3–4; and also "Bad Ideas and Good," *The New Republic.*

32. Robert Leiken, "Reform the Contras," *The New Republic,* 31 March 1986.

33. George Kennan, cited in Merrick Carey, "The Coming Global Democracy," research paper, 29 January 1980, available from the Alexis de Tocqueville Institution.

34. Charles de Gaulle, *Les mémoires de guerre,* vol. 1 (Paris: Plon, 1954), p. 5.

35. Editorial, *The Economist,* cited in Henry Luce, "The American Century," *Life,* 17 February 1941.

36. Luce, "The American Century."

37. Ibid.

INDEX

INDEX

Great Britain, *see* United Kingdom
Greece, 10–11, 40, 185
Greenfield, Meg, 33–34
Greenspan, Alan, 193
Grenada, 42, 72, 147, 164, 224, 234
Griesgraber, Jo Marie, 76
Gromyko, Andrei, 99
Gross, Jan T., 54
Group of 77, 211
Guatemala, 8, 61, 69–70, 72, 147
Guerillas, *see* Third-force movements
Guinea, 205
Gupte, Pranay, 211
Guzman, Antonio, 76

Haig, Alexander: on Central America policy, 166; on human rights policy, 67; policy in Nicaragua and, 147, 164–65, 167; policy in Poland and, 86
Haiti: democracy in, 9, 180–81, 183; human rights policy and, 62, 71; NED and, 72
Hale, Julian, 99, 103
Harkin, Tom, 171
Harris, Lou, 47–48
Háy, Gyula, 92
Heginbotham, Stanley, 60–61
Helsinki Accords, 232, 235
Helsinki Watch, 112
Heritage Foundation, studies on United Nations, 235
Hertzberg, Hendrik, 127
Heuvel, Katrina Vanden, 93
Hitler, Adolf, 116–17
Hobbes, Thomas, 18
Hoffman, Stanley, 65
Holbrook, Richard, 93
Honduras, 8, 73, 147
Hoover, Herbert, 228
Hsin-Huang Michael Hsiao, 6
Human capital, 189
Human Events (magazine), 107, 141
Human rights policy: Abrams doctrine and, 67–71; of Carter, 23, 24, 27–28, 59–67, 74–76; effectiveness of, 27–28; endowment of, 71–75; evaluations of, 60–64; failures of, 77–84, 85–87; ideology and, 64–67; Kirkpatrick doctrine on, 61–64; of Reagan, 59–60, 63, 64, 67–74, 75, 76; *see also* Carter, Helsinki Accords, Reagan, Rights of man
Humphrey, Gordon, 158
Hungary: movement toward democracy in, 11–12; NED and, 72; Soviet invasion of, 88–91; Western broadcasts and, 90–91, 92–94, 100, 102

Ideology, and human rights, 64–67
Ideopolitik, 36–38
Ignatius, David, 226
Iker, Sam, 111
Iklé, Fred C., 9, 171
Illegal aliens, 257*n*32
IMF, *see* International Monetary Fund (IMF)
Immigration: 1986 immigration bill and, 257 *n*32; in U.S. vs. Soviet Union, 48
India, 8, 38, 72, 187, 188, 197
Inflation, and exchange rates, 186, 193, 195–98
Information: international availability of, 43–44; planting of false, 111; political action and, 44; pragmatism and, 109–10; in Western broadcasts, 106–14; *see also* Broadcasts
Interest rates, and exchange rates, 194
International crises, voters' vs. leaders' responses to, 225–26
Internationalism, trend toward, 222
International law: enforcement of, 30–31, 281 *n*27; foreign policy decisions and, 234–35; historical growth in, 232–33; spread of democracy and, 30–31; strengthening of, 233–36; use of force and, 280*n*27
International Monetary Fund (IMF): conditionality and, 183–84, 192, 207–8; foreign aid programs and, 26, 206–8; lending by, 199; Nigerian coup and, 9; origin of, 203; Western banks and, 203, 206
Iran: human rights and, 28, 62, 77, 80; Islamic revolution and, 49; moderates in, 46; reforms in, under shah, 80–81; secret police in, 80, 81; Soviet setbacks in, 40; U.S. intervention and, 84; VOA reporting on, 111
Iron Curtain, *see* Communist bloc countries, Eastern Europe
Islam, and representative democracy, 46
Isolationism, 221–23
Isoventionism, 224–26
Ispahani, Mahnaz, 7
Israel, 38, 41, 99, 115
Italy, 185
Itayim, Fuad, 116
Izvestia, 101

Jackson, Henry "Scoop," 120–21
Jackson, Jesse, 184

INDEX

Libya, 45, 49, 224
Lieberman, Adam, 154*n*
Lincoln, Abraham, 218, 219, 221, 238
Lipset, Seymour Martin, 54, 85, 119
Literacy rates, 44
Locke, John, 19, 218, 219
Low, Robert, 10
Luce, Henry, 240–41

McCarthy, Joseph, 96–97, 107
McFarlane, Robert C., 151, 164–65, 171, 172
Mackinder, Halford J., 35, 36–37
McLaughlin, John, 31
MacMahon, John, 159
McPherson, Peter, 209
Madison, James, 19, 150
Magna Carta, 13
Mahan, Alfred Thayer, 36, 37
Mali, 204
Mandela, Nelson, 135
Manglapus, Raul S., 182
Mao Tse-tung, 126, 127, 149
Marcos, Ferdinand: effect of public information and, 44; human rights policy and, 5, 64, 76–77; U.S. support for, 33, 67–68
Market economy, 50
Marshall Plan, 184, 187–89, 239
Martin, David, 150
Martin, Everett G., 70–71
Martinez-Mont, Lucy, 69–70
Marx, Karl, 178
Marxism, *see* Communism
Matlock, Jack, 105
Mauritania, 204
Mee, Charles L., 187, 191
Meese, Edwin, 172
Mendlicott, W. N., 117
Menges, Constantine, 161–62, 164
Mexico, 9, 210
Meyer, Raymond, 126
Meyerson, Adam, 9, 61
Michie, Allan A., 91, 92, 93, 103
Mickelson, Sig, 93, 95, 96, 109
Military aid: as controversial, 139–49; human rights and, 68; international law and, 233–34; spread of democracy by, 29–30; token assistance and, 151–56
Military strength, and polity, 37
Moderates: in Iran, 79, 82–84; in South Africa, 136
Monarchy, decline of, 43
Mondale, Walter, 66

Monetary stabilization, and economic growth, 190–91, 192
Montt, Efrain Rios, 69
Morgenthau, Henry, 208
Moser, Charles, 174
Most-favored-nation status: Afghanistan and, 158; China and, 127; Soviet Union and, 120–21
Moynihan, Daniel Patrick, 29, 266*n*8
Mujahedin (Afghanistan), 140, 142–43, 149, 158–59, 163
Mundell, Robert, 193, 194, 196
Muravchik, Joshua, 23, 60, 60–61, 75
Murrow, Edward R., 97, 103

Napoleon Bonaparte, 35
National Committee for a Free Europe, 95–96
National Endowment for Democracy (NED), 71–74, 76
Nationalism, and growth of democracy, 48–50
National Opinion Research Center, 221–23
National Review, 33
National Security Decision Directive 17, 167
National Union for the Total Independence of Angola, *see* Unita
NED, *see* National Endowment for Democracy (NED)
Negrin, Juan, 4
Nemschak, Franz, 188
Netherlands, 37
New China News Agency, 126
New Republic, The, 24, 180, 186
New York Times, 5, 9–10, 24, 147–48, 180
Nicaragua: Carter policy and, 28, 132–33, 160–63; derecognition policy and, 175–77; direct intervention in, 78–79, 168–69, 233; human rights policy and, 28, 62, 77–79; importance of opposition to communism in, 147; NED and, 72; populist foreign policy and, 53; sanctions against, 131–33; Soviet Union and, 42, 45, 155; support for contras in, 145–48; World Court and, 233, 235; *see also* Sandinistas
Nicolaides, Phil, 39, 106
Nielsonovich Ratings, 101
Niger, 205
Nigeria, 9–10, 85, 202, 204, 210
Nixon, Richard: approval ratings of, 226; Bretton Woods approach and, 212; China and, 124, 125–27, 128, 151; devaluation and, 192, 194, 212; economics-first model and, 180; international law and, 233–34; on nuclear age

INDEX

INDEX

49; non-nuclear military activity and, 38; postwar condition of, 187; postwar dependence of, 185, 187, 240; U.S. sanctions and, 129

United Nations, 232, 235–36; *see also* International law

U.S. Congress: aid to mujahedin and, 158–59; aid to Unita and, 159–60; Boland amendments and, 170–71; House Foreign Affairs Committee, 105; role of, in foreign policy, 227

U.S. Council on Foreign Relations, 280*n*26

U.S. Department of Defense, 121–22, 150

U.S. Department of State: aid to Afghan mujahedin and, 158–59; aid to Unita and, 160; international support for resistance groups and, 174; Korean politics and, 74; League of Democracies and, 236; policy on Nicaragua and, 164–65; *see also* Diplomatic community

U.S. Federal Reserve system, 199–202

U.S. Information Agency, 27, 97, 113, 227

U.S. National Security Council, 227

U.S. Office of Strategic Services, 95

U.S. Overseas Private Investment Corporation, 7

U.S.-Soviet Standing Consultative Commission (SCC), 31

Urban, Jerzy, 86, 104

Uruguay, 61

USIA, *see* U.S. Information Agency

Vaky, Viron Pete, 78

Valenta, Jiri, 90

Values, U.S. vs. Soviet, 49–50

Vance, Cyrus, 65, 66, 83, 162

Vietnam, 131, 153, 209, 226

Voice of America (VOA): editorials on, 111–12; effectiveness of, 27; function of, 95*n*; Hungary and, 90–91, 93–94; as information source, 93; listenership for, 100; origins of, 94–95, 96; physical plant of, 105–6; populist foreign policy and, 51; programming on, 111–14

Volcker, Paul, 193, 198–200, 202

Vo Nguyen Giap, 149

Walesa, Lech, 12, 102, 104, 130

Wallace, DeWitt, 95

Wallop, Malcolm, 172, 173, 175

Wall Street Journal, 5, 9–10, 12, 24

Waltz, Kenneth, 42

Wan Li, 15

Wanniski, Jude, 123

Warfare, conduct of, 38–39, 232

Warsaw Pact nations, *see* Communist bloc countries, Eastern Europe, *specific nations*

Washington Post, 33–34, 160, 202

Wattenberg, Ben, 47–48, 223

Watts, William, 221–23

Wealth, diffusion of, 254*n*13

Weinberger, Caspar, 27, 31, 79, 165, 170, 227

Wells, H. G., 18–19

Western Europe: democratic progress in, 10–11; Soviet setbacks in, 41; U.S. public diplomacy and, 107*n*; U.S. sanctions against, 129; *see also specific countries*

West Germany (Federal Republic of Germany), 240

Wick, Charles, 106

Wildavsky, Aaron, 55

Will, George, 11, 17–18

World Bank, 127, 183, 203, 207–8

World Court, 30–31; *see also* International law

World War II, Voice of America in, 96

Worldwide Broadcasting Foundation, 96

Yakovlevitch, Aleksandr, 104

Yankelovich, Daniel, 226

Young, Andrew, 184

Youwei, Kang, 182

Yugoslavia, 40, 91

Zahedi, Ardeshir, 82

Zaire, 41

Zalaquette, Jose, 75

Zaslavskaia, Tatiana I., 14

Zero option, 228

Zia ul-Haq, Mohammed, 7, 159

Zimbabwe, 42, 202–3

Zulu, Justin, 207